1 MONTH OF
FREE
READING

at

www.ForgottenBooks.com

By purchasing this book you are eligible for one month membership to ForgottenBooks.com, giving you unlimited access to our entire collection of over 1,000,000 titles via our web site and mobile apps.

To claim your free month visit:
www.forgottenbooks.com/free169125

ISBN 978-0-266-17502-5
PIBN 10169125

CIVIL PROCEDURE REPORTS

CONTAINING CASES UNDER THE

CODE OF CIVIL PROCEDURE

AND

THE GENERAL CIVIL PRACTICE

OF THE

STATE OF NEW YORK.

REPORTED WITH NOTES

BY

HENRY H. BROWNE

OF THE NEW YORK BAR.

WITH A REFERENCE TO THE SECTIONS OF THE CODE OF CIVIL PROCE-
DURE CONSTRUED OR CITED IN THE OPINIONS CONTAINED IN THE
FOLLOWING REPORTS, ISSUED DURING THE PERIOD COVERED
BY THIS VOLUME : NEW YORK REPORTS, VOL. 103 ; RUN'S
REPORTS, VOLS. 41, 42 ; AND NEW YORK CIVIL PRO-
CEDURE REPORTS, VOL. XI.

VOLUME XI.

NEW YORK:

S. S. PELOUBET,

LAW PUBLISHER AND BOOKSELLER,

80 NASSAU STREET.

1887.

CONTENTS.

CONTENTS

vi

CONTENTS.

CONTENTS.

CONTENTS.

CONTENTS.

TABLE OF CASES REPORTED.

CASES REPORTED.

TABLE OF CASES CITED

IN THE OPINIONS.

---

a—affirmed ; ap—approved ; d—distinguished ; ex —explained ; f—
followed ; nf—not followed; o—overruled ; r—reversed.

A.

CASES CITED.

xxiv

CASES CITED.

STATUTES, ETC., CITED.

SECTIONS OF THE CODE OF CIVIL PROCEDURE CITED.

SECSIONS OF THE CODE OF PROCEDURE CITED.

CODE OF 1848.

CODE OF CRIMINAL PROCEDURE.

SESSION LAWS CITED.

NEW YORK REVISED STATUTES CITED.

FIRST EDITION.

REVISED LAWS.

GENERAL RULES OF PRACTICE CITED.

UNITED STATES REVISED STATUTES CITED.

CONSTITUTION OF THE STATE OF NEW YORK CITED.

CONSTITUTION OF THE UNITED STATES CITED.

TEXT-BOOKS, ETC., CITED.

SECTIONS OF CODE OF CIVIL PROCEDURE

CONSTRUED OR CITED IN THE OPINIONS CONTAINED IN
THE FOLLOWING REPORTS, ISSUED DURING THE PERIOD COV-
ERED BY THIS VOLUME ; New York Reports, Vol. 103 ;
Hun's Reports, Vols. 41, 42; Civil Procedure Reports,
Vol. 11.

CIVIL PROCEDURE REPORTS.

CLAY, by STONE her Guardian ad litem, Respondent, v. BAKER and Another, Appellants.

SUPREME COURT, FIFTH DEPARTMENT, GENERAL TERM, JUNE, 1886.

§§ 525, 526.

Guardian ad litem.—Verification of pleading by.

Where the complaint of an infant suing by her guardian *ad litem* was verified by such guardian, in the same form as though he was a party, and without stating any reason why the verification was not made by the infant or any grounds for his information or belief,— *Held*, that the complaint was properly verified; that the guardian was appointed to prosecute the action in behalf of the infant, and the complaint was his pleading and not that of the infant, and in that sense he was a party to the record and the party pleading, and therefore, the party within the contemplation of the statute, providing for verification by a party or by an agent or attorney, who may, as such, verify a pleading; that a guardian *ad litem* does not come within the meaning of the term agent or attorney, as that term is usually understood or applied.

Anable v. Anable (24 *How. Pr.* 92), followed.

It seems, that the guardian *ad litem* by whom an infant prosecutes an action, is not a party plaintiff to the action, but he prosecutes the action and the complaint is his pleading in behalf of the infant plaintiff, and that the infant cannot be required to verify the pleading. nor is it any evidence against her, nor does it conclude her, and the infant has the right to inquire on arriving at full age during the pendance of the action, whether the guardian is prop-

erly prosecuting it, and to abandon it and charge him with costs
if he is not.
(*Decided June*, 1886.)

Appeal from an order of the Erie county court
denying a motion to compel the plaintiff to receive
an unverified answer.

The plaintiff is an infant, and her guardian *ad
litem* verified the complaint by an affidavit, stating that
he was such guardian and that the complaint was true
of his own knowledge, except as to the matters therein
stated to be alleged on information and belief, and as
to those matters he believed it to be true. The defendants served an answer without verification, which was
returned because it was unverified. Thereupon the
defendants moved to require its acceptance as an
answer to the complaint, and from the denial of
the motion this appeal was taken.

Ralph Stone, for plaintiff-respondent.

Where a pleading is verified, each subsequent
pleading, except a demurrer, or the general answer of
an infant by his guardian *ad litem*, must also be verified. *Code Civ. Pro.* § 523. It therefore follows, that
if the plaintiff's complaint is a verified pleading
within the meaning of section 523 of the Code, then
the defendant's answer must be verified. The verification of plaintiff's complaint by her guardian *ad
litem* is sufficient. In Hill *v.* Thacter, 3 *How. Pr.* 407,
the court says, "Had he (the guardian) been in truth
appointed the guardian at this time," *i. e.*, before veri-
fying the complaint, "I think he might in that character have verified the complaint." The guardian of
an infant plaintiff may verify the complaint. The
guardian for this purpose is "the party," within the
meaning of section 157 (of the old Code). *Van Sand-
voord's Pleading*, 374. There is no authority for the

Clay *v.* Baker.

supposition that the new Code has made any change in the practice in this respect. Under the former chancery practice, an infant was not allowed to plead personally, and the answer was termed the answer of the guardian and not of the infant, and in a case where an oath was necessary, it was sworn to by the guardian. 1 *Barb. Ch. Pr.* 148; Bulkley *v.* Van Wyck, 5 *Paige,* 536. The answer of an infant by his guardian cannot be read against the infant, for he cannot make an admission which ought to bind him; though it may be read against the guardian, for it is he alone who makes oath to it. 3 *Greenleaf on Evidence,* § 278; Stephenson *v.* Stephenson, 6 *Paige,* 353. So, also, the infant's answer by his mother may be read against her. 3 *Greenleaf on Evidence, note,* p. 239. Hence, we see that under the Code, the case might easily arise where the guardian would be the only person who could properly verify the pleading. But the courts have gone further, and this precise question was raised at special term in Anable *v.* Anable. In this case Justice PECKHAM says, "The first objection to this motion, that the complaint is not properly verified, being by the guardian instead of the infant, is not well grounded. For this purpose the guardian may be regarded as *the* plaintiff or *a* plaintiff. He is so as to the general proceedings in the cause. He verifies it in such case as a *party,* not as *agent* or *attorney* of the party. Anable *v.* Anable, 24 *How. Pr.* 92. There are no decisions in the courts of the State of New York to be found contrary to the foregoing authorities.

Baker & Schwartz, defendants-appellants, in persons.

The plaintiffs' complaint was not properly verified, it having been verified by the guardian *ad litem,* without stating the grounds of his belief, and the reason

why it was not made by the party. The Code, § 449,
provides that "every action must be prosecuted in
the name of the *real party* in interest;" and section
468 provides that. "where an infant has a right of
action, he is entitled to maintain an action thereon;"
and section 469 provides that "before a summons is
issued in the name of an infant" a guardian shall be
appointed for the purpose of the action. Thus clearly
establishing that the infant and not the guardian is
the real party in interest. Sections 525 and 526, provide that the verification must be made by the affidavit of the party, except under certain circumstances,
and that when made by a person other than the party,
he must set forth in the affidavit "the grounds of his
belief," and, "the reasons why it is not made by the
party." The whole matter then rests upon the question, is the guardian *ad litem* the party, or united in
interest with the infant? It is contended he is not.
He is in no manner interested in the result except in
the performance of such duties as necessarily devolve
upon him by reason of his office. He cannot settle or
compromise the claim of his ward without the consent
of the court. The only cases that can be found mili-
tating against this point are Anable *v*. Anable (24
How. Pr. 92) ; Hill *v*. Thacher (3 *Id.* 407); both special term decisions. The first so far as it related to the
subject matter thereof not necessary to the decision
of the case as the defendant was excused from verify-
ing his answer by reason of the nature of the charge
made against him, and beyond the mere assertion of
the justice having nothing to support his position,
except the *dictum obiter* of Justice WILLARD in Hill
v. Thacer, *supra* (cited by Justice PECKHAM as an
authority on the proposition), that if Hill had been
appointed guardian he thought he might in that character have verified the complaint, making, however,
no distinction between guardian and attorney as to

the manner, or what the affidavit should contain, but simply advancing the opinion that he might make such an affidavit. Granting that the guardian *ad litem* in the case at hand could verify the complaint, it is strenuously contended that in that character he verifies as "a person other than the party," and should state "the grounds of his belief" and "the reason why it is not made by the party." There is no provision of the Code conferring this power upon the guardian. He is appointed to prosecute the action by the court, and his duties are the same towards his ward and the conduct of the case as those of an attorney towards his client; he can sue as guardian, or procure the services of an attorney of the court for that purpose. People *v.* N. Y. Common Pleas, 11 *Wend.* 164, 165.

BRADLEY, J.—The contention of the defendants, is that as the affidavit was not made by the party plaintiff it was ineffectual as a verification, because it did not set forth the grounds of his belief, and the reason why it was not made by such party.

The statute provides that the verification must be made by the affidavit of the party, except that under certain prescribed circumstances it may be made by the agent or attorney (*Code Civ. Pro.* § 525). And that when made by a person other than the party, he must set forth in the affidavit the grounds of his belief as to all matters not stated upon his knowledge, and the reason why it is not made by the party (*Id.* 526). The guardian is not a party plaintiff to the action (Sinclair *v.* Sinclair, 13 *Mees. & Welsb.* [*Eng. Excr.*] 640).

But he prosecutes the action and the complaint is his pleading in behalf of the infant plaintiff. And the latter cannot be required to verify the pleading, nor is it any evidence against her, nor does it conclude the infant party (2 *Kent's Com.* 245 ; 3 *Greenl. Ec.*

§ 278 ; Bulkley v. Van Wyck, 5 *Paige*, 536 ; Stephenson v. Stephenson, 6 *Paige*, 353).

The statute provides for verification by a party and by an agent or attorney only. The guardian *ad litem* does not come within the meaning of the term agent or attorney as that term "is usually understood or applied." And if he cannot be deemed a party the verification of a pleading by him as such is not within the statute or provided for by it. But such guardian was appointed to prosecute the action in behalf of the infant. The complaint is his pleading and not that of the infant, and in that sense he is the party pleading, and therefore the party within the contemplation of the statute who may, as such, verify a pleading.

In Anable v. Anable (24 *How. Pr.* 92) it was remarked that the guardian verifies as a party, and not as an attorney or agent of the party, and although the question was not necessarily decided in that case, the rule there stated is in accord with the view which before the Code prevailed, as to his relations to the pleadings and proceedings in the prosecution and defense of suits in behalf of infant parties. And in those in chancery where oath to bill or answer was made or required it was that of the guardian only, because he was deemed the party or person upon the record prosecuting or defending, and the bill or answer his (1 *Barb. Ch. Pr.* 148–9 ; Rogers v. Cruger, 7 *Johns.* 571). There is nothing in the statute which can fairly be treated as a purpose to change such relation, or to so qualify the term party, as to confine it to the party to the action as distinguished from the party pleading, for the purposes of verification.

The guardian *ad litem* for that purpose is a party upon the record, and by him the infant appears and prosecutes, with the right of the latter to inquire on arriving at full age, during its pendency, whether the guardian has properly prosecuted the action ; and to

abandon it, and charge him with costs if he has not
(Waring v. Crane, 2 *Paige*, 79). This relation to the
record is not questioned in People *ex rel.* Baker *v.* N.
Y. Common Pleas (11 *Wend.* 164).

The affidavit of verification seems to have been
properly made by the guardian, as such, in the form
as by a party.

The order should be affirmed.

SMITH, P. J., BARKER and HAIGHT, JJ., concurred.

CLARK, RESPONDENT, *v.* CLARK, APPELLANT.

N. Y. COURT OF COMMON PLEAS, GENERAL TERM,
JUNE, 1886.

§§ 4, 724, 1773.

*Contempt—Power of court to strike out pleading because of—Exercise of
such power in action for divorce.*

The power to strike out a defense in an action in equity for refusal to
obey orders of the court, existed in the court of chancery, and now
exists, and this irrespective of the question whether the defendant
disobeying is within or without the jurisdiction of the court.[1]
This power is inherent in the court, and can be exercised by it in all
cases where a party is in contempt,[2] and it is not necessary that
there be an order adjudging the party proceeded against guilty of
contempt, but it is sufficient if it appears that he was in fact guilty
of contempt.[3,4]
Where the default of the defendant in an action for divorce in answer-
ing, was opened on condition that he pay certain disbursements and
a counsel fee within a time limited by the order, and the defendant
interposed an answer, but failed to pay a counsel fee, etc., and was
adjudged guilty of contempt because of such failure,—*Held*, that the
court had power to strike out his answer, and this, it seems, even if

it did not possess the general power to strike out the answers of those in contempt.[3,4]

(*Decided June* 7, 1886.)

Appeal by defendant from an order striking out his answer.

This action was brought by the plaintiff, who is the wife of the defendant, for a divorce *ab vinculo*. The answer was substantially a general denial. The order appealed from was made on the ground that the defendant had failed and neglected to comply with an order directing him to pay the plaintiff alimony, and also directing him to pay the fees of the referee and counsel. The opinion states other facts.

E. P. Wilder, for plaintiff-respondent.

Wakeman & Campbell, for defendant-appellant.

BOOKSTAVER, J.—The defendant appeared in the action and opposed the granting of any alimony to his wife, but did not answer. The sum of eight dollars per week was granted as alimony, and because of the defendant's failure to answer, an order of reference was taken in due course. After several hearings before the referee the defendant asked leave to answer, which was granted by an order made by default at first, and afterwards the order was allowed to stand on December 11, 1884; but the court imposed as additional terms that the defendant should pay the referee's fees already accrued, and also $100 counsel fees to plaintiff's counsel, within a time limited by the order. Thereupon defendant interposed the answer in question, and proceeded with the reference for a time, but failed to pay the whole of the alimony, counsel and referee's fees, and on May 19, 1885, an order was made at the special term of this court adjudging the defendant guilty of and in contempt of the court

for such failure, and directing that the defendant
"stand committed to the common jail of the city and
county of New York, there to remain, charged upon
said contempt," until he should pay the sums directed
by that order. This order also directed that a commitment issue unless the amounts by said order directed
to be paid should be paid within five days. It also
provided that defendant should diligently proceed
with the trial of the action.   ·

Some payments seem to have been made under this
order, but they were again stopped, and on July 15,
1885, plaintiff moved the court at special term to strike
out the answer for the non-payment of the residue of
alimony, counsel fees, etc. The court again decided
that the defendant must pay them on or before August
27, 1885, or in event of his failure to do so, an order
was to have been entered striking out his answer. No
formal order was entered on this decision, but some
payments seem to have been made under it.

The defendant, however, again made default, and
on October 26, 1885, the plaintiff moved on all the
papers and proceedings in the case, to strike out
defendant's answer, which resulted in an order of the
special term, dated November 30, 1885, granting
plaintiff's motion unless the defendant should, within
twenty days from the service of the order, pay the
alimony due at the time of the hearing of that motion,
amounting to the sum of $251; and also the referee's
fees, then due, amounting to $72; and the balance of
counsel fees, amounting to $50.

This order recited, among other things, that it was
made upon "the opinions, orders and papers used
upon the former motions herein." On January 11,
1886, the defendant having failed to comply with this
order, a final order was made striking out the answer
which the defendant, after default, had been allowed
to interpose, by order of the court, dated December

11, 1884. The power to strike out a defense in an
action in equity, for refusal to obey orders of the
['] court existed, in the court of chancery, and now
exists (Walker v. Walker, 82 N. Y. 260). This,
irrespective of the question whether the defendant is
within or without the jurisdiction of the court (Brisbane v. Brisbane, 34 *Hun*, 339).

['] The power oi the court over its suitors does not
rest on this ground, but on the ground that the party
is in contempt of court. Indeed, it would seem that
if a suitor, instead of removing from the jurisdiction
of the court, remains in it and defies its authority, he
is more clearly guilty of contempt than if he ran away.
If this power is inherent in the court, and can be
exercised by it in all cases where a party is in contempt, much more has it the power in a case like the
present, where the defendant was permitted to answer
after default ; and from the opinion of the court it is
clearly apparent that the payment of the counsel fee
and referee's fees was intended as a condition of let-
ting the answer stand, although not so expressly
stated in the order allowing it. If defendant failed to
perform the conditions on which he was allowed to
answer, we think the court had the right to strike
['] it out, even if the court did not possess the general power to strike out the answers of those in
contempt. But appellant contends that neither the
preliminary order of November 30, 1885, nor the final
order of January 11, 1886, adjudged the defendant
guilty of contempt. We do not understand that it is
necessary for the order to adjudge the party proceeded
against guilty of contempt, in terms ; it is sufficient if
it appears he was guilty of contempt in fact. But if
the contrary were the case, then the order of
['] November 30, 1885, sufficiently adjudges him
guilty of contempt by reciting the "orders and
papers used upon the former motions," among which

was the order of May 19, 1885, which did, in express terms, adjudge defendant guilty of contempt, and order commitment to issue *nisi*.

This order has never been reversed or appealed from and is in full force.

We think the orders appealed from should be affirmed, with costs.

BEACH, J., concurred.

RUDE, RESPONDENT, *v.* CRANDELL, APPELLANT.

COUNTY COURT, ALLEGANY COUNTY, SEPTEMBER, 1886.

§ 526.

Verification.—Objection to insufficiency of, should point out defect.

Where the complaint in an action in a justice's court was duly verified and the defendant filed an answer verified by an agent, in which the agent did not state the reason why he made the verification, or the grounds of his information and belief, and the plaintiff moved for judgment thereon on the grounds that the defendant "had not presented her answer duly verified as required by law," and judgment was thereupon entered in favor of the plaintiff, and against the defendant for the amount claimed in the complaint, with costs,—*Held*, that the answer was not properly verified, but that the plaintiff's objection thereto was not good because it did not specifically point out the particulars wherein the verification was defective, and that the judgment must therefore be reversed.

Snape *v.* Gilbert (13 *Hun*, 494), followed.

It seems, that if the plaintiff had pointed out the defect in the verification in such a case, and after that, the defendant had failed to file an answer with the proper verification, the judgment might very properly be upheld.

Where the complaint in an action in a justice's court is verified and served with the summons, the answer of the defendant is required by Laws of 1881, chapter 414, § 2, to be in writing, and verified,

and the verification and answer should be in the manner as provided by section 526 of the Code of Civil Procedure.
(*Decided September* 23, 1886.)

Appeal by defendant from a judgment recovered.
against him in a justice's court.

The opinion states the facts.

Wilkes Angel, for defendant-appellant.

Benton C. Rude, for plaintiff-respondent.

FARNUM, Co. J.—The plaintiff commenced this
action in a justice's court, and to the summons which
was personally served upon the defendant, there was
attached a complaint duly verified by the plaintiff.

Upon the return day of the summons the plaintiff
appeared by his attorney, and the defendant appeared
by her husband, Luke G. Crandell. The defendant
through her attorney filed with the justice an answer,
verified as follows: "Allegany County, ss. Luke
Crandall being sworn says, that he is the agent for
the defendant in the above entitled action; that the
foregoing answer is true to his own knowledge, except
as to those matters therein stated to be alleged on·
information and belief, and as to those matters he
believes it to be true, sworn, etc."

The return of the justice recites, "Issue being
joined between the parties the plaintiff moved that
judgment be rendered against the defendant in favor
of the plaintiff for $45.64, besides costs, for the reason
that the defendant has not presented her answer duly
verified as required by law." Without passing upon
this question the justice upon the agreement of the
parties adjourned the cause to March 26, 1885. Upon
the adjourned day the same parties appeared, and the
return then further recites, "Plaintiff renews his
motion that judgment be rendered against the defend-

ant and in favor of plaintiff for $45.64, besides costs, for the reason that the defendant has not presented her answer duly verified as required by law." Whereupon without taking any evidence, the justice immediately rendered judgment in favor of the plaintiff and against the defendant for the amount claimed in the complaint, with costs.

The complaint was verified and served with the summons by virtue of chapter 414 of the Act of 1881. Section 2 of that act requires the answer to be in writing and verified as provided for the verification of the complaint. The complaint and answer in justice's court, under chapter 414, cited above, shall be verified in the manner and as provided by section 526 of the Code of Civil Procedure. The verification of the answer does not state the grounds of the affiant's belief, nor the reason why it was not made by the defendant, and it is conceded, as it must be, that the verification is not a compliance with the requirements of section 526 of the Code of Civil Procedure. However, for all practical purposes it complied substantially with the requirements of the Code.

Had the plaintiff's counsel pointed out the defect in the verification, and after that the defendant had failed to file an answer with a proper verification the judgment might very properly be upheld. The only objection made to the answer was, it is not "duly verified as required by law." It was a technical objection, and if the plaintiff be met with techinicality he cannot complain. Had he specifically pointed out the defect, the defendant might have been able to supply it then and there.

In the supreme court it has been held that a similar objection was not good. An objection of this kind must specifically point out the particulars wherein the instrument is defective (Snape v. Gilbert, 13 Hun, 494). If such an objection be unavailing in a

court of record, where the proceedings in the action
are taken by trained attorneys, certaintly it ought
not to be good in a court where the trials are so often
conducted by the parties without counsel.

The judgment must be reversed.

DEMPEWOLF, APPELLANT, v. HILLS, RES-
PONDENT.

SUPERIOR COURT OF THE CITY OF NEW YORK, GEN-
ERAL TERM, FEBRUARY, 1886.

§ 531.

Bill of Particulars.—Of what required in action for slander.

In an action for slander alleged to have been spoken "in the presence and hearing of divers persons" defendant is not entitled to
a bill of particulars showing the names of all the persons in whose
presence the words were spoken, but the plaintiff should be
required to give the names of some persons in whose presence he
claims the words were spoken.*

It is not the office of a bill of particulars to apprise the defendant of
the nature of the plaintiff's proof or of the names of his witnesses.

(*Decided March* 1, 1886.)

---

* In Kranz v. Dunn (8 *N. Y. Civ. Pro.* 408) the General Term of
the Supreme Court, First Department, held, in February, 1884, that
the order requiring the plaintiff in an action for libel to serve upon
the defendant's attorney "a bill of particulars specifying every per_
son and firm to whom he intended to prove the alleged libellous
statement was published, and giving the name of the town or city in
which such persons respectively reside, or have a place of business,"
was properly granted. See also N. Y. Infants Asylum v. Roosevelt
(7 *N. Y. Civ. Pro.* 307).

† See as to nature and office of Bill of Particulars, Note on Bill of
Particulars, 2 *N. Y. Civ. Pro.* 240.

Appeal by plaintiff from order directing plaintiff to serve a further bill of particulars.

The facts appear in the opinion.

Marshall P. Stafford, for appellant.

The sole purpose of a bill of particulars in an action for slander is that the defendant may have the time and place at which the words were spoken pointed out so definitely and distinctly that he may know with certainty the occasion to which the complaint refers. Jones *v.* Platt, 60 *How. Pr.* 278 ; Solomon *v.* Stock Exchange, 49 *N. Y. Super.* (17 *J. & S.*) 139 : Butler *v.* Mann, 9 *Abb. N. C.* 49.

Even if the name of some one individual were necessary to enable the defendant to know the occasion referred to, the plaintiff ought not to be compelled to give him the names of all the persons she proposes to call as witnesses on the question of uttering the slander.

Edward S. Clinch, for respondent.

The bill of particulars demanded was proper. Stiebeling *v.* Lockhaus, 21 *Hun*, 457 ; Gardinier *v.* Knox, 27 *Id.* 500.

PER CURIAM.—The complaint was upon an alleged slander of plaintiff by defendant, averred to have been spoken "in the presence and hearing of divers persons." The defendant demanded a bill of the particulars of the time and place of the slander. This was served without any information as to the names of persons in whose presence or hearing the slander was claimed to have been uttered. The order appealed from was then made, that plaintiff serve "a statement in writing, of the names of the persons in whose presence or hearing" the plaintiff claimed the slander was uttered.

The defendant claimed that the order was neces-sary to enable him to draw his answer and prepare for trial. Less than the names of all persons claimed to have been present, would enable the defendant to draw a truthful answer which would deny or admit the slander. And to prepare for trial, it was not necessary to do more than specify a particular occa-sion, to which the defendant might direct his prepara-tion. It is not the office of a bill of particulars, to apprise the defendant of the nature of the plaintiff's proof, or of the names of his witnesses. On the trial, it would not be just that the plaintiff should fail be-cause of some person, among others named in the bill, not being present, although there might be no doubt that the speaking relied on by plaintiff was the one actually referred to in the bill served. The order made below should be so modified, that it require a further bill to give the name of some person in whose presence the plaintiff claims the words were spoken.

The order, as modified, is affirmed, with $10 **costs** to abide event.

SEDGWICK, Ch. J. and TRUAX, J., concur.

SPRAGUE, Appellant, v. PARSONS, et al.,
Respondents.

N. Y. Common Pleas, General Term, May, 1886.

§ 481.

Pleading – Complaint in action for damages sustained by levy of an attachment.— When does not state sufficient facts.

An allegation in the complaint in an action for damages sustained by levy of an attachment, that the attachment was wholly illegal and unauthorized by law, and the court had no jurisdiction to issue the same and the same was null and void, is a statement of a conclusion of law only.*

An allegation that the action in which the attachment was issued was one against the plaintiff and others to charge them with the debt of a certain corporation (therein named), of which it was claimed the defendants in that suit were trustees, but it was not stated whether they were sought to be held liable as trustees or as sureties, does not necessarily show that the attachment was unauthorized.

An allegation in a complaint in an action brought against the plaintiff in an attachment to recover damages sustained thereby, that the attachment was vacated on motion, without stating whether it was vacated for irregularity or as unauthorized, is insufficient to sustain the action; unless the attachment was unauthorized or irregular an action for damages not brought upon the undertaking could not be maintained.

(*Decided June* 7, 1886.)

Appeal by the plaintiff from a judgment in favor of defendants entered upon dismissal of the complaint at trial term.

---

* See Sprague v. Parsons, 6 *N. Y. Civ. Pro.* 26, where the justice who wrote the opinion here reported, held, in determining a demurrer to a complaint in this case—since amended—that an action to recover damages sustained by an attachment may be maintained, if the attachment be irregular only, on proof that it has been set aside; but that an allegation in the complaint that the attachment was "illegal, unauthorized and void," was a conclusion of law, and therefore not sufficient to admit proof that the attachment was void.

The complaint was dismissed upon the ground that it did not state facts sufficient to constitute a cause of action. The action was to recover damages sustained by the levy of an attachment in an action brought by defendants against the plaintiff and others in the supreme court, which attachment had been vacated. The defendants asked for a dismissal of the complaint for the reason that the allegations of fact in the complaint did not show that the attachment was unauthorized or was irregular.

W. Z. Larned, for appellant.

Gilbert R. Hawes, for respondent.

DALY, J.—The allegation of the complaint that the attachment was wholly illegal or unauthorized by law, and the court had no jurisdiction to issue the same, and the same was null and void, is a statement of a conclusion of law, and sets forth no fact whatever (Hammond *v.* Earle, 58 *How. Pr.* 426).

The allegation that the action in which the attachment was issued was an action against this plaintiff and others to charge them with liability for the debt of the McKillop & Sprague Company of which corporation it was claimed that the defendants in that suit were trustees, does not show that the action was one in which an attachment was unauthorized. It does not state that the defendants therein were sought to be charged with liability as trustees. The liability with which they were sought to be charged might have been that of surety and yet the allegation would have been true; the claim that they were trustees, not being averred as the ground of action. As, therefore, that action may have been an action for a money demand on contract, for aught that appears in the complaint in this action, it is not shown that the attachment was unauthorized in the action.

Nothing is left, therefore, but the allegation that the attachment was vacated on motion. But it is not alleged that it was vacated for irregularity nor as being unauthorized. It might have been vacated for error upon a question of fact upon opposing affidavits. Unless unauthorized, or irregular, an action of damages (not brought upon the undertaking) could not be maintained (Day v. Bach, 87 *N. Y.* 56).

It appears, therefore, that no facts were stated in the complaint constituting a cause of action, and the complaint was properly dismissed.

On the argument of a demurrer to the original complaint in this action (it has since been amended), I held that the complaint might be sustained as upon an attachment set aside for irregularity but that point was evidently not discussed by counsel.*

Judgment should be affirmed, with costs.

BOOKSTAVER, J., concurred.

---

* The decision here referred to is reported 6 *N. Y. Civ. Pro.* 38.

MOREHOUSE, Respondent, *v.* MOREHOUSE, by
Committee, etc., Appellant.

Supreme Court, Third Department, General
Term, June, 1886.

§§ 829, 830.

*Evidence.—When testimony of party taken on former trial may be used,
because he has become incompetent.— When testimony taken on trial
of action may be used on the trial of a subsequent action,
although the parties are not precisely the same.— When
joint indebtedness becomes several.*

Where devisees of real property partitioned the same between them
and procured a mortgage thereon to be foreclosed, each one agreeing to pay the holder thereof upon the bid, one half the amount
due upon the mortgage with costs,—*Held,* that the holder of the
mortgage could have held them as joint debtors, but that, as he,
at their request, treated each as his separate debtor for the one-
half, and acted to his own prejudice upon that request, he had the
right to treat them as estopped from insisting that they were joint
debtors, and that a payment made by one of said debtors did not
release the other and was not the payment of the other, it being
clear that it was the purpose of all the parties that payment should
be made by each for himself, and for the release of his half premises and not at all for the benefit of the other debtor, or for the
release of his half; and this is so notwithstanding the debtor
making such payment by reason of some mistake in the figures,
paid more than his half of the debt.

It seems, that where the parties to two actions are the same or in
privity, and the issues or the point in issue the same, evidence
given by a witness on the trial of one action is admissible on the
trial of the other.

If the subject matter to be established in an action is the same
against the party against whom testimony given on the trial of a
former action, is offered, and was of as much importance to the
issue in the former as in the present action, and the witness giving
such testimony is dead, it should not be excluded, although the
parties to the two actions were not quite the same.

Philadelphia, &c. R. R. Co. v. Howard (13 *How. U. S.* 334), followed. Section 830 of the Code of Civil Procedure, which provides for the reading, upon the trial of an action, of testimony given upon a former trial by one who has since become incompetent to testify, is remedial and should be liberally construed.

Testimony given on a former trial, by a party to an action, who has since become generally incompetent by reason of the insanity of his opponent may be read on the second trial of the action; it is not necessary that such incompetency result from death to entitle such testimony to be read.

Where, on the foreclosure of a mortgage, the mortgaged premises were struck off to two owners of the equity of redemption, who had apportioned the premises between them, and agreed to each pay half of the sum bid, but the sale was not completed by the payment thereof,—*Held*, that so long as the sale remained incomplete, by the refusal of one of the purchasers to pay his part of the bid, the mortgagee could not be deprived, without his own consent, of the benefit of his mortgage, and could not be compelled against his consent, to waive a good security and take a cause of action as for a simple debt against the purchaser; that the statute of limitations not having run against the mortgage, an action to have an affidavit of foreclosure of sale canceled, and removed from the records so far as they affect that part of the premises set-off to one of said purchasers, unless he pay the balance remaining due on account of his proportion of the bid, with interest and costs, and that if he failed to pay said sum for leave to foreclose the mortgage for that amount, and that the sale under such foreclosure be limited to the part of the premises set off to said purchaser, was not barred by the statute of limitations.

In such a case.—*Held*, that the contention of the defendant that the mortgage could not be satisfied in effect as to one part of the mortgaged premises and remain a lien upon the other part, rested upon no foundation.

(*Decided June*, 1886.)

Appeal by defendant Joel B. Morehouse, by his committee, etc., from a judgment entered upon decision of the Saratoga county special term.

This action was originally commenced, March 2, 1874, against Joel B. Morehouse, impleaded with his wife and Talcott B. Morehouse. It was once tried

and determined in favor of said defendant Joel B.
Morehouse, and afterwards reversed at general term.
In 1883 after the order for a new trial was granted, and
before the case again came on for trial, the defendant
was prostrated by a stroke of paralysis which entirely
destroyed his mind, and a committee of his person
and estate was appointed, by whom this action was
continued without prejudice to any and all proceedings had in the action prior to December 24, 1883.
Subsequently the action was tried at special term in
Saratoga county, and judgment rendered in favor of the
plaintff, from which judgment this appeal was taken.
 The facts as stated in the complaint are substantially as follows : John Morehouse by his last will and
testament, which was on January 15, 1860, duly
admitted to probate, by the surrogate of Saratoga
county, devised unto his sons Joel B. and Talcott B.
Morehouse, his "homestead farm," to be held by
them share and share alike ; which farm the said Joel
B. and Talcott B. Morehouse, afterwards partitioned
between themselves, and the said Joel B., thereby
became seized and possessed in his own right of the
south half thereof. At the time of the death of the
said John Morehouse, said farm was incumbered by a
mortgage, executed by him to Daniel B. Campbell,
dated September 13, 1858, to secure the payment of
$559.68 and interest, which mortgage was on April 8,
1861, duly assigned by said Campbell unto plaintiff.
A short time before taking such assignment it having
been discovered that there not having been sufficient
personal property of the testator John Morehouse to
pay his debts, and that the said farm would be
required by a sale thereof to pay said debts, the said
Joel B. and Talcott B. Morehouse, preferring to take
title thereto by a foreclosure of said mortgage, they
and the executors of John B. Morehouse requested
the plaintiff to purchase said mortgage from said

Campbell, and take an assignment of the same and foreclose it, and such assignment was taken in pursuance of such request, and plaintiff paid therefor with his own money the sum of $651, that being the amount then due thereon. Thereafter, in accordance with said request, the plaintiff commenced proceedings to foreclose the said mortgage by advertising, and in pursuance of the notice contained in such advertisement, the said premises covered by the aforesaid mortgage were struck off to the said Joel B. and Talcott B. Morehouse for the sum of $2,200, which sum it was understood and agreed was sufficient to cover the amount due to the plaintiff on the aforesaid mortgage, the costs of the foreclosure proceedings, and also the balance of the debts and liabilities due from the estate of the said John Morehouse, deceased. The amount due on the mortgage for principal, interest and costs, at the time of the sale was $734.41 ; and it was agreed between the plaintiff and the said Joel B. and Talcott B. Morehouse, and the executors of their father's will, that the plaintiff should receive from them in payment of their said bid, the amount due him in cash, and receipts for the payment of debts against the estate, for the balance of the bid, and in pursuance of such arrangement, the defendant Talcott B. Morehouse paid the plaintiff $215 in cash, and as to the balance produced receipts for the payment of the debts of said estate, but the defendant Joel B. Morehouse did not pay his half of the bid, or any part thereof. The affidavit of publication and other requisite affidavits, relating to the foreclosure and sale were made by and remained in the possession of the plaintiff for some time after the sale, but were subsequently delivered at the request or by the consent of the said Joel B. and Talcott B. Morehouse to one Calvin W. Dake, to be retained by him until the said Joel B. Morehouse paid his proportion of the said bid; and the. said affidavits, etc., were thereafter, without the knowledge or consent of the plaintiff recorded in the office of the clerk of Saratoga county.

The plaintiff demanded judgment "that it be decreed that the aforesaid recording of the afor. said affidavits of foreclosure and sale be canceled or removed from the aforesaid record, so far as the said record and sale affect that part of said premises set off to the said Joel B. or claimed by him, unless the said Joel B. Morehouse shall, within a certain time named in the decretal judgment of this court, pay to the said plaintiff the amount remaining due to him from the said Joel B. Morehouse on account of his proportion of said bid on the aforesaid sale, together with interest thereon from the time of said sale and the costs of this action; and that it be further adjudged and decreed that if the said Joel B. Morehouse shall fail to pay the aforesaid sum of money within the time therein named, that the said plaintiff be at liberty to foreclose the aforesaid mortgage for the principal and interest due thereon, less the said $215 paid by the said Talcott B. Morehouse; and that upon a sale under such foreclosure the said sale be limited and confined to that part of the said premises set off to Joel B. Morehouse, in the partition between the said Joel B. and Talcott B. Morehouse, or to that part of the homestead premises covered by said mortgage that the said Joel now claims to own. And that such other order, judgment or decree may be granted as will be just and agreeable to equity, together with the costs."

The defendant Joel B. Morehouse, who alone answered, among other things: (1.) admitted the purchase of the Campbell mortgage by the plaintiff, and the foreclosure of it and sale of the premises thereunder, and the purchase of them by the defendants at said sale, and denied all other allegations of the complaint ; (2.) set up that the cause of action accrued more than six years before the action was commenced, and that the same was barred by the statute of limitations ; and (3) alleged payment of the amount due to the plaintiff on said bid.

On the second trial at special term the plaintiff put in evidence against the defendant's objection, all the testimony given by both parties on the former trial, including that given by the plaintiff and that given by the defendant, in his own behalf. He also put in evidence the judgment-roll and a portion of the evidence of Joel B. Morehouse and of Calvin W. Dake (who died prior to this trial) in three other actions brought by Freeman Tourtellot, Simeon Scouton and David Bennet, respectively, against the plaintiff herein, and the defendants Joel B. Morehouse and Talcott B. Morehouse, which three actions were tried together.

Said actions were brought for the purpose of charging debts due the plaintiffs therein from John Morehouse, deceased, upon the real property devised by him to the defendants Joel B. and Talcott Morehouse, and to secure the payment of said debts from the proceeds of a sale thereof.

The complaint, among other things, set out the devise of the property in suit to the defendants Joel B. and Talcott B. Morehouse ; that they had accepted the same, and had entered into possession thereof; the purchase and foreclosure of the mortgage by Nelson D. Morehouse, and the purchase of the property covered thereby at the sale by Joel B. and Talcott B. Morehouse, and alleged that such transfer of the mortgage, and sale thereunder, were made for the purpose, and with the intent to cheat and defraud the plaintiff in said action, out of the sum due him, and that by false and fraudulent statements the defendants in said action, deterred and prevented others intending and desiring to bid at said sale, from so doing, and that the said premises were sold at much less than their value. The answer of the defendants denied the allegations of the complaint setting out fraud, and that the defendants, Joel B. and Talcott B. Morehouse accepted the devise ; and averred, that after the executors of John Morehouse, deceased, had become satisfied that his debts "could not be made from the personal estate, and that a sale of the real estate by the order of the surrogate or in some other way, would become necessary for the pay- ment of debts, it was agreed between the said execu- tors and the said Nelson D. Morehouse, that the said Nelson D. Morehouse should purchase from Daniel D. Campbell the aforesaid mortgage and foreclose it, with a view of having the premises sold for the pur- pose of realizing money to apply upon the said debts, the said Daniel D. Campbell having made demands upon the executors for the payment of the amount due upon the said mortgage, threatening to foreclose the same if payment was not made, and the said executors being of the opinion that the said mortgage could be foreclosed at less expense in the hands of the said Nelson D. Morehouse than if foreclosed by the said Campbell, and thereby obtain money without the expense of proceedings before the surrogate, and that the said mortgage was purchased by said Nelson D. Morehouse under the said agreement and foreclosed by him, and the premises were purchased by the said Joel B. Morehouse and Talcott B. Morehouse on or about the twenty-eighth day of October, 1861, at the sum of $2200, being the full value of the said premises, subject to the incumbrances thereon, which incum- brances amounted to about $800 ; that the said sale was in all respects fairly conducted, no representations were made by the said defendants or to their knowl- edge, intended or calculated to prevent competition at said sale ; that the said defendants Joel B. Morehouse and Talcott B. Morehouse have fully paid over to the said Nelson D. Morehouse the whole of said $2200, except their pro rata share of the amount due them from the estate of the said John Morehouse."

The testimony of Joel B. Morehouse in those actions which was received in evidence in this, related to the agreement under which the assignment of the mortgage and sale thereunder were made, and the testimony of Calvin Dake, which was read in evidence, was as follows: ⸙

"I believe I have the affidavits on the last foreclosure ; Nelson Morehouse left them with me to retain until Bradley had complied with the condition of the bid ; he bid it off as I understood. I have never had any instructions to deliver them. ——(sic) any demand made on me for them."

All this evidence was objected to by the defendant and exceptions duly taken.

The testimony of the plaintiff and of Joel B. Morehouse, given on the former trial, was also received in evidence, subject to defendant's exception to its admissibility.

A. Pond (*Pond & French*, attorneys), for defendant-appellant.

The debt created by that joint bid by the defendants constituted a joint debt of the two defendants, Joel B. and Talcott B. Morehouse, for whom the bid was made, and a payment by either of the joint debtors would extinguish it. The plaintiff testified that he had never released Talcott from his liability to him on this bid. Hence, any payment by Talcott on this joint indebtedness of his and Joel B., extinguished the debt, to the full extent of the payment, and operates to the joint benefit of both debtors, and when once made could not be recalled. Le Page *v.* McCrea, 1 *Wend.* 164 ; Hobby *v.* Hobby, 5 *Cush.*

(*Mass.*) 516 ; Marvin *v.* Vedder, 5 *Cow.* 671. . . . A payment on a debt against two joint debtors by one, operates when made, to extinguish the debt, to the extent of such payment, and it cannot be repudiated or taken back by the creditor, and only partly applied, because he says now it will pay more than the proportion of the debt, owing by the joint debtor making such payment. Le Page *v.* McCrea, 1 *Wend.* 164; Hobby *v.* Hobby, 5 *Cush.* 516. Nor could the lien of the mortgage debt so paid by said note of $449, so taken as cash, and thereby discharged to that amount, be again revived, even by an express agreement between Talcott B. and the plaintiff to that effect, if one had been made, which is not pretended. Marvin *v.* Vedder, 5 *Cow.* 671. . . . The rule is, that the evidence given by a witness since dead, in another case between other parties, is admissible, if the issue in the two cases are the same, but not otherwise. 1 *Greenl. Ev.* § 164 ; Jackson *v.* Crissey, 3 *Wend.* 251 ; Osborn *v.* Bell, 5 *Denio*, 370, 378. Greenleaf says : " Where, therefore, the point in issue in both actions was not the same, the issue in the former action having been upon a common or free fishery, and in the latter, it being upon a several fishery, evidence of what a witness since deceased swore upon a former trial, was held inadmissible." 1 *Greenl. Ev.* § 164 ; Malvin *v.* Whiting, 7 *Pick.* 79, 81. . . . The right of action for the debt created by the bid by the defendants at the foreclosure sale, and to secure the payment of which the plaintiff claims an equitable lien on the real estate so sold by him and purchased by them, was itself barred in six years from said sale by the statute of limitations. . . . And after the debt has become extinguished, either by the operation of the statute of limitations, or by bankruptcy or otherwise, in such case, nothing would then remain to support a lien. The debt is the principal, and the lien the incident, and when the former dies, the latter ceases to exist also. This is extremely well settled law. *Code of Procedure*, § 91, subd. 1 ; Borst *v.* Corey, 15 *N. Y.* 505, 511 ; Rundle *v.* Allison, 34 *Id.* 180, 182 ; Loder *v.* Hatfield, 71 *Id.* 92, 103, 104; Am. Bible Soc. *v.* Hebard, 51 *Barb.* 553; S. C., aff'd, 41 *N. Y.* 619 ; Matter of Neilley, 95 *Id.* 382, 390 ; Ocean Nat. Bank *v.* Olcott, 46 *Id.* 12, 22; Linthicum *v.* Tapscott, 28 *Ark.* 287 ; Yates *v.* Wooden, 6 *Bush (Ky.)* 438. . . . Where the remedies at law and in equity are concurrent, the same statute of limitations which bars the legal remedy bars the equitable remedy also. See all the cases above cited, and particularly Borst *v.* Corey, 15 *N. Y.* 505, 510; McCrea *v.* Purmort, 16 *Wend.* 460, 476 ; Rundle *v.* Allison, 34 *N. Y.* 180, 182 ; Coleman *v.* Second Ave. R. R. Co., 38 *Id.* 201 ; Foot *v.* Farrington, 41 *Id.* 164, 171 ; Morris *v.* Budlong, 78 *Id.* 544, 559 ; Am. Bib. Soc. *v.* Hebard, 51 *Barb.* 552, 570 ; Matter of Neilley, 95 *N. Y.* 382, 390. And see Thomas *v.* Dickenson (12 *N. Y.* 364, 370), as to right of vendor to maintain action at law for purchase price of land sold. Pierson *v.* McCready, 22 *N. Y. Weekly Dig.* 258. . . . The answer admits both the sale and bid, and hence the pleadings show a valid sale and a legal bid, as already shown. Now, said sale on foreclosure being valid and regular, it extinguished the mortgage, and the plaintiff's only remedy, while the sale stands, is to collect the bid. Stackpole *v.* Robbins, 47 *Barb.* 212, 217 ; Knower *v.* Reynolds, 99 *N. Y.* 245, 249. . . . And see Coulter *v.* Bower, 64 *How. Pr.* 132, 134.

Nathaniel C. Moak (John C. Hurlburt, attorney), for plaintiff-respondent.

The deposition of plaintiff taken before trial on application of Joel B., was competent on this trial in behalf of plaintiff. Rice *v.* Motley, 24 *Hun*, 143. The testimony of Calvin W. Dake given before Judge

FERRIS, as referee in the suit by Truman Tourtellot against Joel B. Morehouse, Talcott B. Morehouse and Nelson D. Morehouse, was competent. 1. Dake was called, sworn and gave testimony in that suit in behalf of the defendants. 2. The defendants in that suit answered; the answer was sworn to by Joel B. 3. They asserted the legality of the sale, and that plaintiff held himself liable to the estate, less mortgage, debts, costs, etc. 4. The testimony of a witness thus called by Joel B., even though also called by others, and sworn upon material issues, was competent testimony in favor of another party who had answered, and took part in the trial. The competency of the testimony does not depend upon examination of the witness by the party against whom the testimony is offered, but upon the right to examine. Bradley *v.* Mirick, 91 *N. Y.* 293 ; Lawson *v.* Jones, 1 *N. Y. Civ. Pro.* 247 ; Cozenon *v.* Vaughn, 1 *Maule & Selw.* 4. 5. The point in issue in the Tourtellot suit was, whether Joel B. had, under the mortgage foreclosure by Nelson D., obtained a good title to the land in question. The question whether title was held in escrow by Dake, or was held by him, was material. Osborn *v.* Bell, 5 *Denio*, 377 ; Clark *v.* Vorce, 15 *Wend.* 193 ; Jones *v.* Jones, 45 *Md.* 153 ; Jackson *v.* Bailey, 2 *Johns.* 19, 20. It is not necessary the parties should be the same if the parties to the suit were parties in the former suit. Philadelphia, etc. R. R. Co. *v.* Howard, 13 *How. U. S.* 334, 335. On the trial of an action brought by an administrator to recover damages for the death of his intestate, caused by the wrongful act of the defendant, evidence is admissible to prove what was the testimony of witnesses since deceased, on the trial of an action brought by said intestate, and abated by his death, for damages for injuries caused by said wrongful act. Indianapolis, etc. *v.* Stout, 53 *Ind.* 143. The testimony of the plaintiff on the former trial was competent. 1. The

Code (§ 830) entitles it to be read. That section of the Code, as originally passed in 1877 (2 *Laws* 1877, p. 266), simply excluded the husband or wife of a party, when the party was excluded. That section was repealed in 1878, p. 174. The present section was enacted and numbered 830, in 1879 (*Laws* 1879, p. 618). The design of section 830 was, when a party had been properly examined, and was incompetent generally, at the second trial, his testimony, taken at a time when it was properly taken, and the adverse party had an opportunity to, or ought to have answered it, the testimony so taken, should be competent. "A thing within the meaning and intent of a statute, is within it, though not within the language thereof, and even though it seem contrary to the letter of the statute." Jackson *v.* Collins, 3 *Cow.* 89, 96 ; James *v.* Patten, 6 *N. Y.* 9, 13. "The intent and meaning of the statute must be found partly from the words of the statute, and partly from the mischief which the statute was intended to remedy. That intent sometimes becomes so controlling that it is found necessary to expound it against the letter, in order to preserve the intent of the statute ; for a thing which is within the letter is not within the statute, unless it be within the intention of the makers." White *v.* Wager, 32 *Barb.* 253 ; Rice *v.* Mead, 22 *How. Pr.* 449. 2. And it is even immaterial whether the party whose evidence is offered was, or was not cross-examined if he might have been. Bradley *v.* Mirick, 91 *N. Y.* 295 ; Lawson *v.* Jones, 1 *N. Y. Civ. Pro.* 247. 3. The testimony was admissible at common law without any statute. If testimony be competent when given, and the witness be subsequently made incompetent, the testimony given when he was competent may be read. The deposition of an interested witness, taken in an equity proceeding, when both parties are alive, is admissible in evidence after the death of one of said parties, in an action of eject-

ment touching the same subject-matter between the
survivor of the representative of the party deceased.
Galbraith *v.* Zimmerman, 100 *Penn. St.* 374. . . .
Where one sues by a guardian or committee, such
guardian or committee is not a party to the suit. It
is the suit of the party by his protector. Bryant *v.*
Livermore, 20 *Minn.* 314, 342 : George *v.* High, 85 *N.
C.* 113. . . .

LANDON, J.—The finding that Joel B. Morehouse
has never paid anything upon or by reason of the bid
upon the foreclosure sale, is in accord with the evidence of Joel himself. The elaborate argument of the
appellant in opposition to this finding rests upon the
fiction of a constructive payment for Joel by means
of the payment of Talcott, when it is quite clear that
it was the purpose of all the parties that Talcott's
payment should be for himself and for the release of
his half of the farm, and not at all for the benefit of
Joel or for the release of his half. If by means of any
mistake in figures, Talcott should be credited with
more than his half, which is not clear, he did not pay
it for Joel's benefit, did not intend to do so, and it
would be an entire perversion of the understanding of
the parties to give it that effect now. Each was the
devisee of an undivided half of the farm covered by
the mortgage. They partitioned the farm between
themselves ; procured plaintiff to foreclose the mortgage, each one agreeing to pay plaintiff, upon the bid,
one half the amount due upon the mortgage with
costs. The plaintiff could have held them as joint
debtors, but at their request treated each as his separate debtor for the one half, and acted to his own prejudice upon that request, and has the right to treat
them as estopped to insist that they are joint debtors.
Upon the trial, the testimony of Calvin Dake, then
deceased, which he had given in an action in which

one Turtellot was plaintiff and Nelson, Talcott, and Joel B. Morehouse were defendants, was read in evidence against the objection of Joel B. The parties to this action were parties to that action. The issues framed by the pleadings are not precisely the same, but under the issues in each action the point in issue touched by Dake's testimony was the same, and in the former action must have been fatal to the main defense alleged, whereas in this action its force would have been entirely neutralized if the payment alleged by the defendant Joel had been established.

Where the parties are the same or in privity, and the issues, or the point in issue the same, such evidence is admissible (Jackson *ex dem.* Barton *v.* Crissey, 3 *Wend.* 251 ; Osborn *v.* Bell, 5 *Denio*, 370 ; Lawson *v.* Jones, 1 *N. Y. Civ. Pro.* 247 ; Clark *v.* Vorce, 15 *Wend.* 193 ; Bradley *v.* Mirick, 91 *N. Y.* 293).

When the parties are the same, and the point in issue the same, we can clearly see, that the party against whom the testimony is offered had the same opportunity and the same interest as now to resort to every test to probe the witness and his testimony, and we see no reason, although the parties are not quite the same, if the subject matter to be now established is the same against the party against whom the testimony is offered as upon a former trial, and was of as much importance to that issue as it is to this, why the death of the witness should exclude his testimony. The party against whom it is now offered has once had his day in court in the very matter of developing that testimony, and that too under a pressure of interest as great as now exists, so that nothing can be presumed to have been omitted from want of opportunity, care or interest.

In Philadelphia, &c. R. R. Co. *v.* Howard, 13 *How. U. S.* 334–5, the action was between Howard and the Philadelphia, W. & B. R. R. Co. as for covenant broken. There had been a former action between Howard and another, and the Wilmington & S. R. R. Co., as for assumpsit. The Wilmington & S. R. R. Co., and the Baltimore & P. D. Co., were subsequently by the legislature consolidated into the present defendant, the Philadelphia, &c. R. R. Co. The deposition of a witness taken upon the same *subject matter* in issue in this case as in the former,—viz., whether a certain paper, made by one of the constituent companies, was under its corporate seal or not,—was held to be admissible. There the parties were not the same ; one action was assumpsit, the other covenant. See also 1 *Greenleaf Ev.* § 164.

Upon principle and authority, we think the evidence was properly received.

The testimony of the plaintiff given upon the former trial of this action was properly received under § 830, *Code Civ. Pro.*

That section is remedial, and should be liberally construed. It renders competent : 1st, the testimony of a party given upon a former trial, in case such party has since died ; 2d, the testimony given on the former trial of any person who since then has become incompetent to be examined on this trial, by virtue of section 829. Section 829 affects the competency of the witness to be now examined, but section 830 establishes the competency of his testimony given upon a former trial of the same case. A technical reading of the section which should make the death of a party the condition precedent to the competency of the testimony of any witness other than the deceased party, may possibly be made, but the spirit of the statute should prevail, and that gives competency to the testimony previously given in the case between the same parties, before the incompetency attached to the witness.

Pennsylvania cases tend to show that this sensible

Morehouse v. Morehouse.

rule exists at common law (Galbraith v. Zimmerman, 100 *Penn. St.* 374; Pratt v. Patterson, 31 *P. F. S.* [*Pa.*] 114; Evans v. Reed, 28 *Ib.* 415; Hay's Appeal, 10 *Norr.* [*Pa.*] 256); and we think it should not be defeated by an adherence to the letter in opposition to the spirit of the statute.

The objection of the statute of limitations was overruled upon the former appeal.*

The complaint states that upon a foreclosure of the mortgage by advertisement, the mortgaged premises were struck off to Joel B. and Talcott Morehouse, and it characterizes that proceeding as a sale, but it expressly shows that the sale was not completed by payment of the sum bid. So long as the sale remains incomplete by the refusal of the defendant to pay his part of the bid, the plaintiff cannot be deprived, without his own consent, of the benefit of his mortgage. He cannot be compelled against his consent to waive a good security and take a cause of action as for a simple debt against such a debtor. No statute of limitations has run against his mortgage. The contention of the defendant that the mortgage could not be satisfied in effect as to Talcott's share of the farm and be on foot upon Joel's, rests upon no solid foundation.

It was Talcott's duty to protect by payment his own share, under the understanding between Joel, Talcott and the plaintiff.

The judgment is right, and should be affirmed, with costs.

PECKHAM, J., concurred.

BOCKES, P. J., not sitting.

---

* Morehouse v. Morehouse, 15 *N. Y. Weekly Dig.* 575.

WEITKAMP, Respondent, *v.* LOEHR, Impleaded, etc., Appellant.

Superior Court of the City of New York, Special Term, August, 1885 ; also General Term, February, 1886.

§§ 635, 636.

Attachment,—What amounts to non-residence,—Distinction between residence and domicile.

The meaning of residence, inhabitancy and domicile stated, and the distinction between them,—particularly as the terms are used with reference to attachments under the Code of Civil Procedure,— pointed out. [²⁻⁵, ⁸⁻¹¹]*

Actual cessation to dwell within the State for an uncertain period, without definite intention as to any fixed time of returning, even though a general intention to return at some time in the future may may exist, constitutes non-residence, and warrants the issue of an attachment under sections 635 and 636 of the Code of Civil Procedure. [¹²]

De Meli *v.* De Meli (5 *N. Y. Civ. Pro.* 306); [⁸,¹⁰] Depuy *v.* Wurts (53 *N. Y.* 556), [¹⁰,¹¹] distinguished.

Where, on a motion to vacate an attachment granted in April, 1885, on the ground that the defendant was a non-resident of this State, it appeared that in June, 1884, the defendant removed from the city of Brooklyn, in this State, where he had previously resided with his family, to Milwaukee, Wisconsin, with the intention of remaining there for an indefinite period, and then returning to Brooklyn ; that he stored his furniture in the city of Brooklyn, but did not have any place of abode or house in which he could at the time the attachment was issued call his home or residence ; that he occasionally returned to New York on business, and while here stayed temporarily in boarding-houses in Brooklyn, but that during the greater part of the time between his removal and the

---

* The meaning of and distinction between the terms, residence and domicile are considered in a Note on Security of Costs, 4 *N. Y. Civ. Pro.* 82, at p. 87.

Weitkamp v. Loehr.

issuing of the attachment he was absent in Milwaukee, or traveling in relation to his business,—*Held*, that the defendant was a non-resident of the State within the meaning of the provisions of the Code, providing for the issuing of an attachment on that ground ; [⁶, ¹²] that the attachment was properly granted, and should not be vacated. [⁷, ¹³]

It is well settled that a person may have a domicile in this State and at the same time be a resident of another State. [¹]

In re Thompson (1 *Wend.* 43) ; [²] Mayor *v.* Gennett (4 *Hun*, 489) ; [³] Wallace *v.* Castle (68 *N. Y.* 374) ; [⁴] *In re* Collins (64 *How. Pr.* 65), [⁵] followed.

(*Decided at Special Term, August* 29, 1885, *at General Term, March* 1, 1886.)

Motion by defendant, Francis Loehr, that an attachment issued against his property on the ground that he is a non-resident of the State be vacated.

The facts appear in the opinions here reported.

John D. Ahrens, for defendant and motion.

Frank J. Dupignac, for plaintiff, opposed.

INGRAHAM, J.—From the facts as they appear in this application, it is clear that the defendant did not lose his domicile in this State.

[¹]   It is well settled, however, that a person may have a domicile within this State, and at the same time be a resident of another State.

[²]   In the matter of Thompson (1 *Wend.* 43), the supreme court states the distinction, and held that the question is one of actual residence at the time the warrant is issued ; and this case has been approved in Haggart *v.* Morgan (5 *N. Y.* 432.)

[³]   In the case of the Mayor *v.* Genet (4 *Hun*, 489), the supreme court held that where a person left the State with the design of remaining beyond the limits of the State, he became a non-resident, and

liable to have his property seized by attachment ; and
in Wallace v. Castle, 68 N. Y. 374, the court of
['] appeals held, that the fact that a person had a
place of business in the city of New York was
not sufficient to constitute him a resident, so as to
exempt him from attachment.

['] In the matter of Collins (64 *How. Pr.* 65), it
was held, that residence means the act or state of
being seated or settled in a place. It imports not only
personal presence in a place, but an attachment to it
by those acts or habits which express the closest connection between the person and the place, as by usually sitting or lying there.

It appears in this case, from the defendant's own
statement, that about June 25, 1884, the house at which
he then resided with his family was given up, and his
family removed to Milwaukee, with the intention of
remaining there for an indefinite period (at any rate
until the following October), and then returning to
Brooklyn ; that for a considerable portion of the time
between said removal and the issuing of the attachment the defendant was absent in Milwaukee, or
traveling in relation to his business; that while he
was here he boarded at two places in Brooklyn, one of
such places being an hotel ; that on March 15, defendant
left New York city, and was absent from the State
until May 14, 1885. During the time he was absent
it does not appear that the defendant had any place
of abode or residence in Brooklyn, or in this State ; no
house that he could at that time call his home or residence.

Nothing appears that would show that defendant
intended to retain his residence in Brooklyn, and
although the case is a close one, I think that
['] under the rule as stated in the cases above cited,
the defendant was not a resident of this State at
the time the attachment was granted.

[*]   The motion to vacate the attachment must therefore be denied, with $10 costs, to abide the event of the action.

From the order entered on this decision the defend-ant appealed.

William P. Chambers (*John D. Ahrens*, attorney), for defendant-appellant.

Frank J. Dupignac, for plaintiff-respondent.

O'GORMAN, J.—This is an appeal from an order of this court at special term, denying a motion made on behalf of defendant, Loehr, to vacate an attachment issued against the property, on the ground that he was a non-resident of the State of New York.

The material facts, as stated by the defendants, and uncontroverted, are these:

Defendant Loehr, had been, before June, 1884, a commercial traveler for a New York establishment, spending much of his time on the road and outside of the State of New York. He had lived in Brooklyn with his wife and family, and, up to that time, was a resident of the State of New York. Finding his wife and children ill, as he was advised by his physician, of disease contracted by bad sewerage of the house in which he dwelt, and finding change of air necessary for their recovery, he left the house in which he had dwelt. His wife's father and mother resided in Milwaukee, and, his wife being then pregnant, he decided to move her and his family to that city, so that they could have the care of their relatives. It was no part of his or his wife's intention to reside permanently in Milwaukee, but it was his and her intention to return to Brooklyn. They did return to Brooklyn on June 11, 1885. Their absence from the State, in the meantime, is attributed to the illness of defendant's wife, who was delivered of a child in October, 1884, and the subsequent illness of his and her children.

The defendant Loehr, before he left Brooklyn, put his furniture into a storage house there, for safe keeping until his return. During the absence of his wife and family in Milwaukee, the defendant, on his occasional returns to New York from his journeys, had no permanent dwelling in this State, but stayed temporarily in boarding-houses in Brooklyn.

The attachment was issued in April, 1885, during the absence of the defendant from New York.

There is sufficient evidence, in my opinion, to warrant the conclusion, that in leaving Brooklyn, the defendant had not the intention to seek a domicile outside the State of New York, and that the stay of his wife and family in Milwaukee was not intended by him or her to be permanent, but was transitory, and that, during all their absence from New York, they always had the intention of returning to Brooklyn, at some time in the future not fixed.

The question is not wholly free from doubt, and that doubt has been, to some extent, caused by the failure to distinguish accurately between *domicile* and
[*] *residence.* These words are often used indifferently. Generally speaking, domicile and residence mean the same thing (Kennedy *v.* Ryal, 67 *N. Y.* 379). They have, however, at least when used in reference to attachments under the Code, different and distinct meanings.

Residence, combined with intention to remain, constitutes domicile (2 *Kent's Com.* 577).

Inhabitance and residence mean a fixed and permanent abode, a dwelling-house for the time being, as contradistinguished from a mere temporary locality of existence (Roosevelt *v.* Kellogg, 20 *Johns.* 208).

Residence in attachment laws, generally implies

an established abode, fixed permanen ly for a time, for business or other purposes, although there may be an intent existing all the while, to return to the true domicile (Kone v. Cooper, 43 *Ark.* 241).

['] The meaning of the word *resident*, as used in section 1763 of the Code, was discussed in De Meli v. De Meli, and it was held that a natural born citizen of the United States, who had been for some years dwelling in Dresden, but always stated his residence to be in New York, and never had the intention of obtaining a residence anywhere else than in New York, had never acquired a foreign residence ; that the residence of a man is changed only by an aban-, donment of the first place of *domicile*, with the inten-tion not to return, but to permanently settle in another place (De Meli v. De Meli, 5 *N. Y. Civ. Pro.* 308.)

['''] In Dupuy v. Wurtz, 33 *N. Y.* 556, the conten-tion was as to the proper execution of a will by a citizen of the State of New York, who had dwelt con-tinuously in Europe for many years. The will was executed in Nice, and according to the laws of New York. It was held that the testatrix had not aband-oned her original *domicile*, which continued to be in New York.

['''] The question in the case at bar, however, is not as to *domicile*, with reference to proper execu-tion of a will, but as to *residence* or *non-residence*, as the test of the right to attach property of the defend-ant.

['''] In my opinion, actual cessation to dwell within the State for an uncertain period, without definite intention as to any fixed time of returning, even although a general intention to return at some time in the future may exist, constitutes *non-residence*, and warrants an issue of an attachment under sections 635 and 636 of the Code.

["]   The order appealed from should be affirmed, with $10 costs.

SEDGWICK, Ch. J., concurred.

WILLIAMS, AS RECEIVER OF THE BLAIR IRON AND STEEL COMPANY, APPELLANT, v. MEYER, RESPONDENT.

SUPREME COURT, FIRST DEPARTMENT, GENERAL TERM, OCTOBER, 1886.

Limitations to actions.— When cause of action to recover balance of subscription of stock in manufacturing corporation barred by Statute of Limitation.— When such cause of action accrues.

§§ 382, 415.

An action to recover from a stockholder of a corporation a balance due from him on stock, for which he has subscribed, is barred by the lapse of six years from the time that the right to sue therefor accrued.

Where the capital stock of a corporation had been paid up by the transfer of patents, and 9,000 shares thereof transferred by the holders to the corporation to be used as working capital for the company, subject, as provided in the agreement signed by such stockholders, to the order of the board of trustees of said company, excepting $50,000 of the proceeds thereof first to be paid to them by said trustee, and the trustees ordered a sale of 6,000 of said shares for the purpose of raising the present working capital and paying the said $50,000, the minimum price to be $50 per share, and offered the same for sale at said minimum price of $50 a share, to be paid for as follows : One-third thereof as soon as the whole 6,000 shares should be subscribed for, and the remainder in such installments as the board of trustees may call for the same for the purposes of the business, the certificates to be delivered when the whole shall be paid, and one " M." subscribed for 3,000 shares of said stock, paid one-third of the price thereof, and with others signed an agreement reading as follows : " We, the under-

signed,' hereby subscribe to the number of shares of the above
6,000 shares set opposite our names respectively, to be paid for
according to the terms above set forth, but this subscription
not to be binding until the whole 6,000 shares shall have been
reliably subscribed,"—*Held*, that it was competent for the defendant to enter into a contract by which he could be called on to pay
in at the time of making the subscription, but at future periods
continuing for more than six years from the time the original
contract was made, but that the general rule is well settled in this
State that in the absence of a contract to make a payment in future
installments which shall not by the terms of the contract become
due and payable until said future time, subscriptions become payable at once and no call or demand therefor is necessary, and that
this is the case with the agreement made by "M." ; that the
action to recover the balance of "M's." subscription was barred
by the lapse of six years from the date of making the same.

In such case,—*Held*, that evidence offered by the plaintiff in an
action to recover the balance of such subscription, touching the
requirements of the business, was incompetent and immaterial, and
its rejection was not error; that it would not be competent for the
plaintiff to vary the terms of the contract by oral evidence showing the needs of the corporation, nor was there in the contract
anything in the nature of a latent ambiguity which would justify a resort to any testimony of this character.

(*Decided October*, 1886.)

Appeal by plaintiff from judgment in favor of the
defendant.

The facts as agreed upon by the parties for the
purposes of this appeal are stated in the opinion.

James Watson, for plaintiff-appellant.

Upon the agreed statement of facts plaintiff was
entitled to recover, if the Statute of Limitations was
not a bar. The subscription agreement was conditional and created a condition precedent,—viz., a call
or demand by the trustees based upon the requirements of the business of the company,—to the payment
of the subscriptions, except 33⅓ per cent. thereof,
the time for the payment of which was fixed. The Statute of Limitations, in a case of contingency, runs from

the time when the contingency happens. This was
held in Savage v. Alden, 2 *Stark*, (*Eng. N. P.*) 232 ; and
Fenton v. Emblees, 1 *W. Bl.* (*Eng. K. B.*) 353 ; and the
doctrine is unchanged. See *Wood's Limitations of
Actions*, subject "Conditions Precedent." The money
agreed to be paid could not be said to have become due
upon the whole number of shares being subscribed for ;
the terms of the agreement contradict such a construction, because they fix that as the time for the payment
of only a portion of the amount. . . . The question
presented for the determination of this court has been
decided in the supreme court of Pennsylvania, in
Sinkler v. Turnpike Co., 3 *Penn. & Watts*, 149 ; and
in Pittsburg & C. R. R. Co. v. Byers, 32 *Penn. St.* 22 ;
in Maryland, in Glenn v. Williams, 60 *Md.* 93 ; S. C.,
1 *Am. & Eng. Corp. Cases*, 58 ; in California, in Glenn
v. Sexton, 10 *Am. & Eng. Corp. Cases*, 303 ; in Ala-
bama, in Glenn v. Semple, 10 *Am. & Eng. Corp.
Cases*, 297. All of these cases hold that the Statute
runs only from the time of the calls ; and this is laid
down as the correct rule by Wood in his work
on Limitations, and by Thompson in his treatise on
the Liability of Stockholders. See Scovill v. Thayer,
105 *U. S.* 143 ; and Savage v. Medbury, 19 *N. Y.* 32. . .

William H. Williams, for defendant-respondent.

This action not having been commenced within six
years after the cause of action accrued, to wit, within
six years from May 15, 1873, is barred by the statute
of Limitations. *Code of Civ. Pro.* §§ 380, 382, 415.

The law as to a contract or obligation like that
under consideration has long been determined. It
has been declared in an unbroken line of decisions
in the higher courts of this State. It is, that all subscriptions or sums of money, so promised or agreed to
be paid, are due and payable at once, and that no call or
demand before action is necessary. Goshen Turnpike

Co. *v.* Hurtin, 9 *Johns.* 217; Lake Ontario, &c. R. R.
v. Mason, 16 *N. Y.* 451; White *v.* Haight, 16 *Id.* 310;
Howland *v.* Edmonds, 24 *Id.* 307; Tuckerman *v.* Brown,
23 *Id.* 297. To the same effect are White *v.* Smith, 77
Ill. 351 ; Washington Co. Mutual Ins. Co. *v.* Miller,
26 *Ver.* 77. . . . The language employed in the
contract itself calls for this interpretation of it. It
states that the nine thousand shares of stock were "to
be used as working capital for the company," and that
the sale of six thousand of the said shares was ordered
for the purpose of raising a present working capital.
That is to say, to provide a fund for immediate use in
the business of the company, to be at the call and dis-
posal of the board of trustees. . . . Furthermore,
the statute itself provides that the board of trustees
has the exclusive right to manage the affairs of the
corporation—Laws of 1848, chap. 40, § 3 ; and it makes
the subscription, payable at such times, and in such
payments or installments as the trustees shall deem
proper. Laws of 1848, chap. 40, § 6. The special contract, therefore, where it says that the stock is to be
paid for "in such installments as the board of trustees
may call for the same for the purpose of the business,"
in slightly different language, expresses merely the
provisions of the general act. And it has been well
established in the courts, that it is for the trustees of
a corporation to determine whether its business and
necessities demand that subscriptions to its stock
should be called in. Policy and reason alike forbid
that stockholders should be allowed to dispute the
necessity of assessments upon their stock to the hazard
of the business and the rights of creditors. Hoyt *v.*
Thompson, 19 *N. Y.* 207; People *v.* Met. El. R. R. Co.,
26 *Hun.* 82; East N. Y. & Jamaica R. R. Co. *v.* Lighthall,
5 *Abb. Pr. N. S.* 458 ; Judah *v.* Am. Live Stock Ins. Co.,
4 *Porter* (*Ind.*) 336 ; Met. El. R. R. Co. *v.* Manhattan
El. R. R. Co., 11 *Daly*, 375. If it be contended that

this is a case in which a demand was necessary before an action could be maintained that contention will be met by the principle of law that where a demand is necessary, the statute runs from the time when the right to make the demand is complete, which, in this case, was May 15, 1873, more than six years before the action was commenced. *Code Civ. Pro.* § 410 ; Dickinson *v.* Mayor, 92 *N. Y.* 584.

Macomber, J.—Between January 20, 1873, and May 15, 1873, the defendant subscribed for six hundred shares of the stock of the Blair Iron and Steel Company, a corporation organized under the general act of 1848, of which the present plaintiff is the receiver. The action was begun by the company itself, October 14, 1879. At the time of the subscription of the stock, the defendant paid thirty-three per cent. of the amount subscribed, and has paid no other sum. The defense interposed and relied upon, and upon which the complaint was dismissed is, that the action was not brought within six years from the time that it accrued. The sufficiency of this defense is to be determined by the nature and terms of the contract. For if the right of action accrued to the company at the time of the making of the subscription, it is quite clear that the statute has now run against the claim and no action therefor can be maintained. The substance of the papers upon which the liability of the defendant is sought to be made, is the statement of certain persons in writing, to the effect that the capital stock of the company was 25,000 shares of $100 each, making in all $2,500,000 ; that it has already been paid up by the transfer of patents, that 9,000 shares of the stock was to be used as working capital for the company, "subject to the order of the board of trustees of said company, excepting $50,000 of the proceeds thereof first to be paid to us by said trustee. The trustees have, with our consent, ordered a sale of 6,000 of said shares for the purpose of raising the present working capital and paying the said $50,000, the minimum price to be $50 per share. And said trustee, with the approbation of the board of trustees, now offers said 6,000 shares at said minimum price of $50 a share, to be paid for as follows: One-third thereof as soon as the whole 6,000 shares shall be subscribed for, and the remainder in such installments as the board of trustees may call for the same for the purposes of the business, the certificates to be delivered when the whole shall be paid." This proposition was signed by certain persons interested in the enterprise. The paper which the defendant signed is as follows:

"We, the undersigned, hereby subscribe to the number of shares of the above 6,000 shares set opposite to our names respectively, to be paid for according to the terms above set forth, but this subscription not to be binding until the whole 6,000 shares shall have been reliably subscribed."

The amount which the defendant subscribed for was $30,000, one third of which, as has already been stated, was paid in by him on or about May 15, 1873. It was competent for the defendant to enter into a contract by which he could be called upon to pay, not at the time of making the subscription, but at future periods continuing for more than six years from the time the original contract was made. The general rule is well settled in this State that in the absence of a contract thus to make the payments in future installments which shall not become, by the terms of the contract, due and payable until some future time, subscriptions become due and payable at once, and no call or demand before action therefor is necessary (Howland v. Edmonds, 24 N. Y. 307; Tuckman v.

Brown, 33 *N. Y.* 297; Lake Ont. &c. R. R. Co. *v.* Mason, 16 *N. Y.* 451).

The question is whether there is anything in the language of this contract that takes the case out of this general rule. The learned counsel for the plaintiff contends that the expression " one third thereof as soon as the whole 6,000 shares shall be subscribed for, and the remainder in such installments as the board of trustees may call for the same, for the purposes of the business," makes it a contract to become due and payable in future installments, and that, by implication at least, if not by positive language, the trustees had no right to call for the same except for the purposes of the business and as the exigencies of the business would warrant. This, in our judgment, is not tenable. The sum required was for a " working capital for the company," and it was subscribed for solely for the purpose of obtaining a present working capital, so that if the company was to operate at all in its enterprise, and if we are to resort to inferences and deductions, it would seem that the whole of it would be required to be paid at the time of the subscription. The contract does not say, however, that the installments should not be paid except as the purposes of the business might require it, and if it had so stated, the subscribers might have had a defense against the calls that were made by the trustees by showing that the sums called for were not in fact needed for the uses and purposes of the corporation. But this would import into the contract a condition which does not appear to be found there. The expression " for the purposes of the business " has no significance whatever as it seems to us, because in reality and in terms, not only was the contract made for the purposes of the business of the corporation alone, but the trustees themselves would not have any right to call for any sum except for the business of the corporation. The counsel labors under the misapprehension of assuming that the subscription would be tantamount to a condition that the same was payable only according to the exigencies and requirements of the corporation and that these were to be determined wholly by the board of trustees.

If we are right in this construction of the agreement, the evidence offered by the plaintiff touching the requirements of the business, was incompetent and immaterial and its rejection was not error. It would not be competent for the plaintiff to vary the terms of the contract by oral evidence showing the needs of the corporation, nor is there, in the contract, anything in the nature of a latent ambiguity which would justify a resort to any oral testimony of the character offered by the plaintiff and which was rejected by the trial court.

For these reasons, we think the judgment should be affirmed with costs.

BRADY, J., concurred.

DANIELS, J.—(Concurring.)—To hold that the cause of action accrued before the subsequent payments were required to be made, is not consistent with the agreement between the defendant and the company when he subscribed for the stock. And the case of Scovill *v.* Thayer (105 *U. S.* 143), is opposed to that conclusion. But the authorities cited in the opinion, as well as Goshen Turnpike Co. *v.* Hurtin (9 *Johns.* 217), sustain the power of the court, to disregard the terms on which the parties made the money payable, and to hold the contract to be one for the absolute payment of so much money at once. They are controlling, although they do violence to the agreement, and annul the intention expressed in it. In compliance with the superior authority, I agree to the affirmance of the judgment in this case.

PADDOCK, Respondent, v. KIRKHAM, Appel-
LANT.

COURT OF APPEALS, OCTOBER, 1886.

§ 887, *et seq.*

Commission to take testimony of witness in another State.— When
ordered on reference of claim against decedent in surrogate's
court.

The power to issue a commission to take testimony out of the State
depends entirely upon statutory provisions and is now regulated by
section 888 of the Code of Civil Procedure.[1]

Where a disputed claim against the estate of a decedent has been
referred pursuant to 2 *R. S.* 88, § 36, a commission may issue to
take the testimony of a witness without the State, for use on the
reference.[4,6]

Roe v. Boyle (81 *N. Y.* 305);[2] Mowry v. Peet (88 *Id.*'453);[3] Wood
v. Howard Ins. Co. (18 *Wend.* 646);[5] Matter of Whitney (4 *Hill,*
533),[6] distinguished.

Paddock v. Kirkman (38 *Hun,* 376), affirmed.[7]

(*Decided October* 4, 1886.)

Appeal by defendant from an order of the general
term of the supreme court in the second department,
affirming the order of the special term, directing the
issuing of a commission to take the testimony of a
witness without the State.

Reported below, 38 *Hun,* 376.

This is a reference of a disputed claim against the
estate of the defendant's decedent. The reference was
made by consent of the parties with the approval of
the surrogate, pursuant to 2 *R. S.* §§ 36, 37. The
plaintiff upon affidavits and due notice to the defendant, moved for an order directing the issuing of a
commission to William B. Wood, an attorney and
counsellor at law, of Salt Lake city, Utah, to take the

deposition of plaintiff's witnesses residing in that city, and his motion was granted. From the order granting his motion an appeal was taken to the general term which affirmed it, and from that order this appeal was taken by the defendant. The only objec. tion the defendant made to the granting of the motion was that the court was without authority to issue a commission in this proceeding.

H. A. Miller, for defendant-appellant.

William P. Cantwell, for plaintiff-respondent.

RAPALLO, J.—The power to issue a commission to take testimony out of the State depends entirely upon statutory provisions, and is regulated now by ['] section 888 of the Code of Civil Procedure, which is in substance a re-enactment of a like provision of the Revised Statutes.*

Section 888 provides for the issuing of such a commission only where an issue of fact has been joined in an action pending in a court of record.

The appellant contends that this reference was not an action but a special proceeding citing, Roe v. Boyle (81 *N. Y.* 305, 308), and Mowery v. Peet (88 *Id.* 453), and that consequently the power to issue a commission in an action did not extend to it.

['] Roe v. Boyle decided that such a reference being a special proceeding, an appeal from an order made therein was governed by the provisions of the Code expressly applicable to orders in special proceedings.

['] In Mowery v. Peet, it was held that in such a proceeding there was no power in the reference or in the court to render an affirmative judgment against

---

* Section 888 of the Code of Civil Procedure was taken from Laws of 1862, chap. 375, § 1, which superseded 2 *R. S.* 383, § 11.

the claimant on a counter-claim, for the reason that
on such a reference the only question submitted to the
referee was whether the claimant had a just claim
against the estate of the deceased over and above all
off-sets, and although in trying and adjudicating upon
those matters which were within the scope of the reference, the statute (2 *R. S.* 88, § 36), conferred upon
the referee and the court the same powers as if the
reference had been made in an action, yet the proceeding was not an action and no power was given to
render an affirmative judgment for the executors
against the claimant or to certify a balance in their
favor.

As to the powers of the court and referee in such
a proceeding, with respect to the determination of the
matter in controversy, the terms of the statute are
very broad. Section 36 provides for the entry of a
rule in the supreme court or court of common pleas,
referring the matter in controversy, and section 37
provides that "the same proceedings shall be had in
all respects, the referees shall have the same powers
. . . as if the reference had been made in an action in
which such court might by law direct a reference, and
the judgment of the court on the report of the referees shall be valid and effectual in all respects as if the
same had been rendered in a suit commenced by the
ordinary process."

[']   We think this provision is sufficiently broad
to authorize the issue of a commission to take
testimony out of the State. The necessity for such
process is quite as great as in an action, and neither
the executor nor the claimant should be deemed to
have forfeited that advantage by consenting to such a
reference. It is to a certain extent compulsory so far
as costs are concerned (§ 41).

[']   The cases of Wood v. Howard Ins. Co. (18
Wend. 646) and Matter of Whitney (4 *Hill*, 533),

Paddock v. Kirkham.

are cited as authorities for the proposition that the
provision that in cases of reference of disputed claims
against executors, etc., the same proceedings shall be
had in all respects, and the referees shall have the
same powers as if the reference had been made in an
action (2 *R. S.* 89, § 37), is not sufficient to authorize
the issuing of a commission. We do not think that
the cases cited sustain the proposition. The references in those cases were governed by the statute in
relation to the powers and duties of trustees and
assignees of absconding and insolvent debtors (2 *R. S.*
40). That statute authorized the reference of contro-
versies relating to demands against or debts due to
the debtor, and it provides (2 *R. S.* 45, § 24) that the
referees so appointed should have the same powers as
referees appointed by the supreme court in personal
actions. That provision clearly did not affect the
power of the court to issue a commission. It related
solely to the powers of the referees.

[*] The statute in respect to references of disputed
claims against executors, etc., is much more com-
prehensive. It not only provides that in cases of such
references the referees shall have the same powers,
but it contains the further express provision that
" the same proceedings shall be had in all respects"
as if the reference had been made in an action. We
think this includes the proceeding by commission to
obtain the testimony of absent witnesses.

['] The order should be affirmed, with costs.

All concurred.

SCHULTZE ET AL. v. THE MAYOR, ALDERMEN AND COMMONALTY OF THE CITY OF NEW YORK.

SUPREME COURT, FIRST DEPARTMENT, NEW YORK COUNTY CIRCUIT, OCTOBER, 1886.

§ 3253.*

Extra allowance.—*Refused in action to recover back over-payment of assessment.*

An extra allowance will not be granted in an action to recover back part of the sum paid to a city in payment of an assessment subsequently reduced upon a ground purely technical.

(*Decided October*, 1886.)

Motion for an extra allowance under section 3253 of the Code of Civil Procedure.

The action was brought to recover back a part of the sum paid by the plaintiff to the city of New York in payment of an assessment, which was after such payment reduced by order of court.

Other facts appear in the opinion.

Charles A. Murphey, for plaintiff and motion.

G. L. Sterling, assistant corporation counsel, opposed.

ANDREWS, J.—This action was not a difficult or extraordinary one, unless every action which is tried must be considered such. The assessment was reduced upon a ground purely technical, and the

---

* See Note on Additional Allowance, 8 *N. Y. Civ. Pro.* 214.

plaintiff recovered a judgment for $32,460.75, which sum of money, so far as the merits of the matter are concerned, ought to have remained in the city treasury. I am not aware that an allowance has ever been made against the city in an action of this description, and I am not willing to establish so bad a precedent, for which, in my opinion, no justification can be found either in the provisions of the Code or the equities of the case.

Motion denied, without costs.

PEOPLE ex rel. COHEN, *v.* GRANT, Sheriff of the City and County of New York.

Supreme Court, First Department, New York County Special Term, October, 1886.

§ 111.

Imprisonment. — *When person imprisoned under order of arrest in action for separation not discharged therefrom.*

Where the defendant, in an action brought by a wife against her husband for separation, was imprisoned on an order of arrest granted in the action on the ground that the judgment would require the performance of an act ; to wit, the payment of alimony, the neglect or refusal to perform which would be punishable by the court as a contempt, and that the defendant was not a resident of the State, and by reason of his non-residence there was danger that the judgment or an order requiring the performance of the act would be rendered ineffectual, and judgment was afterwards entered directing the payment of alimony and counsel fee and the giving of security for such payment but no proceedings were taken under the judgment, — *Held*, that the defendant could not be discharged from imprisonment under the original order of arrest, under section 111 of the Code of Civil Procedure, as enacted by Laws of 1886, chap. 672, § 3.

People ex rel. Lust v. Grant (10 *N. Y. Civ. Pro.* 158), not followed; People ex rel. Rodding v. Grant (10 *Id.* 174, *note*); N. Y. C. & H. R. R. R. Co. v. Shepard (10 *Id.* 153); Warshauser v. Webb (10 *Id.* 169), followed.

(*Decided October* 20, 1886.)

Motion to discharge the relator from imprisonment under order of arrest.

This is a proceeding by *certiorari* and *habeas corpus* to procure the discharge of the relator from imprisonment. The relator is imprisoned under an order of arrest granted before judgment in an action brought against him by his wife for separation. The order of arrest was granted on the ground that the judgment demanded in the complaint required the performance of an act, to wit:—the payment of alimony, the neglect or refusal to perform which would be punishable by the court as a contempt, and that the defendant was not a resident of the State, by reason of which non-residence, a judgment or an order requiring the performance of the act, would be rendered ineffectual. The sheriff's return to the writs, set forth, that the relator was held by virtue of the order of arrest which was annexed to the papers and that no final judgment had been rendered. It appeared, however, from the petition, that the action had been tried and judgment entered in the plaintiff's favor, and that by such judgment the relator was required to pay the plaintiff alimony at the rate of $7 a week, from April 22, 1886, and $100 counsel fee and expenses, and to give security for payment of such alimony, but that no proceedings had been taken under the judgment; also, that the relator had been imprisoned for more than three months.

Malcolm R. Lawrence (*McCarthy, Lawrence & Buckley,* attorneys), for relator and motion.

William H. Clark (*Cockran & Clark*, attorneys), for the sheriff, opposed.

Aaron Levy, attorney for plaintiff in order of arrest.

ANDREWS, J.—The relator was arrested by the respondent, who is the sheriff of the city and county of New York, under an order of arrest granted in an action brought by Fanny Cohen, the relator's wife, to procure a separation. The action has been tried and judgment entered in the plaintiff's favor, and the defendant is required by such judgment to pay the plaintiff alimony at the rate of $7 a week, from April 22, 1886, and $100 counsel fee and expenses, and to give security for the payment of such alimony ; but no proceedings under such judgment have been taken, and it appears by the return to the writ of *certiorari* that the relator is still held under the original order of arrest.

It was decided by Judge POTTER that an order of arrest is a mandate against the person to enforce the recovery of a sum of money (People *ex rel.* Lust *v.* Grant, and other cases, 10 *N. Y. Civ. Pro.* 158), but this decision is in conflict with those of Judge VAN BRUNT in People *ex rel.* Rodding *v.* Grant (10 *Id.* 174, *note*), of Judge CORLETT in N.Y. Central & H. R. R. R. Co. *v.* Shepard (10 *Id.* 153), and of Judge McADAM in Warshauer *v.* Webb (10 *Id.* 169.)

The three decisions last mentioned were, as I understand, rendered in actions where judgment for a sum of money only was sought, and if they were correctly decided, *a fortiori* an order of arrest in an action brought by a wife to obtain a judgment of separation from her husband is not a mandate to enforce the recovery of a sum of money.

As the relator is not imprisoned under an execution nor under a commitment upon a fine for contempt of court in the non-payment of alimony or counsel fees in a divorce case, nor, according to the weight of authority as the decisions now stand, under a mandate to enforce the recovery of a sum of money within the meaning of section 111 of the Code, as amended by section 3 of chapter 672, of the laws of 1886, I am constrained to deny the motion of his discharge.

An appeal, which presents the precise question involved in this case, is pending in the General Term, and, as the matter is one of great importance, not only to the relator and the sheriff in this case, but in all cases where orders of arrest have been or shall be granted, I have deferred my decision for a short time, hoping that, before rendering it, I might have the benefit of knowing what views are entertained by the appellate branch of the court as to the proper construction of section 3 of said chapter 672.

As it seems to be uncertain, however, when the appeal will be disposed of, I must decide the question according to the light I now have, and the motion will be denied, but without costs.

DALON v. KAPP.

Superior Court of The City of New York, Special Term, October, 1886.

§ 111.

Discharge from imprisonment.— When person imprisoned under order of arrest in action of replevin not discharged.

Where the defendant in an action of replevin was arrested on the ground that he had intentionally disposed of the chattels to recover which the action was brought in such a way that they could not be found or taken by the sheriff, and gave bail for the limits,—*Held*, that a motion by the defendant under section 111 of the Code of Civil Procedure as enacted by Laws of 1886 chap. 672, § 3, that he be discharged from imprisonment on the ground that six months had elapsed since his arrest should be denied; that the weight of authority is that said statute relates to persons detained under final process, and not to such as are detained under order of arrest during the pendency of the action.

People *ex rel.* Cohen *v.* Grant (*ante*, page 55), followed.

(*Decided October*, 1886.)

Motion by defendant for his discharge from arrest under section 111 of the Code of Civil Procedure as enacted by Laws of 1886 chap. 672, § 3, on the ground that six months had elapsed since his arrest.

The defendant was arrested on January 19, 1886, under an order of arrest issued in an action of replevin, on the ground that he intentionally disposed of the chattels to recover which this action was brought, in such a way that they could not be found or taken by the sheriff. He gave bail for the limits under section 149 of the Code of Civil Procedure, and at the time of making this motion was imprisoned within the limits under said order of arrest.

W. F. Severance (*Townsend, Dyett & Einstein*), for defendant and motion.

Wm. H. Clark (*Cockran & Clark*, attorneys), for the sheriff, opposed.

S. F. Kneeland, for plaintiff, opposed.

FREEDMAN, J.—In this action, which is in replevin, the defendant was arrested upon an order of arrest, and gave bail in the sum of $3,000 for the jail limits of the city and county of New York. The ground of

arrest was the intentional disposition by the defendant of the chattels, to recover which this sction is
brought, in such a way that they could not be found
or taken by the sheriff. The defendant moves for his·
discharge from arrest and from imprisonment on the
limits under chapter 672 of the laws of 1886, and the
sole ground of the motion is that, although the order
of arrest has never been vacated, nor the issues in the
action tried, more than six months have elapsed since
the arrest and the giving of the bail. It was shown
by Mr. Justice ANDREWS in People ex rel. Cohen v.
Grant [reported ante, p. 55], that, as the decisions
under the said statute now stand, the weight of authority is that the statute referred to relates to prisoners
, detained on final process and not to such as are held
under orders of arrest during the pendency of the
action.

In following the weight of authority thus pointed
out, I call attention, by way of addition to the well
settled rule of statutory interpretation enforced in
Hickey v. Taaffe (99 N. Y. 204), which is to the effect
that a word, having in general use a broader significance than others in connection with which it is used,
if used with words of limited meaning which have
received in the same act a particular application, must
be referred to things of the same kind as those specified and to which the other words are referred.

The motion must be denied, with $10 costs.

FIRST NATIONAL BANK OF NORTHAMPTON,
Respondent, *v.* DOYING, Impleaded, etc., Appellant.

N. Y. Court of Common Pleas, General Term, June, 1886.

§§ 1775, 3343, subd. 18.

Pleading.—Complaint by corporation.—Failure to properly plead incorporation, how taken advantage of.

The complaint in an action by a corporation alleged to have been organized under an act of congress, should also state whether it is a foreign or domestic corporation; such a corporation is not necessarily a foreign corporation, but is foreign or domestic according to whether or not it is located within this State.

The objection that a complaint in an action which states that a party thereto is a corporation, is insufficient because it fails to state whether it is a foreign or a domestic one, is properly taken by demurrer.

(*Decided June* 7, 1886.)

Appeal from a judgment entered on an order of the general term of the city court of New York, affirming a judgment entered on an order of the special term of that court overruling an amended demurrer as frivolous and directing judgment.

The facts appear in the opinion.

John C. Shaw & C. J. Myers, for defendant-appellant.

Cited *Code of Civil Procedure*, §§ 1775, 3343, subd. 18 ; Baker *v.* Star Printing & Publishing Co., 3 *N. Y. Monthly Law Bul.* 29 ; Clegg *v.* Chicago Newspaper Union, 8 *N. Y. Civ. Pro.* 401.

Charles W. Wetmore (*Barlow, Olney & Wetmore,* attorneys), for plaintiff-respondent.

The failure to allege that the plaintiff is a foreign corporation is not a defect which can be raised by a demurrer, on the ground that the complaint does not state facts sufficient to constitute a cause of action. The demurrer falls under section 488, subdivision 8, and, if valid at all, should have been taken under subdivision 3 of that section. Irving Nat. Bank *v.* Corbett, 10 *Abb. N. C.* 85 ; Phœnix Bank *v.* Donnell, 40 *N. Y.* 410, 414 ; Fox *v.* Erie Railway Co., 93 *N. Y.* 54, 57. Even if the demurrer is good under subdivision 3 of section 488, that ground cannot now be availed of, inasmuch as it was not specified in the demurrer, and the particular defect pointed out, as required by section 490. Phœnix Bank *v.* Donnell (*supra*); Berney *v.* Drexel, 33 *Hun*, 419 ; *Code Civ. Pro.* § 490. Even if the demurrer is sufficient in point of form, it is not well taken. *Code Civ. Pro.* § 1776. It is a fair inference from this provisisn that the legislature could not have intended that a violation of section 1775 should be a ground of demurrer. Where section 1775 is not complied with, the remedy is by motion to make the complaint more definite and certain. If a violation of section 1775 is available on demurrer, a violation of the technical requirements of sections 481 and 483 must be equally so. That a violation of section 483 is not a ground of demurrer, was decided in Townsend *v.* Coon, 7 *N. Y. Civ. Pro.* 56 ; Henderson *v.* Jackson, 40 *How. Pr.* 108.

PER CURIAM.—The action is on a promissory note. The complaint alleges :

"FIRST. That at the times hereinafter mentioned the plaintiff was, and now is a national banking association incorporated and doing business under and by virtue of an act of congress, entitled 'An Act to provide a national currency,' &c., but contains no allegation as to whether it is a foreign or domestic corporation."

For some inscrutable reason section 1775 of the Code requires this allegation in every complaint by or against a corporation.

The court below held that inasmuch as it was alleged in the complaint that the plaintiff was incorporated under the act of congress, it was from the very nature of its incorporation, a foreign corporation, and that where this was a self-evident fact it added no force to the pleading to allege it was a foreign corporation.

The difficulty with this position is that section 3343, subdivision 18 of the Code says a "domestic corporation" is a "corporation created by or under the laws of the State or located in the State, and created by or under the laws of the United States. . . every other corporation is a foreign corporation." Therefore a national bank is either a foreign or domestic corporation according to its location within or without this State, and as this is not specifically stated, the complant is defective in that particular, and this defect can be taken advantage of by demurrer (Baker *v.* Star Printing and Publishing Company, 3 *Law Bull.* 29 ; Clegg *v.* Chicago Newspaper Union, 8 *N. Y. Civ. Pro.* 401).

The judgment must therefore be reversed, but as the defect complained of could mislead no one, and the demurrer is highly technical, the plaintiff is given leave to amend its complaint in any way it may be advised within six days after the service of an order reversing the judgment on its attorneys. The costs of this appeal to abide the event of the action, and with costs of prior proceedings in the court below at the discretion of that court.

ALLEN and BOOKSTAVER, JJ., sitting.

WEBER v. MANNE.

SUPREME COURT, FIRST DEPARTMENT, NEW YORK
COUNTY, SPECIAL TERM, SEPTEMBER, 1886.

§§ 1698, 1704.

*Replevin.—Effect of stating aggregate value of chattels in plaintiff's
affidavit.—Undertaking to be given by defendant to reclaim chattels
replevied.—Amount of, when part of chattel only replevied.*

Where the plaintiff's affidavit to replevy chattels, states only the
aggregate value thereof, and a part only is taken, the defendant to
reclaim the same is not required to give an undertaking conditioned for the delivery of all the chattels sued for; if all the chattels
have been taken the undertaking should, of course, so recite, and
if a part only has been taken, the recital should be so modified as to
conform to the fact, and the undertaking should be for the return
of the articles actually replevied only; the undertaking should also
provide that the defendant will pay the plaintiff any sum which
the judgment awards against him, in the language used in the
statute.

(*Decided September 27, 1886.*)

Exceptions to undertaking to retake chattels
replevied.

The opinion states the facts.

Abram Kling, for plaintiff.

Richard M. Henry and *Charles Meyers,* for
defendant.

ANDREWS, J.—As the aggregate value only was
stated in the plaintiff's affidavit, the undertaking
must be in double the value so stated, which was
$1,415.32. If the value of each article had been stated,
the undertaking would have been in double the value
of the articles actually replevied only. If it be true,

therefore, as claimed by defendant, that the sheriff has actually replevied articles of the value of $300 only, and the value of each of those articles had been separately stated in the plaintiff's affidavit, the undertaking to be given by the defendant would have been for $600 only ; and that undertaking, of course, would not have fully secured the plaintiff, if upon the trial, he proved that the defendant had in his possession all the articles named in the affidavit of the alleged value of $1,415.32.

The position taken by plaintiff's counsel leads to the following result : The plaintiff, by stating the value of the articles named in his affidavit, in the aggregate, can obtain an undertaking for the delivery to him of all the articles named, or the payment of their value, if he succeeds, no matter how small a portion the sheriff may actually take from the defendant ; while, if the value of the articles is stated separately, he can obtain an undertaking for the return of those articles only which the sheriff takes, or for the payment of their value. If a plaintiff requires the sheriff to take one hundred packages of goods of the aggregate value of $100,000, and the sheriff finds and takes one package of the value of $1,000, the defendant, in order to obtain the return of that one package, must give an undertaking in $200,000 that he will deliver all the packages, or their value, if the plaintiff succeeds on the trial ; while if the value of each package had been separately stated in plaintiff's affidavit at $1,000, the defendant could have secured the return of that one package by giving a bond in $1,000 only, for the return of that one package. It certainly would be a novelty in judicial proceedings that a defendant should be required to give security for the payment of $100,000 as a consideration for the privilege of retaining property of the value of $1,000. Section 1698 of the Code declares that the aggregate value, if that only is stated, shall be deemed the value of the part replevied for the purposes of procuring a return thereof to the defendant, but I do not think that that section, and section 1704, should be so construed as to enable the plaintiff, by merely stating the aggregate instead of the separate value of the articles named, to obtain an undertaking conditioned for the delivery to him of all such articles, no matter how small a portion thereof may have been actually taken by the sheriff; while if he had stated the value separately he could only have obtained an undertaking for the delivery to him of the part taken.

I can see no reason why the recital preliminary to the undertaking should contain an admission contrary to the facts. The sheriff either has or has not replevied all the articles mentioned in plaintiff's affidavit, and there can be no difficulty in determining this fact. If he has taken all, the undertaking should, of course, so recite; if he has taken a part only, the recital should be modified so as to conform to the fact; for it would be grossly unjust to the defendant to compel him to give a written admission that the sheriff had taken all the articles if, in fact, he has taken but a small part of them.

I also think that the undertaking of the defendant should be for the return of the articles actually replevied only.

The provision of section 1704, that the defendant will pay the plaintiff any sum which the judgment awards against the defendant, should be retained, in the language used in the statute. What its effect will be, in case the plaintiff proves on the trial that the defendant has more of his (the plaintiff's) property than the sheriff has taken, I do not attempt to decide. It would certainly be strange if the plaintiff, by stating the aggregate value of the articles named in his affidavit, could compel the defendant to give security for the payment of $1,415.32, as well as costs and disbursements, in order to retain possession of articles of the alleged worth of $300 only.

If the plaintiff desires to appeal, a stay will be granted, provided he will print the papers, accept short notice of argument, and be ready to argue the appeal when reached, and will stipulate that, if defeated, he will pay so much of the sheriff's fees and charges as shall accrue pending the appeal.

HUTKOFF, Respondent, v. DEMOREST and Another, Appellants.

CALDWELL, et al., Respondents, v. WALL, Appellant.

GREINER, Respondent, v. HAMBURGER, Appellant.

COURT OF APPEALS, OCTOBER, 1886.

§§ 190, 191, subd. 2.

N. Y. City Court.—Appeal from, cannot be taken direct to court of appeals.—Act authorizing such an appeal unconstitutional.

Jurisdiction to review adjudications of the city court of New York (formerly marine court) is given the N. Y. court of common pleas by the constitution, and chapter 408 of the Laws of 1886 which amends section 191 of the Code of Civil Procedure, in so far as it seeks to deprive the court of common pleas of its jurisdiction and power to review the judgments of the city court, and permits an appeal from the city court of New York to the court of appeals, without a previous review by the court of common pleas, is unconstitutional and void.

The act (Laws of 1883, chap. 26) changing the name of the marine court of the city of New York to the city court of New York, did not change the court itself or make any change in its judges, or officers or jurisdiction, or deprive the court of common pleas of jurisdiction to review its judgments.

(*Decided October* 26, 1886.)

Motion in each case to dismiss appeal from the general term of the city court of New York to the court of appeals.

The appeal in each case, was taken subsequent to the passage of Laws of 1886, chapter 418, amending section 191 of the Code of Civil Procedure, from a judgment of the general term of the city court of New York determining an appeal from a judgment of the trial term of said court. The judgment of the general term had not in any one of the cases, been reviewed by the court of common pleas.

David Leventritt, for respondent and motion in Hutkoff *v.* Demorest.

William F. Mac Rae, for respondent and motion in Caldwell *v.* Wall.

Wehle & Jordan, for respondent and motion in Greiner *v.* Hamburger.

John R. Marvin, for appellant, and opposed in Hutkoff *v.* Demorest, and *W. T. Birdsall,* for appellant, and opposed in Caldwell *v.* Wall.

The court of appeals may lawfully take the jurisdiction the act confers. The constitution (art. 6, § 6), provides that, "there shall be an existing supreme court with general jurisdiction in law and in equity, subject to such appellate jurisdiction of the court of appeals as now is or may be prescribed by law." This provision was interpreted by the court of appeals in Butterfield *v.* Rudde (58 *N. Y.* 490), where the court held, that "the appellate jurisdiction [of the court of appeals] over judg, ments from other courts is subject to the same regulation by the legislature," which means that section 6 is to be construed with the other provisions of the constitution and so construed, the powers and jurisdiction of the courts mentioned in it *eo nomine* or authorized by it are "subject to such appellate jurisdiction of the court of appeals as now is or may be prescribed by law." In other words, the power to regulate the right of appeal to the court of appeals was left to the discretion of the legislature unrestrained by limitations of any kind. Article 14, section 12, of the constitution makes this meaning more plan. It provides that "all local courts established in any city or village, including the superior court, common pleas, sessions and surrogate's courts of the city and county of New York, shall remain until otherwise directed by the legislature, with their present powers and jurisdictions." That this is so is also evidenced by the law regulating appeals to the court of appeals from the city court of Brooklyn. Article 6 of the constitution went into effect January 1, 1870. The People *v.* Gardner, 45 *N. Y.* 812 ; Same *v.* Norton, 59 *Barb.* 169. At that time appeals from the city court of Brooklyn went to the supreme court, general term, and from thence to the court of appeals. In 1871 (chap. 282) leave to go to the court of appeals direct was given for the first time, and thus in face of a constitutional prohibition against impairing the jurisdiction of the supreme court. De Hart *v.* Hatch, 3 *Hun*, 375, approved in the People *v.* Mayor, 79 *N. Y.* 589, 590. And yet the court of appeals has exercised the power to review the judgments of the city court of Brooklyn, under the act of 1871, for over fifteen years. If that act was unconstitutional, it is surprising that the court of appeals, or some other aggrieved litigant, did not find it out before. That the jurisdiction of the supreme court is as inviolate as that of the common pleas, see Butterfield v. Rudde, 58 *N. Y.* 490; De Hart v. Hatch, 3 *Hun*, 375, approved of in People v. Mayor, 79 *N. Y.* 589, 590. If the act relating to appeals from the city court of New York is unconstitutional, that relating to the city court of Brooklyn is open to the same objection.

The act in question, so far as this case is concerned, takes nothing from the common pleas which it had in January, 1870, when the constitution went into effect. The amount claimed and recovered herein exceeds $1,000. The marine court in 1870 had jurisdiction only to the extent of $500, see *McAdam's Marine Court·Pr.* (2 ed.) p. 4. Its jurisdiction was increased to $1,000 May 10, 1872 (chap. 629, § 3), and to $2,000, June 3, 1875 (chap. 479, § 1), so that as to appeals in cases where the recovery exceeded $500 (as in this case), there can be no question but that the legislature creating the new and extended jurisdiction may permit appeals in respect thereto to go to the court of appeals.

It is elementary that an act may be to an extent constitutional and beyond that unconstitutional. The constitutional and unconstitutional provisions may be contained in the same section, and yet be perfectly distinct and separable, so that the first may stand, though the last fall. . . . If a statute attempts to accomplish two or more objects, and is void as to one, it may still be in every respect complete and valid as to the other. *Cooley on Const. Lim.* 3 ed. 177, 178. DENIO, Ch. J., in the People v. Draper (15 *N. Y.* 543, said: "The people in framing the constitution, committed to the legislature the whole law-making power of the State, which they did not expressly or impliedly withhold. Plenary power in legislature for all purposes of civil government is the rule. A prohibition to exercise a particular power is an exception. In inquiring, therefore, whether a given statute is constitutional, it is for those who question its validity to show that it is forbidden." "It has never before been questioned, so far as I know," said RED-FIELD, Ch. J., in Thorpe v. Rutland & B. R. R. Co. (27 Vt. 142) "that the American legislatures have the same unlimited power in regard to legislature which resides in the British parliaments, except where they are restrained by written constitutions." To the same effect see cases collated in 2 Abb. N. Y. Dig. p. 118 . . . . . "The court of common pleas of the city and county of New York is continued with the powers and jurisdiction it has now, and such further civil and criminal jurisdiction as may be conferred by law" (Constitution, art. VI. § 12). The term "powers" as used in this section, is supposed to be synonymous with the term "jurisdiction" therein employed, for the term "jurisdiction" means "power" to hear and determine, &c. (1 Abb. Law Dic. title "jurisdiction," Webster's Dic., title "jurisdiction"). The term "powers" was not intended to apply to remedial legislation, or otherwise every provision of the New Code which takes away or modified any of the remedial powers of the court of common pleas, which it possessed at the time this constitutional provision was adopted, is unconstitutional and void. Every statute since passed limiting or modifying these powers is also unconstitutional and void. The word "powers" therefore, cannot be held to prevent the legislature from changing the remedies of suitors so long as it does not take away the vested "jurisdiction" (properly so called), of the court of common pleas. The Code in existence when this constitutional provision was passed, enumerates and defines the jurisdiction of the court of common pleas (Code of Procedure, §§ 33, 34, 35). None of these sections embrace appeals from the marine (now city) court, so that the constitu-

tion in using the term "jurisdiction" in referring to
the common pleas, did not in the light of then existing litigation intend to include within it appeals from
the marine court. If it be claimed that because the
common pleas, had "power" to hear these appeals,
when the constitutional provision was adopted that it
is to be included in the term "powers" as therein
employed ; then we answer that it was a mere remedial power and subject to the control of the legislature,
and this point will be next considered. The term
"jurisdiction," as used in the constitution in reference
to the common pleas, refers to its original, and not to
its appellate jurisdiction. For the term "appellate"
is not used either with respect to its powers or its jurisdiction. The same article of the constitution (Art.
6, § 6), provides that "there shall be an existing
supreme court with general jurisdiction in law and in
equity, subject to the appellate jurisdiction of the
courts of appeals, as now is or may be prescribed by
law. The jurisdiction of the supreme court is as inviolate as that of the common pleas, and yet in 1871
(chap. 282), the right to hear and determine appeals
from the city court of Brooklyn was taken from the
supreme court, general term, and given to the court
of appeals. The right of appeal exists only by favor
of the legislature, and can be taken away or regulated
at pleasure. It is a mere remedial power, and the
legislature may change existing remedies at will. It
is laid down as an elementary rule, that the "individual citizen with all his rights to protection has no
vested right in what is known in the law as remedies,
nor in any particular existing remedy. He has no
such vested interest in the existing laws of the State,
as precludes their amendment or repeal by the legislature" (*Potter's Dwarris Statutes*, 471, 472). The act
is constitutional in all its parts, as appeal is not a
vested right, but a mere legislative privilege subject

to change by it at will. We will cite a few opinions of the court of appeals on this subject. (*a.*) A statute which takes away a future right of appeal is not unconstitutional (Grover *v.* Coon, 1 *N. Y.* 536). (*b.*) A statute which takes away an existing right of appeal is constitutional (*In re* Palmer, 40 *N. Y.* 561). (*c.*) The act limiting appeals to the court of appeals to judgments wherein the sum in controversy exceeds $500, has been held to be constitutional by the court of appeals (People *v.* Horton, 64 *N. Y.* 58; Roosevelt *v.* Linkert, 67 *N. Y.* 447). (*d.*) All the changes made by the legislature by way of amendments to the Code in respect to appeals, have been held constitutional. (*e.*) The right to a review in civil cases is not a natural and inherent right, which cannot be taken away by legislation, but is created, and the jurisdiction of the court is prescribed by statute (People *v.* Fowler, 55 *N. Y.* 675). . . . As the original and appellate jurisdiction of the city court is purely legislative, it must in the nature of things, be wholly within legislative control. It cannot be that part of it (the incidental branch of appeal to the common pleas) is protected by the constitution, so as to be unalterable, and the root and body subject to legislative control only. Indeed, the legislature has power to entirely abolish the city court as a judicial tribunal, root, body and branches (see Neuzler *v.* People, 58 *N. Y.* 516). These various decisions and suggestions show that there is no such thing as a vested or constitutional right of appeal, but it is matter purely within legislative control.

A. J. Dillenhoefen (*Rose & Putzel*, attorneys), for appellant and opposed in Greiner *v.* Hamburger.

RAPALLO, J.—Article 6 of the Constitution of the State was adopted by the people at the November election in 1869, and declared adopted by the Board of State Canvassers December 6, 1869. One of its provisions was that the superior court of the city of New York and the court of common pleas of the city and county of New York, the superior court of Buffalo and the city court of Brooklyn, were continued, with the powers and jurisdiction they then severally had, and such further civil and criminal jurisdiction as might be conferred by law (Art. 6, § 12).

In the case of Popfinger v. Yutte (102 *N. Y.* 38), we decided that this' provision superseded section 12 of article 14, which declared that those courts should remain, until otherwise directed by the legislature, with their then present powers and jurisdiction ; that after the adoption of article 6, it was beyond the power of the legislature to take from those courts any of the powers or jurisdiction which they had at the time of the adoption of the article, and that consequently subd. 5 of section 263 of the Code of Civil Procedure, which purported to confine their jurisdiction in judgment creditors' actions to cases when the judgment on which the action was founded was recovered in the same court, was inoperative and void, because at the time of the adoption of article 6 those courts had general jurisdiction in equity within their territorial limits, co-extensive with that of the supreme court, and subd. 5 purported to take away part of that jurisdiction by limiting it in judgment creditors' suits to judgments recovered in the same court.

At the time of the adoption of article 6 the jurisdiction and powers of the court of common pleas of the city and county of New York were declared and enumerated in title 5 of the Code of Procedure (§§ 33, 34).

Section 34 is in the following words : "§ 34. The court of common pleas of the city and county of New

York shall also have power to review the judgments of the marine court of the city of New York, and of the justices' courts in that city."

By the act of 1883 (chap. 26), the name of the marine court was changed to the city court, but it still remained the same court, with the same judges and officers and the same jurisdiction, and the power to review its judgments continued in the court of common pleas under its original grant of power.

By chap. 416, of the laws of 1886, it was sought indirectly and by language, the full effect of which would not readily be observed by a casual reading, to take from the court of common pleas the important power of reviewing the judgments of the marine court, now the city court, and to authorize an appeal from those judgments direct to the court of appeals, without requiring that they should first be subjected to review by the court of common pleas. The enactment is as follows:

"Section 1. Subdivision two of section 191 of chap. 448, of the Laws of 1876, entitled, 'An act relating to courts, officers of justice and civil proceedings,' is hereby amended so as to read as follows: 2. An appeal cannot be taken in an action commenced in a court of a justice of the peace, or in a district court of the city of New York, or in the city court of Yonkers, or in a justice's court of a city, unless the court below allows the appeal by an order made at the general term which rendered the determination, or at the next general term after judgment is entered thereupon. An action discontinued because the answer set forth matter showing that the title to real property came in question, and afterwards prosecuted in another court, is not deemed to have been commenced in the court wherein the answer was interposed within the meaning of this subdivision. The city court of

New York shall be deemed a superior city court within the meaning of section 190 of the Code of Civil Procedure.

"Section 2. This act shall take effect immediately, but shall not apply to any actions now pending in which the time to appeal has not already expired."

If the act were construed literally it could not have any operation whatever, for it would have no application to any actions pending at the time of its passage, in which the time to appeal had not then already expired, and it is difficult to suppose any case to which under that restriction it could apply. But reading it as if the word "not" were omitted, it is still subject to the fundamental objection that it contravenes section 12 of article 6 of the Constitution by depriving the court of common pleas of its jurisdiction and power to review the judgments of the marine (city) court which it possessed at the time of the adoption of the article, and which were thereby rendered permanent and placed beyond the power of the legislature to take from that court.

The act authorizing appeals to this court from the decisions of the general term of the city court of Brooklyn (Laws of 1871, ch. 282) and its recognition by this court by entertaining such appeals, are relied upon by the appellants as giving support to their position in the present cases. But we do not see that they affect the question. There is no provision in the constitution in relation to the supreme court which could be construed as restraining the legislature from taking from that court the appellate jurisdiction over the judgments of the city court of Brooklyn which it possessed in 1869 and 1870, and the question now presented could not arise in respect to the act of 1871, before referred to.

The motions to dismiss the appeals in the above

entitled cases should be granted, but as the question is new no costs should be allowed to either party.

All concurred.

DRAKE, APPELLANT, v. DRAKE, ET AL., RESPONDENTS.

SUPREME COURT, FIRST DEPARTMENT, GENERAL TERM,

OCTOBER, 1886.

§ 1866.

Action to construe will.—Jurisdiction of Supreme Court.

Where one J. D. gave by his last will and testament, to one M. H. D., full power and authority to devise or appoint by her last will and testament, or other instrument in writing, certain real property owned by him, and the said M. H. D. subsequently by her last will and testament, and a codicil thereto, devised the said lands, and both said wills and said codicil were thereafter duly admitted to probate,—*Held*, that the Supreme Court had jurisdiction of an action seeking a determination as to the validity, construction and effect, of the will of the said J. D. so far as it is related to said property, and of any attempted testamentary disposition thereof by said will, and of the validity, construction and effect of the will and codicil, of M. H. D. in relation to the same lands, and of any attempted testamentary disposition thereof ; that such an application was a plain application to the court for the construction of a devise of a power in trust by one will, and of the sufficiency of the execution of that power by the other will, under section 1866 of the Code of Civil Procedure, which was specially and particularly designed to meet the questions arising under both wills.

Weed v. Weed (94 *N. Y.* 243) distinguished. Thiers v. Thiers (98 *Id.* 568), followed.

(Decided October, 1886)

Appeal from a judgment of the special term sustaining a demurrer and dismissing the complaint..

The opinion states all material facts.

Joseph F. Choate (*Evarts, Choate & Beaman,* attorneys), for plaintiff-appellant.

James C. Carter (*Crane & Lockwood,* attorneys), for defendants-respondents.

The title asserted by the plaintiff, being a pure legal estate, if he is not in possession, his appropriate, ample, and only remedy is an action in the nature of ejectment to recover possession. If he is in possession, the proof of that title will be a sure defense against any attack. He needs no other remedy. These are very old and familiar rules. Weed *v.* Weed, 94 *N. Y.* 243 ; Wager *v.* Wager, 89 *Id.* 161 ; Chipman *v.* Montgomery, 63 *Id.* 230 ; Post *v.* Hover, 33 *Id.* 602 ; Bowers *v.* Smith, 10 *Paige,* 200. Like most general rules they are subject to some exceptions. None of these, however, embrace the plaintiff's case. 1. Persons standing in the attitude of trustees are sometimes embarrassed by questions of difficulty concerning the course they ought to pursue. . . Courts of equity will entertain a suit by them seeking for instructions, and the decree will give them protection. The questions of doubt in such cases frequently relate to the construction, validity or effect of wills and deeds, and in this form there is a jurisdiction in equity to entertain suits for construction. In some of such cases a *cestui que trust* may bring a like action. 2. Sometimes also the title of the party in possession of an estate in real property, although his actual enjoyment may not be obstructed, may be threatened by a person asserting some right under some deed, judgment, mortgage or other instrument, or making some other adverse claim. Such threat may impair the marketable character of the property, or the party making the adverse claim may refrain from the assertion of his right until the loss of evidence by the lapse of time and the chances and changes of life may render the defense against it difficult or impossible. This is the foundation of those heads of equity known as the jurisdiction for the cancellation and delivery up of deeds, the removal of clouds upon title, and the *quia timet* jurisdiction.

Our statute relative to the determination of adverse claims to real property is founded upon these considerations of policy. The plaintiff's case is wholly outside of this exceptional class. Baily v. Briggs, 56 *N. Y.* 407 ; Scott v. Onderdonk, 14 *Id.* 9 ; Ryerson v. Willis, 81 *Id.* 281. The action cannot be maintained under section 1866 of the Code of Civil Procedure. 1. This crude and unintelligible section, founded upon a misconception of the statutes (Laws of 1853, chap. 238 ; 1879, chap. 316) from which it was drawn, should not be construed as superseding those sound and useful rules of procedure which the long experience of courts has shaped and established. 2. The artificers of this provision seem to have been under the impression that there was a general jurisdiction in equity, or somewhere, to determine " the validity of a deed purporting to convey land " . . " in an action brought for that purpose." It is only in cases where this can be done, and in the manner only in which this can be done, that the validity, construction or effect of a testamentary disposition of lands can under this section be determined. . . . 3. Upon consulting the authorities it will probably be found that the " validity of a deed " cannot be " determined " at all " in an action brought for that purpose alone."

MACOMBER, J.—The demurrers of the defendants Benjamin Drake, Mary F. Drake, Emily T. Smith, Ethelbert H. Smith, Anna T. L. Atterbury and Louis B. Atterbury to the complaint, were interposed upon the ground that the complaint did not state facts sufficient to constitute a cause of action. The demurrer of the defendants Mary K. Black, Charles N. Black and James Drake Black was put upon the same ground and also upon the further ground that the court had not jurisdiction of the subject of the action.

The order sustaining the demurrers is expressly stated to be upon the ground that the court had not jurisdiction of the subject of the action. In so far as this decision affects the demurrers which were interposed for the reason that the complaint did not state facts sufficient to constitute a cause of action, it would be a mis-trial, because it would not be possible to sustain a demurrer upon any ground other than that upon which it was placed. This does not affect the general principle that the jurisdiction of the court may always be questioned at the trial, whether such jurisdiction is challenged by the answer or not (*Code Civ. Pro.* § 499). Nevertheless, inasmuch as one of the demurrers raised the question of the jurisdiction of the court, it was doubtless deemed advisable· by counsel upon both sides to have that question settled for the benefit of all of the parties, and hence no suggestion has been made that the decision was, in part at least, a mis-trial, but, on the contrary, counsel unite in asking us to pass only upon the question that was considered by the special term, namely, that of the jurisdiction of the court to entertain the case as made by the complaint.

The action is brought to determine the validity, construction and effect of certain provisions of the last will and testament of Mary Hopeton Drake and James Drake. The complaint alleges the due execution of

the last will of James Drake, and his death subsequently thereto, and the admission of the same to
probate before the surrogate of the county of New
York, and sets forth the will and codicil in *hæc verba.*
It then proceeds to set out in detail the description of
the several lots of land in the city of New York,
including the eleven lots hereinafter mentioned, owned
by the testator at the time of his death, of which the
plaintiff, with others, is in possession. It also contains suitable allegations showing the relationship of
the plaintiff with the several defendants to the testator, as heirs at law or devisees. The ninth provision
of this will reads as follows: "In case of the
death of the said Mary Hopeton Drake, without leaving lawful issue surviving at the time of her decease,
then, and in such cases, I give and devise to her full
power and authority to devise or appoint by her last
will and testament, or other instrument in writing,
executed by her in the manner hereinbefore mentioned, the said eleven dwelling-houses and lots of
land last above mentioned, and each and every of
them, to all or any or either of my sisters, Susan Ann
Drake, Sarah Ann Lawrence and Mary N. Keene, or
to all or any or either of the lawful issue of my said
sisters from and after the death of the said Mary
Hopeton Drake forever thereafter, and in such shares
and proportions as she may think proper; and in such
case I hereby give and devise the same in case of such
devise or appointment, and in default of said last mentioned devise or appointment of the said Mary Hopeton Drake, and without leaving lawful issue her sur-
·viving, I hereby give and devise the last mentioned
eleven dwelling houses and lots of land to my sisters
above named, and to their heirs and assigns, from
and after the death of the said Mary Hopeton Drake
forever, to be divided among my said sisters in equal
shares; and in case of the death of any or either of

my said sisters during the lifetime of said Mary Hopeton Drake, leaving lawful issue, then in such case last
mentioned the said issue of each one so dying shall
take the share or part thereof which the parent of
such issue would have taken if she had survived."
It is out of the foregoing article of the will of James
Drake that the questions of law designed by plaintiff
to be presented to the court principally arise.

It further appears that Mary Hopeton Drake survived the testator, and after the death and the probate
of the will she took possession of the eleven lots of
land particularly set forth in the complaint, and continued to occupy and possess the same until her
death. Mary Hopeton Drake, it is shown, died on June
24, 1884, unmarried and without issue, having previously made her last will and testament, bearing date
June 14, 1881, and a codicil thereto, bearing date June
21, 1881, both of which instruments are set out in full in
the complaint, and were duly admitted to probate by
the same surrogate. By the second article of her will
she recites the fact of the devise to her of the eleven
houses and lots mentioned in the will of James Drake,
and the authority to devise the same as therein provided, and then proceeds to make a disposition thereof
to sundry persons in different shares. By the first
article of her codicil she revokes the devise made in
the second clause of her will to James Drake Black,
and devises him other property in lieu thereof. She
also revokes the devise to Mary Hopeton Smith, and
in place thereof gives her other property ; and also
revokes the devise to Mary Hopeton Drake, and gives
her other property instead thereof. By the second
clause of her codicil she devises to Hopeton Drake
Atterbury, land on the western side of Broadway, in
the city of New York, describing it, also premises on
Twelfth street adjoining, to have and to hold the same

to the said Hopeton Drake Atterbury, and to her heirs and assigns forever. And if the devisees should not be living at the time of the death of the testator, then the same should go to her lawful issue equally, and in the event of her death before the testator, without lawful issue surviving her, then the property should form a part of her residuary estate and be disposed of as directed in relation to that portion of her property.

The complaint further alleges that article second of said will of said Mary Hopeton Drake, and articles first and second of her codicil thereto, are void, inoperative and of no effect in so far as they relate to or attempt to devise or appoint or dispose of lands in the complaint particularly described, or any part thereof, and that as to said lands and premises the said Mary Hopeton Drake has failed to devise or appoint the same under law by virtue of the power of appointment given to her in and by the last will and testament of James Drake. Thence follows a suitable prayer for relief, based upon such allegations, and a further prayer that the validity, construction and effect under the laws of the State of New York, of the will of the said James Drake, deceased, in so far as it relates to the lands and premises mentioned, and the validity, construction and effect under the laws of any testamentary disposition of said lands, in that will contained, be determined by this court; that the validity, construction and effect of the last will and codicil of Mary Hopeton Drake in relation to the same subject matter, or of any attempted testamentary disposition of those lands and premises or any part thereof, in and by the will of Mary Hopeton Drake, be also determined by the Court; together with a suitable prayer for injunction and appointment of a receiver, &c.

It will thus be seen what was in the mind of the counsel who drew the complaint, and what questions of law may arise for the determination of the court.

Drake v. Drake.

We are not asked to make a construction of any of
these provisions of the wills respectively, nor to pronounce any of their provisions valid or invalid, but are
asked to consider only the question of jurisdiction of
the court to entertain a complaint containing these
allegations, and by which a construction of this nature
is sought. The learned judge, at special term, based
his decision upon the case of Weed v. Weed (94 *N. Y.*
243). That case holds only that a devisee who claims
a mere legal estate in the real property of the testator
where there is no trust, cannot maintain an action for
the construction of a devise, but must assert his title
by legal action, or, if in possession, must await an
attack upon him, and set up the devise in answer to
the hostile claim. The court there held that there was
no element in the case of equitable jurisdiction, or
cognizance, inasmuch as there was no trust provided
for by the terms of the will. That decision was in a
case arising before the enactment of section 1866 of the
Code of Civil Procedure, upon which the complaint in
this action is manifestly based, and furthermore does
not, in our judgment, meet any question that is
designed to be presented by the plaintiff in this action.
The question before us rather is this : assuming the
principle of Weed v. Weed to exist, as it has existed
from time immemorial, is this plaintiff in a situation to
call upon the court for the construction of the particular wills above mentioned ?

Section 1866 of the Code of Civil Procedure is as
follows : "The validity, construction or effect, under
the laws of the State, of a testamentary disposition of
real property situated within this State, or of an interest in such property, which would descend to the heir
of an intestate, may be determined, in an action
brought for that purpose, in like manner as the validity of a deed, purporting to convey land, may be determined. The judgment in such an action may perpetu-

ally enjoin any party, from setting up or from impeaching the devise, or otherwise making any claim in contravention to the determination of the court, as justice requires." It would seem that by reference to the ninth clause of the will of James Drake that a . trust of a most important character was reposed in Mary Hopeton Drake, and that the exercise of that trust or power in trust, if it be that only, calls upon this court for the exercise of its most important equitable jurisdiction, and a power which is not limited altogether either by the section of the Code above mentioned or by previous legislation. This section of the Code is an elaboration only of the statute of 1853 by which the validity of any actual or alleged devise in a will, of real estate, might be determined by the supreme court in a proper action for that purpose in like manner as the validity of any deed conveying, or purporting to convey lands, may be determined by such court. And we are cited to a decision of the general term in the second department,*.by which a complaint was sustaind under chapter 238 of the laws of 1853, which sought to declare a will invalid. The law of 1879 (laws of 1879, chapter 316), simply provides that the validity of a devise or will may be determined by the supreme court in a proper action for that purpose, leaving out entirely the restrictive clause derived from the analogous practice relating to deeds of real estate.

Many cases have been decided by the courts, arising under the statute of 1853, which tend to uphold the contention made by the counsel for the plaintiff, that even without section 1866 of the Code the jurisdiction of the court in this instance could be upheld, and among them are Jones v. Jones, 1 *How. Pr. N. S.* 510 ; Marvin v. Marvin, 11 *Abb. Pr. N. S.* 102 ;

---

* Pryer v. Howe, 40 *Hun*, 383.

Wager v. Wager, 23 *Hun*, 439 ; Ward v. Ward, 23 *Hun*, 431 ; De Bussierre v. Holladay, 55 *How. Pr.* 210.

The case of Tiers v. Tiers (98 *N. Y.* 568), seems to have arisen distinctively under section 1866 of the Code, but authorities are hardly needed in a case that seems to have been so perspicuously placed by the pleader upon the section of the Code already quoted. "The validity, construction and effect of a testamentary disposition of real estate situated within this State, may be determined by the court in an action brought for that purpose," says the statute. The plaintiff brings this action, thereon, and, under suitable allegations, challenging the validity of article two of the will of Mary Hopeton Drake, and articles one and two of the codicil to that will, as the same is to be ascertained under article nine of the will of James Drake, and in the words of the statute asks that this court determine the validity, construction and effect of those instruments. It seems to us to be a plain application to the court for the construction of a devise of a power in trust by one will and the sufficiency of the execution of that power by the other will under a statute that was specially and particularly designed to meet the questions arising under both wills. Being of opinion, therefore, that the special term was in error in sustaining the demurrers upon the ground that the court had not jurisdiction of the subject of the action, it follows that the order and interlocutory judgment should be reversed. It is so ordered without costs to either party, and with directions to the special term to consider the questions which are presented by the other ground of the demurrers, which will necessarily involve the construction and effect of the provisions of the two wills already mentioned.

BRADY and DANIELS, JJ., concur.

THE COLUMBIAN INSTITUTE, Judgment Cred.
ITOR, v. CREGAN, Judgment Debtor.

City Court of New York, Chambers, October,
1886.

§§ 2447, 2464, 2468, 2469.

*Supplementary proceedings.—What property may be reached in — When
salary cannot be—Public officer.*

Proceedings supplementary to execution are statutory and operate
on property which the debtor has at the time the order is obtained
and do not affect property acquired afterwards, and a receiver
appointed therein becomes vested from the time of his appointment with the property which the debtor had at the time the proceedings were commenced, but gets no title to property which the
debtor acquires subsequently.

An order in supplementary proceedings requiring the judgment
debtor to deliver over property or money to be applied on account
of the judgment, can only be made where it appears that the
debtor had the specific property in his possession when the proceedings were commenced, and that he is at the time of making
the order able to comply with its commands.

A judgment debtor cannot be required in proceedings supplementary
to execution, to set apart a portion of his salary, thereafter to
become due, and apply it on account of the judgment and particularly so when he is a public officer.

Public officers cannot, by any act of their own, assign or incumber
their future salary as such, nor can the courts for them assign or
incumber it; such acts are forbidden by public policy.

(Decided October 9, 1886.)

Motion by the judgment creditor in proceedings
supplementary to execution for an order directing the
defendant to pay the judgment out of an installment
of salary due him October 1, 1886, as clerk of the sixth
distict court, or (2) for an order appointing a receiver

and directing the defendant to pay said judgment in installments from his salary as he receives it, until the judgment is paid.

The judgment debtor herein was examined in proceedings supplementary to execution, and at the conclusion of such examination the judgment creditor made this motion.

H. R. Bayne & G. M. Baker, for judgment creditor and motion.

W. Armstrong and *Granville P. Hawes*, for judgment debtor, opposed.

McADAM, Ch. J.—These proceedings are statutory, and operate on property which the debtor has at the time the order is obtained (Potter *v.* Low, 16 *How. Pr.* 549; and cases cited under section 2447 of *Bliss' Code*), and do not affect property acquired afterwards (Merriam *v.* Hill, 1 *N. Y. Weekly Dig.* 260, and cases cited), and the receiver becomes vested from the time of his appointment (*Code*, § 2468) with the property which the debtor had at the time the poceedings were commenced (Dubois *v.* Cassidy, 75 *N. Y.* 302), but gets no title to property which the debtor acquires subsequently (Thorn *v.* Fellows, 5 *Weekly Dig.* 473; Graff *v.* Bennett, 25 *How. Pr.* 470). The application of these rules to the present motion makes it clear that the present motion to be decided is whether the defendant had any specific property in his possession when the proceedings were commenced, that he is now able to deliver over, for the order applied for can be made only where the defendant is able to comply with its command if granted (*Code*, § 2447; Peters *v.* Kerr, 22 *How. Pr.* 3; West Side Bank *v.* Pugsley, 47 *N. Y.* 368).

To make the order without proof of ability

to comply would in effect be reviving in another form imprisonment for debt, which has long since been abolished. The defendant had no property when the proceedings were commenced, and this fact is an unanswerable objection to the application to require him to pay over. To direct debtor to deliver over when he has nothing to pay or deliver over is practically telling the defendant judicially that he must either raise the money and pay the debt represented by the judgment or go to jail and remain there until some friendly hand discharges the obligation for him. Imprisonment for debt in all its rigor meant nothing more.

The branch of the motion which seeks to compel the defendant to set apart a portion of his salary each month as it becomes due, and apply it to the judgment until it is paid, cannot be granted. No court has power to make such a decree in supplementary proceedings. The statute limits the power of the court in such proceedings to existing rights and things *in esse* at the time they are instituted, and does not permit it to anticipate upon what the defendant ought to be able to pay or do in the future. Such a grant of power might be beneficial to debtors as well as creditors. It might teach the former the advantages of economy and at the same time insure creditors the payment of their demands. But the legislature has withheld this power from the courts, and they cannot exercise it until the authority is conferred.

Salaries to become due to employes cannot be reached in any case (Woodman *v.* Goodenough, 18 *Abb. Pr.* 265; Geregani *v.* Wheelwright, 3 *Abb. N. S.* 264; Potter *v.* Low, 16 *How. Pr.* 549; Caton *v.* Southwell, 13 *Barb.* 335; First National Bank *v.* Beardslee, 8 *N. Y. Weekly Dig.* 7). This is particularly so with regard to public officers, who cannot by any act of theirs assign or incumber the future salary of their office,

nor can the court incumber or assign it for them. The
reason is founded on a rule of public policy which forbids such acts (Bliss *v.* Lawrence, 58 *N. Y.* 442). The
court in that case forcibly said : " The public service
is protected by protecting those engaged in performe-
ing public duties ; and this, not upon the ground of
their private interest, but upon that of the necessity
of securing the efficiency of the public service, by see-
ing to it that the funds provided for its maintenance
should be received by those who are to perform the
work at such periods as the law has provided for their
payment."

These views render it unnecessary to consider any
of the suggestions made upon the argument.

If the plaintiff insists upon the appointment of a
receiver of the few effects belonging to the defendant,
is may have that relief.   In other regards, the several
applications will be denied, but without costs.

WHEATON *v.* NEWCOMBE, Appellant.
BAMBERGER & HART, Respondents.

Superior Court of the City of New York, General Term, April, 1886.

§§ 3247, 3352.

*Costs.— When attorney not chargeable with.— When Code of Civil Pro-
cedure applies to costs of action began before its enactment.*

The provision of section 3247 of the Code of Civil Procedure which
exempts an attorney or counsel from liability for the costs of an
action, on the ground that he is beneficially interested therein
where "his only beneficial interest consists of a right to a portion
of the sum or property recovered as compensation for his services

in 'the action " applies to an action began before its enactment, in which costs were not recovered until after it took effect.[2]

It seems, that prior to the enactment of section 3247 of the Code of Civil Procedure, an attorney who had a right to a portion of the recovery in an action as compensation for his services, was liable for the costs of such action.[1,5]

As costs relate merely to the remedy and as their recovery and taxation are regulated solely by the provisions of the statute in force at the time of the recovery of a judgment, a party to whom costs had not been awarded at the time the Code of Civil Procedure went into effect, had not a lawfully accrued or established right thereto within the true intent and meaning of section 3352 of the Code of Civil Procedure which provides, among other things, that said Code shall not render ineffectual or otherwise impair any right lawfully accrued or established before it took effect.[3,4]

(*Decided May* 3, 1886.)

Appeals by defendant from two orders denying motions made to charge the attorneys for the plaintiff, as persons beneficially interested in the action, with a judgment for costs.

The facts appear in the opinion.

Abram Kling, for defendant and appellant.

G. W. Cotterill, for respondent, Ira Leo Bamberger.

Reginald Hart, respondent in person.

FREEDMAN, J.—The appeals present the question whether Hart and Bamberger, the attorneys of record for the plaintiff, are liable to the defendant who recovered judgment, for the costs of the action, on the ground that they were beneficially interested in the action by virtue of an agreement by which they were to have a portion of the recovery as compensation for their services. That under section 44, chapter X., title I., part III. of the Revised Statutes* they would [*] have been so liable, if both shared in the agree-

---

* 2 *R. S.* 619, § 44.

ment, was expressly decided in Voorhees v. McCartney
(51 N. Y. 387). In Sussdorff v. Schmidt (55 Id. 325),
it is true, a statement to the contrary may be found,
but such statement is a mere dictum which was made
without reference to the statute. In case it were necessary to decide which of the two cases should be
followed, the preference would have to be given to
Voorhis v. McCartney, on the ground that it is an
express adjudication on the very point under the
statute.

Section 321 of the Code of Procedure provided a
further remedy against the assignee of a cause of
action after action brought. Section 44 of the Revised
Statutes, and section 321 of the Code, were both
repealed by chapter 245 of the laws of 1880, and in
place thereof a new provision was substituted by section 3247 of chapter 178 of the laws of 1880 entitled
"An Act supplemental to the Code of Civil Procedure." But this new section (§ 3247) expressly
['] exempts attorneys from liability for costs, as follows : "But this section does not apply to a case,
where the person so beneficially interested is the attorney or counsel for the plaintiff, if his only beneficial
interest consists of a right to a portion of the sum or
property recovered, as compensation for his services
in the action."

In the case at bar the action was brought in 1878,
and the judgment for costs for which Hart and Bamberger are sought to be held liable, was recovered in
August, 1882. At the time of such recovery, section
3247 of the Code of Civil Procedure was already in
force, and the question therefore is, whether that section, or the prior law, is to control. There is no claim
that Hart and Bamberger held any assignment. The
most that is claimed is that Hart and Bamberger were,
or that at least Bamberger was beneficially interested
in the action by virtue of an agreement with the

plaintiff for the receipt of a portion of the recovery as compensation for services to be rendered.

The solution of the question of liability depends upon the effect to be given to several saving clauses. They have been carefully examined in the light of the points and the arguments submitted on both sides, and the conclusion reached is somewhat at variance with the view entertained by me in one of the early stages of this litigation, when I did not have the benefit of any argument.

['] Section 3347 of the Code of Civil Procedure saves a great number of proceedings in actions commenced before September 1, 1880, but does not affect the question of liability now under investigation. Section 3 of chapter 245 of the laws of 1880, saves, from the operation of the repealing clauses of that statute, any right "*lawfully accrued or established before this act takes effect.*" Section 3352 of the Code of Civil Procedure contains a similar saving clause in favor of rights *lawfully accrued or established*, &c.

Under the two saving clauses last referred to, and no others having been cited as bearing upon the question under examination, it is not enough that the action was commenced before the enactment of section 3247. To succeed in his application the defendant must show that his right to the costs of the action lawfully accrued or was established before the section went into effect.

['] As costs relate merely to the remedy, and as their recovery and taxation are regulated solely by the provisions of the statute in force, at the time of the recovery of a judgment, the defendant never had a lawfully accrued or established right to the costs of the action within the true intent and meaning of said saving clauses until he recovered judgment against the plaintiff in August, 1882.

['] The conclusion is therefore unavoidable that,

inasmuch as in August, 1882 there was no statute in
existence under which an attorney could be compelled to pay costs on the ground that he had a beneficial
interest in the action by virtue of an agreement for
the receipt of a portion of the recovery as compensation for his services, the orders appealed from were
properly made. This being so, the subordinate questions involved in the appeals need not be considered.

The orders appealed from must be affirmed, with
costs.

INGRAHAM, J., concurred.

BLISS, RESPONDENT, *v.* BLISS, APPELLANT.

N. Y. COURT OF COMMON PLEAS, GENERAL TERM,
MARCH, 1886.

§§ 724, 1011, 1012, 1229, 1757.

Divorce.—Orders of reference, when may be amended, nunc pro tunc.

Where, in an action for divorce, *a vinculo matrimonii*, in which issue
was joined on the question of adultery, a stipulation was made
that the "right to a trial by jury be waived, and that it be referred
to a referee, to take proof and report to the court," and an order
was entered thereon, that the "action be referred to. . . . take
proof of the facts stated in the complaint, and report to the court
with all convenient speed with his opinion thereon," and thereafter a second order was made, directing "that the issues" raised
by a supplemental answer and reply "be tried before. . . .. the
referee heretofore appointed herein, in like manner as if included
in the original order of reference," which order was entered upon
a stipulation that "the issues thus raised be included in the order
of reference already entered, and that an order be entered," etc.,
and the reference thereafter proceeded under said orders before

Bliss v. Bliss.

the referee appointed thereby, who at the conclusion thereof made findings of facts and conclusions of law, and it also appeared that it was the intention of the parties, that the whole issues in the action be referred for hearing and determination,—*Held*, that an order was properly made upon the coming in of the referee's report, amending order of reference *nunc pro tunc*, so as to refer in terms, the action and all its issues to such referee for hearing and determination, and to report thereon.[1,2] [LARREMORE, Ch. J., dissenting.] [3,7]

In such a case, LARREMORE, Ch. J., dissenting,—*Held*, that such a reference could not be ordered without a written consent [4,5] that the court could not so amend the order of reference, inasmuch as the written consent did not in terms provide for such a reference, and the power of the referee was expressly limited, and confined in the consent and order.[6,7]

Wilmore v. Flack (6 *N. Y. Civ. Pro.* 191), followed;[7] and Fisher v. Fisher (unreported);[3] Baird v. Mayor (74 *N. Y.* 382):[8] Renouil v. Harris (2 *Sandf.* 642);[8] McCleary v. McCleary (30 *Hun*, 154),[9] distinguished by LARREMORE, Ch. J., dissenting.

The practice where issues in a divorce case are referred to take testimony and report, stated.[9]

(*Decided June* 7, 1886.)

Appeal by defendant from an order of the special term amending an order of reference, *nunc pro tunc*.

The action was brought to procure a divorce *a vinculo matrimonii*, and the order appealed from amended orders of reference *nunc pro tunc* so that they should read : "Ordered that the above entitled action and all the issues therein be and the same hereby are referred to JOHN A. OSBORN, Esq., as referee to hear and determine the same and report thereon with all convenient speed."

The first order of reference, made upon the original pleadings was : "Ordered that the above action be referred to JOHN A. OSBORN, Esq., to take proof of the facts stated in the complaint, and report to this court with all convenient speed with his opinion thereon : and also to take proof of the service of the summons and complaint upon this defendant."

The second order of reference, made when the supplemental answer was interposed, was that "the issues thus raised by supplemental answer and reply be tried before JOHN A. OSBORN, Esq., the referee heretofore appointed herein in like manner, as if included in the original order of reference."

Further facts appear in the opinions.

Wheeler & Cortis, for appellant.

James E Doherty, for respondent.

J. F. DALY, J.—The intention of the parties as expressed in their stipulations and the orders entered thereon, and in all their subsequent proceedings, was apparently to have the issues tried privately by a referee instead of in open court; and the order appealed from amending the orders of reference so as to carry out that intention, was correct and should be affirmed.

The first order of reference was made upon a stipulation in writing that the "right to a trial by jury be waived, and that it be referred to a referee to be named by the court, to take proof and to report to this court." The reference was first suggested in a letter written before that time and when the cause was reached for trial on the calendar of the court, by the attorneys for the defendant and appellant (who is now objecting to the amendment), to the attorney of the plaintiff and respondent as follows: "We had hardly thought you were serious in pressing the trial of the Bliss Case, but as you now seem inclined to do so we would suggest that it is for the interest of both parties that the cause should be referred to some suitable person. If you approve of this we would be glad to have suggestions from you as to who that person shall be."

A subsequent letter from the same writer says, " You are right in assuming that a reference had been decided upon, but before consenting to Judge Bos. worth we must have our client acquiesce in the choice.

After the entry of the order of reference, a notice of trial was given by plaintiff and accepted by defend. ant. "That the above action will be brought on for trial before JOHN A. OSBORN, Esq., referee appointed by this court to determine the matters in controversy between the parties in the above entitled action at his office," &c.

When the defendant afterwards obtained leave to serve her supplemental answer, her attorneys and the attorneys for the plaintiff entered into the following stipulation : " It is mutually stipulated that the supplemental answer heretofore served herein be received ; that it be considered as denied by the reply already in, and that the issues thus raised be included in the order of reference already entered, and that an order to this effect be entered." It was upon this stipulation that the second order of reference was entered.

In a petition addressed to this court by defendant and appellant while the action was pending before the referee, for an allowance for the expenses of the action, she states that : " The issues in this action as raised by the original answer were referred to JOHN A. OSBORN, Esq., as sole referee to hear and determine the same on November 22, 1884. The issues raised by the supplemental answer have also been referred to him." Accompanying such petition is the affidavit of her attorney and counsel, Mr. Wheeler, which begins by stating, " I am counsel for the defendant and have acted as such since the trial thereof began and prior thereto," and repeatedly afterwards refers to the proceedings before the referee as the trial of the action. Accompanying said petition is the affidavit of Mr. Knevals, one of the defendant's counsel stating among other things that the action " is now and has been since January 20, 1885, on trial before the referee."

Upon the decision of the action the defendant requested findings of fact and of law from the referees as upon trial of the issues, and asked of him " judgment in her favor and against the plaintiff upon the merits," and excepted in writing to his findings of fact and law. It is now her contention that the proceedings before the referee, were not a trial, nor intended to be, but were intended merely for the taking of testimony as preparation for a hearing at special term ; and that an amendment of the orders of reference requires an amendment of the stipulation which the court has no power to order.

['] On the contrary I find the intention expressed throughout the case by the parties, by stipulations and orders, and in every possible form of written declaration and admission, is to try the case out of court, and before a referee, and that the amendment of the orders of reference expresses exactly what they purposed and designed from the time that a reference was first suggested.

The suggestion that the court should impose terms of the amendment is not, in my opinion, reasonable. No favor is extended to plaintiff : he gets only what he is legally entitled to.

The order should be affirmed.

['] Van Hoesen, J.—(Concurring.)—In my opinion, both parties intended that the referee should hear and determine the issues (subject, of course, to the application to the court for its approval of his proceedings that section 1229 and rule 77 make an indispensable preliminary to the entry of judgment in an action for divorce). The attorneys appear not to have had at the time, a clear recollection of the requirements of the law, for they assume that they could select the referee though rule 73 forbids the appointment of a referee selected by the parties. I believe that both parties supposed that the stipulation provided for a trial of the issues, first, and then for the submission of the referee's report to the court in obedience to the requiremnts of rule 77 and section 1229. This was their meaning, imperfectly and inartificially expressed. Judge ALLEN did not make a new stipulation for them, but simply gave form to what both parties intended at the time the stipulation was signed. I concur with Judge DALY.

LARREMORE, Ch. J.—(Dissenting.)—This is an action for divorce. The complaint charges the defendant with adultery, and asks for a dissolution of the marriage. The answer denied the allegations of the complaint, set up counter allegations of adultery and also asked for a divorce *a vinculo.* The action being at issue, upon the consent, in writing, of the attorneys for both parties, it was, on or about November 22, 1884, referred to a referee " to take proof of the facts stated in the complaint and report to this court with all convenient speed, with his opinion thereupon ; and also to take proof of the service of the summons and complaint upon this defendant." Thereafter, a supplemental answer was served by defendant on or about May 19, 1885, upon consent in writing of said attorneys, it was ordered " That the issues raised by said supplemental answer and reply be tried before the referee heretofore appointed, in like manner as if included in the original order of reference to him." Testimony was taken on behalf of both parties before the referee ; proposed findings and conclusions of law were submitted to him upon which he passed. and, on or about September 28, 1885, he rendered his report containing findings of fact and con-

clusion of law to the effect that plaintiff is entitled to
a decree in his favor, and that said plaintiff be absolutely divorced fro.n the defendant. Thereafter, and
on or about November 30, 1885, upon motion of plaintiff's counsel an order was entered at the special term
amending said order of reference *nunc pro tunc* so
that the ordering part of the same shall read as follows :—"Ordered, that the above entitled action and
all the issues therein be, and the same hereby are
referred to John A. Osborn, Esq., referee, to hear and
determine the same and report thereon with all convenient speed." From such order of amendment this
appeal is taken.

[']   If the order appealed from had simply amended
the orders of reference to conform with a consent
given, as in the case of Fisher *v.* Fisher (special
term of this court, June, 1875), the authority of the
court to make such amendment would have been
ample under § 724 of the Code. The difficulty is that
the original order of reference did not conform with
the consent, and if such order is amended the consent
must be amended also. According to § 1757, if the
allegation of adultery is put in issue, the court must,
upon the application of either party, or may of its
own motion order trial of such issue by a jury.
According to § 1012, if such issue is raised, it may, in
the discretion of the court, be tried by a referee,
provided the parties consent to a reference. Section
1011, must evidently be read in connection with section 1012, and it provides how such consent is to be
manifested, *i. e.*, by the written stipulation of the
[']   parties signed by their attorneys. If the issues
are not tried by a jury under section 1757, or by
a referee under sections 1011 and 1012, they must of
course be tried at the special term.

[']   As this case was at issue it could not have
been referred at all, except upon the consent in

writing of the parties. Such consent was signed by the respective attorneys, and plaintiff, in effect, asks the court to declare that it was in reality, though not in terms, a consent to refer the issue to hear and determine. But how can we disregard the explicit language of the consent and hold that the parties [*] meant one thing when they said another? In Renouil *v.* Harris (2 *Sandf.* 642), the court held that when an order is made referring the cause without any limitations, all the issues are referred. In McCleary *v.* McCleary (30 *Hun*, 154), the order was "to hear the same and all the issues therein." In neither of these cases did the court go counter to the language employed ; but in both the decision went on the theory that the intention was incompletely expressed in the order, but was nevertheless apparent from it. In the case at bar the power of the ref- [*] eree is expressly limited and defined in the consent and order ; and, if the latter were amended to be an order to hear and determine, the original intention of the parties, so far as language can express it would be disregarded, and the arbitrary dictum of the court substituted therefor.

"The right to give or withhold the consent does not belong to the court, but to the party ; his free choice and option cannot be taken away under the guise of correcting a mistake or oversight" (Wilmore *v.* Flack, 6 *N. Y. Civ. Pro.* 191).

In the case from which this extract is quoted, the court of appeals decided that it was beyond the power of a court, under the pretence of amendment, to pronounce that a consent existed which had never been given. Equally beyond the court's power would it be to pronounce that a consent did not mean what its unambiguous language expresses. The consent upon which the supplemental order of reference was granted is simply that the issues raised by the supplemental answer, "be included in the order of reference already entered" and cannot be construed to aid plaintiff in his present contention.

[⁸]   Plaintiff further claims, under the authority of Baird v. The Mayor (74 *N. Y.* 382), and many other cases of similar import, that the order appealed from should be affirmed, because, by proceeding with the reference, defendant has waived any irregularity in the original order.   But defendant is not asking to set the reference or its results aside.   She offers to allow the testimony to stand and be used at the trial of the case.   She has not asked to have the reference declared a nullity; but that the effect of a written instrument shall not be extended beyond its actual terms.   Some of the allegations in papers verified by herself and her counsel, and the form of the supplemental order of reference of May 19, 1885, are indeed inconsistent with her present position.   But, on the other hand, it appears that the referee did not consider that he was empowered to hear and determine the action, and that he excluded testimony offered by defendant on this ground.   ¹

The present situation is one which is presented so frequently in divorce cases, that we are led to believe that there is much confusion in the minds of members of the bar as to the proper practice (see remarks of FREEDMAN, J., in Sullivan v. Sullivan, 41 *N. Y. Super. Ct.* [9 *J. & S.*] 519).

Even if both parties were under the impression that they were actually trying the case before the referee, and in many respects acted under such assumption, I do not think that this takes away from defendant the privilege of asserting her strictly legal right (Wilmore v. Flack, *supra*).

In Sullivan v. Sullivan (*supra*), the order of ref-
[⁹]   erence was to take proof and report, as in the present case and upon the coming in of the report

the court refused to confirm it, saying: "There is but one way that I can see in which evidence irregularly taken after issue, by a referee pursuant to an order to that effect, can be used in an action for divorce ; and that is, that by consent of the parties it may be read upon a subsequent trial held before the court and brought on regular notice in the usual way. In such case, it may be treated and will have the force of a conditional examination before trial. But this course must be agreed to by the parties, and, thereupon the court must try the issues and make its own findings of fact and draw its own conclusions of law therefrom."

In that case, no application for an amendment *nunc pro tunc* of the order of reference seems to have been made ; but from the tenor of the learned judge's opinion it is quite clear that he would not have entertained it.

As to the course to be pursued under the circumstance, I think the better rule is that laid down by VAN BRUNT, J., in Wertheimer *v.* Wertheimer (1 *Law Bul.* 34), as follows : "The case must be brought on for trial upon the usual notice, and, instead of the witnesses being sworn in open court, the evidence taken before the referee must be presented " (see also Kane *v.* Astor's Executors, 5 *Sandf.* 467). This view in the main commands itself, but I also think that as the proceeding in court is the trial of the action, the parties should be permitted to present any additional evidence they have to offer ; and that the case should be there heard and decided upon the evidence taken before the referee and in court. It is especially proper in this case that the parties should be accorded such privilege, because it appears that some evidence was excluded by the referee for reason of his want of power.

The order appealed from should be reversed with provision for a trial at the equity term, as above directed.

WILLIS, Respondent, v. BELLAMY, Appellant.

Superior Court of The City of New York, General Term, March, 1886.

§ 1674.

Lis pendens— When not canceled.*—Reviewing decision of motion to cancel.

The determination of a motion to cancel a *lis pendens* is in the discretion of the court and should not be disturbed without manifest cause.

The right to file a *lis pendens* being statutory, the provisions of the statute should be strictly followed in all their essential requirements, and a motion to cancel a *lis pendens* is properly denied where none of the events, which section 1674 of the Code of Civil Procedure shall authorize its cancellation, have occurred.

(*Decided March* 1, 1886.)

Appeal by defendants from an order denying a motion for the cancellation of a *lis pendens* filed by plaintiff.

Burnett & Whitney, for defendants-appellants.

William Settle, for plaintiff-respondent.

O'Gorman, J.—The question in dispute in this case is whether a notice of *lis pendens*, duly filed, should be canceled before the entry of final judgment in the action.

A motion by defendants for cancellation of the *lis*

---

* See Niebuhr *v.* Schreyer, 10 *N. Y. Civ. Pro.* 72.

pendens here, was made at the special term of this court and denied, on the ground that the motion was premature, and from this decision the defendants appeal.

It was a matter resting in the discretion of the court, and the decision should not be disturbed without manifest cause.

The action was to compel specific performance of an agreement to convey title to real estate, or for the return to plaintiff of $500 paid on account of the purchase money. The action was tried at special term, and the court adjudged that the defendants were unable to convey, and that the plaintiff was not entitled to specific performance, but had a lien on the premises in question, for the money so paid by him with interest. From this judgment the defendants appealed to the general term of this court, by which the judgment was reversed and a new trial was ordered as to some of the defendants. An application was afterwards made to the general term for re-argument, which has not yet been decided.

The Code of Civil Procedure provides in section 1674. that after the action is settled, discontinued or abated, or final judgment is rendered therein against the party filing the notice of *lis pendens* and the time to appeal has expired, the court may in its discretion, on motion, direct that the notice of *lis pendens* be canceled of record.

None of these events has taken place in this action.

The right to file a *lis pendens* is statutory (*Code*, § 1670), and the provisions of the statute should be strictly followed in all their essential requirements.

The order appealed from must be affirmed, with $10 costs.

SEDGWICK, Ch. J., concurred.

HENRY AS RECEIVER, ETC. *v.* DERBY, ET AL.
IN RE, APPLICATION OF THE DEFENDANTS FOR AN
ORDER DIRECTING WILLIS M. RANNEY
TO PAY THE COSTS OF THE ACTION.

SUPERIOR COURT OF THE CITY OF NEW YORK, GEN-
ERAL TERM, MARCH, 1886.

§§ 433, 3247.

*Costs—Motion to charge person beneficially interested in action with—
Notice of such motion on whom served—Employment of
attorney when ended.*

An order charging a person not a party to an action but beneficially
interested therein with the costs thereof cannot be made without
service of notice of the application therefor on him, and where
such an order is made without service upon him, his proper proceeding is to move to set it aside.   Accordingly, *Held,* where an order
was made charging a judgment creditor with the costs of an action
brought by a receiver of the property of his judgment debtor, on
the ground that the action was brought at his instance and that
he was beneficially interested therein, and notice of the application
was not served on him, that the order should be vacated ; that
service of notice on his attorney in the action in which the
receiver was appointed and on the attorney for the receiver was not
sufficient.
The authority of an attorney in an action ceases on the recovery of
judgment therein.
(*Decided, March* 1, 1886.)

Appeal by Willis M. Ranney from an order denying his motion to vacate an order directing him to pay
the costs of the action.

The facts appear in the opinion.

Riddle & Ward, and *Charles M. Hough,* for
appellant.

F. A. Burnham, for defendants-respondents.

PER CURIAM.—The action was brought by a receiver appointed in supplementary proceedings, and resulted in the dismissal of the complaint, with costs. Costs having been taxed, the defendant moved under section 3247 of the Code, that Willis M. Ranney be compelled to pay the costs, on the ground that the action had been brought at his request. Notice of that motion was served upon the attorney for the plaintiff, in the action in which the receiver was appointed, and the attorney for the receiver, but was not served on Ranney personally. The court granted the motion. Subsequently a motion was made on behalf of Ranney, who appeared by attorney, for the purposes of that motion only, to vacate the order requiring him to pay such costs. The motion was denied, and from ,the order denying that motion plaintiff appealed.

If the order directing Ranney to pay costs had any validity, proceedings might be taken at once against him or his property to enforce such order. He had an interest in having it set aside so that proceedings upon it might not even be begun. The order adjudicated him to have been beneficially interested in the action brought by the receiver, and that that action was brought at his request. Such an order could not be made without notice to him so that he could be heard and oppose.

The finding in the action that it had been brought at his request, and that he was beneficially interested in it, was without validity as to him, as he was not a party to the action. It cannot be said that the notice to the attorney for the receiver was notice to Ranney, because, before it could be held that the attorney for the receiver was acting for Ranney, the court must find that the receiver brought the suit at Ranney's request, or on Ranney's account, and that fact was in

controversy, and was the fact to be tried on this ·
motion. Nor was notice to the attorney for Ranney in
the action in which the receiver was appointed, notice
to Ranney. That attorney's authority to appear for
Ranney ceased on the entry of the judgment in that
action,* and there is no evidence that he was subsequently employed by Ranney.

The original order having been entered *ex parte* so
far as Ranney was concerned, his proper proceeding
was to move to set it aside, and we think that motion
should have been granted.

The order appealed from is reversed, with $10 costs
and disbursements, and the motion below granted,
with $10 costs.

SEDGWICK, Ch. J., and INGRAHAM, J., concurred.

GILLETT AND ANOTHER, JUDGMENT CREDITORS, *v.*
HILTON, JUDGMENT DEBTOR.

CITY COURT OF NEW YORK, SPECIAL TERM, NOVEM-
BER, 1883.

§§ 2451, 2463.

*Supplementary proceedings—When use of money earned within sixty
days is contempt.*

A judgment debtor who pays a debt with money received by him in
payment of commissions for personal services rendered within
sixty days, violates an injunction order granted in supplementary
proceedings, restraining him from transferring or otherwise disposing of his property, etc., and is guilty of a civil contempt,

---

* See Webb v. Milne, 10 *N. Y. Civ. Pro.* 27.

and it is immaterial that the debts so paid were for money borrowed for, and used in the support of his family.

Hancock v. Sears (93 N. Y. 79), distinguished.

(*Decided November* 18, 1886.)

Motion by judgment creditors to punish the judgment debtor for contempt in violating an injunction order granted in the proceedings supplementary to execution.

On November 1, 1886, an order in proceedings supplementary to execution was served on the defendant, George D. Hilton. judgment debtor, requiring him to appear for examination; and enjoining, restraining and forbidding him from making any transfer or other disposition of his property rights and equitable interests not exempt by law from levy and sale under an execution, and from any interference therewith.

On November 9, his examination was taken pursuant to said order and among other things he testified, —"I am the agent for three flour mills; I receive a commission (at the end of the month) for all orders shipped during the month ; I received my commission for October sales on November 4, 1886, amounting to $175 ; this I received in three drafts. I have received no other money since November 1; I have paid $50 out of this $175 to George Hollister, flour dealer, at the time I got the drafts cashed, on November 4, or 5; that was money I borrowed from him during the month of October ; I also paid $60 out of this $175 received by me on November 4 or 5, to William B. Gottlieb, 12 Bridge Street ; I paid that to him the same day I got the drafts cashed, on November 4 or 5; that was for money borrowed from him during the month of October; I paid $25 out of this money to my grocer ; I paid $10 to my butcher and gave my wife $5 or $10; I also paid rent of my flat in Brooklyn, for the month of November, $25."

An order to show cause was thereupon granted why the judgment debtor should not be punished for contempt by reason of his misconduct in violating and disobeying the order for his examination forbidding and restraining him from disposing of his property, in disposing of said money or a portion thereof.

On the return of the order to show cause, the debtor presented affidavits showing that his family consisted of himself, wife and child ; that in lieu of salary he receives a commission for all orders shipped during each month ; that on October 6, being in need of money for the support of his family he applied to Gottlieb for a loan, and at the same time informed him that there would be due him for commissions from the persons he represented, the sum of $175, for October, and if said Gottlieb would loan him the money desired, he would pay said Gottlieb as soon as he received his said commissions for October, and for the purpose of securing said Gottlieb, he would assign to him, said Gottlieb, so much of said commissions, as would secure the money loaned and advanced by said Gottlieb ; that said Gottlieb relying on said representations loaned to him the sum of $60; that said sum being insufficient to meet the demands necessary for the support of his family he applied to Hollister for a further loan, representing to said Hollister the same facts he represented to Gottlieb, and agreeing to assign to said Hollister, so much of said commissions as would secure the money loaned and advanced by said Hollister; that said Hollister relying on said representations loaned him $50, on or about October 25, and that out of his October commissions, he paid his grocer $25, butcher $10, his rent for November, $25, and to his wife, $5, and paid to Hollister and Gottlieb, the amounts loaned to him, namely $110.

He further swore that the money borrowed from these parties, was all used for necessary and absolute expenses in the support of his family.

Jacob Marks, for judgment creditors and motion.

Argued that no actual assignment of the debtor's commissions, or earnings had been made up to the time of the service of the order ; that having borrowed the money, it became a mere debt due to these two parties, and the debtor had no right to violate the order, by paying the indebtedness, no matter to what purpose the money borrowed was applied ; that section 2463 of the Code of Civil Procedure exempts only earnings for sixty days actually necessary for the use of the debtor's family, and having supported his family and paid his bills for necessary living expenses, rent, &c., on or up to November 4 or 5, he violated the injunction by expending the balance of $110, and that the case of Hancock v. Sears, 93 *N. Y.* 79, did not apply, as the debtor must show, to exempt the earnings, or to relieve himself from contempt, in disposing of his earnings after service of order that they were actually paid after the service of the order for necessary living expenses.

Frank Warner Angel, for judgment debtor, opposed.

Argued that all the payments were necessary for the support of the debtor's family ; that the earnings of defendant for sixty days are exempt ; that Gottlieb and Hollister had an equitable assignment of the debtor's commissions, and cited Hancock v. Sears, 93 *N. Y.* 79 and Miller v. Hooper, 19 *Hun,* 394.

NEHRBAS, J.—The debtor received $175 ; $65 of which was paid out for rent, groceries, &c. But the balance, $110, was paid to two persons in payment of loans of money. It is immaterial to what purpose the money loaned was applied. The return of the money loaned was the payment of an ordinary indebted-ness, which was prohibited by the injunction order. The case of Hancock v. Sears (93 *N. Y.* 79), has no application to this branch of the motion. The debtor is guilty of a civil contempt.

He will be fined the amount so wrongfully paid, namely, $110, besides $20 costs.

TRIPP, Jr., v. DABALL.

Superior Court of the City of New York, Special Term, October, 1886.

§§ 537, 538.

Answer—When not stricken out as frivolous—When not sham.

Where, upon a motion to strike out a portion of an answer as sham, the defendant presented an affidavit of merits, and that the answer was interposed in good faith,—*Held*, that the motion should be denied.

(*Decided, October* 20, 1886.)

Motion to strike out part of an answer as frivo-lous, and part as sham.

The action was brought upon a judgment recov-ered in the State of Rhode Island, and the complaint alleged the recovery of said judgment upon the per-sonal service of the process in the action upon the defendant.

The answer (1) denied on information and belief, that the court of the State of Rhode Island, was a court of competent jurisdiction : (2) denied the personal service of the process upon him in Rhode Island ; (3)

denied on information and belief the recovery of the judgment against him ; averred that if any judgment in said court of Rhode Island was so entered, that the same was erroneously entered; and, (4) denied the indebtedness as stated in the complaint.

The plaintiff moved upon the answer and a copy of the judgment and an affidavit of plaintiff's attorney showing some admissions of the defendant, to strike out subdivision 1 of the answer as frivolous and to strike out the other subdivisions as sham.

The defendant in opposition to said motion, submitted an affidavit of merits and that the answer was interposed in good faith.

Robert P. Lee, for plaintiff and motion.

Every legal presumption will be given in favor of and to uphold the jurisdiction of the Rhode Island court. Beebe v. Marion, 17 *Abb. Pr.* 194; Ray v. Rowley, 1 *Hun*, 614. Facts to negative presumption must appear and be set up. Pringle v. Woolworth, 12 *N. Y. Weekly Dig.* 334; Gaffney v. Bigelow, 2 *Abb. N. C.* 313. In an action brought to enforce a foreign judgment where the answer is a general denial, or on information and belief, the same will be stricken out. Beebe v. Marion, 17 *Abb. Pr.* 194; Richardson v. Wilton, 4 *Sand.* 708 ; Roblin v. Long, 60 *How. Pr.* 200. The Rhode Island court had jurisdiction. See *Public Statutes of R. I.* 1882, chap. 193, § 3, p. 370; also *Public Statutes of R. I.* 1882, chap. 207, § 3, p. 366, as to how writ should be served.

D. McLean Shaw, for defendant, opposed.

A denial on informa ion and belief is not frivolous. Stent v. Continental Nat'l Bank, 5 *Abb. N. C.* 88 ; Metraz v. Pearsall, 5 *Id.* 90. A frivolous answer is one which controverts no material allegations of the complaint. Lefferts v. Snediker, 1 *Abb. Pr.* 40 ; Nichols v.

Jones, 6 *How. Pr.* 355. In this case we deny personal service and we deny the indebtedness as stated in the complaint. If the answer is good upon its face, the motion to strike out must be denied. Hecker *v.* Mitchell, 5 *Abb. Pr.* 453 ; Grocers' Bank *v.* O'Rorke, 6 *Hun*, 18 ; Thompson *v.* Erie Ry. Co., 45 *N. Y.* 468. A sham answer is one that is false. The defendant denies the allegations of the complaint in several important features in a verified answer, and it is settled that a verified answer which denies some of the material allegations of the complaint cannot be stricken out as sham. Law *v.* Maher, 9 *N. Y. Weekly Dig.* 38 ; Wayland *v.* Tysen, 45 *N. Y.* 281 ; Thompson *v.* Erie Ry. Co., 45 *N. Y.* 468. Falsity must appear clearly if not decisively. Lockwood *v.* Salhenger, 18 *Abb. Pr.* 136 ; Nichols *v.* Jones, 6 *How. Pr.* 355 ; Ostrom *v.* Bixby, 9 *Id.* 57 ; Morey *v.* Safe Deposit Co., 7 *Abb. Pr. N. S.* 199. Judge MORRELL, in Morey *v.* Safe Deposit Co, 7 *Abb. Pr. N. S.* 199, says : "In determining that an answer is false, not cnly must the plaintiff have a clear *prima facie* case, but the proof of the falsity of the answer or defense, must be clear and decisive, if not overwhelming. There must not be left in the mind a doubt as to its entire truthfulness. The effect of such a determination is to deprive a party of a trial by jury, and the case presented must therefore be of no doubtful character." A motion to strike out certain defenses as sham must be denied when the defendant interposed an affidavit that the answer was put in in good faith, and not for delay, and made an affidavit of merits. Henderson *v.* Manning, 5 *N. Y. Civ. Pro.* 221 ; Wayland *v.* Tysen, 45 *N. Y.* 281.

FREEDMAN, J.—The defendant's opposing affidavits takes the case out of the doctrine of the authorities cited by the plaintiff.

Motion denied, with $10 costs to abide the event.

ESTATE OF REUBEN P. WILCOX, DECEASED.

SURROGATE'S COURT, MADISON COUNTY, NOVEMBER, 1886.

§§ 2514, subd. 3, 2562, 2749, *et seq.*, 2757, 2758, 2793, subd. 7.

Surrogate's court—When decree awarding costs in action against execu-tor, out of an estate not res adjudicata—When creditors entitled to share in proceeds of real estate sold for payment of debts—Payment of costs out of such proceeds—Amount of costs allowed executor for preparing account.

An action cannot be maintained against an executor in his represen-tative capacity upon a transaction which occurred before the testa-tor's death, the executor in such cases is liable individually.[2]

Where, in an action brought by a widow for admeasurement of her dower in her deceased husband's estate, to recover from the execu-tor thereof, her shares of the avails of crops raised on such estate subsequent to his death, in which the executor and others sup-posed to have interest in the lands or crops were made parties de-fendant, and the plaintiff alleged that no personal claim was made against the defendants, except the said executor and the heirs of her deceased husband, judgment was rendered in her favor for the relief demanded, and costs were directed to be paid out of the rents and profits of the realty in the executor's hands, so far as the same should prove sufficient, and that the remainder, if any, be paid from the other assets of the estate in the executor's hand,—*Held,* that the question of the payments of the balance of such costs out of a fund arising from the sale of the decedent's real estate, was not *res adjudicata*,[3] especially as regards a creditor of the estate who was not a party to such suit:[1] that the supreme court had no jurisdiction to decree that any portion of the costs of such action should be paid out of the assets of the estate.[*, 4]

It seems, in such a case, where an estate is thus situated, the surro-gate's court has a right upon its own motion to appear in the courts of this State, and be heard in opposition to a decree obtained in the manner and for the purpose that said decree was.[4]

Where a debt of a decedent was not due at the time a proceeding

was instituted for a disposition of the debtor's real property for
the payment of his debts, and could not, therefore, be proved
therein, it may be proved upon the hearing of the proceedings for
a decree for distribution, and such creditor is entitled to share in
the proceeds of the sale *pro rata* with those whose debts were proved
upon the first hearing.[5,9]

The word "debts," as used in the provisions of the Code of Civil
Procedure, relating to the sale of a decedant's lands for the payment of his debts, include any claim or demand upon which a
judgment for a sum of money, or directing the payment of money
can be recovered in an action, and the word "creditor," includes
any person having such a claim or demand [5]

The expense incurred by an executor defending actions, concerning
the trust estate, cannot be paid out of the proceeds of the real
property sold pursuant to sections 2749 *et seq.* of the Code of Civil
Procedure, for the payment of the funeral expenses and debts of
the decedent.[10, 11]

Instance of a case, in which an executor was held to be guilty of mal-
administration in defending suits brought against the estate.[12-14]

Where by reason of the fact that an executor did not keep proper
books of account as such, much time and labor was required in preparing his final account, he should not be allowed for the time so
employed, but should be allowed costs only for such time as would
be necessarily occupied in preparing for an accounting, if proper
books of account had been kept.[16]

(*Decided November*, 1886.)

Proceedings for a judicial settlement of Orlando
Woodard, as executor, etc.

The opinion states the facts.

A. N. Sheldon, for executor.

E. H. Lamb, in person, and for Mrs. R. P. Wilcox,
heirs of the deceased.

White & Underhill, for Mrs. Cook, a creditor.

KENNEDY, Surrogate.—On March 28, 1881, Reuben
P. Wilcox, of the town of Brookfield, died, leaving a

will which gave to his widow the use of all his real and personal estate during her life, and at her death the residue was bequeathed to his legal heirs. The will was subsequently admitted to probate and Orlando Woodard, named therein as executor, duly qualified and entered upon the discharge of his duties. Mr. Wilcox, at the time of his death, was the owner and in possession of a farm of two hundred acres in Brookfield, and also the owner of another of sixty-two acres in Oswego. Immediately after the death of her husband, Mrs. Wilcox entered into possession of the farm in Brookfield, and assumed its control and management, Mr. Woodard aiding, assisting and advising with her in regard to the same, and was permitted by her to receive a large portion of the money resulting from the sale of the products of the farm. They appeared to have acted in concert and harmoniously in conducting the business for the season of 1881 until late in the fall of that year, when she served a written notice upon Mr. Woodard that she had decided not to accept the provisions of the will, but had elected to take dower in her husband's estate, and also demanded an accounting of the avails of the farm which came into the hands of Mr. Woodard during that season. Notwithstanding this demand he rendered no account to her for her share of the profits of the farm since her husband's death, whereupon on December 19, 1881, Mrs. Wilcox commenced an action in the supreme court against Orlando Woodard, as executor of the last will and testament of Reuben P. Wilcox, and also against other persons who had, or were supposed to have, an interest in the land or crops raised by her since the death of her husband, for the purpose of having her dower admeasured and set off to her, and also for the further purpose of recovering from Mr. Woodard her share of the avails of the crops raised on the farm during the season of 1881. She also alleged that no personal claim was made against any defendant, except said Woodard, executor, and the heirs of Reuben P. Wilcox, deceased.

The defendant Woodard interposed an answer, and, amongst other defenses alleged that the facts and allegations of the plaintiff's complaint did not constitute a cause of action against him as executor of the will of Mr. Wilcox or otherwise, that he was not a necessary or proper party to the action, and that a cause of action to recover her dower could not be joined with a cause of action for an accounting as executor, or otherwise.

The action was referred to Hon. CHAS. L. KENNEDY to hear and determine, and was subsequently tried before him and the plaintiff's dower in the Brookfield farm duly assigned and set off to her.

The thirteenth finding in Judge KENNEDY's report is as follows: "That the gross proceeds of the rents and profits of the said real estate, since the death of said R. P. Wilcox, deceased, for the year 1881, was the sum of $978.73, of which said Sarah A. Wilcox received $172.82 and the said Orlando Woodard, executor, received the sum of $805.91; that the actual expense producing said profits and income was the sum of $449.35, of which said plaintiff, Sarah A. Wilcox, paid and furnished the sum of $217.71, leaving as the net profits of said real estate the sum of $529.28, and that plaintiff is entitled to receive and to be reimbursed the sum of $217.71 as balance of the expenses paid and incurred, and the further sum of $176.46, being one-third of the net profits as aforesaid, leaving in the hands of Woodard, executor, defendant, the sum of $352.92, being two-thirds of the net profits to be accounted for by him to the proper heirs at law of said Reuben P. Wilcox, or in some other manner provided by law, or for the costs of these proceedings."

One of the conclusions of law found by the referee

was the following : "Fourth, that said plaintiff, Sarah A. Wilcox, is entitled to recover of and from the defendant, Orlando Woodard, as such executor, her costs and disbursements of this action to be taxed, and that said defendant, Orlando Woodard, is also entitled to recover his costs and disbursements of this action, and judgment is hereby ordered accordingly." At a circuit and special term held at Morrisville, on October 16, 1882, Mr. Justice FOLLETT presiding, the referee's report was duly confirmed and an interlocutory judgment entered. This judgment directs the payment of the plaintiff's costs out of the rents and profits in Mr. Woodard's hands and also directs the payment of the executor's costs out of the same fund, so far as the same was sufficient for that purpose, and that the remainder of his costs shall be paid and allowed to him on final accounting or settlement of the estate of said Reuben P. Wilcox, deceased, by said Orlando Woodard, executor as aforesaid."

At a special term held at Syracuse on June 30, 1883, Mr. Justice CHURCHILL presiding, a motion was made to confirm the report of the referee appointed to admeasure the dower. The report was confirmed and the order awards the plaintiff an extra allowance of $30, and directs the payment of this sum and all of plaintiff's other costs out of the rents and profits so far as the same shall prove sufficient, "and the remainder, if any, be paid from the other assets of the estate in his (Woodard's) hands as executor."

At a special term held at Norwich on July 30, 1883, Mr. Justice FOLLETT presiding, a motion was made to correct the interlocutory judgment by striking out the direction that the plaintiff's costs be paid out of the fund arising from the rents and profits. The motion was denied with costs "payable out of the fund in controversy" and with this decision Judge FOLLETT filed this memorandum : "This action was brought to enforce the plaintiff's rights in specific real estate and in the profits arising therefrom.. She recovered. The general rule in such cases is to charge the land or fund with the costs, unless the defeated party is charged personally. There is nothing in· the referee's report to indicate that the costs should be charged against the estate generally, and it clearly appears from the report that the defendant is not to be charged personally. I think that the plaintiff is clearly entitled to costs out of the fund."

The personal estate of the decedent has been exhausted, or nearly so, in expenses of administration, and the proceeds of the sale of the real estate by the executor are not sufficient to pay more than sixteen per cent. of his indebtedness, and, if the costs of this and other litigations are allowed to the executor upon this accounting, they must be charged over to the real estate and paid out of the money arising from the sale of the land.

The counsel for the executor and for Mrs. Wilcox insists that the question of the payment of the $110.05 of the plaintiffs' costs mentioned in the judgment, and Mr. Woodard's costs, $151.46, also therein mentioned, out of the fund arising from the sale of the real estate, is *res adjudicata* and cannot be disturbed by the surrogate.

We cannot adopt this view for the following reasons:

The will gave the executor no authority over the real estate, and it was no part of his duty as executor to take charge of, or to do any act in relation to it, except when it became necessary to institute proceeding for the payment of the decedent's debts. Whatever he did in relation to the management of the real estate, he did, not as executor, but in his individual capacity, and if, by reason of such acts, he incurred any liability to pay costs, he should pay them himself, and there is no reason in law or equity why this estate should be called upon to pay them. Neither the creditors, nor this estate had a dollar's interest in the result of the litigations, and could in no way be legally affected by it, and to hold that the only persons ['] having an interest in this estate are concluded by a judgment to which they were not parties, made in a litigation in which they had not the slightest interest, would be the height of injustice.

Every transaction out of which the claim of Mrs. Wilcox arose for an accounting was subsequent to the death of Mr. Wilcox. It was for the avails of crops grown by her upon the farm while she, and not the executor, was in possession and had control and management of it. In all that Mr. Woodard did he was acting as her friend and agent and was under her authority. If he sold the crops and received the avails of the farm produce he did it upon his own responsibility or as the agent of Mrs. Wilcox. She simply had a demand against him personally for her share of the avails of the farm and not against him as executor, for he did not and could not legally act as such in assisting her in the management of the farm. The fact that the action was brought against him as executor did not change the nature of her claim nor of his defense, if he had any, nor relieve him from personal liability for costs. The judgment of the court was that the avails of the farm for the season of 1881, were not the property of the estate but belonged to others. It would be grossly unjust, if executors, without any authority whatever, could enter upon the lands of others, or take part in their management, and when called upon to pay over the avails of their cultivation which they have received to the rightful claimant, refuse to pay without litigation, and if defeated, have the costs of both parties paid out of

the estates of which they may happen to be at the time, executor. We think we are amply justified in holding that an action cannot be maintained against an executor in his representative capacity, upon a transaction which occurred after the testator's death. The executor is liable in such cases individ-
['] ually (Ferris v. Disbrow, 22 N. Y. Weekly Dig. 330 ; Buckland v. Gallup, 40 Hun, 60 ; Ketchum v. Ketchum, 4 Cow. 87).*

The total amount of the costs and expenses of that litigation as presented to us by the executor for allowance is as follows :

Balance of Mrs. Wilcox costs . .	.$110.88
Motion, costs before Judge FOLLETT .	. 10.00
Costs of executor as taxed . . .	. 151.46
Expenses and disbursements of executor	. 249.96
Services of counsel	. 300.00
	$822.30

Beside the above sum Mr. Woodard paid $295.28 out of the "fund" arising from rents and profits of the farm, making, if allowed, the total costs of this unnecessary litigation, so far as this estate is concerned, the sum of $1,117.58; and this estate is asked to bear $822.30 of it. We believe the whole of it to be an unjust, illegal, and inequitable claim, and that
['] the supreme court had no jurisdiction to decree that any portion of the costs should be paid out of the assets of this estate, and so far as it does make such a decree, that it was inadvertently made by the court.

No creditor of this estate, at least not Mrs. Cook,

* See also Caulkins v Bolton, 98 N. Y. 511 ; Thompson v. Whitmarsh, 100 Id. 35 ; Schmittler v. Simon, 101 Id. 354; Feig v. Wray, 3 N. Y. Civ. Pro. 159.

was a party to this litigation and hence were not in a situation to oppose the entry of the decree which has been entered in the action, nor have they been at any time since its entry in a situation where they could ask the court to modify it in their interest or in the interest of this estate. Nor is any other person that we are aware of so situated that he can, upon this proceeding, oppose the enforcement of this decree save by the action of the surrogate in disregarding it. Where an estate is thus situated we believe this court has the right, upon its own motion, to appear in the courts of this State and be heard in opposition to a decree obtained in the manner and for the purpose that ['] this one was which we are asked to obey. Were it otherwise, a surrogate's court would be compelled to allow large sums of money to be taken from creditors and heirs upon decrees of other courts, obtained by parties interested in shielding themselves from the expenses of litigations which their own acts have brought upon them. We shall, therefore, hazzard the criticism, possibly the censure, of the supreme court, in respectfully disregarding its decree in the above mentioned action.

Another reason for the disallowance of the costs above referred to, and the expenses and disbursements of Mr. Woodard in this action, will be stated in connection with the discussion in regard to the claim of Rosina Cook against this estate and the expenses of the executor in resisting the payment of her claim.

We now come to the discussion of the claim of Rosina Cook. It will be remembered that the decedent died March 28, 1881, and his will was admitted to probate June 20, of that year.

At the time of his death, Mrs. Cook, of St. Johns, Michigan, was the owner and holder of a promissory note against him, of which the following is a copy:

" $3,100. March 29, 1878.

"Six years after date I promise to pay to the order of S. B. Daboll, three thousand one hundred dollars for the value received with use.

"R. P. WILCOX."

"Indorsed S. B. Daboll."

The executor duly published a notice to creditors, and on March 18, 1882, the claim in question was duly presented to the executor and the same was disputed and rejected by him, and the objection was accompanied by an offer to refer the claim under the statute, but the executor having refused to waive the objection that the note was not yet due, and at all times insisted that no action or proceeding could be commenced upon the same until it became due, a reference was deferred until the note matured. On December 29, 1884, the claim was referred under the statute to three referees.

After a trial upon the merits, the referees made their report, awarding to the plaintiff the full amount of her claim. Their report was duly confirmed, and on May 17, 1886, judgment was duly entered thereon for

Damages.	. $4,861.30
Cost.	. 406.58
Judgment.	. $5,267.88

The petition for the sale of the decedent's real estate was filed on May 22, 1882.

The petition refers to the claim in question as having been presented to the executor and rejected by him. Mrs. Cook was duly cited in this proceeding but did not appear and made no effort to prove her claim upon the first hearing.

On March 17, 1883, a motion was made before Surrogate CHAPMAN to open the decree of July 25, 1882, for the purpose of allowing Mrs. Cook to prove her claim and have the same established by and as of the date of said decree.

The surrogate denied this motion upon the ground that the claim was not then due, and without prejudice to its renewal.

The motion was renewed before the present surrogate July 22, 1885, and was denied by him for want of jurisdiction, more than one year having elapsed since the entry of the decree.

Mrs. Cook's claim has been duly proved and established upon the hearing for distribution.

The proceeds of the sale of the real estate are not more than sufficient to pay the claims established upon first hearing.

Upon these facts a serious question arises as to the status of Mrs. Cook's claim, in this proceeding.

Counsel for Mrs. Cook contends that she is entitled to share pro rata with the creditors whose claims were established upon the first hearing and counsel for the executor urges that the claims established upon the first hearing are entitled to payment in full before any portion of the proceeds can be applied to the payment of the claim in question.

The only serious question in the case arises from the fact that at the time of the entry of the first decree the claim in question was not yet due.

['] The Code of Civil Procedure (§ 2758) provides :

"The decree must determine and specify the amount of each debt established as a valid and subsisting debt against the decedent's estate, &c.," and a "debt" is defined by the Code of Civil Procedure (§ 2514, subd. 3), as follows : "The word 'debts' includes any claim or demand upon which a judgment for a sum of money or directing the payment of money could be recovered in an action ; and the word 'creditor' includes any person having such a claim or demand."

In several places in chapter 18, claims which have not matured are referred to, not as "debts" but always as "debts not yet due."

Mrs. Cook's claim was not due at the date of the first decree; she could not at that time be said to have a "valid and subsisting debt against the decedent's estate;" she could not then have instituted proceedings for the sale of the real estate; she could not have established her claim upon the first hearing.

There is no provision anywhere in title V., chapter 18, for the proof of a debt not yet due, upon the first hearing, and Mrs. Cook for that reason was not bound to present her claim at that time, and laches cannot be attributed to her on account of her failure so to do.

In this view of the case the motions to open the decree should have been denied upon the merits, as unnecessary and superfluous.

Under the revised statutes (§§ 37, 38, 39, 43, 71 and 73) claims proven upon the second hearing stood upon an equal footing with those established by the first decree, and there was no preference or priority of payment as between debts of the same class.

But by the Code of Civil Procedure a radical change was introduced, and under the present law there can be no doubt that those claims which were established by the first decree are entitled to priority of payment over those proved upon the hearing for distribution unless there exists a single exception, in favor of a "debt not yet due."

The serious question in this case, therefore, arises upon the construction of subdivision 7, section 2793, of the Code of Civil Procedure, which reads as follows :

Estate of Wilcox.

" Out of the remainder of the money must be paid, in full, the other debts, which were established and recited in the first decree, and were not rejected upon the second hearing ; or if there is not enough for that purpose, they, or so much thereof as the money applicable thereto will pay, must be paid in the order prescribed by law for payment of a decedent's debts by an executor or administrator out of the personal assets, without giving preference to rents, or to a specialty or to any demand on account of an action pending thereupon ; and paying debts not yet due, upon a rebate of legal interest."

The section is ambiguous and is inartificially drawn, and at the first glance there would seem to be doubt as to its true construction and meaning; but upon a careful examination of the section in connection with the revisers' notes and the former statute, we are convinced that the true meaning and intent will be better arrived at by transposing the words after the second semi-colon ("and paying debts not yet due, &c.") to a position immediately after the words " second hearing," before the first semi-colon, thus placing debts not yet due upon the same footing with those established by the first decree.

This is the only construction that gives the subdivision an intelligible meaning, and the last clause of the subdivision would be utterly meaningless under any other construction that has been suggested.

[*]   If the legislature had intended that a debt not yet due should be postponed to one which was due, they would have provided for its payment in subdivision 8; but it appears that the only provision anywhere in the whole title for proving or for paying a debt, not yet due, is contained in subdivision 7, and provision for its payment being made there, and there only, the conclusion is irresistible that it is to be paid with the other debts provided for in that subdivision.

We believe too, that this construction will tend to do substantial justice in all cases.

Under the construction contended for by the counsel for the executor, creditors whose claims are not due at the death of a decedent will be entirely at the mercy of the executors or administrators, who through favoritism or from enmity could so institute and conduct the proceedings as to unjustly and unfairly discriminate between creditors whose claims are equally just and equally entitled to payment.

['] There is no reason why in justice and fairness a claim against a decedent's estate, which is due, should be preferred to another which is not due, and such is not the policy of the law.

This is emphatically indicated by the provisions of the Code of Civil Procedure (§ 2742) with reference to the payment of a claim not yet due upon the judicial settlement of the accounts of an executor or administrator.

Ample provision is here made for the protection of a creditor whose claim is not due upon the same basis as one which is due, and while this is not controlling in this case, yet it is a strong indication that the legislature regarded the two classes of claims as equally entitled to payment.

We are strongly reinforced in our opinion by the notes of the revisers. Section 38 of the Revised Statutes, provided for the payment of all the decedent's debts in full, or in case of a deficiency of assets, in proportion to their respective amounts; section 39 provides that a creditor whose debt is not yet due shall receive his proportion with other creditors upon a rebate of legal interest, substantially the same as the last clause of subdivision 7, section 2793.

The revisers say: "Subdivision 7 has been taken from sections 38, 39 and 73 of the Revised Statutes *without material change, except by the addition of*

the words which connect the provision with subdivision 8, and by the insertion of the provision with reference to the order of payment among creditors."
['] From this language the fair inference is that there was no intention to change the status of a debt not yet due.

The revisers further say : "Subdivision 8, is new. It applies to creditors who come in after a sale as provided in section 2788. The regulation which it introduces appears to rest upon plain principles of justice, especially in view of the amendments to the preceding sections giving to any creditor the right to institute original proceedings ; of his right which the amendments preserve to come in at any time before decree when proceedings have been instituted by another creditor ; of the great publicity required at every step before the decree : and of the embarrassments which will result from the debts subsequently proved, if there is any deficiency. Under such circumstances creditors who neglected to come in until after the decree should be postponed, even when no other property remains, to those who have been diligent to prove their debts in season, and have perhaps borne the expense and labor of the proceedings."

None of this reasoning is applicable to the case before us.

As we have seen, Mrs. Cook was not, at the date of the first decree a "creditor" and her claim was not then a "debt" within the meaning of the statute, and she could not thus have established it. It cannot therefore, be said that she was guilty of laches in not then attempting to establish it.

After a troublesome and expensive litigation she has had the justice of her claim established by law. She has not neglected any proper or necessary step to bring her claim to the attention of the court ; and now for the first time she has an opportunity to prove and establish it in this proceeding.

[']   Every consideration of justice and equity, and we believe, the plain language and direction of the statute itself, require that she should not be placed upon an equality with the other creditors.

The order of distribution will be made accordingly, and the claim of Rosina Cook (exclusive of costs) be paid *pro rata* and in proportion to its amount with the other creditors.

Upon this accounting we are asked by the executor, against the objection of Mrs. Cook's counsel, to allow out of the proceeds of the sale of the real estate, his expenses in defending the suit of Mrs. Cook, amounting to about $600 as well as her costs and disbursements in defending the Wilcox action for dower and an accounting amounting to $822.30. In addition to the reasons heretofore stated for disallowing costs in the Wilcox case, we decline to do so for the additional reason that there is no provision of law which justifies or provides for their payment out of this fund. Independent of any question as to the necessity or propriety of the large expenditure of the executor in litigations it may be seriously doubted whether under any circumstances this expense could be charged upon the real estate, or provision made for their payment out of its proceeds. The law makes no provision [¹⁰] for the sale of real estate to pay cost of litigations or the expenses of administration, on the contrary it provides that the real estate of a decedent cannot be sold by the executor or administrator except for the payment of his debts and funeral expenses (*Code Civ. Pro.* § 2749). Even where a judgment is obtained against an executor upon a disputed claim, the costs in such a judgment cannot be paid from the proceeds of the real estate (§ 2757, *Code Civ. Pro.*). In short, the policy of the law seems to be to carefully guard against the payment, from the proceeds of the real estate, of any claim or demand except a debt owing by the decedent at the time of his death, his necessary funeral expenses, and the actual expense of the proceeding for the sale of the real estate. Were this not so the Code would not have restricted the claims for which land must be sold, to the payment of the decedent's debts and funeral expenses, but would have permitted the executor or administrator to sell the lands for any claims which he might have, arising from expenses incurred by him in the administration of the estate. The language of subdivision 7, section 2793, is imperative as to the class of debts which may be paid under its provisions. It says : "Out of the remainder of the money, must be paid in full, the other debts, which were established and recited in the first decree, and were not rejected upon the second hearing," thus devoting the fund to the payment of certain specific debts and preventing its diversion for any other purpose whatever.

It would be a useless expense, many times, for a creditor to prove his claim in such a proceeding if the statute did not afterwards protect his debt against the claims of executors for expenses incurred, either before or after he is cited to establish his debt in court. The decree of the surrogate upon the first hearing becomes in fact a lien upon the proceeds of the sale of land and thus secures payment of the debts established upon the first hearing, if sufficient for that purpose, against any contingency. No mortgage or judgment could make it more secure than this decree of the court against the subsequent acts of executors, or against those creditors who neglected to establish their debts when invited by the court to do so. The law has wisely appropriated this fund to the payment of those debts which the decedent created in his lifetime, and in our judgment we have no authority to use it for any other purpose. Nor is it any hardship upon, or injustice to an executor thus to hold the law to be, for before he prosecutes or defends an action or subjects an estate to any expense beyond which the law has made provision, he has ample opportunity to ascertain the exact amount of the assets of the personal estate, and then to determine what his course shall be. In plain and unmistakable language the law has said to him that the real estate of a decedent cannot be sold for any other purposes than those we have stated and we know of no reason why he should not act accordingly. Had all the expenses which this executor had incurred in his litigations existed before any proceedings were taken to sell the land for the payment of debts he would then have been compelled to see the land of the decedent ordered sold for the payment of debts existing at the death of Mr. Wilcox, for he could not have proven his claim in that proceeding nor made use of it to institute measures for the sale of the decedent's land to procure its payment, so that, at no stage of his administration, has it been in the power of the court to aid him in the ["] collection of his disbursements in the litigations in which he has been engaged out of the real estate or its proceeds, and his application to be repaid in this manner for this class of expenses must therefore be denied. It may be claimed that under the provision of subdivision 5, section 2793, these expenses may be allowed as against the real estate, but in our opinion this provision is only intended to cover payments made by an executor or administrator on account of debts of the decedent and funeral expenses.*

---

* In Estate of Meakim, 5 *N. Y. Civ. Pro.* 421, it was *held*, that the surrogate has no power to direct the payment out of a fund arising from the sale of a decedent's real property for the payment

["]   But there are other grounds for rejecting the·
claim of the executor to be reimbursed the expenses of the Cook litigation. They are as follows : At
the time her claim was referred the condition of the
estate was nearly as follows :

Total amount of the proceeds of
. the real estate $1731.00
Total amount of personal estate   .   483.00

                                 ——————
                                 $2214.00

Claims of creditors allowed by the
  surrogate on proceedings to sell
  the land of Mr. Wilcox   .   . $1195.00
Expense of proceedings to sell land   596.00
Costs and expenses of Wilcox' suit   822.00

                                 ——————
                                 $2611.00

So that the estate according to his figures was
utterly bankrupt. There was not a dollar which
could be reached by Mrs. Cook, if she got a judgment,
provided the law is as claimed by the executor. If so,
why subject her to the costs of a litigation which
would be fruitless in the end. But one motive is
apparent, because but one result could be obtained, and
that was to subject the assets of this estate to a further reduction by means of costs and expenses, and
thereby deprive, if possible, creditors whose claims
had been proven and established in the first decree,
from any share in the avails of the real estate. Such

_____

of his debts, etc., of allowances made on the contest of a will ;
that such fund can only be applied to the payment of such claims
and debts of the decedent as would authorize the surrogate's
court to order a sale of the real estate ; and the court conld not
order a sale for the purpose of paying the expenses of administration,
and the fund arising from the sale cannot be applied to their
payment.

is the result as shown by the claims of the executor presented for our consideration, for his total claim amounts to the sum of $2,815, while the total avails of the estate amount to the sum of $2,214. But not content with deciding to contest the note the executor compelled Mrs. Cook to wait two years before referring the claim for trial upon the frivolous pretext that it was not due, thus unnecessarily delaying the settlement of the estate, preventing creditors from receiving the amount due them and subjecting the estate to many hundred dollars interest. This claim, if the executor had not needlessly raised his technical objection that the note was not due could, although disputed, have been tried before the surrogate in the proceedings to sell the land, or it could have been referred to some referee approved by the surrogate and tried, and thus the useless and vexatious delay avoided. No interest upon debts would have accrued, the expenses incidental to such delay in the settlement of estates would not have been incurred, and the estate settled within the eighteen months usually taken by executors for that purpose. For four years this executor has prevented this estate from being settled by his litigations and the manner in which he has conducted them, and in that time has accumulated a bill of costs and expenses amounting to a sum sufficient to bankrupt it, provided the view which we have taken of the law does not, to some extent, prevent it. We do not believe such a result was necessary or proper in the administration of this estate, nor do we believe that he was justified in pursuing the course he has pursued from the beginning to the end. He begins and ends his administration with litigation. He has needlessly kept it in court for nearly five years and then seeks to charge the expenses he has incurred to a fund set apart for the payments of debts which the decedent owed in his life-time and thus prevent the creditors from receiving a single dollar upon their claims. We believe it to be the duty of courts to allow executors and all others who have the official care of estates all just and reasonable expenses in their management, but we do not believe it to be their duty to permit an executor to transform an entire estate amounting to $2,214 into a bill for costs and expenses and so leaving nothing for the heirs or creditors. Here is the condition of the estate as presented to us by the excutor for settlement :

Total assets	. $2214.00
Executor's claim for services and expenses	. 1711.65
Executor's expense for attorney and counsel . . .	. 1103.80
	$2815.45
Creditors and heirs . . .	. Nothing

No debt of the decedent's, however trivial, has been paid, even his grave being paid for from the private purse of the widow.

[''] Such a result bears upon its face the stamp of *mal administration* and bad faith ; it shows that his services have been of no benefit to the estate, but on the other hand have been a positive and irreparable injury. Some higher court may enable us to see our way clear to turn the assets of this estate into a bill of costs, but until then we shall hold that it has not been legally or properly administered, and that the account of such an executor for services and expenses ought to be cut down to such an amount as would fairly and reasonably pay for its proper administration. The sum of $247.06 is allowed for this purpose as per statement filed with this decision.

[''] In conclusion we desire to call attention to another fact in connection with the history of this case. From the time the executor commenced the discharge of his duties, down to the end of these proceedings he has kept no account of his services or the expenses of his administration. His account for nearly $3000 of alleged indebtedness of this estate to him is made up from diaries, which he fails to produce for the inspection of the court or of parties, interested in this proceeding ; from entries made by his counsel in law registers and papers in his possession ; from his memory of the various services he has performed, and money expended, and from various other sources of information. An account thus kept or made up is suspicious upon its face, for it gives opportunity for mistake, and worse still, an easy method for fraud and dishonesty. We do not claim the executor has not rendered the services nor expended the money he has charged and testified to, but we claim he has violated his duty to this estate, by not keeping his account in the usual and regular manner. It should have been kept distinct from his dealings with others, in a book kept for that purpose, and in such a manner that persons interested in the estate could inspect them at any time, if they desired to know its standing or condition. They should not have been so kept as to be the occasion of doubt and uncertainty, and require a long contest in the courts to ascertain their truthfulness. No one needs to be learned in the intricacies of book-keeping to keep the accounts of an estate in such manner, that people unlearned in such matters, can readily and without expense or assistance from counsel, know its true condition or make such investigation as they desire in regard to it.

Nine days were spent in investigating the accounts of the executor because of the manner in which he had kept them and the character of some of his claims, while in our judgment if he had kept his account in a regular and orderly manner, setting down the items

therein as they occurred, there need not have been
two days spent in submitting them to the court. We
shall therefore not allow him for his own time or
["] expenses, or for the expense of his counsel upon
this accounting, more than would be reasonable
for the time and labor spent in establishing an account
kept and made out in such manner as the law requires.
We decline to subject this estate to any expense for
the carelessness and negligence with which he has kept
the records of its business. We have no doubt, that
he, as well as his counsel, have spent the time charged,
in straightening out and making up his account, and
believe the services were worth what has been charged
but out of his commissions or from some other source
it is his duty to pay for preparing accounts thus kept,
and not this estate.*

The accounts of the executor will be settled in
accordance with this decision and a decree entered
accordingly.

* Section 2562 of the Code of Civil Procedure provides that "the
surrogate may allow an executor, administrator, guardian or testamentary trustee, upon the settlement of his account. . . such a
sum as the surrogate deems reasonable for his counsel fees and other
expenses, not exceeding ten dollars *for each day.* . . *necessarily
occupied* in preparing his account for settlement," etc. In Estate of
Withers (2 *N. Y. Civ. Pro.* 169), it was held that an administrator
was " necessarily occupied " with the business of an estate only for
such time as his devotion thereto " was substantially to the exclusion
of other employment and was essential for the proper discharge of his
duties."

Smith *v.* Chenoweth.

SMITH, Respondent, *v.* CHENOWETH, Appellant.

City Court of New York, General Term, October, 1886.

§ 66.

Attorney's lien—When prevents set off of judgment.

The right to set off one judgment against another does not exist where one judgment is for costs only and where the effect would be prejudicial to an attorney equitably or legally entitled thereto, and this, although the judgments were recovered in the same action, if they were recovered on different causes of action.

Where a complaint set up three distinct causes of action, and the plaintiff was successful upon the trial of an issue of fact joined as to two of them, and the defendant was successful as to the third upon the trial of an issue of law, and recovered a judgment thereon for costs.—*Held*, that the judgment in favor of the defendant for costs could not be set off against the judgment in favor of the plaintiff rendered on the two causes of action; that the defendant's attorney had a lien upon the judgment for costs, and this prevented a set-off; that *it seems*, that this lien could not be evaded by the payment of the judgment in favor of the defendant to the sheriff, and the making of a levy thereon, under an execution issued by the plaintiff on the judgment in his favor.

New Haven Copper Co. *v.* Brown (46 *Me.* 418); Prince *v.* Fuller (34 *Id.* 122), distinguished; Turnstall *v.* Winton (31 *Hun,* 219, aff'd 96 *N. Y.* 660), followed.

(*Decided October* 22, 1886.)

Appeal from an order made herein, granting plaintiff's motion to set off judgments.

The opinion states the material facts.

J. C. O'Connor, Jr., attorney for defendant-appelant.

Raphael J. Moses, Jr,. attorney for plaintiff-respondent.

HYATT, J.—The plaintiff brought an action, setting up three causes of action ; defendant demurred to the complaint ; as to the first and second causes of action, the demurrer was overruled ; as to the third cause of action, the demurrer was sustained, and then the defendant answered the other two causes of action ; upon issue joined the plaintiff recovered judgment for $307.72. Judgment for the third cause of action was entered in favor of the defendant, from which the plaintiff instituted an appeal. The appellate court affirmed the judgment with costs to the respondent ; the same were taxed at $72.06.

The plaintiff then moved to set off defendant's judgment against the plaintiff's judgment, or in other words to credit the judgment of $307.72 with $72.06.

The plaintiff in fact seeks to avoid the costs of an appeal instituted by her, and decided adversely to her, and now seeks to apply those costs upon an execution issued upon other and different causes of action against the defendant.

The demurrer to the plaintiff's third cause of action was sustained upon the ground that such cause of action did not accrue to her in her individual capacity ; the affirmance of this decision resulted in the judgment against her for costs.

I understand the law to be well settled that costs are the property of the attorney and are not the subject of set-off, that "the right to set off one judgment against another is not allowed, where the judgment to be extinguished is for costs only, and where the effect would be prejudicial to the attorney equitably and legally entitled to them" (Linderman v. Foote, 5 N. Y. Civ. Pro. 154, note).

An attorney has a lien on a judgment recovered by him (Code Civ. Pro. § 66). This judgment sought to be set off was for costs only and solely ; it belongs to the attorney ; it is well settled law in this State, that it will be protected and secured to him against any act by or between the parties themselves, that would tend to deprive him of it.

A judgment for costs such as this one, cannot be made the subject of a set off as between the parties to the action, in respect of another judgment recovered on a different cause of action. Plaintiff's judgment is such a one (Place v. Hayward, 8 *N. Y. Civ. Pro.* 352 ; Perry v. Chester, 53 *N. Y.* 243 ; Ennis v. Curry, 22 *Hun*, 584).

It is ingeniously suggested that the plaintiff could pay the amount of the judgment against her for costs to the sheriff, and he pay it to the defendant ; that it would then be money belonging to the judgment debtor (the defendant), and that under section 1410, Code of Civil Procedure the same sheriff would be required to levy upon the same money and pay it over to the plaintiff immediately that it is paid by him to the defendant.

The answer to this proposition is, if the money belonged to the attorney as his costs, it could not, by this device, become the property of the judgment debtor. In this case, however, the sheriff has not had the opportunity to create such a situation.

The cases of the New Haven Cooper Company v. Brown (46 *Me.* 418), and Prince v. Fuller (34 *Id.* 122), cited by plaintiff's counsel do not avail him, they simply hold that " on motion the court will order a set-off, if other rights do not interfere."

In this case, the judgment being for costs only, the right of the attorney equitably or legally entitled to them, unquestionably interferes.

We are of the opinion therefore, that the order should be reversed, with costs.

McADAM, Ch. J.—I concur on the authority of Tunstall v. Winton (31 *Hun*, 219, affirmed, 96 *N. Y.* 660).

which in effect overrules the decision in Hoyt *v.* Godfrey (3 *N. Y. Civ. Pro.* 118). I believe the principle laid down by Judge HYATT to be the correct one, and to be in accordance with the controlling authorities upon the subject.

THE FLOUR CITY NATIONAL BANK OF ROCHESTER, RESPONDENT, *v.* DOTY, AND ANOTHER, APPELLANTS.

SUPREME COURT, FIFTH DEPARTMENT, GENERAL TERM, JUNE, 1886.

§ 1274.

Confession of judgment— When statement for, insufficient—Insufficiency renders judgment void— When referee may discredit witness.

A confession of judgment which does not state sufficiently the facts out of which it arose is regarded in law as fraudulent and void, and may be attacked and set aside by a subsequent judgment debtor in an action prosecuted for that purpose.[b]

Where the statement in a confession of judgment relating to the indebtedness was as follows: " that the debt for which this judgment is confessed arises upon three several promissory notes in writing,"—describing them—"that all the said notes are past and the sum of $5,713.77, is now due and owing the plaintiff from me upon the said notes this day; that the three several notes above stated and upon which this judgment is confessed, were given by the defendant. . . to the plaintiff. . . at the dates above stated and for the amounts above stated and all said notes were so given by said defendant to pay for money loaned by the plaintiff to defendant, and the amount now due and owing to me by the defendant upon said notes for borrowed money, borrowed of plaintiff is the sum of $5,713.77,"—*Held,* that this statement was defective for the reason that there was a failure to state the sum of money borrowed; [1] that it is insufficient to make a general statement that the indebtedness arose upon a promissory note describing the same.[2]

Where, in such a case it appeared that one of the notes was not given for money loaned and advanced by the plaintiff to the defendant, but that the plaintiff had signed a note for that amount for the defendant, and pledged securities of her own for its payment, and that the proceeds of the note had been used by the defendant, and it remained unpaid,—*Held*, that while the plaintiff could have taken a confession of judgment to secure herself against the contingent liability assumed on signing the note as surety, the statute required that the facts should be concisely stated, and as there was a failure to comply with the requirements of the statute, the confession of judgment was regarded in law as fraudulent and void.[4,5]

The object of the requirement in section 1274, of the Code of Civil Procedure, that a statement for confession of judgment should contain concise statement of the facts constituting the liability, stated.[3]

Where, in an action to set aside as fraudulent, a deed of real property executed by a judgment debtor to his wife, the circumstances connected with its execution and delivery were such as to call upon the wife to show the real transaction, and that it was entered into in good faith and without any intent to hinder, defraud, or delay the creditors of her husband, and the only consideration for the conveyance was the discharge of an alleged indebtedness from her husband to herself, the only evidence of the existence of the indebtedness was the wife's own naked statement of loans and advances made by herself directly to her husband after her marriage and many years prior to the conveyance,—*Held*, that it was for the referee before whom the case was tried to determine from her appearance and manner whether her uncorroborated statement was entitled to full credit.[6]

(*Decided June* 17, 1886.)

Appeal by defendants from a judgment entered on the report of a referee.

The facts appear in the opinion.

T. P. Heddon, for defendants-appellants.

C. F. Bissell, for plaintiff-respondent.

BARKER, J.—The plaintiff is a subsequent judgment creditor of the defendant, John C. Doty, and this action is to set aside a judgment confessed by him to Susan F. Doty, his wife, and also a conveyance of lands made by the said Doty to his said wife, as fraudulent and void. The deed of conveyance is dated March 15, 1884, for the sum of $5,713.77. The judgment is attacked upon the ground that it is fraudulent and void and made with intent to hinder and delay the creditors of the said John C. Doty in the collection of their debts; and also upon the ground that the statement signed and verified by the defendant is not in compliance with section 1274 of the Code of Civil Procedure, for the reason that it fails to state concisely the facts and circumstances out of which the debt arose and does not show that the sum for which the judgment was confessed, was justly due or to become due the plaintiff.

The statement relating to the indebtedness is as follows: "That said debt for which this judgment is confessed arises upon three several promissory notes in writing. One dated April 1, 1873, made and given by this defendant to the above named plaintiff for the sum of $650, payable two years after date, to Susan F. Doty or bearer, with use, for value received. One note dated December 10, 1874, made and given by this defendant to this plaintiff for the sum of $1,200, payable five years after its date to Susan F. Doty or bearer, with use, value received. One note dated July 2, 1883, made and given by this defendant, John C. Doty, to the plaintiff herein, Susan F. Doty, for the sum of $3,000, payable six months after its date to Susan F. Doty or bearer, with use. That all of the said notes are past due, and the sum of $5,713.77, is now due and owing the plaintiff from me upon the said notes this day. That the three several notes above stated and upon which this judgment is confessed, were given by the defendant, John C. Doty, to the plaintiff, Susan F. Doty, at the dates above stated, and for the amounts above stated, and all said notes were so given by said defendant to pay for money loaned by the plaintiff to defendant, and the amount now due and owing to me by the defendant, upon said notes, for borrowed money, borrowed of plaintiff, is the sum of $5,713.77.''

[¹]   This statement is defective for the reason that there is a failure to state the sum of money borrowed. At the most it is only a statement that the defendant, John C. Doty, borrowed of his wife a sum of money, and the statement would be literally true if the real sum borrowed was less than the face of either of the notes.* The statute requires that the confession must state concisely the facts out of which the indebtedness arose. It is insufficient to make a general

[²]   statement that the indebtedness arises upon a promissory note setting forth and describing the same. No one can determine from this statement the exact amount of money loaned, for which each of the said notes was given, which constitute the basis of the alleged indebtedness for which the judgment was confessed.

The object of the statute in requiring a detailed statement of the facts and circumstances, out of which the indebtedness arose, is to inform other credit-

[³]   ors of the dealings and transactions which had taken place between the parties to the judgment, that they might ascertain by proper inquiry that the indebtedness was real and not fictitious, and satisfy themselves, if such was the fact, that the judgment was based upon a good consideration, and valid in law. The statute looks not to the evidence of the demand, but to the facts out of which it originated; in other

* See Terrett *v.* Brooklyn Imp. Co., 18 *Hun,* 6; Marvin *v.* Marvin, 27 *Id.* 601.

words, to the consideration which sustains the promise. The law requires this to be concisely set forth in the statement which is to form a part of the record ; and in this way only does the provision furnish any additional security to creditors against the fraudulent combination of the parties to the judgment (Chappel v. Chappel, 12 *N. Y.* 215 ; Citizens' National Bank v. Allison, 37 *Hun*, 137).

[*]   On the trial the plaintiff was examined as a witness in her own behalf, and it appears from her own evidence that the $3,000 note was not given for money loaned and advanced by herself to her husband, but that she, on the day this note bears date, signed a note as security for her husband in the sum of $3,000, payable at the Canandaigua Bank, and pledged securities of her own for its payment, and that the proceeds of the loan were used by her husband, which note remains unpaid.

[*]   She could have taken a confession to secure herself against the contingent liability assumed on the signing of the note as surety, but the statute requires in such a case that the confession must state concisely the facts constituting the liability assumed, and must show that the sum confessed does not exceed the amount of the liability. As there was a failure to comply with the requirements of the statute, the confession of judgment is regarded in law as fraudulent and void, and may be attacked and set aside by a subsequent judgment creditor in an action prosecuted for that purpose* (Dunham v. Waterman, 17 *N. Y.* 9 ; Lawless v. Hackett, 16 *Johns.* 149 ; Symson v. Silhe mer, 40 *Hun*, 116).

The value of the morgagor's interest in the real estate conveyed to his wife, Susan F. Doty, was found

---

* See as to power of court to amend confession *nunc pro tunc*, Symson v. Silheimer, 40 *Hun*, 116.

by the referee to be $5,000. And he also finds that no consideration was in fact paid by the grantee at the time of the execution and delivery of said conveyance, the express consideration being arbitrarily used and not representing any specific financial transaction between the parties. He also found as a matter of fact that the deed of conveyance and confession of judgment were, and each of them was made, executed and delivered by the debtor, John C. Doty, with an intent to hinder, delay and defraud the plaintiff in this action, and for the express purpose of preventing the plaintiff from collecting his judgment.

[°]   The circumstances connected with the execution and delivery of the deed were such as to call upon Mrs. Doty to show the real transaction, and that it was entered into in good faith and without any intent to hinder, defraud or delay the other creditors of her husband. The only consideration for the conveyance was the discharge of an indebtedness equal to the amount expressed as the consideration claimed to be due from her husband to herself. The only evidence produced on her part was her own naked statement of loans and advancements of money by herself directly to her husband, made after her marriage and many years prior to the conveyance. Not one independent fact or circumstance was proved on the trial in corroboration of her own evidence. As she was an interested witness, it was for the referee to determine, from her appearance and manner, whether her uncorroborated statement was entitled to full credit. We are unable to discover any reason for reversing the judgment, and are satisfied with the conclusions reached by the referee on the facts and law of the case.

Judgment affirmed, with costs.

SMITH, P. J., HAIGHT and BRADLEY, JJ., concurred.

GOODRICH, as Administrator, etc., Respondent, v. McDONALD, Impleaded, etc., Appellant.

Supreme Court, Fourth Department, General Term, July, 1886.

§ 66.

Attorney's lien—How enforced—When payment of judgment does not extinguish.

An attorney who prosecutes an action, has a lien on the cause of action and the proceeds thereof, and a judgment recovered therein in whosoever hands they may come for the value of his services, and such lien cannot be effected by any settlement between the parties either before or after judgment, and does not rest upon possession, but can be actively enforced.[1,2]

The distinction between an attorney's general or retaining lien, and an attorney's lien upon a judgment recovered by him, or on its proceeds for the value of his services, and expense in recovering such judgment, stated.[2]

When the administrator of an attorney consented that a judgment upon which a lien existed in favor of his decedent for professional services should be paid to the judgment creditor, and the judgment discharged at the same time, stating that he would look to such judgment creditor for the amount coming to the estate,—
Held, that he did not thereby waive such lien;[3] that an action could be maintained to enforce the lien and compel payment of the debt as ascertained;[4] that one who took the assignment of a bond and mortgage purchased with a portion of the moneys received on said judgment in payment of a debt due from the judgment creditor, and with full notice of the attorney's lien took it subject to such lien;[3,5,6] that the lien attached to the money and mortgage in the judgment creditor's hands [3,6] and was not lost by the transfer,[6] and that an action could be maintained charging such lien upon said bond and mortgage.[3,5,6]

In such a case, where the judgment was recovered by an administratrix as such, the action to charge the attorney's lien upon the proceeds of the judgment is properly brought against her personally.["]

(*Decided July*, 1886.)

Appeal by defendant from a judgment rendered upon a trial at special term.

The facts are stated in the opinion.

George E. Goodrich, plaintiff-respondent, in person.

Pond, French & Brackett, for defendant-appellant.

BOARDMAN, J.—Milo Goodrich, plaintiff's testator, as an attorney for the defendant, Jennie L. Graves, administratrix of her deceased husband, recovered a judgment in 1877 for some $12,000, and afterwards, and before the same was collected, died. Mr. Kernan thereafter attended to the case for Mrs. Graves, and in 1882 the proceeds of said judgment including Milo Goodrich's costs and counsel fees, were paid to Mrs. Myers. In the meantime plaintiff had been duly appointed the administrator of Milo Goodrich. On being informed by Mr. Kernan that the money was ready to be paid upon a proper discharge of the judgment, he wrote Mrs. Graves, January, 1882, among other things, as follows : " I am willing to allow you to receive the money and discharge the judgment. . . my father's estate will look to you alone for the amount coming to us." On the same day he wrote to Mr. Kernan as follows : " While my father's estate is interested in the judgment, I am willing to look to Mrs. Graves alone for the share of the judgment coming to us, and she may therefore, discharge the judgment and receive all of the proceeds, after settling with you, so far as the claims of our estate are concerned. I am sole administrator of my father's estate, and as such consent that the judgment be discharged upon payment to Mrs. Graves. In pursuance of such authority, the money was paid to Mrs. Graves, and the judgment satisfied by her.

The most difficult, as well as the most important question for our consideration is presented by these facts, viz. : Had the estate of Milo Goodrich a lien or interest, by way of equitable assignment to the extent or value of his services, upon the proceeds of such judgment, before the same were paid to Mrs. Graves ; and if so, was such lien waived or interest released by plaintiff's acts and declarations so as to preclude him from following the funds in the hands of Mrs. Graves?

That the plaintiff had a valid lien upon the judgment and its proceeds before payment of the same to Mrs. Myers, cannot be doubted. Section 66 of the ['] Code of Civil Procedure must set that at rest. . By that section the attorney had a lien upon Mrs. Graves' cause of action which attached to the judgment in her favor, "and the proceeds thereof in whosesoever hands they may come," for the value of his services, and such lien cannot be affected by any settlement between the parties before or after judgment (Marshall v. Meech, 51 N. Y. 143). The learned counsel for the appellant contends that no lien can exist without possession. We think he has overlooked the ['] distinction between a general lien resting upon possession and giving the right to retain until the attorney's whole bill is paid, and the lien upon judgment recovered by him, or its proceeds, for the value of his services and expenses in recovering such judgment The latter form of lien does not rest on possession and can be actively enforced. The former cannot exist without possession and the lien is not confined to a specific claim or debt. The distinction and authori-

ties are quite fully discussed by BROWN, J. (*In re*
Wilson & Gregg, 2 *N. Y. Civ. Pro.* 343 ; *Code Civ. Pro.*
§ 66).* In the present case the lien is not general and
does not depend upon possession, but is specific upon
the judgment or its proceeds to the extent of the value
of the services of Milo Goodrich in the litigation.

Was such lien waived by plaintiff's letters to Mrs.
Graves and Mr. Kernan under which the money was
paid? That depends upon a proper construction of
the language used in said letter. There is no express
waiver. If any is found it must be inferred or spelled
out of the words used. There must be something
indicating an intention to release the lien. Nothing
of the kind exists. The evident purpose was to allow
the judgment to be satisfied by Mrs. Graves and for
that purpose allow her to receive the proceeds from
the defendant. Without such action the defendants
could not safely pay over the money to her and doubtless would not have paid. Plaintiff preferred to have
the proceeds in Mrs. Graves' hands, but beyond such
transfer no intent was shown to change his relations
to the fund. He simply consents to the discharge of
the judgment upon its payment. He calls attention
to his father's interest in the judgment and consents
to hold Mrs. Graves for the claim of his father's estate.
The interest and claim so referred to was an attorney's
lien upon the proceeds of the judgment in " whosesoever hands they may come." The estate was the
['] equitable assignee and owner of that portion of
the proceeds due for costs.† The payment to Mrs.
Graves only changed the possession. It did not
extinguish plaintiff's ownership nor the lien.‡ She

---

* See Dimick v. Cooley, 3 *N. Y. Civ. Pro.* 141.

† Naylor v. Lane, 5 *N. Y. Civ. Pro.* 149 ; Smith v. Chenoweth,
ante, p. 137.

‡ See *In re* Bailey, 4 *N. Y. Civ. Pro.* 141; Merchant v. Sessions, **5**
Id. 24; Ward v. Craig, 87 *N. Y.* 559.

took with full knowledge, and no reason is apparent, why, under the facts, a court of equity should hold, that she of all persons should take such moneys released from plaintiff's lien and title. It would be the height of injustice to so hold. The court at special term has found that the payment did not constitute a waiver or release of the lien, and we think such finding is just and true.

[*]   If we are so far right Mrs. Graves took such moneys subject to plaintiff's right under his lien and as equitable assignee. In her hands equity would seize upon and compel the payment to plaintiff of the claim for services of Milo Goodrich. An action was brought against her to enforce the lien and compel payment of the debt so ascertained, and judgment establishing the lien and ordering the payment, was entered against her. As against Mrs. Graves such judgment is conclusive and the rights of plaintiff to equitable relief are adjudged. It turns out, however, upon examination of Mrs. Graves that she had bought the Crane mortgage, now sought to be charged, for $6,000, and that the remainder of the proceeds of the collection had been paid out and expended for various purposes, so that, at that time, this $6,000 Crane mortgage, constituted the only part of the proceeds which could be identified or found. Even this mortgage had been assigned to defendant, McDonald, by Mrs. Graves before judgment recovered against her. So that the plaintiff could obtain no relief under his judgment against Mrs. Graves. He then brought this action against Mrs. Graves, Mrs. McDonald and Crane to establish his lien and procure payment of his claim out of the amount secured by the mortgage. Judgment was recovered in his favor and Mrs. McDonald appeals.

When Milo Goodrich undertook Mrs. Graves' case it was understood that payment for his services must be dependent on his success, since Mrs. Graves and her husband's estate were both insolvent. As a part of such original agreement Mrs. McDonald undertook to advance the necessary money to cover the expenses of the litigation, and in consideration thereof she was to have one-half of the recovery. The support of Mrs. Graves' other children by Mrs. McDonald was also alleged as a further consideration. Mrs. McDonald did furnish some money towards the expenses and did support her daughter and children. About May 1, 1882, the Crane bond and mortgage was assigned by Mrs. Graves, as administratrix, to Mrs. McDonald as and for her one-half of the recovery. It is apparent that Mrs. McDonald took the same with full knowledge of plaintiff's rights and the court so finds. It is also found that she took such assignment in bad faith with intent to hinder, delay and defraud the plaintiff out of his debt and lien.

Mrs. McDonald's objections to the judgment are:

First. That plaintiff never had any lien on the proceeds.

Second. That he waved his lien when he consented that they might be paid to Mrs. Graves.

Third. That she is the owner by a valid assignment of the bond and mortgage under the agreement above stated and for a valid consideration, and that in equity she is entitled to priority over the plaintiff's claim.

Fourth. That plaintiff's judgment against Mrs. Graves did not reach or bind this bond or mortgage, it having been assigned prior to such judgment.

Fifth. That appellant had no notice of plaintiff's claim when she took the assignment.

Sixth. That the action should have been against Mrs. Graves, as administratrix, she having received and invested the money and made the assignment as administratrix of her husband.

The first and second objections have already been considered and decided adversely to the appellant.

The third, fourth and fifth may be considered together.

[*]   Mrs. Graves held such bond and mortgage subject to plaintiff's equity. When she assigned them to Mrs. McDonald the latter took them subject to plaintiff's equities, because she thus parted with no new consideration and for the further reason that she took them with full notice of such equities (Weaver v. Barden, 45 N. Y. 286), and in bad faith, as the court has found. The judgment against Mrs. Graves may not be binding upon Mrs. McDonald because she was not a party to the action. But if the plaintiff's claim was a lien upon the bond and mortgage in Mrs. Graves' hands, it continued to be after the assignment to Mrs. McDonald. She was a party to the original arrangement, by which Milo Goodrich undertook the litigation. She was to make certain advances and to have half of the recovery. She was a party in interest in that litigation, and might under the agreement have properly been made a co-plaintiff as half owner of the claim to be prosecuted. As such she would have become entitled to one-half of the amount collected after payment of the costs and expenses. But she has taken in this more than one half and holds it charged in her hands with plaintiff's equitable claim. She and Mrs. Graves stand on the same plane. She is charged with the same knowledge possessed by Mrs. Graves, and has no equities superior to those of plaintiff (31 Alb. Law J. 304, 305). Especially is this so if she took this mortgage with int nt to

[*] defraud plaintiff. In such case the fraud would avoid the assignment. In our opinion the lien of plaintiff attached to the money and mortgage in Mrs. Graves' hands, and was not lost by the transfer to Mrs. McDonald (Ward v. Craig, 87 N. Y. 560.)

The plaintiff seeks to charge property in the hands of Mrs. Graves and by her transferred to appellant by reason of the lien upon it. It is not an action for money only. Mrs. Graves' possession of the property sought to be reached is the reason why she is ['] made the party. The claim is not against her husband's estate nor against her as its representative. As equitable assignee of so much money or such a proportion of this mortgage the plaintiff makes his claim against the persons in possession of such property for his share. That share does not belong to the estate of Graves but to plaintiff, and this remedy is to reach the property to satisfy his claim (*In re* Knapp, 85 *N. Y.* 297). Besides an action against Mrs. Graves personally, upon a contract made by her after her husband's death was proper. She alone incurred the obligation (Austin *v.* Munro, 47 *N. Y.* 360).* Again, the assignment was a personal transaction because it was not made in payment of any debt due from the estate. It was mainly to pay for the support of herself and her children (Le Baron *v.* Long Island Bank, 53 *How. Pr.* 286). And the lien may be enforced in such case against the avails of the property in lieu of the property or money itself (Hale *v.* Omaha National Bank, 49 *N. Y.* 627 ; 3 *Rom. Eq. Jus.* § 1280).

The inherent justice of plaintiff's claim requires us to sustain it if consistent with the rules of law. After a careful examination we are convinced of the justness and truth of the various findings of fact, and that the conclusions of law founded thereon are well sustained upon principle and authority.

We think the judgment should be affirmed, and with costs against the appellant.

FOLLET and HARDIN, JJ., concurred.

---

* See Estate of Wilcox, *ante,* p. 115, and cases cited in foot-note, *ante.* p. 122.

In re Petition of BRIDGET HYDE for an Order Directing and Requiring ELLEN GAGE to Produce John Lane and Others, Tenants for Life of Certain Real Estate.

HYDE, Appellant, GAGE, Respondent.

Supreme Court, Fifth Department, General Term, June, 1886.

§§ 2302, *et seq.*

Life tenant.— When order for production of, not made.— When will give contingent estate in fee, and not life estate.

hose provisions of the Code of Civil Procedure (§§ 2302, *et seq.*), which provide for the granting of an order for the production of a life tenant, apply only to a case where the prior estate is held by one who is a life tenant proper in the legal and technical sense of that term, and do not apply where such person is the holder of a contingent fee, which may be reduced to a life estate.

tenant for life of real estate is one to whom lands or tenements are granted or devised, or to which he derives title by operation of law for the term of his own life, or the life of another.

Where a will devised lands to one M. her heirs, and assigns forever, but provided that in case said M. should die without issue the lands should go to one J. L. during his natural life, and after his death to one B., and her heirs and assigns forever,—*Held*, that M. was not given by the will a life estate only, but was given a contingent fee, liable to be reduced to a life estate upon the happening of a contingency, and that the case was not one in which a proceeding for the production of a life tenant could be maintained under sections 2302, *et seq.* of the Code of Civil Procedure.

In such a case,—*Held*, that the only questions of fact that the court would have power to try in a proceeding for the production of a life tenant were whether M. and J. L. were living or dead, and that it would not have jurisdiction to determine whether M. left descendants surviving her, who, under the express terms of the will would take an absolute fee as her heirs at law.

(Decided June, 1886.)

Appeal from order denying petition for an order directing the production of life tenants of certain real property.

The petitioner bases the proceedings which she has instituted upon the provisions of section 2302 of the Code of Civil Procedure. She claims to be entitled to the real estate described in the petition if Maria McLean be dead without issue of her body surviving, and if one John Lane be also dead, as is averred in the petition. By the last will and testament of John McLean which was admitted to probate in the surrogates' court of Erie county on February 17, 1865, he gave and devised to his daughter, the said Maria McLean, her heirs and assigns forever, the lands in question, upon this proviso or contingency: "But in case my said daughter, Maria McLean, should die without issue, then I give and devise to my nephew, John Lane, son of my brother Patrick Lane, the above described premises to have and to hold the same during his natural life, and after his death to my daughter Bridget McLean, and to her heirs and assigns forever.

The petitioner is the Bridget McLean mentioned in this clause of the will. It is averred in the petition upon information and belief that Maria McLean intermarried with one Clark and that she died more than one year ago without issue, and that she believes that John Lane is now dead. The respondent, Ellen Gage, is in possession of the premises, and in her answer she denies that Maria McLean or John Lane is dead and averred that both are living. The petition was presented at the Erie county special term, and after hearing the parties the court denied the application without costs, and from that order the petitioner appealed.

O. O'Cottle, for the petitioner, appellant.

Tracy C. Becker, for the respondent.

BARKER, J.—The special term properly dismissed the petition and the order should be affirmed. We place our concurrence upon the ground that upon the conceded facts no case was made within the statute requiring the respondent, Ellen Gage, to produce Maria Clark the alleged life tenant of the premises. Whether or not she was a life tenant depends upon the provisions of the will of John McLean. The respondent contends that by that will Maria Clark took a fee simple absolute, and that the petitioner Bridget Hyde, named in the will as Bridget McLean, the daughter of the testator, would have no estate in the lands although Maria Clark be dead, and left no issue surviving as she survived the testator. This contention on her part, is placed upon the ground that the proviso or contingency expressed in the words : " but in case my said daughter Maria McLean, shall die without issue," refers to the time of her death happening in the life time of the testator, and as she survived the testator she at once, upon his death, became the absolute owner.

The petitioner maintains that Maria McLean took only a contingent estate in the fee which was reduced to a life estate when the contingency named in the will happened, to-wit: "her death without issue." In support of her position as to the proper construction to be placed on the will, her counsel cites Buel v. Southwick (70 *N. Y.* 581); Nellis v. Nellis (99 *N. Y.* 505; S. C., 2 *East Rep.* 423).

It was held that by the respective wills under consideration in those cases the primary devisee took only a contingent estate in fee which was liable to be reduced to a life estate in case of the devisees death without children or any descendants of children. The petitioner bases her claim of title and the right to the possession of the premises upon the ground that by the will of John McLean, Maria Clark took only a life estate in case she died without issue.

The statute authorizing summary proceedings for the purpose of ascertaining whether a life tenant is dead or not has no application to a case like the one now presented. The title of the Code regulating the proceedings is entitled "proceedings to discover the death of a life tenant." The section upon which the petition is based provides, "a person entitled to claim real property after the death of another who has a prior estate therein, may, not oftener than once in each calendar year, apply by petition to the supreme court . . . for an order, directing the production of the tenant for life, as prescribed in this title by a person named in the petition, against whom an action of ejectment to recover the real property can be maintained, if the tenant for life is dead ; or, where there is no such person by the guardian, husband, trustee, or other person, who has, or is entitled to, the custody of the person of the tenant for life, or the care of his estate." In case an order is granted, the person to whom it is directed is required, at a time and place therein to be mentioned, before the court or a referee therein designated, to produce the person upon whose life the prior estate depends, or, in default thereof, to prove that he is living (§ 2305).

The form and effect of the final order, if one is granted in support of the proceedings, is found in section 2310, which provides, that if it appears that the person upon whose life the prior estate depends, was not produced ; and if the party required to produce him, or to prove his existence, has not proved to the satisfaction of the court that he is living, a final order must be made, declaring that he is presumed to be dead for the purpose of the proceeding, and directing that the petitioner be forthwith let into possession of the real property as if that person was actually dead.

This title of the Code is but a reproduction of the Revised Statutes on the same subject, with some added provisions as to the mode and manner of procedure. It is manifest that the statute applies only to a case where the prior estate is held by one who is a life tenant proper in the legal and technical sense of that term. A tenant for life, of estates, is one to whom lands or tenements are granted or devised, or to which he derives title by operation of law for the term of his own life, or the life of another. This will, in terms, does not give the devisee, Maria McLean, a life estate only. On the contrary she is given a contingent fee as the petitioner admits, but claims that the contingency has happened upon which the fee was reduced to a life estate. The petitioner is necessarily forced to maintain, as her learned counsel has argued before us, that the prior estate devised to Maria Mc Lean, although properly denominated a fee because it might last forever, was, nevertheless, a base or determinable fee, because it was liable to be defeated by the happening of the contingency upon which it was limited. In other words, that the estate devised to the first taker by the will, was a determinable or qualified fee. Therefore, in a strict sense, Maria was never a life tenant of the premises. Assuming that she is now deceased, yet, at the time of her death, she was in possession, as owner of the fee, and if she in fact left children surviving, then they would take an absolute fee as her heir-at-law by the express terms of the will, and this the petitioner admits.

The only fact which the court has the power to try and determine in these proceedings is whether Maria McLean and John Lane, are now dead or living. If it should be found that they are dead, then it does **not** follow, that the respondents should be required to surrender up the possession of the premises to the petitioner, for Maria may have left descendants who would have a fee in the premises, a fact this court has no jurisdiction to determine, in this matter.

We purposely refrain from expressing any opinion as to the proper construction which should be given to the will of John McLean beyond expressing the opinion that Maria McLean, the first taker, was not a tenant for life of the premises, in the sense in which that term is used in the statute upon which these proceedings are based.

The order should be affirmed, with $10 costs and disbursements (*Code,* § 2316.)

SMITH, P. J., HAIGHT and BRADLEY, JJ., concurred.

SARGENT, APPELLANT, *v.* WARREN, RESPONDENT.

SUPREME COURT, FOURTH DEPATMENT, GENERAL
TERM, JUNE, 1886.

§ 3256.

Witness fees—What must be shown to entitle party to tax—When not allowed.

Where the defendant, in an action upon the taxation of his costs, upon the dismissal of the complaint at a special term held in Rochester, sought to have allowed him as a disbursement $32 travel fee, of a witness who resided and did business in Rochester, upon an affidavit showing that such witness was necessary and material for the defendant, and that at a term of the court when the case was on the calendar, the witness was in New York, and came to Rochester from that place at the special request of the defendant's attorney, to be a witness on the trial for the defendant,—*Held*, that this item should be rejected, as it did not appear that the witness returned from New York to his home in Rochester, for the sole purpose of attending the court as a witness for the defendant, and that he actually returned to the city of New York to complete the business which detained him there when requested to come to Rochester as a witness, but that if it had been made to appear that the witness had actually and necessarily made the journey from New York, and returned to that place, to comply with the defendant's request, then the item would have been taxable, unless it appeared that the party for whom he attended was in fault, and guilty of negligence in omitting to subpœna him before he left his permanent home for the temporary absence.

It is incumbent upon the party who subpœnas a witness while away from his home, and pays an additional travel fee to make it appear that the witness was necessarily compelled to travel an increased distance, and had a legal right to demand an increased fee, and the necessity of subpœnaing the witness away from his home must be clearly shown, or the party will not be entitled to an allowance of the increased travel fee.

Pfandler Barm Extracting Bunging Apparatus Co. *v.* Pfandler (39 *Hun*, 191).

(*Decided June* 16, 1886.)

Appeal from order of Monroe county, special term, denying a motion made by a plaintiff for a re-taxation of defendant's costs.

The plaintiff's complaint having been dismissed with costs, at the Monroe county special term, held in December, 1885, without trial, the defendant presented a bill of costs to the clerk of that county for adjustment, in which, among the items of disbursements, was one for $32 travel fee of one Hawley, witness in behalf of the defendant, from the city of New York to the city of Rochester, for attending at the February term, at which term this case was on the calendar, but was not disposed of. The clerk allowed this item upon the affidavit of the defendant's attorney, who stated therein that Hawley was a necessary and material witness for the defendant, and that at the February, 1885, term, the witness was in New York,

and came to Rochester from that place, at his special
request, to be a witness on the trial for the defendant,
and that he paid him the sum of $32 for traveling
fees. The defendant's attorney stated in another
affidavit that the place from which said witness was
brought was correctly stated and set forth in the items
of disbursements.

Other facts appear in the opinion.

John J. Van Voorhis, for plaintiff-appellant.

James B. Perkins, for defendant-respondent.

BARKER, J.—The witness, Hawley, was a single
man, doing business in the city of Rochester, which
was his permanent place of residence. When
requested by the defendant's attorney to attend the
term of court in February, he was temporarily in the
city of New York. Upon the affidavits presented to
the taxing officer the item of travel fee from New York
to Rochester should have been rejected. It is not
made to appear that the witness returned from New
York to his home in Rochester for the sole purpose of
attending the court as a witness for the defendant, and
that he actually returned to the city of New York to
complete the business which detained him there when
requested to leave that place and come back to Rochester as a witness. If it had been made to appear that
the witness actually and necessarily made the journey
from New York and returned to that place to comply
with the defendant's request, then the item would
have been taxable. The rule is to allow travel fee
when paid to a witness in such cases, unless it appear
that the party for whom he attended at the term of
court was in fault and guilty of negligence in omitting
to subpœna the witness before he left his permanent
home for a temporary absence. When a witness is

Sargent *v.* Warren.

subpœnaed at a place where he is found during a temporary absence from his permanent place of residence, the necessity of subpœnaing him away from his home must be clearly shown to entitle the party to an allowance of the increased travel fee (Mead *v.* Mallory, 27 *How. Pr.* 32.)

" The only facts established by the defendant's affidavit, are, that when he requested the witness to attend the court he was in the city of New York, and he came to Rochester and was paid the travel fee between the two cities. It does not appear that he returned to New York, or that the journey made was any inconvenience to him.

We are cited to our decisions made in January, 1886, in the case of the Pfandler Barm Extracting Bunging Apparatus Co. *v.* Pfandler (39 *Hun*, 191), as authority for allowing this travel fee. But that case is not at all in point, as the facts are essentially different. There it was established as a fact that the witness who lived in Rochester was temporarily in the city of New York on business, and that he refused to attend the term of court in Rochester unless he was paid the statutory travel fees, and the plaintiff, thereupon, to secure his attendance, complied with the demand of the witness and paid him the fee. The witness' own affidavit in that case was made and read, in which he positively stated that he was obliged to travel from the city of New York to the city of Rochester for the purpose of attending the trial, and after it was over he returned to the city of New York.

It is incumbent upon parties who subpœna witnesses while away from their homes, and pay an increased travel fee, to make it appear that the witness was necessarily compelled to travel an increased distance and had a legal right to demand an increased fee. Otherwise it would be easy to practice fraud and imposition upon the adverse party.

The other item of travel fee allowed for the attendance of the same witness from the State line to Roches
ter, on his journey home from Chicago, should have
been rejected for the same reasons.

The order appealed from should be reversed and a
re-taxation ordered, with permission for either party
to read new affidavits on the re-taxation, with costs
and disbursements of this appeal to the appellant.

SMITH, P. J., HAIGHT and BRADLEY, JJ., con
curred.

ESTATE OF JOHN BAIRD, DECEASED.

SUPREME COURT, FIFTH DEPARTMENT, GENERAL
TERM, JUNE, 1886.

§§ 829, 2618.

*Probate of will—Examination of witnesses—What witnesses should be
examined upon contestant's demand—Evidence—When irrelevant.*

The surrogate is not required to compel the attendance upon the probate of a will of any witness other than the subscribing witnesses,
on the demand of the contestants, unless he is satisfied that they
will be material to the issues of fact to be determined by him.[1]

Where, in a proceeding for the probate of a will, the contestants,
before the proofs are closed, file a notice requiring the examination
of certain witnesses, all of them who are within the state and are
competent and able to testify, must be examined, if the surrogate
is satisfied that they are material, and it is not necessary to entitle the contestants to the examination of witnesses, that such witnesses be present at the execution of the will.[2]

Where a surrogate refused to require the attendance and examination
of witnesses on the probate of a will, pursuant to a demand made
by the contestants, under section 2618 of the Code of Civil Procedure, on the ground of want of power in the court to make the
order, the case will be regarded on appeal, the same as if it had

Estate of Baird.

been specifically determined by the surrogate, on proper proof, that the evidence of the witnesses was material.[2]

Where, in a proceeding for the probate of a will, the contestants require the examination of witnesses who are within the State, and competent and able to testify, and whose evidence is material, it is incumbent upon the proponents of the will to produce such witnesses, and the law imposes upon the surrogate the duty to examine them relative to the execution of the will, whether the contestants be present or not.[4]

The parties who in a proceeding for the probate of a will, demand the production of a witness, thereby waive all objection to his incompetency, as against themselves [5]

Where a widow and her daughter took, by the terms of a will, all the estate of a decedent, and each a greater sum than they would receive under the statute of descent and distribution if he had died intestate, and were therefore interested in supporting the will,— *Held*, that the daughter could not raise the question that her mother was an incompetent witness in a proceeding for the probate of the will, on the ground that her interest was hostile to her own.[5]

Testimony to prove that the widow of a testator, who was a legatee under his will, before her marriage with him was not virtuous, is not involved in the issue on the probate of the will, and is properly rejected.[6]

(*Decided June* 17, 1886.)

Appeal from a decree of the surrogate of Monroe county, admitting to probate the will of John Baird, deceased.

The decedent died on November 30, 1883, at the age of sixty five years, leaving him surviving Isabella McL. Baird, his widow, and three children, being the owner of both real and personal property to the aggregate value of $12,000. On April 3, 1882, the deceased executed an instrument purporting to be his last will and testament, by which he gave all his property to his widow and an infant daughter, Helen A. Baird, making no provision for his other children, James C. and William Baird. By the terms of the will, his widow received a greater interest in his property than

she would have done under the statute of distributions
if he had died intestate. The sons, James and William, resisted the probate of the will, alleging that at
the time of its execution the decedent was not of
sound mind and memory and was incompetent to
make a will devising his property ; that the execution
of the instrument purporting to be his last will and
testament was procured by fraud, circumvention and
undue influence practiced upon him by his wife, Isabella Baird.

The surrogate, on admitting the will to probate,
found specifically, as fact, that at the time of the execution of the instrument the testator was of sound and
disposing mind and memory, and he did the same as
his free and voluntary act, and that he was not under
any restraint or undue influence at the time of its execution.   In the matter of form and manner of execution the will was in full compliance with the statutes.
His sons, James and William, were children of a former marriage, and he intermarried with Isabella, his
widow, in May, 1876, by whom he had two children,
of which Helen A. named in the will, is the survivor.
The widow and Henry J. Hetzel were named as executors, and the will was presented for probate upon the
petition of the executor Hetzel, in which the widow
joined.   There were two subscribing witnesses only,
both of whom were called and sworn.   Both the contestants join in the appeal from the decree admitting
the will to probate.

George A. Benton, for the contestants and appellants.

E. Werner, for the proponents and respondents.

Barker, J.—The will should have been denied
probate for the reason that Isabella McL. Baird, the

widow, was not produced and examined as a witness, as demanded by the contestants. By section 2618 of the Code of Civil Procedure it is provided that: " Any party who contests the probate of the will, may by a notice filed with the surrogate at any time before the proofs are closed, require the examination of all the subscribing witnesses to a written will, or any other witness, whose testimony the surrogate is satisfied may be material, in which case, all such witnesses, who are within the State, and competent and able to testify, must be so examined."

Before the proponents had closed their proofs, the contestants filed with the surrogate a written notice requiring the examination of Isabella McL. Baird, Henry Achilles and William H. Whitney, under and in pursuance of the provisions of the said section.

Immediately after the proponents had rested their case, the contestants demanded that the persons named be produced as witnesses, and examined as required by the said notice. The record states that this application was denied by the surrogate, upon the ground that the words of the section : "Any other witness " applied only to such persons as were present at the execution of the will, and that it appeared that Achilles and Whitney were not present at that time, and that Isabella Baird was in a bed room with the door closed. It was admitted that the notice was duly filed and served. The contestants duly excepted to the ruling.

['] The surrogate is not required to compel the attendance of any witness other than subscribing witnesses, on the demand of the contestants, unless he is satisfied that the testimony of such persons will be material on the issues of fact to be determined by him.

The application was denied on the ground of the want of power in the court to make the order, and not because it was satisfied that the testimony of the witnesses was not material on the questions of fact litigated.

[²]   In determining whether the ruling was erroneous or not, we should regard the case the same as if it had been specifically determined by the surrogate, on proper proof, that the evidence of each of these witnesses was material. The contestants were not called upon by the proponents to produce proof of the materiality of the testimony, and it is manifest that the surrogate made his decision declining to require the production of the witnesses, on the assumption that their evidence was material, or that the contestants were ready to make it appear to his satisfaction that such was the fact. The question is therefore fairly presented whether the proponents were required, under the provisions of section 2618, above quoted, to produce before the surrogate the persons named in the notice, and for the reason that one of them was not produced and examined, the surrogate should have denied probate to the will. The language of the statute is plain and positive, that "all such witnesses," that is, all those named in the notice, "who are within the State and competent and able to testify must be so examined."

[³]   The ruling that the statute has no application unless the witnesses named were present at the execution of the will, is adding to the requirements of the statute, which no court has the power to do. If the surrogate is satisfied that the witnesses named and required to be produced and examined can give material evidence, then, as a matter of right, the contestants can insist on their production and examination, before the will can be admitted to probate. In this respect, the statute is as imperative as its other provisions requiring that at least two of its subscribing witnesses shall be produced and examined, if living and within the jurisdiction of the court.

The proceedings relating to the probate of a will are in the nature of proceedings *in rem*. When a will is allowed probate it becomes an instrument affecting the title to property, both real and personal. It has been for a long time the policy of the law that instruments of this character shall be executed with great formality and in a particular manner, and many arbitrary requirements have been enacted by the legislature to prevent fraud in imposing such instruments upon the heirs and next of kin of deceased persons.

·The provisions of the section now under consideration are not novel, and are, in substance, the mere compilation of previous statutes. By section 10 of chapter 460 of the laws of 1837, at least two of the subscribing witnesses, if not disabled by age, sickness or infirmity from attending before the surrogate, were required to be produced and examined. By the eleventh section of the same act the contestants against the probate could, by filing with the surrogate a request, require all the subscribing witnesses, if there were more than two, to be produced and examined by the surrogate, before the will could be admitted to probate. In 1841 (chapter 129), section 11, was amended so as to apply to all witnesses, whom any person interested in the proof of the will shall request to be examined, whether such witnesses be subscribing witnesses to the will or not, provided the surrogate before whom the proceedings were pending was satisfied that the testimony of the witnesses so requested to be examined was material.

[']   We are also of the opinion that it is incumbent upon the proponents of the will to produce the witnesses named by the contestants, and when produced, the law imposes upon the surrogate the duty to examine such witnesses relative to the execution of

the will, whether the contestants be present or not.
It is made the surrogate's duty, by a statutory requirement, " to inquire particularly into all the facts and
circumstances," and not until he himself is "satisfied
of the genuineness of the will, and the validity of its
execution, can he admit it to probate" (*Code Civ.
Pro.* § 2622).

Similar views as to the true interpretation which
should be put upon the sections of the Code which
have been quoted, were expressed by the surrogate of
the city and county of New York, whose experience
in administering the law relative to the probate of
wills is very great, and his opinions on such matters
are worthy of the highest consideration and respect.
(Matter of Jesse Hoyt, 67 *How. Pr.* 57 ; S. C., *sub.
nom.* Hoyt *v.* Jackson, 2 *Dem.* 443). The question
is not before us as to the course of procedure to be
adopted in the surrogate's court as to the mode and
manner of producing to the surrogate, proofs as to the
materiality of the witnesses whom the contestants may
require to be examined.

Two of the witnesses mentioned in the notice,
Achilles and Whiting, were sworn after the ruling
made by the surrogate, and examined fully upon the
questions of fact in issue, both by the proponents and
contestants. It does not appear, however, that Mrs.
Baird, the other witness, was personally present before
the surrogate, but she was within the jurisdiction of
the state and amenable to the process of subpœna.
She was one of the proponents of the will for probate,
and interested in having it established as the valid
will of her late husband, and it is now suggested by
the respondents that, therefore, she was not a competent witness.

['] The contestants, by demanding her examination, waived all objections to her incompetency as
against themselves, and the infant, the only other per-

son interested who declined to produce the witness, is in no situation, at least at this time, to present that point in support of the surrogate's ruling. The widow and her daughter, who, by the terms of the will, take all of the estate of the decedent, and each in a sum greater than they would receive under the statute of descent and distribution if he had died intestate, are interested in supporting the will, and we think that the daughter, one of the proponents, cannot raise the question that her mother is an incompetent witness on the ground that her interest is hostile to her own.

[*]   On the hearing the contestants offered to prove, and the same was rejected, that the life of Mrs. Baird, before her marriage with her husband, was not virtuous, and the same was rejected. This ruling, we think, was correct, as that question was not involved in the issue.

We have read all the evidence with much attention, with a view of forming a judgment of our own upon the questions of fact litigated before the surrogate, but we withhold any expression of our own judgment upon those questions, for the decree of the surrogate should be reversed upon the question of law as indicated. This is more proper, for the reason that much of the evidence upon which the contestants rely in support of their charge of fraud and undue influence on the part of Mrs. Baird, was given by the contestants themselves, and the wife of James, as to whom the proponents made the objection that they were incompetent under section 829 of the Code of Civil Procedure, which was overruled by the surrogate. We refer to that part of the evidence relative to the transactions and communications between themselves individually and the deceased (*Greenl. Ev.* §§ 390, 397, 399 ; Steele *v.* Ward, 30 *Hun*, 555 ; Holcomb *v.* Holcomb, 95 *N. Y.* 316).

It will not be of advantage to either party for the

court on this appeal to pass upon the many other exceptions taken by the contestants, for it is not likely that they will again arise on the rehearsing in 'the precise manner in which they were presented by this record.

The decree of the surrogate is reversed, and the proceedings remitted to the surrogate of Monroe county, with directions to proceed, etc., with the costs of this appeal to the appellant, to be paid out of the estate.

SMITH, P. J., HAIGHT and BRADLEY, JJ., concurred.

PEOPLE, EX REL. PICKARD *v.* THE SHERIFF
OF CHAUTAUQUA COUNTY.

COUNTY COURT, CHAUTAUQUA COUNTY, DECEMBER, 1886.

§§ 2015, *et seq.*, 2031, 2043.

Habeas corpus — What may be inquired into on—When validity of bench warrant and indictment, on which issued, may be inquired into Grand jury—Powers of—Indictment—When not void—Constitutional law—Meaning of "law of the land" and "due process of law."

The "law of the land" referred to in article 1, section 1, of the constitution of this State, providing that "no member of this State, shall be disfranchised, or deprived of any of the rights or privileges secured to any citizens thereof, unless by the law of the land, or the judgment of his peers," is the general law, a law that hears before it condemns, which proceeds upon inquiry and renders judgment only upon trial [¹]

The words "due process of law" as used in the fifth amendment to the constitution of the United States, providing that "no person shall be. . . . deprived of life, liberty, or property, without due process of law," mean such an exercise of the powers of the government as the several maxims of the law permit, and sanction; they mean the due course of legal proceedings, according to those rules and forms that have been established for the protection of private rights, and that if the person be imprisoned by virtue of process, there being error in the proceeding resulting in that process, yet, if the law is valid, under which the proceeding is had such imprisonment is not without due process of law."[³]

Upon *habeas corpus*, the judge before whom it is returnable, may go beyond the warrant and return of a committing magistrate in the inquiry as to the validity of the process;[⁴] every officer having power to grant a writ of *habeas corpus*, may exercise in the forms prescribed by law, all the powers exercised at common law by the Kings Bench, in England, and the supreme court of this State,[³] and the fact that the warrant was issued out of court of jurisdiction, upon an indictment found by a grand jury thereat, does not change the general rule;[⁵] it merely changes the rule of evidence and reduces the number of matters subject to inquiry from lack of evidence, not from lack of power to make the inquiry, for while in the case of a magistrate the judge may look into the evidence returned by him, in the case of the grand jury a statute has always existed inhibiting the disclosure of the testimony before it, except for certain purposes.[⁵]

Where a person was imprisoned by virtue of a bench warrant, regular and fair upon its face, issued upon an indictment found against him in the court of oyer and terminer, charging him with the crime of forgery,—*Held*, that to warrant his discharge upon *habeas corpus* the warrant and indictment must be absolutely void,[¹⁶] and not merely irregular and voidable, and to ascertain whether such is the case, the court may go beyond the warrant and indictment upon which it was issued.[¹⁹,¹⁴]

People *v.* Nevins (1 *Hill*, 154);[⁶] *In re* Moses (13 *Abb. N. C.* 189);[¹] *In re* Serafino (66 *How. Pr.* 179);[⁹] *In re* Prime (1 *Barb.* 340);[¹⁰] People *v.* Martin (1 *Park.* 187);[¹¹] People *v.* Petrea (92 *N. Y.* 128),[¹²] distinguished. *In re* Edymoin (8 *How. Pr.* 483),[⁸] not followed.

A grand jury is defined by the statute to be a body of men returned at stated periods from the citizens of the county, before a court of competent jurisdiction, and chosen by law, and sworn to inquire of crimes committed or triable in the county; it is no part of the court, the court can exist without it, and it is there in a certain sense under the instruction of the court, as its assistant, but the court has no control over it, in regard to when or how long it may sit.[¹⁶]

People ex rel. Pickard v. Sheriff.

A grand jury is dissolved by the final adjournment of the court,[17] but it is not adjourned by a temporary adjournment or recess thereof, and an indictment found during a recess of the court is not void by reason of that fact.[10,17]

A grand jury has full control of every charge which is the subject of investigation until its final discharge, and during the same session it may reconsider its own actions.[18] *Accordingly held*, where a grand jury passed upon a charge, and voted no bill, and subsequently reconsidered the same charge without leaving the court and found an indictment, that such an indictment was not void.[18]

Section 270 of the Code of Criminal Procedure, which provides that the dismissal of the charge does not prevent its being again submitted to a grand jury, as often as the court may so direct, but that without such direction it cannot be again submitted, does not prevent the resubmission to the same grand jury of a charge already considered by it [19] *It seems*, that if such a direction were necessary, its absence would be but an irregularity, and would not avoid an indictment found.[19]

(*Decided September* 2, 1886.)

Habeas corpus to inquire into the cause of the detention of the relator by the defendant.

The facts are stated in the opinion.

Alonzo C. Pickard, relator in person.

Arthur B. Ottaway, district attorney, opposed.

SMITH, Sp. Co. J.—"No freeman shall be taken or imprisoned nor will the king pass upon him or commit him to prison, unless by the judgment of his pe rs or the law of the land," says Magna Charta, the so called great charter of English liberty, wrung from king John by his barons assembled in arms on June 19, 1215, and violated and disregarded by him and succeeding kings, each of whom, when wishing to do a popular thing, confirmed it—and then violated it again. Nevertheless, grounded upon this charter, thirty two times confirmed between 1215 and 1416, the fabric of constitutional liberty was slowly and patiently erected ; parliamentary institutions under the House of Lancaster, assumed form and acquired strength ; and though the promise of a regular administration of the law was as often violated as kept, the right of the subject to its benefits was never surrendered, and at length, in the reign of the first Charles, it received further assurance and confirmation in his assent to the petition of right, in which it was prayed, although the same had been guaranteed for more than four centuries, that freemen be imprisoned only by the law of the land or due process of law, and not by the king's command without any charge.

This petition was brought about through a multitude of outrages against the guaranties of the charter, chief among which was Darnell's Case (3 *Car. I.* 1627) in which the judges held that the command of the king was sufficient answer to a writ of *habeas corpus.* This writ is supposed to have existed before Magna Charta, traces of its existence may be found during the time of the third Edward, and it appears to have been familiar to the times of the fourth Henry, but no where does it appear to have been granted against the crown or the officers of the crowd until the reign of Henry VII. The petition of right, however, made other answer necessary, upon the return of the writ, than that the prisoner was detained by special command of the crown. Even now the crown through its ministers and judges, by delays and evasions, defeated the object of the writ ; it was absolutely inefficacious for want of a stringent system of procedure. What was needed was not a new right, but a prompt and searching remedy. England was denied that remedy until May 26, 1679, that eventful day in her history, when Charles II gave his assent, which he would have gladly withheld, to that famous measure known as— the *Habeas Corpus* Act—a measure which British authors say "extinguished all resources of oppression," yet a measure that left in doubt the extent to which and as to what matters inquiry might be had upon the return of the writ.

Such, substantially, was the law of England, adopted in 1777, by the first constitution of this State, and the constitution of this State and that of the United States have always guaranteed to the citizens, the privilege of this writ, and our constitution declares that no person shall be deprived of his liberty without due process of law,* and " no member of this State " says the constitution and bill of rights as well " can be disfranchised or deprived of any of the rights or privileges secured to any citizen thereof, unless by the law of the land or the judgment of his peers."† In most of the States, our own among them, statutes have been passed, not only providing what courts and officers may issue the writ of *habeas corpus*, but regulating the practice under it, but in all states the proceeding retains its distinctive feature and merit—that of a summary appeal for immediate deliverance from illegal imprisonment. The statute of this State became a part of the first revision of our statutes,‡ and with no important change now forms a part of the sixteenth chapter of the Code of Civil Procedure.

The relator, in the case at bar, claiming that he is restrained in his liberty without due process of law, nor by the law of the land, sued out a writ of *habeas corpus*, directed to the sheriff-defendant, commanding him to have the body of the relator, together with the time and cause of his imprisonment and detention,

---

* *Constitution of the United States*, Fifth Amendment.
† *Constitution of the State of New York*, Art. 1, § 1.
‡ 2 *R. S.* 563, § 21, *et seq.*

People ex rel. Pickard v. Sheriff.

immediately after the receipt of the writ, before the special county judge of the county of Chatauqua, to do and receive what should then and there be considered concerning the relator.

The sheriff obeyed the writ and made return that he had the relator in his custody by virtue of a bench warrant, which is regular and fair upon its face, issued upon an indictment found against him, as is therein recited, on September 25, 1886, in the court of oyer and terminer of said county, charging him with the crime of forgery, and commanding his arrest, and that he be taken before said court, or if the court were adjourned, his delivery into the custody of the defendant-sheriff.

The relator, availing himself of that provision of the Code of Civil Procedure (§ 2039), that permits a prisoner, produced upon the return of a writ of *habeas corpus*, to deny any material allegation of the return, or make any allegation of fact, showing either that his imprisonment or detention is unlawful, or that he is entitled to his discharge, controverted the return, claiming that the indictment, by virtue of which the warrant was issued, was void—that is, he stood imprisoned without due process of law, and without the sanction of the law of the land.

The defendant-sheriff, although no further pleading seems to be required by the statute and for the obvious reason that the relator would be required to prove his impeachment in any event, demurred to the traverse, which overruled, he put it in issue by a general denial.

The evidence under the issue thus made developes a state of facts the like of which has never had judicial exposition, nor can a similar case be found in the books. Decision is called for upon questions upon which volumes have been written. subjects often before the courts, yet unsettled except as applied to the particular case, and as to which the courts in many cases are at a difference.

What is meant, as applied to this case, by those terms known to the law since Magna Charta, and found in the constitution, the terms " law of the land," and " due process of law ?" That ascertained, how far, and to what length may the judge out of court go in ascertaining whether the process by virtue of which a citizen is restrained in his liberty is due process of law or not ?

A solution of these questions was approached with considerable embarrassment, and with but little aid from counsel, and after an examination of many authorities it is, as to the first proposition, concluded : That as applied to this proceeding, due process of law and law of the land have one and the same meaning.

Law of the land is the general law, a law that
['] bears before it condemns, which proceeds upon inquiry and renders judgment only after trial. Due process of law in each particular case means such an exercise of the powers of the government as
['] the settled maxims of the law permit and sanction,
—it means the due course of legal proceedings according to those rules and forms which have been established for the protection of private rights, and that if a person be imprisoned by virtue of process, there being error in the proceedings resulting in that process, yet if the law is valid under which the proceeding is had, such imprisonment is not without due process of law (Davidson *v.* New Orleans, 96 *U. S.* 103 ; Daniel Webster's argument in Dartmouth College Case, 4 *Wheat.* 518 ; Johnson, J., 4 *Id.* 235 ; Westervelt *v.* Gregg, 12 *N. Y.* 209 ; Murray's Lesees *v.* Hoboken Land Co., 18 *How.* (*U. S*) 272–6 ; *Cooley's Const. Lim.* 437, 572 ; Deady, J., 4 *Fed. Rep.* 899).

The bench warrant and indictment by virtue of which the relator is imprisoned must necessarily then be void, not merely irregular and voidable, but absolutely void, or the relator is not imprisoned without due process of law.

The learned district attorney, citing many cases, asserts that when the relator is held by virtue of a bench warrant a judge at chambers, upon the return of a writ of *habeas corpus*, may not go beyond the warrant, nor the indictment upon which it was issued. Such, however, is not the law. Every officer having power to grant a writ of *habeas corpus*, has, and [*] may exercise, in the forms prescribed by law, all the powers exercised at common law by the Kings Bench, in England, and the supreme court of this State (People *ex rel.* Tweed *v.* Liscomb, 60 *N. Y.* 567), and it has always been held that upon [] *habeas corpus* the judge might go beyond the warrant and return of a committing magistrate in an inquiry as to the validity of the process (People *v.* Martin, 1 *Park.* 187). Because the warrant in this case is issued out of a court of general jurisdiction [*] upon an indictment found by a grand jury thereat does not change the general rule. It simply changes the rule of evidence and reduces the number of matters subject to inquiry for lack of evidence, not from lack of power to make the inquiry. In the case of the magistrate the judge may look into the evidence returned by him ; in the case of the grand jury, a statute has always existed inhibiting a disclosure of the evidence before it, except for certain purposes (*Code Crim. Pro.* 265-6 ; People *ex rel.* Tweed *v.* Liscomb, *supra;* People *v.* Martin, *supra*).

In discussing the cases cited by the district attorney, much need not be said. In Mr.'Hill's notes (3 *Hill.* 661) cases are cited holding that inquiry can not be had as to whether a crime had really been committed, or whether there was sufficient proof to warrant issuing the process. Mr. Hill does not pretend

to say that inquiry can not be had as to whether
there was any proof. The difference between on
[*] proof at all and sufficient proof is obvious. In
People *v.* Nevins (1 *Hill*, 154), the decision is
simply that in respect to mere irregularities the remedy is by motion. That is admitted. The matter
['] of Moses (13 *Abb. N. C.* 189) has nothing to do
with the case. The habeas corpus was sued out
after final judgment, and by statute (*Code Civ. Pro.* §§
2016, 2032) in such a case the privilege of the writ is
denied. The case of Edymoin (8 *How. Pr.* 483) is
[*] a county court decision way back in 1852, and follows no authority when it attempts to lay down
the rule that records, deeds and papers, fair on their
face cannot be impeached. In the Serafino Case
['] (66 *How. Pr.* 179) it was held, as it always has been,
that the court have no power to retry questions of
fact. The matter of Prime (1 *Barb.* 340) is far from
authority in favor of the proposition of the dis-
["] trict attorney. In this case it is held : "If the
court find that the warrant under which the relator is imprisoned is *prima facie* sufficient to justify
the imprisonment and, if, in looking beyond the warrant, and examining the affidavit upon which the same
was issued, it is satisfied that there was at least colorable proof before the officer issuing the warrant, on
which he might exercise his judgment in awarding the
process, that is as far as the court will go upon a writ of
habeas corpus." That is the law exactly, and stated
['] to a nicety. In the Martin Case (People *v.* Martin, 1 *Park.* 187) the judge went beyond the depo-
sitions, return and warrant of the magistrate, and
inquired into the cause of commitment, incidentally
remarking in his opinion, (pp. 190–1) with his mind
upon looking into the evidence before a grand jury,
speaking of the McLeod Case,* says : "The question

---

* People *v.* McLeod, 25 *Wend.* 483 ; S. C., 1 *Hill*, 377.

raised there was whether after indictment the court on *habeas corpus* would entertain the question of guilt or innocence, and on that question the authorities have been very uniform that they would not." This

["]   goes far from saying that for the purpose of ascertaining whether an indictment was void the court would not go behind it. The case of People *v.* Petrea (92 *N. Y.* 128) is an appeal from a conviction, and not one involving the questions here presented. If the defendant in that case had sued out a *habeas corpus* after his conviction, the court probably would have applied the rule that upon *habeas corpus* the question of the constitutionality of a law will not be passed upon.

["]   The proposition made by the district attorney cannot be law, if it is, it should not be. The law was not so understood by the courts in any of the following cases : Matter of Prime (1 *Barb.* 340); People *v.* Martin (1 *Park.* 187) ; People *ex rel.* Tweed *v.* Liscomb (60 *N. Y.* 559) ; People *ex rel.* Frey, Warden, etc. (100 *N. Y.* 20). Suppose for an instant that the district attorney had issued this bench warrant without an indictment ; suppose there was an indictment but no evidence of any kind or character, was before the jury ; suppose twelve men did not concur in it ; suppose a bill had been presented, ignored, and by inadvertence signed a true bill by the foreman, could none of these facts be proved upon *habeas corpus?* With such a state of facts would an imprisonment under the warrant be legal, and what is *habeas corpus* for but to relieve from illegal imprisonment ?

For nearly five hundred years, although Magna Charta said no freeman should be imprisoned except by the law of the land, it was an answer, which could not be disputed, to a writ of *habeas corpus* directed against the officers of the crown, that the imprisonment was by the command of the king. That answer

was a perfect answer until the people said in the Petition of Right that no freeman in such manner should
be imprisoned or detained.   What did that mean ?   It
meant   that   thereafter   the   judges, when it was
        impeached, must go beyond the warrant and com-
["]   mand of the king and see whether or no the
        imprisonment was by due process of law,—by such
process as the settled maxims of the law permitted
and sanctioned.   To hold that in this case no inquiry
may be had beyond the warrant and indictment,
inquiring whether they are void or not, is to put the
law of this land back into those elder days two hundred years ago.   It is to say that the people, our sov-
ereign power, the king, may imprison without due
        process of law.

["]   But the warrant and indictment can not be
        invalidated, proceeding under a *habeas corpus*, by
errors which only render them irregular.   The defects,
to entitle the relator to a discharge, must be such as
to render the process void.

A court of oyer and terminer, in and for the
county of Chantauqua, convened at the court house in
Mayville, September 20, 1886, and a grand jury was
duly sworn and retired to the grand jury room for the
transaction of business.   On September 23, the court
adjourned to Saturday, September 25, at 11 o'clock
in the forenoon.   The justice holding the court left
Mayville on the 23, went to Fredonia, said county,
and there remained until Saturday morning when he
left for Mayville, arriving there at 11.27 o'clock in
the forenoon.   During the absence of the justice, on
Friday, a charge of forgery of a certain note was preferred to the jury against the relator, witnesses were
examined, and the jury voted upon the proposition of
" Bill " or " No Bill."   Twelve members of the jury
did not vote in favor of a " Bill."   No direction was
asked for from the court, nor did the court direct the

charge to be again submitted to the jury. During
the examination of the charge other notes were
brought in question, and on Saturday, before the
return of the justice, at the instance of some member
of the jury, an inquiry was instituted as to these other
notes, and witnesses were sworn, and, after the evidence was in, a vote was again taken upon the question of bill or no bill upon the charge preferred Friday, and the indictment in this case was found, a
bench warrant issued thereon by virtue of which the
relator stands imprisoned. The indictment charges
the relator with the forgery of a promissory note, and
in a second count with uttering a forged promissory
note.

At the close of the evidence the relator asked his
discharge upon four grounds, the first of which was
not argued : 1. The indictment is void upon its face ;
2. After a grand jury has passed upon a charge it
cannot subsequently consider the same charge without leave of the court; 3. The indictment is void by
reason its containing a count that never was passed
upon by the jury ; 4. That a grand jury cannot exist
without an oyer and terminer; that the grand jury
stood adjourned during the adjournment of the court
from Thursday to Saturday noon.

As to the first and third grounds. The indictment
is valid upon its face, and questions as to whether
various offenses should be joined in an indictment,
and whether the prosecutor can on the trial be compelled to elect under which count he will proceed,
cannot be determined in this proceeding. (People *ex
rel.* Tweed *v.* Liscomb, 60 *N. Y.* 559). The witness
Preston says, upon the examination, that, "the
indictment was found," and is must be assumed that
both counts were passed upon.

[*] "A grand jury " is defined by the statute to be
"a body of men, returned at stated periods from

People *ex rel.* Pickard *v.* Sheriff.

the citizens of the county, before a court of competent jurisdiction, and chosen by lot, and sworn to inquire of crimes committed or triable in the county."* Note the language, "returned before a court." All through the chapter of the Code of Criminal Procedure, devoted to the grand jury, it is recognized as a body separate and distinct from the court before which it is returned. It is no part of the court, the court can exist without it. The court of oyer and terminer is composed of a justice of the supreme court without an associate. The grand jury is there, in a certain sense under the instructions of the court, for the purpose of inquiring as to crimes and making its presentments to the court. It is required after the court have advised it as to its duties. to retire to a private room, and it may there stay until it is through with its inquiries or until the final adjournment of the court. The court have no control over it in regard to when and how long it may sit. The court is the adviser of the jury ; the jury the assistant of the court. If, as the relator claims, the jury stands adjourned when the court stands adjourned, the only safe way for courts in the future is to call the jury from its private room to the court room just before every adjournment, even from night to morning, so that the court and jury will adjourn simultaneously, and on the instant. This is not the practice nor was it ever, nor is it contemplated by the statute : Section 251 of the Code of Criminal Procedure provides : "The grand jury on the completion of the business before them, must be dis-
["] charged by the court ; but whether the business be completed or not, they are discharged by the final adjournment of the court." The last section but one before this requires the grand jury to retire to a private room, the next section relates to the appoint-

---

* *Code of Criminal Procedure,* § 223.

ment of a clerk and his duties, and then comes the section quoted. For all the law provides, the grand jury is not required from the time of its compulsory retirement to set foot in the court until the completion of its business. If the grand jury stood adjourned every time the court adjourned, why did the legislature deem it necessary to enact that the final adjournment acted as a discharge of the jury? If a final adjournment of the court would not discharge the jury, without an express statute to that effect, then no adjournment of the court will adjourn the jury without a statute to that effect.

Clearly the indictment is not void by reason of having been found during a recess of the court.

The theory of the law is that a bill of indictment is prepared by the public prosecutor and presented to the grand jury to pass upon it, after hearing the evidence in support of the bill. The jury either find the indictment "a true bill," or ignore it and find it "not a true bill" (4 *Blackstone Com.* 305). The practice, however, is for the district attorney to inform the jury of the charge to be investigated, and if a bill is found, to prepare an indictment such as the jury conclude to present. The law gives the jury full
["] control of every charge until it is finally discharged, and during the same session it may reconsider its own actions, and the law contemplates that the jury shall give each case a full and complete investigation before it finally comes to a conclusion. See Regina *v.* Newton, 2 *Moody & Rob. (Eng. N. P.)* 503, where the jury was allowed to find a second bill for the same offense at the same term.

The relator bases his second ground for a discharge upon section 270 of the Code of Criminal Procedure which reads : "The dismissal of the charge does not, however, prevent its being again submitted to a grand jury, as often as the court may so direct. But with-

out such direction, it can not be again submitted."
In view of the theory and practice already alluded to,
this section was not intended to apply to the same
grand jury, it has reference to the future. There is
no adjudicated case giving construction to this section.
The case of People *v.* Lynch, blindly reported in 20
N. Y. Weekly Dig. 9, came up in a different way than
this and the point is not decided.

Moreover, if the statute contemplates a re-submis-
sion of a charge at the same grand jury, would it be
aught but an irregularity, a departure from the
["] form or mode prescribed by the Code, to again
submit a charge without the direction of the court.
Is the case not covered by section 684 which provides
that "Neither a departure from the form or mode
prescribed by this Code, in respect to any pleading or
proceedings, nor an error or mistake therein, renders
it invalid, unless it have actually prejudiced the
defendant, or tend to his prejudice, in respect to a
substantial right." Where is the substantial right in
this case? The statute does not prescribe or contemplate that a person charged before the grand jury
shall have notice of an application to the court for an
order directing it to be again submitted after once
being dismissed. If he have no notice his constitutional rights as a citizen are not infringed upon.
Without notice to him, if an order of resubmission be
granted, an indictment and a warrant issued, that warrant and that indictment are still due process of law
(Happy *v.* Mosher, 48 *N. Y.* 313).

Lawful cause for the imprisonment and restraint
of the relator is shown, and an order will be made, he
being entitled to be bailed, fixing the amount of bail
at $1.000, in the meantime remanding the relator to
the custody of the sheriff-defendant.

GANNON and Another v. MYARS.

SUPREME COURT, FIRST DEPARTMENT, NEW YORK
COUNTY, SPECIAL TERM, NOVEMBER, 1886.

§§ 451, 488, 721 subd.9.

*Misnomer.—Remedy of defendant sued by wrong name.—When defect
not cured by judgment.*

The remedy of a person sued by a name not his own is not by
demurrer, but by answer.

The verdict or judgment in an action will not cure a defect in the
name of a defendant, unless the correct name of the party has once
been rightly stated.

Where the summons and complaint in an action against a person
designated therein as "Abraham Myars, first name being fictitious
as full name is unknown to plaintiff," was served on one Alexander
M. Christalar,—*Held*, that in case of default in pleading, the only
judgment that could be entered would be against Myars, and no
execution on that judgment would run against said Christalar
unless his real name be Myars; that a demurrer by Christalar to the
complaint, on the ground that it did not state facts sufficient to
constitute a cause of action *against him* was frivolous.

(*Decided November,* 1886.)

Motion by defendant for judgment on demurrer to
complaint as frivolous.

The summons and complaint in this action were
served upon one Alexander M. Cristalar, but the
defendant was designated therein as follows: "Abraham Myars (first name being fictitious, as full name
is unknown to plaintiff):" The person so served
appears specially in the action and demurred to the
complaint, on the ground that it did not state facts
sufficient to constitute a cause of action against him.

Charles Bulkley Hubbell, for plaintiff and motion.

Frank N. O'Brian, for Alexander N. Cristalar, opposed.

BARTLETT, J.—The complaint, which is entitled as above, sets out a good cause of action against the defendant. A special notice of appearance has been put in for Alexander M. Cristalar, stating that he is the person upon whom the summons was served. Alexander M. Cristalar has also interposed a demurrer upon the ground that the complaint does not state facts sufficient to constitute a cause of action against him. In this he is quite correct, unless he is identical with the defendant My⁀rs. The plaintiff now moves for judgment on the demurrer as frivolous.

Section 451 of the Code of Civil Procedure permits a plaintiff who is ignorant of the name or part of the name of a defendant to designate that defendant by a fictitious name, or by as much of his name as is known. The plaintiff here professes to know that the surname of the defendant is Myars and his suit must stand or fall by the correctness of his position in that respect; for a verdict or a judgment will not cure the defect unless the correct name of the party has once been rightly stated (*Code Civ. Pro.* § 721, subd. 9).

In case of a default in pleading the only judgment that could be entered would be against Myars, and no execution on that judgment could run against the Alex. M. Cristalar, who has specially appeared and demurred herein, unless his real name be Myars. If there has been a misnomer the defendant's remedy is by answer; under the circumstances, the demurrer by Cristalar presents no defense.

There must be judgment for the plaintiff, with leave to defendant to answer, if so advised, on payment of $10 costs of motion.

WHITTAKER *v*. THE NEW YORK AND HARLEM RAILROAD COMPANY.

SUPERIOR COURT OF THE CITY OF NEW YORK, SPECIAL TERM, NOVEMBER, 1886.

§ 66.

Attorney's lien—When attaches to judgment and proceeds thereof—When not affected by settlement between the parties—When satisfaction of judgment set aside because of.

Under the Code of Procedure, the lien of an attorney for compensation did not exist before verdict or judgment, except on the papers in his hands, and it was only in the case of a settlement privately effected between the parties, with the design of defrauding the attorney, that the court would insist upon the payment to him of at least the taxable costs before granting a discontinuance of the action, or leave to serve a supplemental answer showing settlement ; the Code of Civil Procedure as originally passed, did not change the law upon this point, but the amendment of section 66 thereof in 1879, for the first time gave to every attorney and counsellor, from the commencement of an action, or the service of an answer containing a counter-claim, a lien upon his client's cause of action or counter-claim, which attaches to a verdict, report, decision or judgment in his client's favor, and the proceeds thereof into whosoever's hands they may come, and which cannot be affected by any settlement between the parties before or after judgment.[1]

The lien of a plaintiff's attorney extends to the whole of the compensation to which he is entitled for his services, whatever they may be, but the lien is upon the actual cause of action, and not upon the one alleged in the complaint.[2]

The attorney's lien given by section 66 of the Code of Civil Procedure attaches in every action, and the rule that a personal cause of action founded upon a tort is not assignable, cannot be invoked to defeat the legitimate claim of an attorney for which he has a lien.[3]

The extent of the compensation of an attorney for his services is governed by the agreement existing between him and his client, which may be either expressed or implied,[4] but the courts exercise a strict supervision over such contracts, and whenever a contract between an attorney and his client gives benefits or advantages to the attorney, the court will scrutinize it with care;[5] all presumptions are in favor of the client and against the propriety of the transaction, and the burden rests upon the attorney to show by extrinsic evidence that all was fair and just, and that the client acted understandingly,[5] but where such facts are shown the contract must be upheld and enforced, although by it the attorney's compensation may have been made contingent upon success, and payable out of the proceeds of the litigation.[6]

Fowler v. Callan (9 N. Y. Civ. Pro. 384), followed;[7] Coughlin v. N. Y. C. & H. R. R. Co. (71 N. Y. 443); [8] Tuttle v. Village of Cortland (21 N. Y. Weekly Dig. 528),[18] distinguished.

Where an attorney was retained as counsel for the plaintiff in an action for damages, for personal injuries, and as such tried the case which resulted in a verdict in favor of the plaintiff for $10,000, and thereafter was substituted as attorney for such plaintiff in the place of his previous attorney of record, and previous to such substitution, it was agreed betweeen him and the plaintiff and the attorney of record, that he should receive as compensation for his services, one-half of the sum recovered and the whole of the costs of the action and interest thereon from the date of recovery, and he gave due notice of such lien to the attorneys for the defendant, and the defendant thereafter settled with the plaintiff by paying him $3,500; but both parties in making such settlement, expressly excepted the claim of the attorney therefrom, —Held, that as the attorney did not obligate himself to pay the costs and expenses of the litigation, and in no manner stirred up strife and induced litigation, the agreement for compensation was not void under any law now in force relating to the doctrine of champerty and maintenance;[9] and there being no suggestion of fraud, and many and valuable services having been performed, said agreement was a fair one;[10] that, as it was such between the attorney and his client, the defendants in the action could not claim the contrary;[11] that such attorney had a lien on the judgment for the amount of his fees,[14] and was entitled to have a satisfaction of judgment set aside so far as it applied to his lien, and to proceed with the action for the enforcement thereof.[16]

Where a case is settled before final judgment, the attorney who has a lien upon the cause of action for his compensation, while he need no longer prove fraud or collision, must go on with the litigation until final judgment; and the defendant cannot be compelled to pay by a mere order.[15]

(*Decided November* 3, 1886.)

Motion by Chauncey S. Truax, attorney for plaintiff, to vacate satisfaction of judgment, etc.

The opinion states the facts.

Chauncey S. Truax and *Chauncey Shaffer*, for the motion.

Anderson & Howland, for the defendant, opposed.

FREEDMAN, J.—This is a motion made by Chauncey S. Truax, attorney for the plaintiff herein, for an order vacating and setting aside the satisfaction of the judgment for $10,646.73 entered herein March 24, 1884, in favor of the plaintiff and against the defendant, and for other and further relief. The satisfaction took place upon a satisfaction piece executed by the plaintiff purporting to have been executed August 4, 1886, and filed in the office of the clerk of this court October 7, 1886.

The papers submitted on both sides are quite voluminous, but there is no substantial conflict as to the material facts which, briefly stated, are as follows, viz. :

The action was brought by the plaintiff to recover damages for a personal injury in consequence of having been run over by a car of the defendant. Truax was not the attorney who brought the action. He was retained as counsel during the pendency of the litigation, and as such he tried the case. The trial resulted in a verdict in favor of the plaintiff for $10,000, upon which a judgment was entered March 24, 1884, for $10,646.73.

On that day, and before the entry of the judgment, Truax, by agreement with the attorney then of record and with the plaintiff, was duly substituted as attorney of record, and from that time on he acted as the attorney and counsel of the plaintiff in the proceedings hereinafter referred to, and was recognized as such by the defendant. As such he entered the judgment already spoken of. About a month thereafter the defendant, upon voluminous affidavits, moved to set aside the verdict, to vacate the judgment, and for a new trial, upon the ground of surprise at the trial. This motion was denied October 11, 1884. From the order denying the same defendant appealed, but the general term affirmed the order. The defendant also perfected an appeal from the judgment, but after argument the judgment was affirmed by the general term in February, 1885, with costs. The defendant thereupon perfected an appeal to the court of appeals from the judgment entered on the verdict, and from the judgment of the general term affirming the first judgment, and this appeal is still pending.

For all the services thus rendered, Truax never received any compensation. It was agreed, however, between him and the plaintiff and the attorney in whose place and stead he had been substituted, that his compensation for his services in the action should be fixed at the sum of $5,000, which was one-half of the verdict, and that in addition he should have the whole of the costs of the action and interest on the total amount coming to him from March 24, 1884.

On November 22, 1884, Truax caused to be duly served upon the defendant and its attorneys a notice stating that he had an interest in and lien upon the judgment to the extent of one-half thereof, besides the costs of the action, and warning them against making any settlement or compromise without his knowledge or consent.

After the service of this notice Truax heard of several attempts made on behalf of the defendant to bring about a settlement with the plaintiff, and he thereupon, on or about August 1, 1885, caused to be duly served upon the defendant and its attorneys of record a second notice, which stated that he had an interest in and lien upon the judgment to the extent of $5,000, with interest thereon from March 24, 1884, and of the costs inserted in the judgment, amounting to $600, with interest thereon from March 24, 1884, and which warned them against making any settlement or compromise without his knowledge or consent.

Notwithstanding the service of these notices the defendant persisted in attempts to settle with the plaintiff directly, and the final result was that the plaintiff, eventually, in consideration of $3,500 paid to him, executed and delivered to the defendant, without the knowledge or consent of Truax, a satisfaction piece of the judgment. This satisfaction piece purports to have been signed and acknowledged by the plaintiff on August 4, 1886, but it was not filed until October 7, 1886.

It is now shown by the affidavit of the plaintiff and his wife that, in making this settlement, the plaintiff intended to release to the defendant only his interest in the judgment ; that, at the time of making it, the plaintiff in the most unequivocal terms stated to the agents of the defendant who negotiated the settlement, that he would only make it subject to whatever interest or lien, Truax, as his attorney, might have, and that he finally made it upon the assurance of said agents that Truax's interest would be respected and taken care of by the defendant.

Upon the argument of the motion, the learned counsel for the defendant conceded that Truax had an interest in the judgment which the court would protect, but they strenuously contended that defendants' liability for such interest extends only to the reasonable value of the services rendered by Truax as attorney ; that the agreement between him and the plaintiff was void as against the defendant under the rules relating to champerty and maintenance ; and that the amount claimed by him was unreasonable.

This contention calls for a determination of the precise nature, character and extent of the said interest.

[']   As shown by me in McCabe v. Fogg,* the lien of an attorney for compensation did, under the old Code, not exist before verdict or judgment except on the papers in his hands, and it was only in the case of a settlement privately effected between the parties, with the design of defrauding the attorney, that the court could insist upon the payment to him of at least the taxable costs before granting a discontinuance or leave to serve a supplemental answer showing settlement. The Code of Civil Procedure, as originally passed, did not change the law upon this point, as it then stood, and Quincy v. Francis (5 *Abb. N. C.* 286) is simply a decision to this effect. The amendment on section 66 of the Code of Civil Procedure, passed in 1879, for the first time gave to every attorney or counsellor, from the commencement of an action, or the service of an answer containing a counter-claim, a lien upon his client's cause of action or counter-claim which attaches to a verdict, report, decision or judgment in his client's favor, and the proceeds thereof, in whosoever hands they may come, and which cannot be affected by any settlement between the parties before or after judgment.

[']   The lien of a plaintiff's attorney extends now to the whole of the compensation to which he is entitled for his services, whatever that may be (Albert

---

* 2 *N. Y. Monthly Law Bul.* 71.

Palmer Co. v. Van Orden, 64 *How. Pr.* 79),* which statement must be taken, however, with the qualification that the lien is upon the actual cause of action, and not upon the one alleged in the complaint (S. C., 4 *N. Y. Civ. Pro.* 44, 89).†

['] ˆ   Nor does section 66 apply only to actions on contract. It gives a lien in every action. This being so, the rule that a personal cause of action founded upon a tort is not assignable, can no longer be invoked to defeat the legitimate claim of an attorney for which he has a lien.

Having a lien under all circumstances for his legitimate claim, it becomes necessary to consider to what extent the attorney of a plaintiff can make a claim for compensation which the law will uphold.

['] The extent of the compensation of an attorney for his services, is governed by the agreement existing between him and the client, which may be either express or implied. Formerly an attorney was under a disability so to contract. This disability was removed by the old Code,‡ and thereupon attorneys were left free to contract with their clients as to their compensation beyond the allowances given by statute. The freedom so to contract was continued by section 66 of the Code of Civil Procedure.

['] Notwithstanding these facts, the courts exercise a strict supervision over such contracts. Whenever a contract between an attorney and his client gives benefits or advantages to the attorney, the

---

* See also *Code of Civ. Pro.* § 66; Coster v. Greenpoint Ferry Co., 5 *N. Y. Civ. Pro.* 146; *In re* Knapp, 85 *N. Y.* 284; Lewis v. Day, 10 *N. Y. Weekly Dig.* 44; Wilber v. Baker, 24 *Hun,* 24; Jenkins v. Adams, 22 *Id.* 600; Schwartz v. Schwartz, 21 *Id.* 33.

† The decision reported in 4 *N. Y. Civ. Pro.* 44, is by the general term of the New York superior court, and is odified that of the special term reported in 64 *How. Pr.* 79.

‡ Code of Procedure § 303, and Code of 1848, § 258.

court will scrutinize it with care. All presumptions are in favor of the client, and against the propriety of the transaction, and the burden is upon the attorney to show, by extrinsic evidence, that all was fair and just, and that the client acted understandingly (Haight *v.* Moore, 37 *N. Y. Super. Ct.* [5 *J. & S.*] 161, and cases there cited ; Allison *v.* Sheeper, 9 *Daly*, 365).

[⁶]　　But where an attorney does show that all was fair and just, and that the client acted understandingly, the contract must be upheld and enforced, although by it the attorney's compensation may have been made contingent upon success, and payable out of the proceeds of the litigation (Forstman *v.* Schulting, 35 *Hun*, 504, and cases there cited ; Fowler *v.* Callan, 9 *N. Y. Civ. Pro.* 384).

[⁷]　　In the case last referred to, the court of appeals of the State of New York went so far as to hold that an attorney may now not only agree with his client that his compensation shall be contingent upon his success and payable out of the proceeds of the litigation, but that he may also, without violating the statute relating to champerty and maintenance,* agree to assume all costs and expenses of the litigation, and indemnify his client against them, as long as he did not, by the promise of such an agreement, or by the agreement, stir up the strife and induce the litigation.

[⁸]　　Coughlin *v.* N. Y. C. & H. R. R. R. Co. (71 *N. Y.* 443), upon which the defendant in the case at bar strongly relies, was a case which arose before the amendment of section 66 of the Code of Civil Procedure, in 1879, and in which it, moreover, conclusively appeared that the agreement of the attorney had induced the client to place the claim into the hands of the attorney for prosecution. It is clearly distinguishable from the case before me.

---

* *Code Civ. Pro.* §§ 74, *et seq.*

[*]   In the case at bar the complaining attorney is not the attorney who commenced the action, nor had he any interest in it at that time. No collusion between him and the attorney who brought the action is even suggested. By his agreement he did not obligate himself to assume the costs and expenses of the litigation and to hold the client harmless. He stirred up no strife and induced no litigation. It is clear, therefore, that the agreement is not void under any rule still in force, re ating to the doctrine of champerty and maintenance.

[*]   But the question still remains whether, under all the circumstances, the agreement was a fair one. Upon this point it appears that the agreement made with him concerning his compensation was made by the client, with the sanction of the attorney then of record : that the client has never complained of any unfairness, but has steadily insisted, and still insists, that the said complaining attorney is entitled to the whole of the compensation secured to him by the agreement. Under these circumstances, and in view of the many valuable services successfully rendered by said attorney, I cannot see how the court can pronounce the agreement an unfair one.

["]   If, then, the agreement was a fair one between attorney and client, how can the defendant claim the contrary ? There is neither authority nor principle for such a claim. As already shown, section 66 of the Code of Civil Procedure expressly provides that the compensation of an attorney or counsellor at law for his services is governed by agreement, express or implied. To that extent he has a lien. To uphold the contention of the defendant, the court would have to say that, though there may be one agreement between attorney and client as to the attorney's compensation, which is in all respects fair, the court may make another and different one between the attorney and the defendant, whenever the defendant sees fit to settle with the plaintiff, without the knowledge or consent of the attorney. If this can ever be done, it certainly cannot be done in a case like the present, in which the defendant settled in the face of express notice, and subject to the rights of the attorney, the full extent of which were made known.

["] In this connection reference should be made to the reasoning of the court at general term, in Tuttle v. Village of Cortland (21 *N. Y. Weekly Dig.* 528), which has been cited by the defendant, but which does not support defendant's contention. It was there said that section 66 of the Code of Civil Procedure is not designed to prevent litigants from fairly composing and settling their suits without the assent of their attorneys, but simply to protect attorneys from being deprived of their compensation by settlements which deprive them of the means to recover their compensation. But this was said concerning a settlement which in nowise impaired or imperiled the attorney's lien upon the judgment. The attorney claimed but $243.53. By the terms of the settlement, the good faith of which was not impugned, the sum of $1,112.53 was agreed to be paid at a future period, and upon that the lien of the attorney remained. It was for these reasons that it was held, and very properly held, that the attorney had no right to have the settlement set aside.

["] The examination so far made fully establishes that the complaining attorney had, at the time of the satisfaction of the judgment, an interest in and lien upon the judgment to the extent of $5,646.73, with interest thereon from March 24, 1884 ; that the defendant not only had constructive notice under section 66 of the Code, of the existence of a lien, for every person is presumed to know the law, but also had actual notice of the precise amount of the lien ; and that consequently the satisfaction of the judgment was in violation of the rights of said attorney. Moreover it was further shown that the said attorney also holds in his own right an absolute assignment to him by the plaintiff of one-half of the verdict and of all the costs of the action, and that the plaintiff is wholly insolvent.

Under these circumstances the attorney must be protected to the full extent of his rights in the premises, and the only remaining question is as to the manner in which it shall be done.

As pointed out in McCabe v. Fogg* the amendment of section 66 of the Code, passed in 1879, though giving a more extensive lien, provided no new remedy for the enforcement of the lien. In order to enforce it, therefore, in the case of a settlement before final judg-
["] ment, the attorney, while he need no longer prove fraud or collusion, must go on with the litigation until final judgment, as under the former practice.† The defendant cannot be compelled to pay by a mere order. To the same effect are Forstman v. Schulting (35 *Hun*, 504), and Albert Palmer Co. v. Van Orden (64 *How. Pr.* 79 ; as modified in 4 *N. Y. Civ. Pro.* 44).

How this practice probably originated was pointed out by EARL, J., in delivering the opinion of the court of appeals in Coughlin v. N. Y. C. & H. R. R. R. Co. (71 *N. Y.* 443).

["] My final conclusion is that the satisfaction of the judgment must be vacated and set aside except as to the sum of $5,000 released by the plaintiff, by virtue of his settlement, and that Mr. Truax, as attorney of the plaintiff, must be left at liberty to prose-

---

* 2 *N. Y. Monthly Law Bul.* 71.

† The attorney before proceeding in the action for the purpose of enforcing his lien must secure leave of court, Tullis v. Bushnell, 65 *How. Pr.* 465; Goddard v. Trenbath, 24 *Hun*, 182; Coster v. Greenpoint Ferry Co., 5 *N. Y. Civ. Pro.* 186.

cute the appeal still pending in the court of appeals,
and, in the event of an affirmance of the judgment, to
enforce the judgment to the extent of his rights in the
same manner as if no settlement between the plaintiff
and the defendant had taken place.

The motion is therefore granted to the extent indicated, with $10 costs.

HOFFMAN *v.* SCHWARTZ and Another.

City Court of New York, Special Term,
November, 1886.

§§ 723, 1189, 3176.

*Judgment—Where entered, where verdicts for different amounts found
against two defendants.*

Where, in an action against two defendants, to recover damages for
assault and battery committed by one defendant under the direction of the other, the jury found a verdict in favor of the plaintiff,
for $50 as against one defendant, and for six cents as against the
other,—*Held*, that the plaintiff properly remitted the six cents damages, and entered judgment for $50 and costs against the defend-
ants jointly, and that a motion to set aside a judgment so entered,
as irregular, should be denied.

(*Decided November* 1, 1886.)

Motion by defendant, J. Schwartz, to set aside the
judgment recovered against him, as unauthorized by
the verdict.

The opinion states the material facts.

Albert Steckler, for defendant and motion.

Gilbert D. Lamb, for plaintiff, opposed.

For the jury to sever the damages in an action of tort proved against two defendants is improper, but that irregularity in the verdict may be cured in either of two ways : (1) By entering a *nolle prosequi* as to one defendant and entering judgment against the other defendant for the damages assessed against him ; or, (2) by entering judgment against both defendants for the largest damages found against either, and remitting the lesser damages. The plaintiff has pursued the latter course here. The entry of judgment against both defendants in this action for the larger damages, the lesser having been remitted, is in accordance with the New York practice, and cures the irregularity in the verdict. Beal *v.* Finch, 11 *N. Y.* 128 ; O'Shea *v.* Kirker, 4 *Bosw.* 120 ; 3 *Wait's Law & Prac.* (5 ed.) 823. . . . The entry of judgment herein is correct and cures the irregularity of the verdict according to the Massachusett's Practice and the Common Law Practice. Halsey *v.* Woodruff, 9 *Pick.* (*Mass.*) 555 ; Sabin *v.* Long, 1 *Wils.* (*Eng. C. P.*) 30. . . . The verdict against defendant Schwartz for six cents, determines that he advised the assault, and that fixes his liability for the $50 damages awarded against Stenberger. *Sedgwick on Dam.* 73 : " In regard to the right invaded, a verdict and judgment for the smallest amount is as effectual as any sum, however large ; for it establishes the fact of the plaintiff's title. And in the common case of trespass to lands, the main object usually being to determine the right, this principle becomes very important." In actions in tort, where it is determined that several defendants participated in the wrong, each is liable for damages which the most culpable ought to pay. Berry *v.* Fletcher, 1 *Dill.* (*U. S. Circ. Ct.*) 67 ; 2 *Addison on Torts*, 1197 ; Brown *v.* Allen, 4 *Esp.* (*Eng. N. P.*) 158. The judgment, as entered herein, is correct in principle. The verdict herein necessarily

determines three facts and those sustain the judgment
as entered.   (1) The verdict determines that Stenberger
committed the assault.   (2) The verdict determines
that Schwartz ordered it.   (3) The verdict determines
that the damages according to the acts of the most
culpable was $50.   The law now steps in and says on
that verdict the plaintiff is absolutely entitled to a
judgment against both defendants for $50 damages.
By section 723 of the Code of Civil Procedure: The
court may at any stage of the action conform the
pleading or other proceedings to the facts proved.
"And in every stage of the action, the court must disregard an error or defect in the pleadings or other proceedings, which does not affect the substantial rights
of the adverse party."   The plaintiff having remitted
the six cents damages the judgments entered is in conformity to the verdict as required by section 1189 of
the Code of Civil Procedure.   That part of the verdict
having been remitted, as authorized by section 3176 of
the Code, the verdict signifies: " We find for plaintiff
against both defendants and assess the damages at
$50," and accordingly, the judgment is correct.   Bos-
worth, J., in O'Shea v. Kirker (4 *Bosw.* 120, at p.
129): "The severing of the damages, like the severance of damages by a jury, may be regarded as an
irregularity, not affecting any substantial right.   All
directions based on such irregularity may be corrected,
and judgment given according to the justice and law
of the case.   A correct judgment has been entered.
If any irregularity, error or defect in the pleadings or
proceedings, has occurred in the progress of the trial
up to or in entering the judgment, which shall not
affect the substantial rights of either defendant, the
court is required by section 176 to disregard it, and is
prohibited from reversing the judgment by reason
thereof."   All the authorities without exception sustain the proposition that when a verdict is rendered

against two defendants in action of tort, in which both parties participated, and the jury severed the damages, the verdict is cured by an entry of judgment against both for the larger damages and remitting the former. There is not a single case on record, where, in an action of tort proved against two defendants, the jury having undertaken to sever the damages , and plaintiff having remitted the lesser damages and entered a joint judgment against both, such a judgment was held irregular, vacated, and severed on appeal. A case in which precisely such an application as this was denied was that of Bulkley *v.* Smith (1 *Duer*, 643), decided in 1352 (though reversed on another point in 2 *Duer*, 271), and sustained in 1859 by O'Shea *v.* Kirker (*supra*) . . . . . The plaintiff's practice must not be confounded with that in such cases as · Hill *v.* Goodchild, 5 *Burr.* 2791 (Opinion by Lord MANSFIELD in 1771), where the plaintiff's judgment was reversed on appeal because he had entered judgment against all the defendants for the total amount of damages.

HALL, J.—Defendant Schwartz moves to set aside the judgment entered against him as unauthorized by the verdict and void.

This action was brought against the defendants for damages for a joint assault and battery committed upon him by defendants. The complaint, instead of merely charging a joint assault and battery, sets forth the facts which plaintiff claims makes the defendant Schwartz jointly liable with the defendant Sternberger viz. ; that Schwartz directed the commission of the assault by Sternberger, his servant. I fail to discover how this could injure the defendant. It gave him notice of the grounds upon which the plaintiff sought to hold him liable, instead of merely stating the commission of the assault, and proving the facts and applying the law which would fix his liability.

The case was tried before the court and a jury, and the evidence was very conflicting, and the jury, after long deliberation, found a verdict against both defendants, assessing damages against defendant Sternberger at $50, and against defendant Schwartz at six cents, and upon that verdict judgment has been entered against both defendants for $50 and costs.*

The verdict of the jury clearly establishes the fact that both defendants committed the assault, but they attempt to apportion the damages between them ; this has never been allowed, because the verdict establishes the amount of money in which the plaintiff has been damaged under the rules of law laid down by the court, and the law says that the defendants are jointly liable for the entire damages without regard to the proportionate part of the injury which was inflicted by either.†

The authorities cited by plaintiff abundantly sustain this view, and it is founded in sound reason.

No motion was made at the close of the trial to correct the verdict, or for further instructions to the jury.

The judgment entered is correct, and the motion to vacate it is denied, without costs.

---

* The plaintiff remitted the six cents damages. *Ed.*

† As to the effect of the payment of one of two judgments recovered against joint tort feasors in separate actions for the same wrong, see Lord *v.* Tiffany, 98 *N. Y.* 412, 421, and cases there cited.

MOODY, Appellant, v. STEELE, Respondent.

City Court of New York, General Term, November, 1886.

§ 501, sub'd 2.

Counter-claim.—What causes of action cannot be set up as.

In an action on contract, a counter-claim consisting of another cause of action on contract, to be available to the defendant, must both have existed and belonged to the defendant at the time the action was commenced.*

Where, in an action on contract the answer set up as a counter-claim, a cause of action on a note, and it did not appear when the defendant became the owner thereof,—*Held*, that the counter-claim was insufficient and the objection appearing on the face of the answer, it was properly taken by demurrer.

Moody v. Steele (10 *N. Y. Civ. Pro.* 67), reversed.

(*Decided November*, 1886.)

Appeal by plaintiff from interlocutory judgment overruling demurrer to counter-claim set up in answer.

Reported below, 10 *N. Y. Civ. Pro.* 67

The action was brought to recover $345 for board and lodgings furnished defendant by the plaintiff. The answer, without putting in issue any of the allegations of the complaint, set out as a counter-claim, a cause of action for $240 and interest, from June 1, 1880, on a promissory note made by the plaintiff to one Mary E. Steele, and by her transferred to the defendant. The answer did not state when such transfer was made, and the only allegation in the answer respecting

---

* See note on counter-claims, 3 *N. Y. Civ. Pro.* 212, 215, where the principle here laid down is stated to be the general rule.

it was as follows: "That said note has been duly indorsed by said Mary E. Steele, to and is now the property of this defendant, and the amounts due thereon belong to this defendant."

The plaintiff demurred to the counter-claim on the grounds:

"1. That the said alleged counter-claim is not of the character specified in section 501 of the Code of Civil Procedure.

"2. That the said alleged counter-claim does not state facts sufficient to constitute a cause of action.

"3. That the said alleged counter-claim is insufficient in law."

This demurrer was overruled by the special term, and the plaintiff appealed.

Christopher Fine, for plaintiff-appellant.

In order that a claim alleged to exist against the plaintiff in an action, may be available as a counter-claim in favor of the defendant, the fact must be, and the answer must allege that the defendant was the owner and holder of such claim, before the time of the commencement of the action. The law will not encourage litigation by allowing a defendant, after an action has been commenced against him upon a just claim, to fish up, hunt up, stir up, or buy up doubtful or other claims against the plaintiff, and interpose them as a defense against a claim to which otherwise the defendant has no defense. We submit that would be worse than any champerty or barratry yet heard of. The learned judge below concedes and states in his opinion that prior to the Code of Civil Procedure (§ 501), no claim against the plaintiff could be available to a defendant in the action as a counter-claim, unless the defendant was the owner of that claim before the commencement of such action. The learned judge failed to observe that the provisions of the Code of

Civ. Pro. § 501, as to what constitutes a counter-claim, and may be set up as such, are the same as were those of section 150 of the old Code of Procedure on that subject. Section 501 of the Code of Civil Procedure provides amongst other things, that "The counter-claim. . . . must be one of the following causes of action against the plaintiff. . . and in favor of the defendant. . . . 2d. In an action on contract, any other cause of action on contract existing at the commencement of' the action." Now the Code of Procedure, section 150 (of which section 501 of the Code of Civil Procedure is a mere re codification on this subject), provided that—"The counter-claim. . . must be one existing in favor of the defendant and against the plaintiff. . . arising out of the following causes of action : . . . . 2d. In an action (arising) on contract, any other cause of action (arising also) on contract, and existing at the commencement of the action." It is thus seen that the law of counter-claim must necessarily be the same under the old and the new Code, for the respective provisions of each are exactly the same—the Code of Civil Procedure merely dropping the words "arising" and "arising also" appearing in parenthesis, the above quotation from the old Code—which, of course, in no way affects the character of the respective provisions.

The authorities under the Code of Procedure, section 150, very plainly and without exception sustain the plaintiff's contention in the case at bar. "A counter-claim must exist in favor of the defendant, and against the plaintiff, at the time the action was commenced, and an answer alleging that the plaintiff is indebted, &c., and that the sum claimed is now due and, &c., is bad on demurrer." Rice v. O'Connor, 10 Abb. Pr. 362, 364. "The rights of the parties to a legal action must be determined as they existed at the commencement of the action." Wisner v. Occum-

paugh, 71 *N. Y.* 113, 117. . . . . . . "A counter-
claim must have belonged to the defendant at the
commencement of the action." Chambers *v.* Lewis, 11
Abb. Pr. 210, 213. . . . The general term of the
New York superior court, in speaking of this subject,
say : " In an action arising on contract the defendant
may set up as a counter-claim any other cause of
action arising also on contract. . . and existing at the
commencement of the action. . . and owned by
such defendant at- the time of the commencement of
the action and due at said time," citing many cases
and old Code, § 150, subd. 2. Chamboret *v.* Cagney,
32 *N. Y. Super. Ct.* 382. "A defendant cannot set
up as a counter-claim, a note made by the plaintiff,
unless it was due and belonged to the defendant when
the action was commenced." Van Valen *v.* Lapham,
13 *How. Pr.* 240, 247. . . . The court here also
considers the provisions of the Revised Statute (2 *R.
S.* 354, § 12, subd. 4), as to set-offs. See also Andrews
v. Artisans' Bank, 26 *N. Y.* 298 ; Willover *v.* First
Nat'l Bank, 10 *N. Y. Civ. Pro.* 80.

The learned judge below, if I may beg to suggest,
seemed to have been led into the error, complained of
on this appeal by a note in Bliss' Code of Civ. Pro. to
section 501, to the effect that, in the opinion of the
editor, it was supposed that such sections of the
Revised Statutes relating to set-offs as were not superseded by, or inconsistent with Code of Procedure, section 150, remained in force, and then adds, that the
following portions of the section of the Revised Statutes, regulating set-offs, are regarded as thus abrogated, to wit: 2 *R. S.* 354, part 3, ch. 6, tit. 2, § 18, subd.
1 to 6 (3 *R. S.* 634, 5 ed.), the fourth subdivision of
which reads as follows : " It (the set-off) must have
existed at the time of the commencement of the suit,
and must then have belonged to the defendant." By
looking at this note and a similar one, now appearing

in Throop's Code of Civil Procedure, edition of 1886, to section 501, it will be found, we think, that such note was not meant to affect or question the law as established by the above authorities, but quite the contrary. (1st.) It relates to set-offs as such, under the Revised Statutes. (2d.) The Code of Procedure § 150, and the Code of Civil Procedure, § 501, only supersede and only by superseding abrogate those provisions of the Revised Statutes as to set-offs as such, but do not repeal or destroy the legal principle involved, but express the same thing as to counter-claims in a different form of language. The Revised Statutes on this subject are codified, and the same principle preserved in the counter-claim of section 501 of the Code of Civil Procedure. Van Valen v. Lapham, 13 *How. Pr.* 240, 247 ; Chambers v. Lewis, 11 *Abb. Pr.* 210, 213.

Demurrer is the proper remedy and practice. *Code of. Civ. Pro.* §§ 494, 465. . . . "The defendant should have alleged in his answer which professes to set up new matter as a defense [or a counter-claim] that the amount [set up as a counter-claim] was due and owing to him from the plaintiff before and at the time of the commencement of the action. Not having alleged this, the demurrer to the defense (counter-claim), was properly sustained." Rice v. O'Connor, 10 *Abb. Pr.* 362. . . An answer which sets up new matter as a defense (or counter-claim), and does not state facts sufficient to constitute such defense, may be demurred to for insufficiency. Merritt v. Millard, 5 *Bosw.* 645, 652, 653 ; Rice v. O'Connor, 10 *Abb. Pr.* 362, 364 ; Bates v. Rosekrans, 37 *N. Y.* 409, 411 ; Allen v. Haskins, 5 *Duer*, 332, 335 ; Vasseur v. Livingston, 13 *N. Y.* 248, 251.

McAdam, Ch. J.—The court below properly held that under the former Code (§ 150) a counter-claim to be available to a defendant must have belonged to him at the commencement of the action, but erred in holding that under the present Code of Civil Procedure (§ 501) no such requirement exists. Subdivision 2 of that section, following the language of section 150 of the old Code, provides that the counter-claim pleaded must' be one "existing at the commencement of the action," which means that it must be a counter-claim held and owned by the defendant at that time. To permit a claim existing before, but acquired after the action had been commenced to be interposed as a counter-claim, would be a departure from the rule by which actions are to be determined according to the rights of the parties as they existed at the time they are commenced. It would also encourage barratry, a practice which receives no favor from the courts. The law never intended to permit a defendant, after an action had been commenced against him, to buy up, for purposes of litigation and defense, doubtful or other claims against the plaintiff, and then interpose them to defeat in whole or in part, a demand against which the defendant had no defense at the time the suit was brought. The statute in regard to counter-claims was intended as a shield to protect defendants from being required to pay more than the amount actually owing by them over and above all counter-claims existing at the time suit was brought, without requiring them to institute cross actions for the recovery of their cross demands. It was also intended to prevent multiplicity of suits, and to prevent, not encourage, litigation. The cases sustain these propositions (Rice *v.* O'Connor, 1 *Abb. Pr.* 362 ; Wisner *v.* Occumpaugh, 71 *N. Y.* 113 ; Chambers *v.* Lewis, 11 *Abb. Pr.* 210 ; Van Valen *v.* Lapham, 13 *How. Pr.* 240 ; Chamboret *v.* Cagney, 32 *N. Y. Super. Ct. R.* 382). The objection in the present instance appeared on the face of the answer and was properly presented by demurrer. It

follows, therefore, that the interlocutory judgment for
the defendant and the order directing its entry must
be reversed and judgment ordered for the plaintiff on
the demurrer, with costs.

HYATT, J., concurred.

ÉSTATE OF FRÉEMAN J. FITHIAN, DECEASED.

SURROGATE'S COURT, NEW YORK COUNTY, NOVEM-
BER, 1886.

§ 2606.

*Executor and administrator—Extent of account of trust estate required
of personal representative of deceased executor or administrator—
To whom should be required to deliver trust property.*

The personal representative of a deceased executor or administrator,
A., of the estate of one B., should, upon an accounting as to B.'s
estate account not only in respect to the assets of B.'s estate,
which came into her hands, but also in regard to her decedent's
administration from the day of his appointment until his death.

The personal representative of a deceased executor or administrator,
can only be required to deliver trust property of such executor's
or administrator's decedent into court, or to a newly appointed
representative of the decedent's estate, and cannot be required to
deliver it to any person claiming as legatee, next of kin or creditor
of such decedent.

The authority of the surrogate to compel the personal representative
of a deceased executor or administrator to deliver over trust property of the executor's or administrator's decedent, is limited to
such property of said decedent, as has come to the possession or
under the control of the personal representative of said executor
or administrator.

(*Decided November* 29, 1886.)

(1) Proceeding against Mary J. Clark, executrix, etc.,
of Lemuel B. Clark for the making and settlement of

the accounts of her decedent, as executor, etc., of Freeman J. Fithian, deceased ; also (2) Petition for the delivery by said executrix of the property of said Fithian.

The facts appear in the opinion.

Cornell, Secor & Page, for heirs of decedent and motions.

G. W. Cotterill, for Mary J. Clark, opposed.

NUMBER ONE.

ROLLINS, S.—The will of this decedent, who died on August 4, 1884, named Lemuel B. Clark as its executor. Mr. Clark was granted letters testamentary on October 15, 1884. He died on June 9, 1886, having rendered no account of his administration. He left a will, of which his widow, Mary J. Clark, is executrix. She qualified as such on July 7, 1886. On the succeeding day a proceeding was instituted in this court by Mrs. Harriet J. Fithian, widow of the testator, and beneficiary under his will, for an order requiring Mrs. Clark, as executrix of her late husband's estate, to render and settle his account as Mr. Fithian's executor.

On October 14, 1886, the respondent filed an account, the scope and character whereof are indicated by its opening sentence, which is as follows: " I, Mary J. Clark, executrix of Lemuel B. Clark, deceased, who was himself executor of Freeman J. Fithian, deceased, do hereby account for all money and other property received by me as such executrix belonging to the estate of the said Freeman J. Fithian, deceased."

It is insisted on behalf of the petitioner that by virtue of section 2606 of the Code of Civil Procedure (and it is upon that section that the present proceeding is founded), she is entitled to an accounting from this respondent not only as regards all money and property of the testator's estate which have come to the respondent's hands, but also as regards all such money and property as came at any time to the hands of the respondent's late husband.

I had occasion in several reported cases which arose before the enactment of chapter 399 of the Laws of 1884 to consider the extent of the surrogate's authority to require the executor or administrator of a decedent A, who had acted in his lifetime as the executor or administrator of a decedent B, to account for A's dealings with B's estate (Le Count *v.* Le Count, 1 *Dem.* 29 ; Maze *v.* Brown, 2 *Dem.* 217 ; Murray *v.* Vanderpoel, 2 *Id.* 311 ; Bunnell *v.* Ranney, 2 *Id.* 327).

In the cases just cited it was held that such accounting could be insisted upon only to the extent that the representative of the deceased executor or administrator had come into possession of assets belonging to the estate of such deceased executor's or administrator's decedent.

These limitations were removed by the act of 1884, above referred to, and section 2606 was so amended as to provide that, " where an executor or administrator dies, the surrogate's court has the same jurisdiction to compel the executor or administrator of the decedent" (that is, of such deceased executor or administrator) " to account which it would have against the decedent" (such deceased executor or administrator meaning) "if his letters had been revoked by a surrogate's decree."

Now, in the present case, if this respondent's testator were alive he could be required, even though his letters testamentary had been revoked, to account for his entire administration of this estate. And such an account is precisely what may be required of his executrix, *i. e.*, and account of her husband's administration from the day of his appointment until his death. The only important practical change effected by the act of 1884 is one that relates purely to methods of procedure. But for that act the cause which any person interested as legatee in the estate of this testator would be obliged to pursue in bringing about an adjustment of the claims of such estate, upon the estate of the testator's deceased executor, Clark, would have been that which is pointed out in the cases above cited. The new statute has provided a short and simpler method of adjustment. 1 must, therefore, sustain the petitioner's objection that the account of the respondent is on its face incomplete. It may be amended, and after amendment the petitioner will be allowed to file new objections.

NUMBER TWO.

In the foregoing memorandum I have held that this respondent, as executrix of her late husband, must account not only for such assets of Mr. Fithian's estate as have come to her hands, but for all assets of that estate that at any time came to the hands of her deceased husband. But the authority of the surrogate under section 2306 of the Code of Civil Procedure, to compel an executor or administrator of a deceased executor or administrator of a decedent "to deliver over trust property" of such decedent, is limited to such property as has come to the possession or is under the control of the representative of such decedent's deceased executor or administrator. And even as regards such property the surrogate cannot direct a delivery to any person claiming as legatee, next of kin or creditor of such decedent. The statute contemplates a delivery into court or to a newly appointed representative of the decedent's estate. By no other course could the rights of all persons interested in such estate be properly protected (Spencer v. Popham, 5 *Redf*. 425). This application must be denied.

GARSDEN, Respondent, v. WOODWARD, Appellant.

DIXON, Respondent, v. SAME, Appellant.

COURT OF APPEALS, OCTOBER, 1886

§§ 523, 837.

Verification.—When answer need not be verified*—Action against trustee of corporation for penalty for failure to file report.*

An action to recover a debt due by a manufacturing corporation, from one of its trustees on the ground that he has failed to file an annual report, is an action for a penalty or forfeiture ; any admission made in the answer, in support of the plaintiff's allegations, would necessarily tend to expose the defendant to a penalty, and he, therefore, need not verify his answer, notwithstanding the plaintiff verified the complaint.

Garsden v. Woodward (38 *Hun*, 548), reversed.

(*Decided October* 5, 1886.)

Appeal by the defendant in each action from an order of the general term of the supreme court in the first department, affirming an order denying a motion to compel the plaintiff to receive an unverified answer. Reported below (38 *Hun*, 548).

The facts appear in the opinion.

James B. Dill, for defendant-appellant.

Wilmot & Gage, for plaintiff-respondent.

RAPALLO, J.—The Code of Civil Procedure provides that the verification of an answer may be omitted—where not otherwise expressly prescribed—where

---

* See note on Verification of Pleadings, 8 *N. Y. Civ. Pro.* 438, 441.

the party pleading would be privileged from testifying as a witness concerning an allegation or denial contained in the pleading (§ 523).

Section 837 declares that a witness shall not be required to give an answer which will tend to expose him to a penalty or forfeiture.

This action is brought against the defendant to recover a debt due by a manufacturing corporation of which he was trustee, and he is sought to be made liable therefor on the ground that he failed to make the annual report required by the general manufacturing law. The action is not to recover a debt which he owes, but to impose upon him, as a penalty for his default, the payment of the debt of the corporation.

We have repeatedly held that such an action is an action for a penalty or forfeiture. Any admission which he might make in his answer, in support of the plaintiff's allegations, would, therefore, necessarily tend to expose him to a penalty (Merchants' Bank v. Bliss, 35 N. Y. 412 ; Veeder v. Baker, 83 Id. 156 ; Stokes v. Stickney, 96 Id. 326).

The liability sought to be enforced against the defendant does not arise out of any contract obligation, but is imposed by the statute as a penalty for disobedience of its requirement.

The distinction between the nature of this liability and that of stockholders under the same statute is clearly pointed out in Wiles v. Suydam (64 N. Y. 173) ; Veeder v. Baker (83 Id. 153, 160).

This action is not founded on any debt owing by the defendant. The debts owing by the company are made the measure of the penalty.

The orders should be reversed, and the motions granted, with costs in the court below, and one bill of costs in this court.

All concurred, except MILLER, J., absent.

LATTEMAN v. FERE, et al.

N. Y. Court of Common Pleas, Special Term, November, 1886.

§§ 2944, 3216.

N. Y. court of common pleas—Power of, to amend pleadings in action removed to it from district court.

In an action in a district court of the city of New York, to recover for work, labor and services, the court has power to permit the amendment of an answer, which is substantially a general denial, so that it will set up payment,[2] and it is the duty of the court to allow amendments to the pleadings in furtherance of justice, at any time before final judgment.[3]

The New York court of common pleas has the same power to permit the amendment of pleadings in an action removed to it from a district court, as the district court would have had if the action had not been removed.[1]

Smith v. White (23 N. Y. 572);[4] Salter v. Parkhurst (2 *Daly*, 240);[5] Fagan v. Poor (11 *N.Y. Civ. Pro.* 220, *note*),[6] distinguished.

Where, on a motion for leave to amend the answer, consisting of a general denial, so as to set up payment in an action removed from a district court to the New York court of common pleas, it appeared that a bill of particulars was served September 27, but that the defendant's attorney being sick, did not see it until a few days before making the motion, and until then did not know of what items the claim sued on consisted; and it also appeared that pending the proceedings for removing the cause, a bill of particulars was served by mail, which the defendant's attorney never received.—*Held*, that the defendant was not guilty of such laches as would defeat the motion,[1] and that it should be granted.[2]

(*Decided November* 27, 1886.)

Motion by defendant for leave to serve a supplemental answer setting up payment.

The material facts are stated in the opinion.

George F. Duysters, for defendant and motion.

Henry A. Vien, for plaintiff, opposed.

BOOKSTAVER, J.—Motion for leave to serve an amended answer setting up the defense of payment.

This action was commenced in the eight district court, February 6, 1886.

Issues were joined in that court February 11, 1886.

The pleadings were oral, the complaint being for work, labor and services ; and the answer a general denial.

At the time of joining issue, defendants gave a bond to remove the action to this court; and the sureties having justified, the action was removed to this court February 17, 1886.

Defendants noticed the action for trial March 23, 1886; but the order requiring written pleadings was not made until September 23, 1886.

On September 27, a written complaint was served, which was substantially the same as the oral complaint in the court below.

Defendants' time to answer was extended until November 6, 1886, when they served an answer, which was in substance a general denial.

On November 17, 1886, defendants served an amended answer, setting up the defense of payment.

This answer was returned to the defendants' attor. ney on the ground that it did not conform to the pleadings in the court below.

The defendants thereupon moved to amend the order directing written pleadings to be served, by striking out that portion directing such pleadings "to conform to the oral pleadings" in the court below, and for leave to serve an amended answer setting up payment.

To this plaintiff interposes two objections :

First. That the defendants have been guilty of laches.

Second. That this court has not power to grant amendments to the pleadings in actions removed from the district courts.

[']   In respect to the first objection, it is sufficient to say that the written complaint and bill of particulars were not served until September 27 ; that the defendants' attorney was then sick and had been for some time, and that he did not see the bill of particulars showing that a part of the claim was for salary for the month of December, 1885, until a few days ago, and that he moved promptly as soon as the fact of this claim was discovered.

It is true, the plaintiff's attorney claims that he served a bill of particulars before the cause was removed from the district court; but this service, the plaintiff admits, was made by mail, pending the proceedings to remove the cause.

I can see no reason why this should have been done ; but if it was, defendants' attorney denies having received it. And I think, upon the papers submitted to me, the defendants should be allowed to serve the amended answer, if this court has power to grant amendments in such cases.

[']   Had this case remained in the district court, that court would undoubtedly have had the power to allow the amendment now proposed (Reeder v. Sayre, 70 *N. Y.* 180 ; Stern v. Drinker, 2 *E. D. Smith*, 402).

[']   Indeed, it is made the duty of these courts to allow amendments to the pleadings in the furtherance of justice at any time before final judgment (*Code Civ. Pro.* § 2944).

Has this court less power, when such actions are removed to it?

Plaintiff contends that the issues made by the

Latteman v. Fere.

pleadings in the court below are those to be tried on
the removal of an action to this court and that there
can be no amendment to them. In aid of his contention he cites Smith v. White (23 *N. Y.* 572); Salter v.
Parkhurst (2 *Daly*, 240); Fagan v. Poor (*Daily Reg.*
August 17, 1886).*

---

* As the *Daily Register* of August 17, 1886, contains only a memorandum of the decision in Fagan v. Poor, the following more complete report of the case is given.

FAGAN v. POOR.

N. Y. COURT OF COMMON PLEAS, SPECIAL TERM, AUGUST, 1886.

§§ 2944, 3216.

*Amendment of answer.— When not allowed in action removed from dis-
trict court to N. Y. court of common pleas.*

The issues to be tried in an action removed from a district to the
N. Y. court of common pleas are the same as those created by the
pleadings in the court below. Accordingly,—*Held*, where in an
action to recover rent and for money expended for the defendant's
account, the answer in the district court was a general denial, that
the answer could not be so amended after the action was removed
to the N. Y. court of common pleas, as also to set up the defense
of payment.

(*Decided August* 16, 1886.)

Motion by defendant for leave to amend his answer herein.

The action was brought in the third district court to recover $35,
money alleged to have been expended by plaintiff for the defendant, and at his instance "in shoring up the stoop of premises No. 105
West eleventh street, in the city of New York," also, to recover $125,
rent of said premises for the month of April, 1886. The answer
was a general denial. The action was removed to the N. Y. court
of common pleas, and the defendant served an answer denying the
allegations of the complaint respecting the first cause of action—to
recover money expended;—admitting the hiring of the said premises,
but denying "the remaining terms of the lease as set forth" in the
complaint, and alleging payment "of any and all rental agreed to be
paid by her in and by the terms of said lease." The answer was
returned and the defendant moved for leave to serve it as an amended
answer.

Lauterbach & Spingarn, for defendant and motion.

I do not think these cases support him.

[']   Smith *v.* White only decides that where an action has been removed from a district court to this court no appeal will lie to the court of appeals from a judgment of this court without an order of the general term allowing such appeal.

This decision is based upon the theory that the action continues in its nature to be an action in a district court, although removed to this court for trial.

As a corollary to this it would seem that neither party should be deprived of any of the rights which they would have in the court below by reason of such removal, including, of course, the right to amend the pleadings to the same extent, and within the same limits, that might have been allowed had no such removal taken place; and I find nothing in the opinion of the court of appeals in variance with this view.

[']   The case of Salter *v.* Parkhurst (*supra*), at first sight, lends more countenance to plaintiff's contention. In that case, after the removal of the action to this court, it was referred. On the trial before the referee he allowed the complaint to be amended so as to charge the defendant's separate estate, she being a married woman.

This amendment made the gist of the action one of which the district court did not have original jurisdiction, and this court decided that it was error to allow such an amendment. This was all there was before the court for decision, and, I think, was all the court intended to decide.

William C. Carpenter, for plaintiff, opposed.

ALLEN, J.—The issues created by the pleadings in the court below, are those to be tried on the removal of the action to this court (See Salter *v.* Parkhurst, 2 *Daly*, 240, and Smith *v.* White, 23 *N. Y.* 572).

Motion for leave to amend answer denied, with costs.

It is true that in the course of the decision, BRADY, J., in speaking of Smith *v.* White, says that that case "determines that the issues created by the pleadings in the court below are those to be tried on its removal to this court;" but he immediately adds, that it "continues in all respects to be an action in a district court, the trial of which is to be had in this court."

If it continues to be, in effect, an action in a district court, then it must be subject to the incidents of such an action, among which is the right of amendment of the pleadings, within the limits of the jurisdiction of the district courts.

And this seems to have been contemplated by the general term, for BRADY, J., says, "The removal cannot be made until after issue joined; and the issues cannot be so changed that a subject, not of original jurisdiction, may be litigated against the consent of one of the parties." This must be read in connection with the passage before quoted and is very far from deciding that no amendment of the pleadings can be allowed by this court. On the other hand, I think it implies that they may be amended within the limits of original jurisdiction, and the power of the court below to grant, which, as we have seen, is very great.

['] I do not know the facts in the case of Fagan *v.* Poor; but the decision manifestly is based upon and follows Salter *v.* Parkhurst, and I presume was decided under a similar state of facts.

['] I am, therefore, of the opinion that this court has power to permit amendments to pleadings, within the limits above indicated, where a proper case has been made out. And I am confirmed in it by the views expressed in Ludwig *v.* Minnot (4 *Daly*, 481).

If no such power existed in this court justice might miscarry, as in this case, if it is true that the plaintiff's salary for the month of December, 1885, has been actually paid, and the defendants were not permitted to show that fact.

[*] Motion granted upon the payment of $10 costs to plaintiff, and defendants stipulating not to postpone the trial of the action on account of such amendment being allowed.

BROWNING, Respondent, v. HAYES, Appellant.

Supreme Court, Second Department, General Term, July, 1886.

§§ 2434, 2442.

Supplemental proceedings—Form of order made in one county for examination in another.

Where an order is made by a justice of the supreme court in one judicial district for the examination of a judgment debtor, in proceedings supplementary to execution in another judicial district, the order must be made returnable before a judge of the district in which the examination is to be held. Accordingly,—*Held*, that an order made by a judge of the supreme court in King's county for the examination of a non-resident judgment debtor, having a place of business in New York city, before a referee in that city, which did not direct that subsequent proceedings be before a judge of the supreme court, in the first judicial district, was irregular, and should be set aside.

(*Decided July* 23, 1886.)

Appeal by judgment debtor from order denying motion to vacate order for his examination in proceedings supplementary to execution.

The order for the examination of the judgment debtor, after reciting the facts, read as follows:

"I do hereby order and require the judgment debtor to appear before Samuel W. Bower, Esq., a counsellor of this court, who is hereby duly appointed a referee herein at his office, No. 35 Pine street, in the city of New York, on the 24th day of March, 1886, at 2 o'clock in the afternoon, and on such further days as the court or referee duly appointed shall name, to make discovery on oath concerning his property. And the said judgment debtor is hereby forbidden to transfer or make any other disposition of the property belonging to him not exempt by law from execution, or in any manner to interfere therewith, until further order in the premises.

"Dated at Brooklyn, at the Court House, the 19th day of March, 1886.   "C. E. PRATT
                                                    "J. S. C."

The judgment debtor moved to vacate this order, and his motion was denied, and from the order thereupon entered he took this appeal.

Other facts appear in the opinion.

William R. Garrard, for judgment-debtor, appellant.

An order to examine a debtor residing, or having a place of business out of the judicial district of the justice making the order, should require all subsequent proceedings to be had before a judge in the county where the debtor resides or has a place of business. Shaltz *v.* Andrews, 6 *N. Y. Weekly Dig.* 156 ; Pardee *v.* Tilton, 83 *N. Y.* 623.

Charles S. Simpkins, for judgment-creditor, respondent.

It will be seen by section 2434 of the Code of Civil Procedure that the judges of the supreme court are only called in to act where other judges are unable to act, in judgments obtained in their courts. The supreme court is excluded from this provision, and this section only provides in the event of such disqualification of the judges as mentioned, that the order to examine or the warrant to arrest a judgment debtor, shall be returnable before the supreme court judge residing in the district where the judgment debtor is to be examined, and that the order to examine the judgment debtor in that event, should direct that all proceedings be had in the county where such judge resides, and where the judgment debtor is to be examined, and not otherwise. This section is entirely different from section 292 of the old Code, under which some decisions have been made as to the directions in the order, that the examination shall be had in the county where the judgment debtor resides, or has a place of business. Baldwin *v.* Perry, 1 *N. Y. Civ. Pro.* 118.

BARNARD, P. J.—The plaintiff obtained a judgment in Kings county in the supreme court. A transcript was filed in the county of New York, and an execution was issued to the sheriff of that county and returned unsatisfied.

The defendant is a non-resident of the State, and has a place of business in the county of New York. An order was made by a judge of the supreme court in Kings county that the defendant appear before a referee in the city of New York.

The order does not provide that the subsequent proceedings be had before a justice of the supreme court of the first judicial district. I think the order is irregular in this respect, and cannot stand. Section 2434 of the Code of Civil Procedure is not very plain. It can be gathered therefrom, by a very strict reading, that it is only in cases where a supreme court justice makes the order in the place of other inferior judges, that a provision must be inserted making the order returnable before a supreme court justice or other local magistrate of the judicial district where the order is to be executed.

This reading is not the true one. A debtor non-resident cannot be taken out of the county where his place of business is. When, therefore, an order to examine a judgment debtor is made by a justice of the supreme court to examine a debtor in another judicial district, the order must be made returnable before a judge of that district, and the words, " in that case," in section 2434, do not alone refer to orders made by inferior judges, but are intended to embrace all orders to be made " before a justice of the supreme court." By section 2442 the referee must certify the evidence to the judge before whom the order is made returnable. This language would not be proper in the ordinary case of an order made in a county where the debtor resided by an officer therein.*

The order should, therefore, be reversed, with costs and disbursements, and the motion granted, with costs, all costs to be applied on the judgment.

DYKMAN, J., concurred ; CULLEN, J., not sitting.

---

* Mr. Justice BARTLETT, in making the decision on which the order appealed from was entered, said in reference to this point : " It is urged that the order is defective, in not requiring all proceedings hereafter to be had in New York county before a justice, to be specified in the order, but that requirement of the old Code does not appear to be retained in the present Code of Civil Procedure; the judgment debtor is entitled. if a non-resident, as in this case, to be examined in the county where his place of business is situated (*Code of Civ. Pro.* § 2459). But he may be examined there before a referee, and, in that event, the referee must certify the evidence and other proceedings to the judge to whom the order is returnable (*Code of Civ. Pro.* § 2442). It is not entirely clear what this expression means in such a case as the present, but I am inclined to think it means the judge by whom this order is granted, and that the proper course for the referee herein will be to report the testimony to Mr. Justice PRATT."

IN RE CHARLES E. HAIGHT, AN IMPRISONED
DEBTOR.

COUNTY COURT CHAUTAUQUA COUNTY, MAY, 1886.

§ 2200 *et seq.*, 2204, 2208.

Discharge of judgment debtor from imprisonment—What use of property will prevent.—Fourteen day act.

To entitle a judgment debtor, imprisoned by virtue of an execution to collect a sum of money, issued in a civil action or proceeding, to be discharged therefrom under section 2200 *et seq.* of the Code of Civil Procedure his proceeding must be "just and fair," [¹] *i. e.,* the affidavit that the debtor is required by section 2204 of the Code of Civil Procedure to make must be true in its letter and spirit. [²]

A judgment debtor cannot be discharged from imprisonment under execution, pursuant to sections 2200 *et seq.* of the Code of Civil Procedure who has disposed of property with the intent to defraud existing creditors, and that whether the disposition was made before or after the action in which he was arrested; [³] but to prevent a discharge there must have been an intent to defraud existing creditors of whom the creditor contesting the discharge is one. [²]

Where, in a proceeding under section 2200 *et seq.* of the Code of Civil Procedure for the discharge from imprisonment of a judgment debtor, it appeared that the judgment upon which the execution under which he was imprisoned was issued was rendered in 1881 in an action to recover $500 with interest alleged to have been obtained by the defendant from the plaintiff through duress and by means of threats on November 13, 1875; that he defended the action and moved for a nonsuit but offered no evidence himself, and appealed to the general term from an order denying a new trial which was there affirmed, and the debtor swore upon his examination in said proceedings that he never had said $500,—*Held,* that his failure to account for the disposition of the $500 would not prevent his discharge; [⁴] that the fact that 17 or 18 years before the time of applying for his discharge (1886) he caused property belonging to him to be conveyed to his wife, would not prevent his discharge as

In re Haight.

the judgment creditor's debt did not then exist; [',*] that the use of
money ($998.40) received by the debtor in the December preceding
the January in which the action against him was tried, to defend
the action and take the appeal, and in traveling about out of the
State,—which he left to escape arrest, for the purpose of " killing
time " and looking for a situation, was a disposition of his property
with intent to injure and defraud his creditor and prevented his
discharge, [']* and this although he swears that he did not intend
to injure or defraud any creditor. [']
The occasion and history of the " Stillwell Act " and the practice
  before its passage and under it, stated.†
(*Decided May* 25, 1886.)

Application by Charles E. Haight, a judgment
debtor, imprisoned by virtue of an execution to collect a sum of money, issued out of the supreme court
in a civil action, to be discharged from imprisonment.

The facts appear in the opinion.

Silas . W. Mason, for the judgment-debtor and
application.

Walter W. Holt, for judgment-creditor, opposed.

MARVIN SMITH, Sp. Co. J.—The statute abolishing
imprisonment for debt adopted in 1831, known as the
    Stillwell Act, forbids arrest and imprisonment up-¹
['] on civil process in all suits and proceedings founded
    upon contract, except where the action is. brought
to recover for a debt fraudulently contracted and like
cases, and provides for the application of the debtor's
property, if he have any, toward the payment of the

---

* See *In re* Lowell, 8 *N. Y. Civ. Pro.* 5; *In re* Caamano, 8 *Id.* 29;
Bradford *v.* People, 20 *Hun*, 309.

† For a review of the history of the legislation for the relief of
debtors see *In re* Audriot, 2 *Daly*, 35.

fraudulently contracted debt, and, if he have no property, for his discharge under what is known as the *Fourteen Day Act.*

Prior to the passage of the Stillwell Act there was no distinction, in the law, between one debtor and another,—the fraudulent, and the honest but unfortunate debtor were each, equally liable to arrest and imprisonment for the failure to pay judgments recovered in civil actions against them. The English process which we call an execution against the person, or body execution, is intended to confine the debtor until he satisfies the debt. It is not a satisfaction, strictly speaking, but the means of procuring, or rather coercing, satisfaction. Imprisonment is no part of the contract, and a release from imprisonment does not satisfy the debt nor impair the obligation, but leaves it a charge against property. Prior to the adoption in 1789, of the Fourteen Day Act, re-enacted with modifications in 1801, imprisonment for debt meant perpetual imprisonment, no matter how the debt was contracted, whether honestly or fraudulently, until the debt was paid, as said Lord HYDE (Many *v.* Scott, 1 *Mod.* 132) : " If a man be taken in execution and he lie in prison for debt, neither the plaintiff, at whose suit he was arrested, nor the sheriff who took him, is bound to find him meat, drink or clothes ; but he must live on his own, or on the charity of others, and if no man will relieve him, let him die in the name of God, says the law, and so say I."

There being no relief for the judgment debtor once imprisoned nor any provision for his maintenance while in prison, the abuse of his power by the over-severe creditor, and the poverty of the people in that early day, induced the adoption of the Fourteen Day Act, which, as modified in 1831, provides for the absolute discharge of the imprisoned debtor, upon peti-

tion, after certain specified terms of imprisonment
regulated according to the amount of the debt, if he
"be minded to deliver up to the creditor or creditors
who shall so charge him in execution all his estate
and effects towards satisfaction of the debt or debts
with which he stood charged." The petition, it was
provided, should be accompanied by a true account of
the debtor's estate, and, if the court so required, as it
always did, he must take an oath that the account
was, in all respects, just and true, and that he had
not at any time or in any manner or way whatsoever
disposed of or made over any part of his estate real or
personal, in law or in equity, with the view to the
future benefit of himself or family, or with the view
or intent to injure or defraud any of his creditors.
The act then provided that, if the court should be satisfied that the proceedings on the part of the prisoner
were just and fair, it should order an assignment and
discharge. This act made no distinction between
classes of debtors, but all were equally entitled to a
discharge if their proceedings were just and fair.

This act was again modified in 1833 (1 *R. L.* 348),
and afterwards, with further modifications, became a
part of the Revised Statutes (2 *R. S.* 32–39), but none
of these modifications affect in anywise the general
scope and theory of the act. The proceedings upon
the part of the debtor have always been required to
have been just and fair, and it has always been
required that he swear, in substance, that he has not
disposed of any part of his property with intent to
injure or defraud any creditor, and such is the statute,
which has become a part of the Code of Civil Procedure (art. III, title I, chap. XVII, §§ 2200, *et seq.*),
wherein it is said that a person imprisoned by virtue
of an execution issued in a civil action to collect a
sum of money may apply for his discharge at any
time, unless the sum for which he is imprisoned

exceeds five hundred dollars, in which case he may
not present his petition until he has been imprisoned
at least three months (§ 2202). To the petition must
be annexed a schedule containing a just and true
account of all the property of the petitioner (§ 2203),
and to the petition and schedule the petitioner must
annex his affidavit that the matters of fact stated in
the petition and schedule are, in all respects, just and
true, and that he has not, "at any time or in any
manner whatsoever, disposed of" or made over any
part of his property, not exempt by express provision
of law from levy and sale by virtue of an execution,
for the future benefit of himself or his family, "or
disposed of" or made over any part of his property
"with intent to injure or defraud" any of his creditors (§ 2204). If the court is satisfied that the petition
and schedules are correct "and that the petition
['] er's proceedings are just and fair" (§ 2208), and
     unless the opposing creditor satisfies the court
"that the proceedings on the part of the petitioner
are not just and fair," the court must direct an assignment and grant a discharge (§ 2210).

We have no inquiry, then, other than into the
question whether or no, in the eye of the law, the
proceedings of the petitioner are just and fair, and to
that end we must ascertain the construction given by
the courts to this expression which, as we have seen,
has been uniform in all the statutes.

The precise force and meaning was first defined, by
the courts of this State in People *v.* White (14 *How.
Pr.* 501, 502), by Mr. Justice SMITH who says: "The
word proceeding ordinarily relates to forms of law,
to modes in which judicial transactions are conducted.
It seems to be used inartificially in this place and in
an untechnical sense. These words apply to moral
qualities or acts, dealings and transactions, but not
fitly to formal legal proceedings. . . . The allegation

that the proceedings of the debtor are not just and
fair must be based upon and refer to some other class
of facts or transactions of the debtor. The policy and
spirit of the insolvent law is to discharge debtors
from imprisonment on their giving up honestly all
their property to creditors. The affidavit which appli-
cants under this article are required to make is, I
think, a key to the meaning of the words in the connection in question. . . This affidavit must be true in
its letter and spirit, or the proceedings of the
['] applicant can not be just and fair within the sense
and meaning and true intent of the statute."
This construction seems to have been followed in all
the cases we have examined, and adopted by the court
of appeals in the Matter of Brady in which Judge
EARL says (69 *N. Y.* 217), "The affidavit is a part of
the proceeding, and that can not be just and fair
unless it is true."

No claim is here made that the affidavit of the
petitioner, which is in the form required by the statute, is untrue in any regard except that the opposition to the petitioner's discharge, claim and insist that
he has disposed of property with the intent to injure
and defraud the judgment creditor at whose instance
he is now imprisoned.

['] Whenever it appears in these proceedings that
the debtor has . disposed of property, with the
intent to injure and defraud existing creditors, he can
not obtain a discharge (Matter of Brady, *supra ;* Coffin *v.* Gourlay, 20 *Hun*, 308), and any disposition of
property, which is intended to defraud existing
creditors. whether made before or after the action in
which the arrest is made, will bar a discharge (Matter
of Watson, 2 *E. D. Smith*, 429 ; Gaul *v.* Clark, 1 *W.
Dig.* 209 ; People *v.* White, *supra ;* Matter of Finck,
59 *How.* 149). That such a disposition of property
should operate as a bar to a discharge, there must

have been an intent to defraud existing creditors, of whom the creditor contesting the discharge is one.*

It is perfectly clear that an imprisoned debtor who has, at any time, made any disposition of his property, with intent to injure and defraud any creditor, and such disposition has that effect, he will be denied a discharge.

There are many frauds that may be practiced by debtors that will work injury to creditors though not effected by means of fraudulent conveyances. In the Matter of Benson (1 *Insolv. R.* 301), it was held, that where the proceeds of certain property purchased by an insolvent firm came into the hands of one of the partners, who failed to give a satisfactory explanation of the disposition thereof, he could not obtain a discharge from imprisonment under an execution issued upon a judgment recovered by the vendor of the property. In the Matter of Watson (*supra*), it was earnestly contended that the fraudulent disposition of property contemplated by the legislature is a disposition made by the debtor between his arrest and examination, and that, if he disposed of the property fraudulently, before any proceedings were instituted against him, that would be no bar to his discharge. This view of the statute did not, in this case, nor has it in subsequent cases, met the approval of the court. The petitioner, so say the courts, "is obliged to swear that he has made no such disposition *at any time.* These words are plain and unmistakable. To attempt to limit their signification by declaring them to be understood as applying only to a particular period would be departing from the obvious meaning of language."

The judgment by virtue of which in execution the

---

* See on this point *In re* Brady, 69 *N. Y.* 215; Matter of Pearce, 29 *Hun*, 270; Coffin *v.* Gourlay, 20 *Id.* 308.

petitioner in the matter at bar stands charged and
imprisoned was recovered in an action brought against
him, by one Mary Tompkins, in November, 1881, to
recover five hundred dollars, with interest, alleged to
have been obtained by him through duress and by
means of threats on November 13, 1875. The petitioner answered to the complaint in the action and
denied all the allegations thereof, and set up the statute of limitations. These issues were tried at a circuit
term of the supreme court held in and for Chautauqua
county in January, 1884. The petitioner was present
at the trial with counsel, and at the close of the plaintiffs case moved a nonsuit and asked the court to
direct a verdict, which denied, he offered no evidence,
nor was he sworn himself. The plaintiff had a verdict
upon which, January 24, 1884, judgment was entered
against the petitioner for $874.83. The petitioner
moved for a new trial and appealed to the general
term from the order denying it which was affirmed.

The real facts in issue were whether the petitioner
obtained the money, when and in what manner. Upon
his examination he denies that he ever had it and
swears that he did not. Judgments are the sayings of
the law and are to be taken as true. By this judgment, as to all the facts necessary to be shown in order
to sustain the actions which are common both to the
action and this proceeding, the petitioner is concluded.
To find out whether he did or did not have the money,
and, if he had it, when he got it is what that action
was about. The finding of these facts was indispensable to a recovery. *Impotentia excusat legem.* We do
not think, however, that the judgment is conclusive to
the extent that, he here denying that he ever received
the money, the petitioner will be required to
['] account for its disposition or be open to the
charge of having disposed of it with intent to
injure his creditors within the rule laid down in the

Matter of Brady, which in general principle is applicable to this case, but vastly different in essential facts. That is to say, the judgment, no matter whether he had the money or not, no matter how much of a hardship it may be, is conclusive that the debt is a just debt and came into existence November 13, 1875.

[*]   It was shown by the evidence of the petitioner upon the examination that some seventeen years ago he caused to be conveyed to his wife eighteen or twenty acres of land. This is of no avail here for the only creditor contesting this application is Mary Tompkins, and her debt did not exist until the year 1875, and to prevent a discharge the disposition must be intended to defraud existing creditors.

[*]   The disposition therefore of the money obtained, to recover which the action in the supreme court was brought, nor the disposition of the land will neither bar a discharge. The disposition of the money received by the petitioner, nearly one thousand dollars, from Mrs. Brownell presents an entirely different case.

In his story, as detailed upon the examination, the petitioner tells us that, in the December before the January in which the action against him was tried, he received from Mrs. Brownell $998.40. The petitioner and his family, wife and children, then lived in the town of Westfield, in this county, in which town they have resided many years. Mrs. Brownell then lived in that town. She received about this time a draft for about $1,800, and she and the petitioner made a journey to Northeast, Pennsylvania, and got the draft cashed there instead, as would have been the natural thing to do, of getting it cashed at some Westfield Bank. Of the proceeds of this draft while at Northeast the petitioner received the $998.40. The petitioner says he was "hunted out of the country in this case,"

and left the town of Westfield January 17, 1884, the
day of the trial, and went out of the State, and did
not return until September 25, 1885, the day before he
was arrested.   During this prolonged absence he visited upon no errand but "killing time" and looking
for a situation, Pennsylvania, Ohio, Indiana, Illinois,
Iowa, Minnesota, and Dakota.   He made his headquar-
ters at a hotel in Northeast, fifteen miles west from
where his wife was living, and, occasionally, was in
this State for short intervals, taking pains to avoid
arrest, coming and going on Sundays, instructing his
family not to open the door of the house until they
knew who asked admittance, intending that no sheriff
or official should arrest him.   In speaking of this
$998 40 the following questions were asked him to
which he made the following answers: "In traveling
over these States you have mentioned of course it
would cost you money? It cost money, yes, sir.   How
much money did you expend in traveling over these
States to kill time? Considerable.   As near as you
can tell how much ; about how much did you spend?
I got through near about $900.   How much? About
$900.   And your object was, as you said, to keep out
of the way of this trouble? It was."   A prudent man
would have deposited this money in some banking
institution ; a man, had he not wished to conceal that
he had it, would not have left as did the petitioner
during his journeying, the much greater portion of so
large a sum in his satchel at his room at the hotel in
Northeast, taking with him but sufficient to pay his
expenses till his return.   In response to questions put
him by his counsel the petitioner accounts for this
money, of which when arrested he had but $40 60, in
this manner ; paid counsel for defending the action,
witness's fees and board $203, of which $193 was paid
counsel ; expenses in the west $197 ; expenses of a five
weeks' stay in the oil regions $193 ; board bill at.

In re Haight.

Northeast $65 ; expenses of another trip in Pennsylvania $125; toward maintenance of family $123; clothing $35, making in all $941.

['] The petitioner, it is true, swears that he disposed of none of this money with the intent to injure and defraud any creditor. We cannot agree with him. Intentions are subservient to the law, not the law to intentions. Fraud is to be proved and not presumed. It is seldom, however, that it can be directly proved, and usually it is deduced from other facts that naturally and logically indicate its existence. They must not be when taken together and aggregated, when interlinked and put into proper relation with each other consistent with honest intent. Were the proceedings of the petitioner in regard to this money, sufficient in itself to have paid this debt that the court have said is a just one, just and fair toward this creditor; were they consistent with honest intent? We cannot say they were. Of this money he paid $193 to employ counsel to interpose an answer; put his creditor to a trial at which he does not produce or swear a witness; and to the expense and trouble of an appeal resulting against him, thus delaying judgment for over three years. For the very purpose of avoiding the judgment, when finally obtained, on the day of the trial, he takes himself and the money he has left out of the jurisdiction of our courts, and spends nearly $600 of it traveling about killing time. For the very purpose of preventing his creditor from recovering her debt by means of the only process the law furnishes in such cases, to keep her from reaching his person, resulting in keeping her from reaching this money, which in right belonged to her, which he ever had upon his person or hidden away, he kept himself and it beyond the reach of execution, and then disposed of the money to suit his own pleasure. The case is as aggravated as the Matter of Watson, in which the learned judge, who delivered the opinion, said : " I cannot persuade myself that a man may, for the express purpose of defrauding his creditors, hinder, delay, and prevent their collecting their debts, . go ' out of the State' and take all his property with him, and then by expenses of living, or unforeseen losses, or even inevitable calamity, he loses his money, return here and ask his discharge."

The construction put upon the statutes affecting imprisonment for debt by the courts, will lead in some instances, and perchance in this, to perpetual imprisonment; nevertheless, courts have no other power or duty than to construe and enforce the law as they find it. They may not modify it nor soften, however much they might so desire, any of its hard provisions. They are able to do that only which can be lawfully done. They declare the law as it is ; the people make the law. The courts say : It is so written, and it can not be abrogated or modified but by the power that made it. If, as counsel said upon the argument, public opinion is opposed to imprisonment for debt in every case, and the time is come when it should be abolished in all cases, especially when, like the petitioner, the debtor has no property with which to pay his creditor, the public must look to the legislature, not the courts, for relief.*

The court is satisfied that the petitioner has disposed of property with intent to injure and defraud an existing creditor, and that the petition and schedule, in that regard, are not correct, and that the petitioner's proceedings are not just and fair ; therefore, the prayer of the petitioner is denied, with costs to be taxed.

* See section 111 of the Code of Civil Procedure as amended by Laws of 1886, chap. 672.

THE GAS LIGHT COMPANY OF SYRACUSE v. THE ROME, WATERTOWN AND OGDENSBURG R. R. CO.

SUPREME COURT, FOURTH DEPARTMENT, ONONDAGA COUNTY, SPECIAL TERM, DECEMBER, 1885.

§§ 1502, 1515, 1531.

Ejectment—What proof of defendant's possession sufficient—Demand when not necessary—Damages recoverable when plaintiff's title extends to center of the street.

A railroad company that has laid a track consisting of iron rails securely fastened to wooden ties embedded in the earth, on the land of another, over which trains of cars pass and re-pass at intervals, has such occupancy or possession of the land as to authorize an action of ejectment:[1,5] although a person can walk over the structure without difficulty the most of the time, it is for all the purposes of a railroad operated by steam, at all times in the exclusive possession of the railroad company.[2]

Carpenter v. Oswego & Syracuse R. R. Co. (24 *N. Y.* 655), followed.[5]

Possession of land means not only that it is physically possible to use and occupy it oneself, but that every other person is excluded from using or occupying it except by permission.[3]

The Code of Civil Procedure authorizes an action of ejectment where the defendant exercised acts of ownership upon the premises at the time of the commencement of the action.[4]

Where a railroad corporation, S. N. R. R. Co. intruded and built its track upon the land of one A., and thereafter was succeeded in such occupancy by a new corporation, S. & N. R. R. Co., which was afterwards consolidated with another corporation the R. W. & O. R. R. Co. which thereby came into possession and thereafter continued in possession of said land, and there was no privity either of contract or estate between A. and the R. W. & O. R. R. Co. and the latter was not even the tenant by sufferance of "A.,"— *Held*, that it was not necessary that "A." demand possession of said land from the R. W. & O. R. R. Co. before bringing an action of ejectment therefor.[6]

Gas Light Co. *v.* Rome, &c. R. R. Co.

In such a case, the plaintiff, if he succeeds, is entitled, as damages, to the absolute value of the use and occupation of said land for the period it was in possession of the R. W. & O. R. R. Co,[16] and the defendant is not liable for the depreciation in the value of the land, caused by the laying of the track.[16]

If the defendant, in an action of ejectment, is not a tenant for years, or from year to year, or from month to month, or at will, or even by sufferance, there can be no pretense that a notice to quit or demand of possession is necessary before the action is brought.[7]

Where a street was not laid out by the process of condemnation or other legal proceeding, but by the dedication of the owners, the fee thereof remained in the owner, while the public acquired a right of way only.[8]

Where land is laid out as blocks bounded by streets dedicated by the owners to that use, which blocks are subdivided into lots, and premises are conveyed as a lot by number in a block by number, the presumption is raised thereby that the title extends to the center of the adjacent streets,[9]—accordingly *Held,* where premises so described were conveyed by one owning the fee to the center of the street, that the presumption was that she intended to convey to the center of the street, unless from the language used by her in conveying, a contrary intention appeared so clearly as to make any other construction unreasonable;[10] that where the premises were described as commencing at "the north east corner of said block at the intersection" of two streets (named), and proceeding "thence south on" one of said streets, and the block extended to the center lines of the said streets, the starting point was at the intersection of the center lines, and the first course on one of said streets meant on the center line thereof;[11] that an inconsistency in the second course or distance must yield to the starting point which, under ordinary circumstances, controls all other courses and distances.[12]

The plaintiff, in an action of ejectment, who owns land and the fee of the adjacent street to the center thereof, is entitled to recover from a railroad company which has intruded thereon his land and the adjacent street to the center thereof, subject to the easement of the public.[13]

The damages recoverable in an action of ejectment are limited to the real property recovered, and do not include the injury to adjacent property;[17] but its situation with reference to the adjacent lands may be considered,[17] where there are no rents and profits, the damages are the value of the use and occupation for the period not exceeding six years, that the defendant has been in

Gas Light Co. *v.* Rome, &c. R. R. Co.

possession,[14,15] and damages caused by his predecessors are not included.[15,16]

(*Decided December* 31, 1885.)

Action of ejectment.

The facts are fully stated in the opinion.

A. H. Green and *George F. Comstock*, for plaintiff.

E. B. Wynn and *P. B. McLennan*, for defendant.

VANN, J.—Block No. 85, Syracuse, as laid out prior to October 20, 1831, is bounded on the north by West Genesee street, and on the east by Franklin street. Since the year 1369 the plaintiff has been seized in fee of a parcel of land on the north-east corner of said block with a frontage of sixty-one feet on West Genesee and ninety feet on Franklin streets, and has, during the period of its ownership, been in the actual possession of all of the same, except a small triangular strip hereinafter described.

In the fall of 1871, the Syracuse Northern Railroad Company, a corporation organized under the General Railroad Act, constructed a railroad track from its former terminus, at a point north of West Genesee street, southerly across said street through Franklin street to its present terminus south of the Erie canal. Such extension was, so far as appears, without any authority from the city government.

The westerly rail of said track was laid eleven and one-half inches west of the north-east corner of said block as it is bounded by the outer lines of said streets. Said rail extended thence diagonally, in a southerly course, about twelve feet until it crossed the westerly exterior line of Franklin street, thus cutting off a triangular strip containing about six square feet, from said corner of said block, with a frontage of eleven and one-half inches on West Genesee and about twelve feet on Franklin street.

Said track continued diagonally west of the center line of Franklin street for about forty-five feet, when it crossed the center line and proceeded on the easterly half of said street until it passed the premises of the plaintiff. The projection of railroad coaches run upon said track, is from twenty inches to two feet beyond the rail on either side. The Syracuse Northern Railroad Company thus occupied said portion of the plaintiff's premises from the fall of 1871 until August, 1875, when, through the foreclosure of a mortgage, it was succeeded in such occupation and in the ownership of said railroad by a new corporation known as the Syracuse *and* Northern Railroad Company, which, in December of the same year, was consolidated with the defendant. During these changes in ownership of the railroad the location of said track on said part of plaintiff's premises and in said streets has remained unchanged.' So far as appears, the plaintiff never consented or objected to such occupation by any one of said railroad companies, nor received any compensation for its land or damages.

On April 4, 1883, the plaintiff commenced this action against the defendant, alleging in its complaint that since July 31, 1875, it has been the owner of said parcel of land, "bounded on the north by West Genesee street, and on the east by the center of Franklin street;" and entitled to the possession thereof ; that on August 1, 1875, the defendant entered "into said premises and ousted the plaintiff and has ever since unlawfully withheld from plaintiff the possession thereof, running and operating its said railroad upon and across the same, greatly depreciating and injuring said property and the value thereof, to the great damage, &c."

The demand for relief is that "the defendant be adjudged to surrender the possession of said real estate to plaintiff, and to pay plaintiffs said damages to the sum of $5,000 besides costs." No demand of possession is either alleged or proved.

The action by mutual consent was tried before the court without a jury, and toward the close of the evidence the plaintiff moved to amend its complaint so as to recover the difference between the value of the premises described in the complaint before and after the railroad was constructed, and to obtain other relief; but the motion was denied upon the ground that it was substantially the commencement of a new action under the form of an amendment to the complaint, and the action proceeded upon its original theory.

The answer admits the corporate character of the plaintiff and the defendant, and the ownership by the latter of the railroad in question, but, as to all the other allegations of the complaint denies knowledge or information sufficient to form a belief. Neither in its pleadings nor proof does the defendant claim any title to or interest in the premises in question.

The cause was submitted upon oral argument and written points on April 10, 1886.

From the foregoing facts, with others not recited, several important questions arise for decision, which will be briefly discussed in their natural order.

I. Is the nature of defendant's occupancy or possession such as to authorize an action of ejectment ?*

The complaint sets forth an action to recover the possession of real property with damages for withholding the same. It neither alleges any other cause of action nor demands any other relief, not even by a

---

* See *Abb. Trial Ev.* 714; *Sedgwick & Wait on Trial of Title to Lands,* § 721; *Code Civ. Pro.* § 1502.

general prayer. This is, therefore, an action of eject-ment, and the defendant insists that there has been no ouster of the plaintiff, that its occupancy is not to the exclusion of the plaintiff, and that the plaintiff is in the actual possession of the whole of the premises in question.

['] The undisputed evidence shows that defendant's track is partly upon plaintiff's land. Its iron rails are securely fastened to wooden ties which are embedded in the earth, and thus a solid and perma-nent structure is erected over which at intervals trains of cars pass and repass. Although a person can walk over this structure without difficulty the most of the time, no one can walk over it or stand upon it when a train is passing. It is then in the exclusive posses-sion of the defendant. For all the purposes of a ['] railroad operated by steam, it is at all times in the exclusive possession of the defendant, as it runs its cars upon said track without permission or notice at any hour of the day or night that it chooses. It is physically impossible for the plaintiff or its agents to use or enter upon the premises thus occu-pied by the defendant, except when the defendant is not using them, and then only by passing over said structure.

['] Possession of land means not only that it is physically possible to use and occupy it one's self, but that every other person is excluded from using or occupying it, except by permission. According to either branch of this definition the plaintiff is not, while according to both branches the defendant is, in possession.

['] Under the Code it is sufficient if the defendant exercised acts of ownership upon the premises at the time of the commencement of the action (*Code Civ. Pro.* § 1502 ; 2 *R. S.* 304, part 3, ch. 5, tit. 1, § 4).

In Carpenter *v.* Oswego & Syracuse R. R. Co. (24

N. Y. 655), the defendant had laid down a single
[*] railroad track across the plaintiff's land in a street
of a city, but had not used the track or the land
upon which it stood, or any part of it, except by laying
the track upon it. Such track was not even connected
with the main track of the railroad company. It was
held by six of the eight judges at that time composing the court of appeals, that the act of the defendant
was sufficient occupation to support the action.

The learned counsel for the defendant insists that
the plaintiff has never been out of possession, because
its president for the past thirty years so testified when
upon the stand, and that there is no evidence to contradict such statement. An examination of the sten-
ographer's minutes shows that that gentleman did so
testify in a general way, both on his direct and cross-
examination, referring to the entire property of the
plaintiff on the corner of West Genesee and Franklin
streets. Reading his whole testimony together, however, it is evident that he did not intend to include
the property in dispute, but only that part in the
undisputed possession of the plaintiff. No fair mind
can conclude that he intended to be understood as ·
denying that the defendant's track and ties are upon
the triangular strip in question. Moreover, it was
admitted by the defendant upon the trial, subject to
correction, that it went into possession "about 1878."
The uncontradicted evidence of the engineer called by
the plaintiff, the map treated as correct by both
parties, and the examination of the experts as to
value, all show that the defendant's railroad track is
upon a corner of the plaintiff's land.

II. Is it necessary to allege or prove a demand in
order to maintain this action?

No privity either of contract or estate existed
between the plaintiff and defendant. The latter was
not a tenant of the former, even by sufferance. It

claims no right to possession in its answer. It never had the consent of the plaintiff, so far as appears, either to take or to continue in possession. It was a mere intruder, taking the place of an original ['] trespasser, innocently perhaps, but still without any right whatever. Under these circumstances no demand was necessary.

[']   If the defendant in ejectment "is not a tenant for years, or from year to year, or from month to month, or at will, or even by sufferance, there can be no pretense that a notice to quit, or demand of possession, is necessary before the action is brought" (*Sedgw. & Wait on Trial of Title to Land*, §§ 375–377; Wood *v.* Wood, 83 *N. Y.* 575; Livingston *v.* Tanner, 14 *Id.* 64; Jackson *v.* Cuerden, 2 *Johns. Cas.* 353; Jackson *v.* Tyler, 2 *Johns.* 444).*

III. The extent of the plaintiff's recovery in land. The proof shows that the plaintiff has an indefeasible title in fee simple to the small triangular strip at the corner of West Genesee and Franklin streets, with a frontage of eleven and one half inches on the former and about twelve feet on the latter. Its right to recover this strip cannot be successfully disputed, but its claim to also to recover the fee to a part of the western half of Franklin street, subject to the easement of the public to use it as part of the highway, is not so clear.

[']   Franklin street was not laid out by the process of condemnation or other legal proceeding, but by the dedication of the owners. Hence the fee remained in the owners, while the public acquired a right of way only.

Block No. 85, which includes the premises in question, was laid out as a block bounded on the north by West Genesee street and on the east by Franklin

---

* See also *Abb. Trial Ev.* 714; *Code Civ. Pro.* § 1515.

street, and was subdivided into lots, prior to October 20, 1831, the date of the earliest conveyance read in evidence. From and including that deed the premises have been conveyed as a lot by number in a block [*]· by number, which raises the presumption that the title extends to the center of the adjacent streets (Bissell *v.* N. Y. C. R. R. Co., 23 *N. Y.* 61 ; Perrin *v.* N. Y. C. R. R. Co., 36 *N. Y.* 120).

The plaintiff acquired title to that part of the premises affected by this litigation on May 27, 1869, by conveyance from one Thankful W. Sprague, who, without question, owned to the center line of Franklin street. Two years before, she had conveyed the adjacent lands on West Genesee street, and hence, when she conveyed to the plaintiff, she had no motive for reserving the west half of Franklin street. As [**] she owned to the center of the street, the presumption is that she intended to convey to the center, unless, from the language used by her in conveying, a contrary intention appears so clearly as to make any other construction unreasonable (*Sedgw. & Wait Trial of Title to Land*, § 857 ; 3 *Kent Comm.* 433–4). She commences her description at "the [**] north-east corner of said block (85), at the intersection of West Genesee and Franklin streets," and proceeds "thence south on Franklin street." There can be no doubt from the evidence, under the authorities, that block 85 extended to the center lines of said streets, and therefore it is clear that the starting point is at the intersection of the center lines, and that the first course on Franklin street means on the center line of that street (Seneca Nation *v.* Knight, 23 *N. Y.* 498 ; Bissell *v.* N. Y. Central R. R. Co., 23 *Id.* 61 ; Luce *v.* Carley, 24 *Wend.* 451). The admitted inconsistency of the second course or distance is all that there is to base an argument upon that Mrs. Sprague intended to reserve that part of the street

lying in front of the premises, but this must yield to
the starting point, which under ordinary circumstances controls all other courses and distances (White's
Bank of Buffalo *v.* Nichols, 64 *N. Y.* 65). It is prob-
able that if she intended to make any reservation at
all, it was a portion of the west part of her premises,
which would be of some value, and not a part of the
street, which would be of no value to her as she owned
no abutting lands.

These views are confirmed by the reference to the
mortgage, that follows the description by metes and
bounds, and especially by the final clause, which sums
up the intention of the grantor and conveys by lot
and block number.

["]   The plaintiff is, therefore, entitled to recover
not only the triangular strip, in fee, but also, subject to the easement of the public, that part of Franklin street lying east of its premises occupied by the
defendant's railroad track (Wager *v.* Troy Union R.
R. Co., 25 *N. Y.* 526 ; Carpenter *v.* Oswego & Syracuse
R. R. Co., 24 *Id.* 655 ; Williams *v.* N. Y. C. & H. R.
R. R. Co., 16 *Id.* 97 ; S. C., on second appeal, 78 *Id.*
423)..

IV. The extent of the plaintiff's recovery in money.
By section 1531 of the Code of Civil Procedure, it is
provided that in an action to recover real property,
"the plaintiff, where he recovers judgment for the
property, or possession of the property, is entitled to
recover, as damages, the rents and profits, or the
value of the use and occupation, of the real property
recovered, for a term not exceeding six years."

["] As in this case there were no rents or profits, the
precise question is, what was the value of the use
and occupation of the real property recovered ?

In its complaint the plaintiff claims the right to
recover the whole of lot 7, in block 85, but as it has
been in the uninterrupted possession of all of that lot

except the triangular piece on the north-east corner, and that part of the west half of Franklin street adjacent to said lot occupied by the track of the defendant, or a strip about forty-five feet long, it can recover only the latter.

["] The ultimate question as to the amount of damages, therefore, is, what is the value of the absolute use and occupation of the triangular piece that the plaintiff is to recover in fee, and the value of the limited use and occupation of the strip in the street about forty-five feet long, that it is to recover subject to the easement of the public ?.

["] The access of the plaintiff to its land from Franklin street was so obstructed when the railroad track was first laid down, as, according to the evidence, to immediately depreciate the value of such land, but the defendant is not liable for that depreciation, for it did not cause it. The original damage, inflicted when the road was built, the damages accruing from that time until the organization of the Syracuse *and* Northern Railroad Company, a period of four years, and the damages accruing from the latter date until April 4, 1877, or six years before the commencement of this action, cannot be considered except to separate that which was done by others from that which was done by the defendant and to entirely exclude it in the assessment of damages.

There can be no recovery, in this action of ejectment, for damages to the adjacent property, for that is not recovered. The damages are limited to "the real property recovered" (*Code Civ. Pro.* § 1531). Its situation with reference to the adjacent lands may, however, be considered.

. Under these circumstances, the evidence of the experts, which was not limited to the property to be recovered, but included the entire lot, or in some instances the eastern half thereof, is of comparatively little value.   Even upon this basis they varied in their estimate of the depreciation in value, from $3,000 to nothing whatever.

Limiting the damages to the land recovered, situated as it was with reference to the remaining land of the plaintiff, under all the circumstances, I have concluded that the sum of $50 per year since April 4, 1877, is the amount of damages sustained by the plaintiff that I am at liberty to award in this action in its present form.

Findings may be prepared accordingly and served with a copy of this opinion upon the attorney for the defendant, who is at liberty to suggest amendments if he so desires.

LIBBEY, Appellant, v. MASON, Respondent.

Estate of LYDIA C. LIBBEY, Deceased.

Supreme Court, Second Department, General Term, December, 1886.

§ 2662.

Letters of administration—When not necessary to cite non-resident on application for—Effect of non-residence on right to.

Where a resident of this State died intestate, within the State, leaving a married daughter who was also a resident of this State, and a husband who resided in the State of Maine, and the daughter petitioned for letters of administration on the decedent's estate, but no citation was issued to the husband, and thereafter, and before letters were granted to her, the decedent's husband also petitioned for letters of administration,—*Held*, that letters of administration were properly granted to the daughter and denied the decedent's husband ; that the husband being a non-resident, it was not necessary to cite him, and when it is not necessary to cite a person, letters may be granted to the petitioner ; and that the petition filed by the husband had no relevancy in the daughter's proceedings beyond what it might declare, respecting his residence.

Where it appears that a person owns a place in the State of Maine and has been accustomed to pass most of his time there, and, above all, has voted regularly in that State, the proof is decisive of residence in Maine, as well under the laws of that State as under our laws.

Where a wife dies intestate, leaving her husband and an only daughter surviving, the husband, by the Revised Statutes (2 *R. S.* 290, § 27), has the better right to administer on the estate of the decedent.

(*Decided December* 28, 1886.)

Appeal from an order of the surrogate of Kings county refusing administration to the husband of the intestate, and granting it to the married daughter of the intestate.

The intestate, Lydia C. Libbey, was the wife of the appellant. She died in the city of Brooklyn, in February, 1886, leaving her husband and one daughter, the respondent, her only next of kin. She left both real and personal property. The respondent is intestate's daughter by a first husband and is the wife of one Summer A. Mason. There is no issue of the second marriage between John Libbey, the appellant, and the intestate. A contest arose before the surrogate of Kings county between the husband and daughter, each claiming administration. The husband based his claim upon prior right under the Revised Statutes. The daughter opposed, stating as the principal ground his alleged residence in Maine, and objecting also to his age (eighty-two years) and consequent incapacity. The surrogate granted letters to the daughter and refused them to the husband. An

order was entered by the surrogate adjudging appellant a non-resident and awarding to respondent letters
of administration. From that order this appeal was
taken.

Chauncey B. Ripley and *A. B. Tappen*, for
appellant.

The husband is fully qualified and is entitled to
administration on the estate of his wife in preference
to any other person. The husband is primarily entitled to administration under the statute. 3 *R. S.*
(7th ed.) 2290, §§ 27, 28, 29, 32. . . . . . In Estate
of Curser (89 *N. Y.* 401), the court of appeals declares
that the statute giving preference to single before married women in the grant of administration and other
similar provisions are in force ; and at page 404 the
court presents forcible reasons why married woman
may not satisfactorily administer an estate, to wit :
"The possible influence of the husband over the wife,"
etc., etc.

The daughter's right is subordinate and cannot in
this case be preferred to the right of the husband. 3
R. S. (7th ed.) 2290, §§ 28, 29 ; Estate of Curser, 89
N. Y. 401.

The surrogate erred in claiming that he could
exercise judicial discretion under section 2662 of the
Code to the prejudice of the husband. The Code,
section 2662, does not change any of the statutory
provisions above quoted ; nor does it apply to the case
at bar. That section of the Code permits the surrogate to cite or not cite non-residents of the State in
his discretion. If not cited, the non-resident is in no
respect prejudiced by this section, provided he appear
voluntarily. The surrogate did not in this case cite
the husband as a non-resident ; the husband came
before the court voluntarily with his petition and
bond and oath of qualification. He was the first to

comply with the statute in filing his bond, and he came with all his rights unimpaired. If the husband had been cited, he could have come in and claimed his right to administer to the exclusion of the married daughter (*Code Civ. Pro.* § 2662) . . . Section 2662 of the Code does not impair any right of the applicant John Libbey, unless as therein expressed—namely, the right to service of citation in case he be a non-resident. The Revised Statutes (3 *R. S.* 7th ed. 2290, §§ 28–32) are not repealed by the Code (§ 2662); nor are the two enactments inconsistent or repugnant. If the Legislature had intended to repeal the former by the latter enactment it would have said so directly in terms or by necessary implication. The statutory right of the husband to administer on the personalty of his wife has existed from the earliest times, and he cannot be deprived of it by wrong inferences or an erroneous exercise of judicial discretion (Matter of Curser, 89 *N. Y.* 405 ; Harrison *v.* McMahon, 1 *Bradf.* 286).

The bad logic which the respondent relied upon in the surrogate's court seemed to be this : Under section 2662 of the Code, the surrogate may omit to cite before him a non-resident who, if he were a resident, would be entitled to citation and to administration. The surrogate did not cite the husband in this case, and therefore he lost all his rights to administration. This reasoning is fallacious because of the fact that the husband (John Libbey) appeared without any citation, voluntarily, and asserted his rights, which the statute never contemplated preventing (*Code Civ. Pro.* § 2662). Under the section of the Code invoked, the case of John Libbey is precisely the same, whether he be a resident or a non-resident of the State. The section has no application. To apply that section three things must be conceded : (1) that he was a non-resident of this State ; (2) that he was not cited by the surrogate ; (3) that he did not appear.

"The person entitled to a preference in administration cannot be excluded from his right, except in
the cases enumerated in the statutes" (Harrison v.
McMahon, 1 *Bradf.* 283). The Revised Statutes (3 *R.
S.* 7th ed. 2291), enumerate the disabilities as follows:
§ 32. A person convicted of an infamous crime ; a person incapable by law of making a contract ; an alien
not a resident of the State ; a person under twenty-
one years of age ; a person adjudged incompetent by
reason of drunkenness, improvidence, or want of
understanding. Married women and unmarried have
not equal claims.

Nathaniel B. Cooke, for respondent.

Section 2662 of the Code of Civil Procedure is new ;
so noted by the codifier. It undoubtedly confers upon
the surrogate power to disregard priority of right in
a non-resident and commit administration to a resident petitioner. The language is unmistakable ; the
non-resident need not be cited ; and when that is not
necessary, the surrogate is empowered to grant letters
"to the petitioner . . . upon presentation of the
petition." By section 2666, even where a citation has
been issued, the surrogate is directed to make "such
a decree in the premises as justice requires. The decree may award administration to any party to the
special proceeding." Does not this language, with
reference to the grant, indicate that the surrogate has
the right of selection ? There certainly is no question
that in the present case,—Mrs. Mason's petition having been first filed and no citation " to non-residents "
having been issued,—the surrogate might, as he did,
make "a decree granting to the petitioner letters"
(§ 2662).

BARNARD, P. J.—The conclusion of the surrogate
that the petitioner Libbey is a resident of the State of

Maine is well supported by the evidence. The proof shows that he owns a small place in Orono, Penobscot county, in that State ; that he has been accustomed to pass most of the time there ; and, above all, that he has voted regularly in that State. This is a decisive proof of residence under the laws of Maine, as well as under our laws. The evidence also shows that the petitioner Mason resides in Brooklyn, New York. A temporary change of domicile for the purpose of educating his children (Dupuy v. Wortz, 53 *N. Y.* 556).

The sole question then is whether the granting of the letters to Mrs. Emma Mason was proper. The petitioner Libbey was the husband of Lydia C. Libbey, the deceased, intestate. The petitioner, Mrs. Mason, was the daughter (only daughter) of the intestate. The husband by the Revised Statutes had the better right (3 *R. S.* 7th ed. 2290, § 27).

By the Code of Civil Procedure, however, it is provided that non-residents of equal or better right than a petitioner to administration upon the estate of a deceased person need not be cited, and that, when it is not necessary to cite a person, letters may be granted to a petitioner (§ 2662).

The petition of Mrs. Mason was presented to the surrogate, and no citation was issued to the husband. Letters to her were therefore properly granted under this section, if the husband was a resident of the State of Maine—about which fact there is no doubt. His petition, even if made before the actual granting of letters to Mrs. Mason, had no relevancy beyond the fact that he declared himself therein to be a resident of Kings county, N. Y. If that was true, then a citation should have been issued to him ; but it was not the fact, and the petition failed.

The surrogate's decree was therefore right, and should be affirmed, with costs.

DYKMAN, J.—[Concurring.]—Lydia C. Libbey resided in Brooklyn, and died there intestate, leaving Emma J. Mason, her only child, who resided in Brooklyn at the time of her mother's death, and now resides in the city of New York, and John Libbey, her husband, who resides in the State of Maine.

Emma J. Mason presented a petition to the surrogate of Kings county praying for the issuance of letters of administration upon her mother's estate to her. A few days subsequently, John Libbey, the husband, also presented a similar petition to the surrogate, who thereupon decided that letters should issue to the daughter. From that decree the husband has appealed.

Section 2662 of the Code of Civil Procedure is this : " Every person, being a resident of the State, who has a right to administration prior or equal to that of the petitioner, and who has not renounced, must be cited upon a petition for letters of administration. The surrogate may, in his discretion, issue a citation to non-residents, or those who have renounced, or to any or all other persons interested in the estate, whom he thinks proper to cite. Where it is not necessary to cite any person a decree granting to the petitioner letters may be made upon presentation of the petition."

Under this law it was not incumbent upon the surrogate to issue a citation to the husband, and it was entirely within his competence and discretion to issue letters to the daughter immediately upon the presentation of her petition.

The failure to issue letters to the daughter previous to the presentation of the petition of the husband did not divest the surrogate of his discretion, and he could exercise the same thereafter as well as theretofore.

We do not find that the discretion of the surrogate was improperly exercised, and the decree should be affirmed with costs, to be paid by the appellant personally.

PRATT, J., concurred.

SMITH *v.* JOYCE.

N. Y. COURT OF COMMON PLEAS, GENERAL TERM, NOVEMBER, 1886.

§§ 757, *et seq.*, 763.

Abatement and revival.—Effect of death of plaintiff in foreclosure action before entry of judgment—Report of referee to compute amount due.

The report referred to in section 763 of the Code of Civil Procedure, —which provides that "if either party to an action dies . . . . after a verdict, report or decision, or an interlocutory judgment, but before final judgment is entered, the court must enter final judgment in the name of the original parties," unless the report, &c., is set aside,—is a decision by a referee which determines the rights of the parties to a controversy as they would be determined by a verdict, decision of a judge or interlocutory judgment, and does not include the report of a referee to compute, take proofs, &c., in a foreclosure suit.

It seems, that said section does not embrace judgments by default.

Where, in an action for the foreclosure of a mortgage, in which all the defendants except infants made default in pleading, and the latter interposed the usual general answer by guardian *ad litem*, the plaintiff died after the report of a referee appointed "to compute the amount due to the plaintiff for the principal and interest upon the bond and mortgage set forth in the plaintiff's complaint, and also to take proof of the facts and circumstances stated in the plaintiffs' complaint, and to examine the plaintiff or his agent on oath as to any payments which have been made,"—*Held*, that the action should have been revived before judgment was entered on such report, but that the failure to revive it did not render the judgment void but irregular ; that a sale thereunder was not void but merely irregular, and that only because of the irregularity of the judgment, and that the title of a purchaser thereat was not unmarketable.

De Forest v. Farley (62 *N. Y.* 628), followed; Gerry v. Post (13 *How. Pr.* 118), not followed.

The title of a purchaser at a judicial sale is not affected by defects in proceedings which rendered the judgment irregular and in consequence of which it might have been set aside.

It seems, that it is only where a party against whom a judgment is rendered dies before the verdict, report, or decision against him, that the judgment is absolutely void.

It seems, that the death of a party to a foreclosure action, whether plaintiff or defendant, after judgment, does not affect a sale thereunder or necessitate the revival of the action.

(*Decided November*, 1886.)

Controversy submitted without action under sections 1279 *et seq.* of the Code of Civil Procedure.

Plaintiff contracted to sell to defendant a certain plot of land. Defendant objected to the plaintiff's title upon the ground that it was derived through a judgment of foreclosure and sale, made in an action in which the sole plaintiff died three days before the signing and entry of said judgment, and no proceedings to revive said action were ever taken. Plaintiff delivered a deed of said premises and defendant paid the purchase money therefor, but upon condition that the same should be refunded in case this court should hold that said title was defective or unmarketable, and thereupon said premises should be reconveyed to plaintiff.

The title of the plaintiff herein to said premises was derived from and through a judgment of foreclosure and sale, signed January 22, 1879, in an action in the supreme court of the State of New York, and filed in the office of the clerk of the city and county of New York, on January 23, 1879, to which action the plaintiff herein, being the mortgagor, was a party defendant.

It was conceded that the action was regularly commenced and prosecuted down to the making, on
November 1, 1878, of an order appointing a referee
" to compute the amount due to the plaintiff, for the
principal and interest upon the bond and mortgage set
forth in the plaintiff's complaint, ... and also to
take proof of the facts and circumstances stated in the
plaintiff's complaint, and to examine the plaintiff or
his agent on oath as to any payment which may have
been made." This order was made upon the consent
of the attorneys for the guardian *ad litem* of infant
defendants, and recited that due proof had been filed
" of the service of the summons in this action more
than twenty days since, either personally within this
State, or by publication, on all the defendants, and
that no answers or demurrers to the complaint have
been put in by any of them, except the infant defendants, who, by their guardian *ad litem*, have put in the
usual general answer ; and that the time to answer or
demur has expired as to all of them."

The referee made his report in accordance with
said order, and delivered it to the plaintiff's attorney
therein on January 18, 1879, who on the same day
served notice of motion for the relief demanded in the
complaint. On January 19, 1879, three days before
the hearing of said motion, the plaintiff in said action
died, leaving a last will and testament, in and by
which he appointed executors thereof, which will was
proved and letters testamentary issued thereon, March
18, 1879.

No motion or proceedings to revive said action of
foreclosure and sale were ever made or taken.

On January 22, 1879, an alleged judgment of foreclosure and sale, in the usual form of such judgments,
was granted in said action, in the name of the original
plaintiff (then deceased), and entered on January 23,
1879. Thereafter, a certified copy of said judgment of

foreclosure and sale was delivered to the referee therein named by the attorney who had represented the original plaintiff in his lifetime. The premises were thereafter advertised for sale, as required by law, and on February 15, 1879, sold under said judgment by the referee named therein to the plaintiff herein, to whom the referee's deed was delivered in February, 1879, and who thereupon entered into possession of said premises.

The plaintiff herein did not have knowledge at the time of the delivery of the referee's deed to him of said premises, and the payment by him of the consideration therefor, that the plaintiff in said foreclosure suit was then dead, or had died at the time herein set forth, and only learned of the facts set forth regarding the time of such death, since entering into the contract with the defendant herein.

That said Joyce objected to the title to said premises, upon the ground that the said alleged judgment of foreclosure and sale was voidable, invalid and of no force and effect, inasmuch as the same was made subsequent to the death of the sole plaintiff in said foreclosure action, also, because the said foreclosure action had not been revived in the name of the legal representatives of said William Sidney Smith, deceased, prior to said alleged judgment of foreclosure and sale, and also upon the ground that the said alleged foreclosure judgment was delivered to said referee after the death of William Sidney Smith, and also, because the alleged sale thereunder was void.

The questions submitted to the court upon this case were as follows: I. Was it necessary, after the defendants in the foreclosure suit of Smith v. Smith were in default, and the matter had been referred to a referee to compute the amount due, take proof of facts and circumstances and the referee had made and delivered his report, and a notice of motion had been served to confirm said report, and for final judgment of foreclosure and sale, all during the lifetime of the plaintiff, that said foreclosure suit should have been revived in the name of the executors of the plaintiff, because the plaintiff died three days before the granting and entry of said final judgment of foreclosure and sale? II. If so, did the omission to revive said foreclosure suit in the name of the executors of the plaintiff under the final judgment of foreclosure and sale rendered and entered therein, and the sale under such judgment, render the title of the purchaser at such sale void and legally defective, he having had no knowledge of the death of the said plaintiff at the time he took title to said premises? III. Was the title of Joseph Finley Smith unmarketable, because the judgment of foreclosure and sale was delivered to the referee to be carried into effect after the plaintiff's death and before the appointment of any executor or administrator upon his estate? IV. Was the title of Joseph Finley Smith unmarketable at the time of the conveyance to said Joyce as aforesaid, for any of the matters hereinbefore stated? The agreement to submit the case provided that if these questions were answered in the affirmative, then judgment should be entered in favor of said Robert A. Joyce, the defendant, against said Joseph Finley Smith, the plaintiff, for the sum of $3,500, and interest from September 22, 1886, and the further sum of $35 expense of searching title, but without costs, and said Joyce is to immediately reconvey said premises and deliver the possession thereof to said Joseph Finley Smith on payment of said judgment, and if the questions were answered in the negative, then judgment is to be rendered in favor of said Smith against said Joyce, but without costs.

P. Van Alstine (*James A. Ross*, attorney), for plaintiff.

It was not necessary to revive the foreclosure suit after the plaintiff died, because said plaintiff died after the referee therein had made and delivered his report, and a motion was pending to confirm such report, and for final judgment . . . *Code Civ. Pro.* § 763 . . . By section 3343, subdivision 5 of Code of Civil Procedure, "the word 'report,' when used in connection with a trial, or other inquiry, means a referee's report." . . The death of plaintiff after judgment is entered in a foreclosure suit, does not affect the power of the referee, in going on to sell and executing deed to purchase ; it is not necessary to revive action. Lynde *v.* O'Donnell, 21 *How. Pr.* 34 ; Hays *v.* Thomas, 56 *N. Y.* 522 . . . The plaintiff was an innocent purchaser at a judicial sale, and his title is not affected by errors in entry of judgment. De Forest *v.* Farley, *N. Y.* 628.

Meyer Butzel, for the defendant.

The death of a plaintiff, in a foreclosure case, before judgment of foreclosure and sale entered, renders the judgment, entered in his name therein, and the purchaser's title under it void. Gerry *v.* Post, 13 *How. Pr.* 118, and cases there cited.

"At common law death abated all actions so as to put an end to them and compel the representatives of the decedent to begin, as if the action had never been instituted." "Various statutes were passed to cure this evil ; but in all it will be found that the action was suspended by the death, and that no proceedings could be had in it until the new parties were brought in, except in two special cases." Gerry *v.* Post, *supra*.

By the Revised Statutes, if a sole plaintiff died after interlocutory, but before final judgment, the action did not abate, but still it was not to be continued in the name of the deceased—his executors or administrators were to sue out a *scire facias*, &c. 2 *R. S.*

387, part 3, ch. 7, tit. 1, § 2 ; 2 *Edm.* 402 ; 3 *R. S.* 5th ed. 669. If either party died after verdict, or a plea in confession, the court could enter final judgment in the names of the original parties at any time within two terms after the death (2 *R. S.* 387, part. 3, ch. 7, tit. 1, § 4; 2 *Edm.* 402). In chancery also, the same statutes provided that no suit should abate when the cause of action continued, but still the new parties were to be brought in before the action could proceed. Gerry *v.* Post, *supra.* . . .

It is contended on behalf of the plaintiff that the report of the referee computing the amount due, &c., is a report within the meaning of Code Civ. Pro. § 763. This section is but a re-enactment of like provisions of the Revised Statutes (*supra*) as construed by the decisions of the courts, except that the provision requiring judgment to be entered within two terms after verdict or plea was omitted. Comr.'s Notes to section 763, Throop's Ed. of New Code. . . .

The term "report," as used in this section, refers to a report upon the issues in an action. Any other construction would lead to an absurd result ; it might as well be contended that a report of a referee to whom it was referred to take the deposition of a party who had refused to make an affidavit in the action was a "report" within the meaning of this section. The word "report" was evidently inserted in this section in accordance with the construction of the sections of the Revised Statutes (*supra*) in the case of Scranton *v.* Baxter, 3 *Sand.* 660, where it was held that a referee's report upon the issues had all the force and effect of a verdict, and that judgment could be entered thereon after death of the sole party. The construction of the word " decision " in said section was likewise limited to the findings of fact and conclusions of law signed by the judge, and held not to include an opinion of the judge delivered upon the merits of the

case, notwithstanding that such opinion stated the
facts and conclusions fully, and the proper judgment
to be rendered thereon ; and it was further held that
no judgment could be entered thereon after death of
party. Adams v. Nellis, 59 *How. Pr.* 385. . . .

The delivery of the judgment of foreclosure and
sale to the referee, for execution, after plaintiff's
death, was analogous to the issue of execution upon a
judgment after plaintiff's death. It has been repeatedly held that such an execution was void, and that
an action in the nature of a writ of *scire facias* by the
legal representatives of the deceased plaintiff was
necessary to issue such execution. Ireland v. Litch-
field, 8 *Bosw.* 634; Thurston v. King, 1 *Abb. Pr.* 126;
Wheeler v. Dakin, 12 *How. Pr.* 537 ; Jay v. Martine,
2 *Duer*, 654. In Lynde v. O'Donnell, 12 *Abb. Pr.* 286 ;
S. C., 21 *How. Pr.* 34, the court said : "A certified
copy of the decree of foreclosure and sale resembles a
fi. fa. upon a common law judgment," although it was
held that a referee had power to execute the decree
notwithstanding the death of the plaintiff after its
entry, and after it had been placed in the referee's
hands for execution, and pending the advertisement
of sale ; the distinction was clearly made between the
death of the party *before*, and *after*, the delivery of
the decree for execution. . . .

A title open to a reasonable doubt is not a marketable one, and the court cannot make it one by passing
upon an objection depending on a disputed question
of fact, or a doubtful question of law, in the absence
of the party in whom the outstanding right is vested.
Fleming v. Burnham, 100 *N. Y.* 1.

J. F. DALY, J.—The first question in the case
arises upon the construction of section 763 of the
Code of Civil Procedure, which provides : "If either
party to an action dies, after an accepted offer to

allow judgment to be taken, or after a verdict, report, or decision, or an interlocutary judgment, but before final judgment is entered, the court must enter final judgment, in the names of the original parties ; unless the offer, verdict, report or decision, of the interlocutory judgment is set aside." The question is, whether in an action for the foreclosure of a mortgage, where all the defendants, except infants, have made default, and the latter have interposed the usual general answer by guardian *ad litem*, the report of a referee appointed " to compute the amount due to the plaintiff for the principal and interest upon the bond and mortgage set forth in the plaintiff's complaint, and also to take proof of the facts and circumstances stated in the plaintiff's complaint, and to examine the plaintiff or his agent on oath as to any payments which have been made," is a report within the above quoted section of the Code.

In this case it was the plaintiff who died after the filing of the report, and before the entry of final judgment, and final judgment was entered upon the motion of the plaintiff's attorney of record.

The second question submitted is, whether the sale of the premises under such judgment was valid without a revivor by the personal representatives of the deceased plaintiff, and the whole controversy is whether the title of the purchaser at such sale (who was the mortgagor and a defendant in the action, and who had no notice of the death of the plaintiff) is affected by the omission to revive the action, either before or after judgment ; the deceased plaintiff left a last will and testament appointing executors, to whom letters were issued after the sale.

The title of a purchaser upon a judicial sale is not affected by defects in proceedings which rendered the judgment irregular and in consequence of which it might have been set aside (De Forest v. Farley, 62 N.

Y. 628). I am inclined to the opinion, that the report of a referee appointed to compute, take proof, &c., in a foreclosure suit, is not the report meant by section 763 of the Code above quoted, but that the provision contemplates a decision by a referee which determines the rights of the parties to a controversy as they would be determined by a verdict, decision of a judge, or interlocutory judgment. It has been held by the supreme court that the section does not embrace judgments by default, and I think the conclusion is correct (Grant *v.* Griswold, 21 *Hun*, 509–513).

The action should have been revived by the personal representatives of the plaintiff, because he died before any decision in the action (Gerry *v.* Post, 13 *How. Pr.* 118); but the omission to take the step was an irregularity merely and did not render the judgment void, because it was in favor of the deceased party. It is only where a party against whom the judgment is rendered dies before the verdict, decision or report against him, that the judgment is absolutely void (*Code Civ. Pro.* § 765). This express provision for the particular case, excludes the construction that the judgment in any other case is absolutely void. If not absolutely void, it is voidable only because irregular, and therefore, under the decision in De Forest *v.* Farley above cited, the title of the purchaser is not affected.

The view of the learned justice in the special term case of Gerry *v.* Post, above, to the effect that the judgment and sale are void, must be deemed to be in conflict with the later decisions of the court of appeals.

The proceeding to sell under the judgment without the revival by the personal representatives of the plaintiff is also a mere irregularity,—and that only because of the irregularity of the judgment, not otherwise. Had the death of the plaintiff occurred after the

judgment and before the sale, it would not have
affected the sale (Lynde v. O'Donnell, 21 *How. Pr.*
34). Even upon the death of the defendant, the mortgagor, after decree and before its enrollment, it would
not be necessary to revive the action before the sale
(Harrison v. Simons, 3 *Edw. Ch.* 416, cited and
approved in Hays v. Thomae, 56 *N. Y.* 522).

The answer to the second, third and fourth questions submitted in the case must be in the negative,
and judgment upon the agreement rendered in favor
of Joseph Finley Smith, without costs.

LARREMORE, Ch. J., and VAN HOESEN, J., concurred.

SIMON v. THE ALDINE PUBLISHING COM-
PANY.

CITY COURT OF NEW YORK, SPECIAL TERM, DECEM-
BER, 1886.

§§ 14, 812, 2266, *et seq.*

*Perjury—When not punishable as a contempt—False justification by
surety on appeal.*

A surety upon an undertaking on appeal who falsely testifies to his
responsibility upon his justification as such, cannot be punished
for his perjury as for a civil contempt.*
Moffatt v. Herman (8 *N. Y. Civ. Pro.* 369 ; as reversed 17 *Abb. N. C.*
107), followed; Hull v. L'Eplatinier (5 *Daly*, 534), not followed.
It seems, that perjury is no longer a great contempt of court; and
that although a party to an action by a false pleading which is a
proceeding of the court, has effectually deprived his adversary of
the legitimate relief sought by him, he is not guilty of a contempt
of court.
(*Decided December* 7, 1886.)

---

* See Norwood v. Ray Manufacturing Co., *post*, p. 273.

Motion by plaintiff to punish James Sutton for falsely testifying to his responsibility as a surety upon an undertaking upon appeal in this action.

The opinion states the facts.

E. J. Myers, for plaintiff and motion.

Thomas Darlington, for surety, opposed.

Neiirbas, J.—This is a motion to punish for contempt James Sutton, one of the sureties on the undertaking given herein by the defendant upon an appeal to the court of common pleas, on the ground that upon the justification he made oath to statements, which were known to him to be false, whereby the undertaking became worthless.

The examination taken under proceedings supplementary to execution herein, before a referee, in which said surety as well as his co-surety, and other witnesses testified, and the additional affidavits submitted, satisfy me that some of the statements made by said surety (who was also the president of the defendant corporation), upon his justification as such surety, were not true, and were known to him at the time to be untrue; and that he was then insolvent, with no present means of meeting the obligation into which he had entered as surety, and with no intention of paying the same.

For instance, he swore upon the justification on January 7, 1886, that his total indebtedness was between $300 and $400, whereas he admitted upon his examination before the referee in September last that he was then indebted to his wife in the sum of at least $5,000 upon a note made to her in 1883, for $20,000, which he had reduced to the former amount in the interim.   His wife, in the affidavit now submitted by her, relinquishes all claim to any indebtedness due her from her husband, but this cannot alter the facts sworn to.

The surety's intention not to pay appears, from the fact sworn to by him, that although not personally liable upon any paper issued by the defendant corporation prior to January 7, 1886, either as indorser or maker, still, a few days thereafter, on the 12th and 16th of the same month, he personally indorsed all the renewal notes given by the defendant to parties to which it was indebted, in various large amounts, he knowing its then financial condition. Shortly thereafter the corporation failed, and its president, the surety aforesaid, succumbed with it. A new corporation was immediately formed, and named the Aldine Press, of which Mr. Sutton now appears to be the general manager, at a salary of $250 a month. From the manner in which the business of the defendant was conducted, mainly through its president, as general manager, the sale of the machinery, fixtures, etc., the repurchase thereof at a loss by the president, their resale to creditors, and the subsequent leasing of the same to the defendant and the new corporation, the Aldine Press, and the management of both corporations, which were principally composed by the president and treasurer (the sureties on the undertaking) and their wives, and the foreman of the printing presses, I am satisfied that the sureties on the undertaking referred to were fictitious.

Thus far I agree with the plaintiff upon this motion. But now comes the question of the power of this court to punish these offenses as for a contempt.

Subdivision 2 of section 14 of the Code provides that a court of record has power to punish "a party to the action or special proceeding for putting in fictitious bail, or a fictitious surety, or for any deceit or abuse of a mandate or proceeding of the court."

It is manifest that this does not cover the present case. The person sought to be punished is not a party to the action. It has been held that a corporation may be fined as for a contempt (Mayor, &c. v. N. Y. & S. I. Ferry Co., 64 *N. Y.* 622). So that the defendant might have been so fined. But as it is now insolvent and has practically ceased to exist, that remedy would be fruitless.

But it is claimed that under subdivision 8 of the same section, a person not a party to the action may be reached under the present proceeding; and in support of this position, the case of Hull v. L'Eplatinier (5 *Daly*, 534), is relied upon. In that case it was held that a stranger to the suit may be punished as for a contempt for conspiring with another to become surety on an undertaking on appeal, by falsely swearing to the ownership of property, when he is in fact insolvent, under the eighth subdivision of section 1, title 3, 2 Rev. Stat. 534, which is substantially re-enacted into subdivision 8 of section 14 of the Code (*supra*). Judge DALY, delivering the opinion at special term, says: "Perjury has always been held a great contempt of court (citing Stockham v. French, 1 *Bing. [Eng. C. P.]* 365). . . . . Any person who adopts any means to prevent the course of justice, will be liable to punishment for contempt (13 *Mees. & Welsby [Eng. Excr.]* 593). And strangers as well as parties to suits, are liable to punishment for contempt, for using force or fraud to prevent the course of justice (citing Smith v. Bond, 2 *D. & L. [Eng. Bail. Ct.]* 460; also 9 *Jur.* 20, and 14 *L. J. Exch.* 114)." This was affirmed by the general term, DALY, Ch. J., writing the opinion, who says: "If the defendant had had what he was entitled to, a responsible surety upon the appeal, it would have been a security for the amount of the undertaking. This he lost by the fraudulent acts and misconduct of

Lee and the false swearing of the minor, whom he procured to become a surety ; and the amount of the judgment upon the undertaking was, therefore, a proper measure of the defendant's loss and injury, it appearing, by the issuing and return of an execution, that nothing could be collected from either of the sureties upon the judgment. It does not follow that because the surety might be indicted for perjury in the making of such an affidavit, or that Lee might be indicted for what he did, that the court have not the power, under the provision referred to in the Revised Statutes, to punish Lee for his misconduct by imposing upon him a fine sufficient to indemnify the defendant in the action for the loss and injury which Lee was chiefly instrumental in producing." This decision was rendered in June, 1875.

Since then, the case of Moffatt v. Herman was decided by the general term of the court of common pleas. In that action an order was made punishing the defendant as for a contempt, for putting in a verified answer, known to him to be false, whereby the plaintiff was defrauded out of the amount of his claim. Judgment was obtained by defraud, and an execution returned unsatisfied. The day subsequent to the service of the false answer, the defendant transferred all his property to a corporation, receiving in payment certain stock, which he immediately disposed of to other alleged creditors. The defendant was fined the amount of the judgment and costs of the proceedings under subdivisions 2 and 8 of section 14 of the Code, already referred to, as for "an abuse of a proceeding of the court." The general term of this court affirmed the order of the special term in an opinion reported in 8 *N. Y. Civ. Pro.* 369. Upon appeal to the general term of the court of common pleas, that court reversed the order appealed from, without writ-

ing an opinion (See 17 *Abb. N. C.* 107). This decision
was rendered in March, 1886.

The conclusion necessarily following from this
decision is twofold, namely, that "perjury is no
longer a great contempt of court," and that "although
a party to an action by a false pleading, which is a
proceeding of the court, has effectually deprived his
adversary of the legitimate relief sought by him," the
former is not guilty of a contempt of court. It
might well be said in that case : "If the plaintiff had
had what he was entitled to—a judgment by default
for failure to answer—he would have been able to collect his judgment. This he lost by the fraudulent
acts, misconduct and false swearing of the defendant
in putting in a false answer ; and the amount of the
judgment recovered and the costs of the proceeding
was therefore a proper measure of the defendant's loss
and injury, it appearing, by the issuing and return
of an execution, that nothing could be collected upon
the judgment.

It seems to me, therefore, that the principles laid
down in Hull v. L'Eplatinier (*supra*), have been overruled by Moffatt v. Herman (17 *Abb. N. C.* 107),
and that the former case cannot be considered as
decisive of the present motion.

When the personal liberty of a citizen is involved
it behooves me to hesitate, when the decisions on the
subject of contempt, of the court of final resort, so far
as this court is concerned, are diametrically opposed.
It would be manifestly unjust to incarcerate the surety
for several months, upon a fine of some fifteen hundred
dollars when the question of punishment for his misconduct is involved in so much doubt. The accused
person is certainly entitled to the benefit of that doubt,
and the present motion should be decided in his favor.

While this result may work a hardship upon the
plaintiff, it would operate still more onerously upon

the delinquent surety, were he to be committed erroneously, and thus be deprived of his liberty, for which money is, at best, an inadequate indemnity.

The motion to punish will, therefore, be denied, with $10 costs.

NORWOOD v. RAY MANUFACTURING COMPANY.

SUPREME COURT, SECOND DEPARTMENT, KINGS COUNTY, SPECIAL TERM, NOVEMBER, 1886.

§§ 14, 812, 2266, *et seq.*

Contempt.—Perjury when not a.—Power of court to punish surety testifying falsely on justification.

The perjury of one who falsely justifies as a surety upon an undertaking on appeal is not a contempt, and cannot be punished as such.

At common law a person not a party to an action and not representing a party as an agent or attorney, could not be punished as for a contempt for perjury committed in such action.

In re A'Becket (5 *Taut.* 776); Anonymous (1 *Strange*, 384); Smith *v.* Bond (2 D. & L., *Eng. Bail. Ct.* 460), distinguished. Hull *v.* L'Eplatinier (5 *Daly*, 534); Nathan *v.* Hope (5 *N. Y. Civ. Pro.* 401), not followed.

An act which is not a private contempt, and is not enumerated among criminal contempts is not a contempt at all.

People *ex rel.* Munsell *v.* Court of Oyer and Terminer (101 *N. Y.* 245), followed.

(*Decided November* 30, 1886.)

Motion to punish surety on undertaking on appeal for contempt in falsely justifying as such.

The opinion states the facts.

Frank E. Blackwell, for plaintiff and motion.

The court has power to punish Cowenhoven for contempt in committing willful and deliberate perjury by which the execution on the judgment herein was stayed pending the appeal. *Code Civ. Pro.* § 14, subd. 8 ; 2 *R. S.* 334 ; Hull *v.* L'Eplatinier, 5 *Daly*, 534 ; Stockham *v.* French, 1 *Bing.* (*Eng. C. P.*) 365 ; *In re* A'Becket, 5 *Taunt.* (*Eng. C. P.*) 775 ; Anonymous, 1 *Strange* (*Eng. K. B.*) 384 ; *Code Civ. Pro.* § 2266.

Arthur Howes, for defendant, opposed.

BARTLETT, J.—This is an application by the plaintiff to punish Randall G. Cowenhoven for contempt of court in having sworn falsely to an affidavit as to his qualifications as a surety upon the defendant's undertaking on appeal. It directly presents the question whether such false swearing on the part of the surety, assuming the offense to have been committed, constitutes a contempt of court under the laws of the State as they now exist.

In the recent case of the People *ex rel.* Munsell *v.* The Court of Oyer and Terminer,[*] the court of appeals expressly held that an act which is not a private contempt and is not enumerated among criminal contempts is not a contempt at all. Criminal contempts are defined in section 8 of the Code of Civil Procedure, but perjury is not among them. Private or civil contempts are defined in section 14 of the same Code, but there I am equally unable to find any language which will include the offense of perjury by a surety, unless it be in the 8th subdivision, which gives the court power to punish acts of misconduct in any case not previously mentioned, "where an attachment or any other proceeding to punish for contempt has been

---

[*] 101 *N. Y.* 245 ; S. C., 3 *East. R.* 563.

usually adopted and practiced in a court of record, to enforce a civil remedy of a party to an action or special proceeding, or to protect the right of a party."

Under this provision, which was formerly found in the Revised Statutes,* the New York court of common pleas, at special and general term, held that it had power to punish an agent of the party to the suit for contempt in knowingly procuring a minor to become a surety on the undertaking on appeal.† The same court adjudged a surety guilty of contempt for falsely swearing that he was worth a certain amount ; but the court of appeals reversed this decision on the facts of the case without passing upon the questions of law which it involved.‡ The New York superior court also held that sureties were punishable for contempt in swearing falsely as to their pecuniary responsibility.§ An examination of cases shows that they do not warrant the inference that perjury by a surety was ever punished as a contempt of court " to enforce a civil remedy of a party to an action or special proceeding or to protect the right of a party." . . . " Perjury is undoubtedly a great contempt of court," said Mr. Justice PARK, "but a contempt can only be visited summarily while the parties are yet in view of the court. At present the plaintiff's only remedy is by indictment."‖

The case of A'Becket (5 *Taunt.* [*Eng. C. P.*] 776) seems to be an authority against the power to punish perjured bail as for a contempt, instead of in favor of it. The entire opinion is in these words : " If the plaintiff can by any means connect the defendant or the defend-

---

* 2 *R. S.* 534, § 1.

† Hull v. L'Eplatinier, 5 *Daly*, 534.

‡ Nathan v. Hope, 5 *N. Y. Civ. Pro.* 401 ; rev'd 2 *East. R.* 655; S. C., 100 *N. Y.* 615.

§ Eagan v. Lynch, 3 *N. Y. Civ. Pro.* 236.

‖ Stockham v. French, 1 *Bing.* [*Eng. C. P.*] 365.

ant's attorney with the false swearing of the bail, the court will punish them, and the court has means so to do ; for the one is a suitor, and the other an officer of the court ; but if the bail have falsely sworn without the privity of the others, the plaintiff has no other remedy than by indictment for perjury. It is clear that the punishment administered in the anonymous case reported by Strange (Anonymous, 1 *Strange* [*Eng. K. B.*] 384), was for a contempt deemed criminal, and that it had no reference to the enforcement of the civil remedies, or the protection of the rights of the parties to the litigation." "Two people put in bail in feigned names," says the reporter, "and because there were no such persons, they could not be prosecuted for personating bail on the statute 21 Jac. I. c. 26. So the court ordered them and the attorney to be set in the pillory, which was done accordingly."

This was punishment pure and simple for an offense which tended to bring discredit upon the administration of public justice, and its infliction had no reference whatever to the particular rights of private suitors. The case is therefore not a common law precedent under subdivision 8,.of section 14, of the Code of Civil Procedure.

In Smith v. Bond* no question arose as to the liability of any one but the plaintiff to be punished for contempt. He had caused an untrue account of his address and abode to be delivered to the defendant. The court refused to issue an attachment against the plaintiff, because no harm appeared to have been done, but expressed an opinion that "whether it be by force or fraud, especially by those who are suitors before the court, and consequently peculiarly amenable to its jurisdiction, the parties will be liable to be punished by attachment, if they adopt any means wil-

---

* 2 D. & L. (*Eng. Bail Ct.*) 460.

fully to prevent the course of justice which they are bound to obey." Chief Baron POLLOCK adds that it is not even necessary to decide this proposition. At all events, it has no application to a proceeding to punish a person not a party to the action, nor representing a party as agent or attorney.

This review of the precedents relied upon in the L'Eplatinier case, fails to disclose any authority for holding that the perjury of a surety was punishable as a civil contempt at common law, and I have been referred to no such authority by counsel, unless we so consider the cases cited by counsel.

These are special term decisions, except Nathan *v.* Hope, and even then the only opinion delivered in the court of common pleas was at special term, as appears by an examination of the appeal-book (see court of appeals cases for October, 1885), while, as already observed, the court of appeals finally reversed the order upon the facts, significantly refusing to pass upon the other questions in the case. We have, therefore, only the special term opinions which have been mentioned, none of them in the supreme court, upholding the power to punish false swearing by a surety as a private contempt.

In an ordinary case I should follow an adjudication of the New York superior court or court of common pleas, although not binding here ; but in disposing of an application like the present, which involves personal liberty, I feel constrained to act upon my own view of the law, notwithstanding these decisions. I cannot find enough in the cases upon which they are based to justify the conclusion that perjury by a surety is a case " where attachments and proceedings as for contempts have been usually adopted and practiced in courts of record to enforce the civil remedies upon any party to a suit in such a court, or to protect the right of any such a party." The English precedents relied upon to sustain that conclusion do not support it. They tend rather to show that only criminal proceedings are available for the punishment of the offense, and that the appropriate remedy is by indictment.

Furthermore, I do not think it is proven beyond a reasonable doubt that the surety there has intentionally sworn to the statement which he knew to be false. Even if the power exists thus to punish a surety as for civil contempt, it would seem that his offense (of perjury) ought to be made out beyond a reasonable doubt, and the denial of the present application might well be based upon the insufficiency of the papers to establish Mr. Cowenhoven's guilt thus conclusively. I prefer, however, to place my decision wholly on the want of power to grant the application.

Motion denied, without costs.

BLANCHARD v. REILLY.

SUPREME COURT, FOURTH DEPARTMENT, ONONDAGA COUNTY, SPECIAL TERM, NOVEMBER, 1886.

§§ 2434, 2457.

Supplementary proceedings.—Jurisdiction of justice other than one for whom proceedings instituted.—Power of justice in one judicial district to order the continuance of proceedings before a justice in another district.

There is now no general provision of law which authorizes a justice granting an order for the examination of a judgment debtor in proceedings supplementary to execution to make all subsequent proceedings returnable before another justice residing in a different judicial district; section 2434 of the Code of Civil Procedure, is limited in its application to those cases where the execution was issued out of a court other than the supreme court, and yet the proceeding is instituted before a justice of that court.*

Where an order for the examination of a judgment debtor in proceedings supplementary to an execution, was made by a justice in one judicial district returnable before a referee in another judicial district, in which latter district the debtor resided, and directed that all the proceedings thereafter had therein be taken before a justice named in said order residing in the latter judicial district, —*Held*, that this provision was unauthorized and the order was irregular in that respect; that a motion to punish the judgment debtor for disobeying a stay contained in said order could only be made before the judge who granted the order, or at a special term of the court out of which the execution was issued.

(*Decided November* 29, 1886.)

Motion to punish the defendant for disobeying an order in proceedings supplementary to execution.

The opinion states the facts.

C. A. Fuller, for judgment-creditor and motion.

John Hopkins, for judgment-debtor, opposed.

VANN, J.—On May 13, 1884, the plaintiff recovered a judgment in this court against the defendant, for $219.85, and the roll thereof was on that day filed in the clerk's office of Chenango county. On May 15, 1884, said judgment was docketed upon a transcript filed in the clerk's office of Onondaga county. Subsequently an execution against the property of the defendant was issued to the sheriff of the county last named, within which the defendant then resided, and in due time the same was returned wholly unsatisfied. Upon an affidavit showing these among other facts, an order, dated December 18, 1884, was granted by a justice of this court, residing in the sixth judicial district, requiring the defendant, who still resided in the

* *Contra,* Browning *v.* Hayes, 11 *N. Y. Civ. Pro.* 223.

fifth judicial district, to appear before a referee and submit to examination concerning his property. Said order contained a clause restraining the defendant from transferring or interfering with his property, and was in the usual form of orders for the examination of judgment-debtors in proceedings supplementary to execution, except that the last paragraph thereof was in these words: "All subsequent .proceedings shall be had before Hon. J. G. VANN, a justice of the judicial district in which the debtor resides."

The order was served upon the defendant, who appeared and was examined, and the proceedings were from time to time adjourned.

Upon affidavits tending to show that the defendant had disobeyed the restraining clause of said order, a motion was made before me at chambers, on September 29, 1886, to punish him for contempt. He appeared by counsel, and opposed the motion on various grounds, but did not contend that I had no jurisdiction to entertain the proceeding to punish him. The proofs presented satisfy me that he is guilty of contempt, and that he should be punished therefor. The question, however, arises whether, under the circumstances, I have jurisdiction to adjudge him guilty or to inflict punishment upon him. When the proceeding is based upon a judgment of the supreme court, can the justice before whom it is initiated confer jurisdiction upon another justice residing in the same district as the judgment-debtor as to all subsequent proceedings? This practice was expressly authorized by the Code of Procedure, which provided that "in case of an order made by a justice of the supreme court all subsequent proceedings" should "be had before some justice in the judicial district where the judgment-debtor resides, to be specified in the order" (*Code of Pro.* § 292).

While this provision was in force it was held to be irregular for a justice of the supreme court, in granting an order for the examination of a judgment debtor without the judicial district of such justice, to direct the referee to report to him (Pardee v. Tilton, 58 *How.* 476).

The Code of Civil Procedure contains an analogous provision, but limits its application to those cases where the execution was issued out of a court other than the supreme court, and yet the proceeding is instituted before a justice of that court (*Code Civ. Pro.* § 2434).

There is no general provision now in force, applicable to judgments rendered in the supreme court, that authorizes a justice granting an order for the examination of a judgment debtor, to make all subsequent proceedings returnable before another justice residing in a different judicial district.

The order in question, was therefore unauthorized and irregular in directing that all subsequent proceedings should be had before me. This clause, being part of an old printed blank prepared for use under the Code of Civil Procedure, doubtless escaped the attention of the learned justice who granted the order.

It is provided by section 2457 of the Code of Civil Procedure, that disobedience of an order in supplementary proceedings "may be punished by the judge, or by the court out of which the execution was issued, as for a contempt."

This means the judge before whom the proceeding was initiated, or the court at special term out of which the execution was issued (Lathrop v. Clapp, 40 *N. Y.* 328; Dresser v. Van Pelt, 15 *How. Pr.* 19; Shepherd v. Dean, 13 *Id.* 173; *Riddle & Bullard's Supplementary Proceedings*, 207–209).

There seems to be no provision applicable to this

case that authorizes the proceeding to be continued, either to punish for contempt or for any other. purpose, before an officer other than the one before whom it was instituted.

Section 26, which authorizes one judge to continue a special proceeding instituted before another, is limited to the city and county of New York.

Section 52 authorizes the substitution in special proceedings of one officer for another when the latter is unable to act from death, sickness or other disability.

Section 279 has a local application only, and does, not affect this case.

These sections are made applicable to proceedings supplementary to execution by section 2462, but it is evident from mere inspection that they do not authorize one justice to continue a proceeding commenced before another, except as expressly permitted under circumstances such as do not exist in this case.

Clearly, therefore, no jurisdiction was conferred upon me either by the order itself, or by the statute independent of the order.

It is equally clear that jurisdiction was not conferred by the appearance of the defendant, and his failure to raise the objection (Sackett v. Newton, 10 How. Pr. 561 ; Carter v. Clarke, 7 Robt. 490, 497 ; Riddle & Bullard's Sup. Pro. 457).

It follows that the motion should be denied, but as all of the essential parts of the order in question are valid, without prejudice to a motion to punish the defendant for contempt, if made before the justice who granted the original order, or before the court at special term.

As the defendant prevails only upon a ground not suggested by him, no costs are allowed.

RUNBERG, Respondent, v. JOHNSON, as Treas-
URER OF THE VALHALLA COUNCIL OF THE
ORDER OF CHOSEN FRIENDS, APPELLANT.

CITY COURT OF BROOKLYN, GENERAL TERM, DECEM-
BER, 1886.

§§ 2320, 2322, 2340.

*When judgment not reversed because plaintiff is insane—When proof
of insanity sufficient to authorize recovery of sick benefits from
a mutual benefit society not sufficient to require
dismissal of action.*

Where, in an action against a mutual benefit society for sick benefits,
the benefits were claimed on the ground that the plaintiff was insane,
and a release signed by him was avoided on that ground, but the
plaintiff had not been judicially determined to be a lunatic in any
proceeding brought for that purpose,—*Held*, that the finding of the
court that the plaintiff was *non compos mentis* when he executed
the release, had no effect beyond setting aside that instrument ;
that the finding that he was insane at the time of the commencement of the action was material only so far as it showed that he
was disabled from following his usual business pursuits, or other
occupation, and therefore entitled to benefits ; that until after
office found the presumption prevailed that the attorney who
appeared for the plaintiff had competent authority to do so, and a
contention that the attorney was without authority, because the
plaintiff was insane could not be sustained on appeal from the
judgment ; but if there was an absence of such authority the error
should have been reached by a direct motion for the interposition
of the court.

Valentine v. Rickhardt (*unreported*), distinguished.

An action may be commenced in the name of a person of unsound
mind before he has been judicially declared such ; the Code of
Civil Procedure does not prohibit the bringing of an action and
does not change the legal status of the lunatic until the court interposes its jurisdiction.

It seems, that where an attorney is responsible and brings an action

without authority, the party in whose name the action is brought
is bound by the judgment therein and must seek his remedy
against the attorney; and that this is so although such party is a
lunatic.

(*Decided December*, 1886.)

Reargument of appeal from judgment of the special
term.

This action was brought by the plaintiff to recover
$85.00 due him as a sick benefit under and by virtue
of the by-laws of the association represented by the
defendant.   Said association is an unincorporated
council of the Order of Chosen Friends, the supreme
body of which order is incorporated under the laws of
Indiana.
   The by-laws provide for the payment by the society
of five dollars per week to any member, who "shall
become disabled by sickness or other disability from
following his or her usual business," such payment
being restricted to twenty-six weeks in each year.
   The plaintiff joined the society at the time of its
organization in 1881, and it is conceded that he has
ever since been a member in good standing.   In August, 1883, the plaintiff received a severe sunstroke,
which resulted a week thereafter in his becoming
insane.   On September 8, 1883, he was conveyed to
the insane asylum at Flatbush, after examination by
Doctors Young and Stone, who pronounced him insane.
From the time he entered the asylum up to the present
he has been continuously insane. During this period he
has been under the care of Doctor Ferris, one of the
physicians connected with the asylum, who testified
that the plaintiff's case was incurable.   When he
entered the asylum the society began paying him five
dollars per week and continued such payment regu-

larly for the full period of twenty-six weeks of the first year, as provided for by the by-laws of the society, such payments dating from September 1, 1883. When one year had elapsed the society began making payments for the second year, commencing September 1, 1884, and continued such payments for nine weeks, when they were discontinued, leaving unpaid seventeen weeks of the second year. The refusal of the society to make further payments, was based upon the opinion of one of its members, a physician, who claimed that the plaintiff was sane, and who upon the trial testified : "He is not insane. I decidedly disagree with Doctors Young, Stone and Ferris on this point."

Five days after the commencement of this action the president of the society, for the purpose of defeating the plaintiff's claim, went to the asylum, saw the plaintiff, and had him sign a general release, which was introduced in evidence upon the trial.

Defendant appealed to the general term, which reversed the judgment, the opinion being written by CLEMENT, J., and concurred in by REYNOLDS, Ch. J. (*Quid vide, post,* p. 291, note).

Thereafter plaintiff's attorney moved for a reargument which was granted.

H. H. Morse (*Leeds & Morse*, attorneys), for defendant appellant.

In 2 *Barb. Ch. Pr.* 224, it is said : "Suits cannot be prosecuted by a lunatic except through the appointment of a committee of his estate, he being alone responsible for the conduct of his suit." See *Code Civ. Pro.* § 2340. In *Tyler's Milford's Pr.* 200, it is said : "It has always been the practice in England, that a lunatic should sue or defend in the name of the committee of his estate." Section 449 of the Code of Civil Procedure provides that all actions must be prosecuted in the name of the real party in interest, except a trustee of an express trust, who may sue without joining with him the person for whose benefit the action is prosecuted. The committee of a lunatic is a trustee of an express trust. Person v. Warren, 14 *Barb.* 488. If the plaintiff in a suit appears to be a lunatic, and no next friend or committee is named, the defendant may demur. *Mitford's Ch. Pl.* 229.

If the plaintiff is a lunatic, then proceedings for the appointment of a committee of the person and of the property should have been instituted and such committee appointed before bringing this suit. See *Code Civ. Pro.* § 2320, 2322. Section 2322 provides that the jurisdiction of the court over the property of a lunatic must be exercised by means of a committee, and section 2340 provides for the bringing of actions by a committee in his own name adding his official title.

In view of these provisions the court below erred in denying defendant's motion for a non-suit duly made. If the plaintiff is not a lunatic, then his repudiation of the suit and general release should have defeated the recovery.

J. Edward Swanstrom, for plaintiff-respondent.

If the fact was that the attorney had no authority to bring this action it would be no ground for reversing the judgment. It is settled law in this State that where an attorney is responsible (and no doubt here exists upon that point) the judgment stands, and the party must seek his remedy against the attorney who appeared without authority. Brown v. Nichols, 42 *N. Y.* 30 (citing Denton v. Noyes, 6 *Johns.* 296); Ferguson v. Crawford, 70 *N. Y.* 256; Hamilton v. Wright, 37 *Id.* 502; American Ins. Co. v. Oakley, 9 *Paige*, 499, where it is said "not necessary to protection of rights, proceedings should be set aside as unauthorized, even if want of authority of attorney was fully established." U. S. supreme court refused to reverse for want of authority. Osborn v. U. S. Bank, 9 *Wheat.* 831. In these cases the whole subject is thoroughly discussed *pro* and *con.* Sane or insane, a party is bound by an unauthorized appearance, except it be that the attorney is not responsible. In the case of Brown v. Nichols, above cited, the party was a lunatic. The law is the same, whether the party is plaintiff or defendant. Brown v. Nichols (*supra*); Denton v. Noyes, (*supra*); Sternberg v. Schoolcraft, 2 *Barb.* 155; McKillip v. McKillip, 8 *Id.* 552; Crippen v. Culver, 13 *Id.* 424. Should the plaintiff recover his reason, he could not disturb this judgment. Any committee hereafter appointed could not have any greater right than a sane plaintiff. The only remedy for either plaintiff or his committee would be to sue the attorney. It would be the same had the judgment been against the plaintiff. He or his committee would be bound by such a judgment. See remarks Lord ABINGER in Rock v. Slade, 2 *Jurist*, 993.

But there is nothing to show want of authority either in the complaint or in the proof. It is at the best only an inference from the proof of plaintiff's insanity. (If it be said that the declarations of the plaintiff that there was no authority are in evidence and uncontradicted, the reply is that it does not appear that the court believed that evidence. The circumstances and the position of the witness who testified as to those declarations fully warranted the court in rejecting that testimony, even if uncontradicted.) Elwood v. Western Union Tel., 45 *N. Y.* 549; Kavanagh v. Wilson, 70 *Id.* 177; Koehler v. Adler, 78 *Id.* 289; Tolman v. Syracuse, 31 *Hun*, 398; Gildersleeve v. Landon, 73 *N. Y.* 609. The record shows that plaintiff appeared by attorney, and nothing can be assigned for error which contradicts the record. King *v.* Robinson, 54 *Am. Dec.* 614. The want of authority should have been set up by answer as it does not appear on the face of the complaint. *Mitford's Pleadings*, 227. . . .

The plaintiff, being a lunatic, not found, could bring this action. By the common law, an action brought to assert the title of a lunatic to real or personal property must be brought in his name. Fields *v.* Fowler, 2 *Hun*, 400, quoting McKillip *v.* McKillip, 8 *Barb.* 552 ; 1 *Chitty's Pleadings*, 18, where it says : " Contract with lunatic, action must be in his name, not in name of committee." The appointment of a committee did not divest the lunatic of his estate or rights of action. The court took charge of the lunatic and the committee was only its bailiff. This is the law now. People *ex rel.* Smith *v.* Commissioners of Taxes, 100 *N. Y.* 218 ; 2 *Hun*, 400. The New York statute of 1845 first gave to the committee the right to bring actions in his own name. It specified the actions, and only in those specified actions could the committee sue in his name. The Code of Civil Procedure has merely enlarged the scope of that statute. . . . . It has been frequently held that lunatics may be sued whether committees have been appointed or not. Chancery may restrain, but if it does not, the judgment is neither void nor voidable. Sanford *v.* Sanford, 62 *N. Y.* 553 ; S. C., 32 *Am. Dec.* 70.

Two defendants in a partition suit were lunatics for whom no committee had been appointed. Both personally served ; one appeared by attorney. Purchaser at sale refused to take title. Court at general term, second department, in 1883, held he must. They say, " Assuming defendants were *non sui juris* at commencement of the action, nevertheless they were liable to be sued. Mental incapacity or incompetency present no interference with the enforcement of legal liabilities. Institution of legal proceedings against lunatics is not inhibited. Whether their insanity constituted defense depends on circumstances of case," quoting Sandford v. Sandford, 62 *N. Y.* 553 ; Mutual Life Ins. Co. v. Hunt, 79 *N. Y.* 541 ; S. C., 14 *Hun*, 169. "The judgment was not even erroneous," quoting Crippen v. Culver, 13 *Barb.* 428, and Sternberg *v.* Schoolcraft, 2 *Barb.* 153. See also Prentiss v. Cornell, 31 *Hun*, 167 ; affi'd, 96 *N. Y.* 665. . . . That an idiot has appeared and defended by attorney can not be assigned for error. 2 *Saund.* 336. Judgment will not be reversed for error on ground of lunacy. Must restrain. Attempt to enjoin on the ground of insanity not sufficient; must be other facts. Sandford v. Sandford, 32 *Am. Dec.* 70. In Maryland, Owney's Case, 17 *Am. Dec.* 317, a bill was filed to relieve from a deed. Plaintiff was in her dotage. The court granted the relief. That case resembled this in that the plaintiff here was relieved from the effect of his release. It may be said in passing, that in Owney's case the old maxim that no man can stultify himself was discussed. That maxim has been rejected in New York. Rice v. Peet, 15 *Johns.* 503. King v. Robinson, 54 *Am. Dec.* 614, contains an elaborate opinion upon the question under discussion.

An idiot or lunatic may sue at law after the execution of the commission of lunacy and after his person is placed under the care of a committee, though the court will always permit his committee to assist in managing the prosecution. Crippen v. Culver, 13 *Barb.* 428. A lunatic confessed by attorney. Objection he had no authority. Held, on review of authorities, judgment good. Stigers v. Brant, 50 *Md.* 214 ; 33 *Am. Rep.* 317. As already stated, the law is the same, whether the lunatic is plaintiff or defendant. The citations in defendant's points on the former argument of this appeal, from 2 *Barb. Ch. Pr.* 200, and *Tyler's Milford's Pleadings in Chancery*, 200, are not

in point. In these passages reference is to persons
who have been found lunatics on inquisition. Both,
of course, are chancery books of practice. The passage
in Barbour is copied from Daniels, and the authorities
are very old English cases. . . . Turning now to
English cases, we find the following recent cases in
chancery and at law, where the question is discussed
on principle and authority. Jones v. Lloyd (9 *Moak's
Eng. Rep.* 792), was a suit brought by the next friend
of a lunatic not found, for dissolution of a partnership,
alleging the plaintiff's insanity. There was a demurrer interposed that suit could not be maintained,
which was overruled. . . . See also *Pierre William*,
111 *note ;* Rock v. Slade, 2 *Jurist*, 993.

A wife has authority arising out of the marital
relation to sue in her husband's name and to employ
an attorney for the purpose where the sum recovered
is necessary for her support, under circumstances such
as those in this case. See Rock v. Slade, *supra*. See
also Read v. Legard, 4 *Eng. L. & E.* 323; S. C., 15
Jurist, 494.

REYNOLDS, Ch. J.—The issues really litigated upon
the trial, were first, whether the plaintiff had become
sick and disabled from following his usual business,
as alleged in the fourth paragraph of the complaint,
the same being denied by the defendant, and second,
whether the plaintiff had discharged and released his
claim subsequent to the commencement of the action.

The court finds that the plaintiff, in August, 1883,
became and *still continued* sick, " *insane, and disabled from following his usual business or other occupation,*" and that the release purporting to be executed by him was procured from him after the
commencement of the action, " and while the plaintiff
was *non compos mentis.*"

The evidence abundantly sustains the first finding,

at least to the extent that the plaintiff was, during the time for which he claimed benefits, "disabled by sickness or other disability, from following his usual business, pursuit, or other occupation," in the language of the by-law set out in the complaint ; and it also sustains the finding as to the *release*, and thus avoids the effect which it would otherwise have had.

The defendant now seeks to reverse the judgment on the ground that as it appears the plaintiff was insane at the time of the commencement of the action, he was incompetent to employ an attorney, and the attorney was therefore without authority to appear for him.

I originally concurred, not without doubt, in the forcible opinion written by Judge CLEMENT to show that this was a fatal objection to the judgment, but on further reflection since the reargument, I have come to a contrary conclusion.

The plaintiff has not been judicially determined to be a lunatic on any proceeding brought for that purpose. The finding of the court that he was *non compos* when he executed the release, has no effect beyond setting aside that instrument.

The other finding (which covers the time of the commencement of the action), that he was "insane and disabled from following his usual business or other occupation," is material only so far as to bring him within the scope of the by-law above referred to, viz: to show that he was "disabled from following his usual business, pursuit, or other occupation."

It is not clear that the court meant more than this by the use of the word "insane," in the connection in which it is used. His mind was so far unsound as to incapacitate him from pursuing his business (that of an upholsterer), but until "after office found," the presumption must still prevail that the attorney who appears in his name has competent authority. Be-

.sides, the issues made by the pleadings having been
rightly decided in favor of the plaintiff, even if there
has been an irregularity such as is claimed, how can
it be corrected on appeal from the judgment?

The judge correctly declares the rights and liabili-.
ties of the parties. If the attorney appeared without
proper authority, that error should have been reached
by a direct motion for the interposition of the court.

I do not see that the decision of this court in
Valentine v. Rickhardt (unreported), is in point here.

In that case, a person without notice to the nominal
plaintiff, and in fact in open hostility to her, had procured an order appointing him her next friend, for the
purpose of commencing an action to set aside a conveyance of real estate made by her, and the action was
brought in her name *by him as next friend.*

We held that such a procedure was unauthorized
by any law or practice in this State. That was entirely
a different question from the one now presented.

Counsel for the appellant contends that the provisions of the Code of Procedure, §§ 2320 *et seq.* prohibit the bringing of an action in the name of a person
who is a lunatic.

The first section declares that the jurisdiction of
the court extends to the custody of the *person* and the
care of the *property* of a person incompetent to manage himself or his affairs in consequence of lunacy,
idiocy or habitual drunkenness, and section 2322
declares that such jurisdiction must be exercised by
means of a committee of the person or property. But
until the court interposes its jurisdiction, these provisions do not change the legal status of the persons
named in section 2320.

Before the court puts forth its arm, it would hardly
be claimed that an habitual drunkard can not employ
an attorney, and prosecute a suit in his own name. If
he may do so, the argument against a suit by a person

incompetent, from any of the other causes named, fails, as far as this statute is concerned. The only regulation as to actions is found in section 2340, which provides that a committee *when appointed* may maintain in his own name as committee, any action which the person for whom he is appointed, "might have maintained if the appointment had not been made." The right to commence an action in the name of a person of unsound mind before he has been judicially declared to be such, is implied rather than taken away by this statute.

It is said that the judgment ought not to stand, because, if the defendant had recovered judgment, it could have been avoided by the plaintiff, on the ground that his attorney had no authority to commence the action. This seems to be a begging of the question. It assumes one side of the very question under discussion ; and I think the assumption is wrong. It seems to be settled that where the attorney is responsible (and there is no question here on that point) the party is bound by the judgment, and must seek his remedy against the attorney who appeared without authority (Brown *v.* Nichols, 42 *N. Y.* 30 ; Ferguson *v.* Crawford, 70 *N. Y.* 254).*

I can see no reason why a lunatic before office found should not be subject to this rule as well as any other person. He has the same legal standing to appear as a party in his own name, till a committee has been appointed in the manner provided by law. The parties litigated upon an equality, and the judgment is binding upon both.

With this view of the case I think the judgment should be affirmed.

CLEMENT, J. — (dissenting.) — The plaintiff has been insane since the month of August, 1883, and

---

* See *contra*, Gilman *v.* Prentice, *post*, p. 311.

from that date till the trial of this action was an inmate of the lunatic asylum, at Flatbush, and from the proofs it is fair to assume that he has been *non compos mentis* all of that time. After the commencement of this action the plaintiff executed a release of the claim in suit, which the learned judge before whom the case was tried has found to be invalid, for the reason of want of mental capacity of the plaintiff to execute same. The plaintiff has recovered for sick benefits of the defendant on the ground that he was insane and has avoided his release on that ground. Suppose the judgment had been for defendant at special term, and the plaintiff, after proceedings in lunacy, should by his committee bring an action for the same claim, the judgment could be avoided on the ground that the attorney for the plaintiff had no authority to commence the action. If the plaintiff is incompetent to give a release he is not competent to employ an attorney.

A person of sound mind cannot now sue by next friend, and it is clear that this action has been commenced by authority of some friend of plaintiff in his name and not by his authority, because he has been mentally incompetent to employ an attorney. The defendant, if he recovered a judgment in his favor, would not have a judgment of any validity, and a judgment in favor of the plaintiff cannot therefore stand.

The defendant has full notice that the plaintiff is of unsound mind, and could not say that he paid the claim in good faith without knowledge of the want of capacity of plaintiff.

The remedy of the relatives of plaintiff is to apply for an adjudication of lunacy. In England there are authorities that actions have been permitted to be brought to protect the personal property of lunatics, in their names, by next friend, but in these cases judgment cannot be entered till after the appointment of a committe. In the case of Valentine *v.* Richardt, decided February 24, 1885, by the general term of this court, we held that an action could not be brought in the name of a party without his consent, and the remedy of the friends of the alleged lunatic is to apply for an adjudication in lunacy.

The proofs in this case show that the plaintiff stated that this action was brought without his knowledge or authority. Until he has been adjudged a lunatic in the manner prescribed by the Code, the plaintiff has certainly a right to say whether an action shall be brought. His right of property has been taken from him without a hearing, and he has been adjudged a lunatic and has had no opportunity to be heard on the question. It would be unsafe to allow an action to be brought in the name of a party, or what is the same thing, to take his property from him, on the theory that he was a lunatic, when the Code prescribes the only manner in which that question can be determined. The judgment must be reversed and a new trial granted, costs to abide the event.

NOLAN ET AL. *v.* COMMAND ET AL.

SUPREME COURT, FOURTH DEPARTMENT, ONONDAGA COUNTY, SPECIAL TERM, MAY, 1886.

§§ 1532, 1538, 1539.

Partition—When may be maintained by alien resident—Effect of law of escheat—Necessity of making State a party.

A resident alien may take real property as an heir, and his title thereto is good as against everybody but the State; the title vests in him but is to be divested in proceedings instituted by the State, unless before the commencement of such proceedings he files the deposition required by law; until such proceedings are taken the alien is entitled to the use and enjoyment of his share of such property, and is a tenant in common with the other heirs to the same property, and as such is deemed to be in possession, and may maintain an action for its partition.

Where, in an action for partition it appeared that the plaintiff and certain of the defendants were aliens, who had not declared their intentions to become citizens,—*Held*, that this fact did not prevent the maintenance of the action, but that the State was a necessary party defendant ; that the fact that the plaintiff had declared his intentions pending the action could be set up by supplemental complaint; but this would not obviate the necessity of making the State a party, inasmuch as certain of the defendants were aliens who had not declared their intentions, and it appeared that the premises must be sold.

(*Decided May* 10, 1886.)

Action for partition of real property.

The facts appear in the opinion.

W. M. Morrissey. for plaintiff.

M. E. & G. W. Driscoll, for defendants.

MERWIN, J.—In June, 1885, Joanna Feagan, who was then the owner of the premises in question, died intestate, leaving as her heirs and next of kin, three sisters and two brothers, all of full age and residing in the United States ; and also five children of a deceased sister Mary Nolan, who was an alien, and lived in Ireland, and died some years ago. All of these five children are of full age, and three of them, Ellen Nolan, Mary Ann Mangan and Jeremiah Nolan, reside in Ireland, and the other two, Bartholomew Nolan and the plaintiff John Nolan, reside in the United States.

This action was commenced on June 19, 1885. At that time the plaintiff had not filed the deposition required by the statute (3 *R. S.* 7 ed. 2164, § 15 ; chap. 261 of *Laws of* 1874; chap. 38 of *Laws of* 1875) to enable him to hold real estate as against the State. It appears, however, that he did file such a deposition on January 16, 1886. No deposition has been filed by Jeremiah or Bartholomew Nolan.

The question is whether the plaintiff, at the time of the commencement of this action, was in a position to maintain partition (Wisner v. Ocumpaugh, 71 *N. Y.* 113).

Under the provisions of chap. 115, of *Laws of* 1845, as amended by chap. 38 of *Laws of* 1875 (3 *R. S.* 7 ed. 2170, § 4), the title of the plaintiff, as heir, was good, as against everybody but the State. The title vested in him, subject to be divested in proceedings instituted by the State, unless, before the commencement of such proceedings, he filed the requisite deposition (Goodrich v. Russell, 42 *N. Y.* 177; Maynard v. Maynard, 36 *Hun*, 227). As said in the case cited, no such proceeding has been instituted, and therefore the State has not acquired any right or interest in the premises.

The plaintiff is entitled to the use and enjoyment of his share of the premises. He is a tenant in common with the other heirs, and as such is deemed to be in possession.

By section 1532 of Code, where two or more persons hold, or are in possession of real property as tenants in common, in which either of them has an estate of inheritance, or for life, or for years, any one or more of them may maintain an action for partition. All of the other heirs except the two brothers of plaintiff took absolute estate in fee.

The right of the estate is somewhat analogous to the outstanding optional power of sale, with no present right of possession. Such a power would not, as I suppose, interfere with the right of one of the holders of the title and possession to maintain partition (see Morse v. Morse, 85 *N. Y.* 58).

Though very likely the holder of the power would be a proper party defendant (48 *Ill.* 111).

Under the provisions of the Code referred to, I think the plaintiff is in position to maintain the action. The State, however, is not made a party, but no objection of this kind is taken by answer.

So far as the plaintiff's interest is concerned, if the fact of filing the deposition, which has occurred since the commencement of the action, was set up by supplemental pleading, that would, I think, obviate the necessity of making the State a party. But there are two defendants to above interest: the State may lay claim, and, as it is conceded here, that the premises must be sold, it looks to me that the State is a necessary party defendant, in order to a complete determination of the matter, and a passage of a good title. Anything that either party has to say about this, I will hear on the settlement of the order or findings to be made herein.

LARKINS, Respondent, *v.* MAXON, as Administrator, &c., of ORVILLE C. SPRAGUE, Deceased, Appellant.

Court of Appeals, November, 1886.

§§ 1835, 1836, 3246.

Reference of claim against administrator—Right of successful party to disbursements—Repeal of § 317 of the Code of Procedure

The successful party, upon a reference of a claim against the estate of a deceased person, is entitled to recover disbursements as a matter of right ; so much of section 317 of the Code of Procedure as provided for the granting of disbursements on such a reference has not been repealed.

Miller v. Miller (32 *Hun*, 481); Daggett v. Mead (11 *Abb. N. C.* 116), overruled; Krill v. Brownell (10 *N. Y. Civ. Pro.* 8); Sutton v. Newton (7 *Id.* 8); Overheiser v. Moorehouse (8 *Id.* 11); Hull v. Edmunds (67 *How. Pr.* 202), approved.

A domestic may be treated in many respects like a daughter, without holding that relation to the employer, and the finding of a referee upon reference of a claim against a decedent's estate, that the claimant's relations to the decedent's family were affectionate and kindly, like those of a daughter, is not inconsistent with a finding that she performed work, labor and services, at the decedent's request, as a domestic in his family.

(*Decided November* 23, 1886.)

Appeal by defendant from an order and judgment of the general term, of the fourth department, affirming a judgment in favor of the plaintiff, entered at the special term, upon the report of a referee, in a reference under 2 *R. S.* 88, § 36, of a claim against the estate of the defendant's decedent.

The defendant-appellant is the administrator, &c. of Orville C. Sprague, deceased. The plaintiff-respondent presented a claim to him for services claimed to have been rendered the decedent as a domestic in his family. The claim was referred pursuant to the statute, and the referee found among other things, "that between October 5, 1867, and February 20, 1880, plaintiff rendered and performed work, labor and services, for said Orville C. Sprague, at his request, as a domestic in his family for the term of six hundred and two and one-third weeks, and that said services were worth $1.50 per week ; that plaintiff's relations in Sprague's family were affectionate and kindly, like those of a daughter, and that her services prior to the time she talked of leaving, in or about 1875, were not done under any express contract, and no such contract existed before that time."

The special term confirmed the report of the referee, and, holding that the plaintiff was entitled to her dis-

bursements, granted the same to her; the general
term, on appeal from the order and judgment entered
thereon, modified the judgment by striking therefrom the award of disbursements, and, as modified,
affirmed it with costs; and the defendant thereafter
took this appeal from the judgment and order thereupon entered.

Elon R. Brown (*Dorwin & Brown*, attorneys), for
defendant-appellant.

W. H. Gillman, for plaintiff-respondent.

PER CURIAM.—We do not think that the findings
of the referee were inconsistent. A domestic may be
treated like a daughter, without holding that relation
to the employer. The facts were sufficient to establish at least an implied contract for compensation,
and so far as there was an express one, it had not been
fulfilled by the devise and legacy given by Mrs.
Sprague. The destroyed wills of Sprague and his wife
bore somewhat on the actually existing relation
between the parties, and formed incidents in the history of these relations. Since the referee found, as a
fact, the existence of an implied contract, his opinion
about an understanding " not amounting to contract"
was immaterial.

From the judgment entered on the report of the
referee the general term struck out the disbursements
taxed and allowed, upon the ground that section 317
of the old Code of Procedure, which provided for their
taxation, was repealed by the repealing act of 1880,
and the right was not preserved by subdivision 8 of
section 3 of that act. Upon the construction of that
saving clause there has been a difference of opinion in
the supreme court. In Miller *v.* Miller (32 *Hun*, 481),
and Daggett *v.* Mead (11 *Abb. N. C.* 116), the saving
clause was held to prevent the destruction only of the

right to such disbursements as were provided for in the Revised Statutes, and, there being none such in a case like the present, there was nothing saved. To the contrary, are Krill v. Brownell (10 *N. Y. Civ. Pro.* 8) ; Sutton v. Newton, (7 *Id.* 333) ;* Hall v. Edmunds (67 *How. Pr.* 202) ; and Overheiser v. Morehouse (8 *N. Y. Civ. Pro.* 11). We think these last cited cases establish the true construction of the subdivision referred to, and that it was intended and did preserve the right to disbursements given by the former Code upon the reference of a claim against a decedent.

The order of the general term striking out disbursements should be reversed, and the judgment as entered at special term be affirmed, with costs of the appeal to this court.

All concurred.

EASTON, Respondent, *v.* CARDWELL, Impleaded, &c., Appellant.

City Court of Brooklyn, General Term, December, 1886.

§§ 549 *et seq.*

Arrest—What amounts to disposition of property with intent to defraud creditors.

A person who, in consideration of his debtor's taking a note payable in thirty days for the amount due, agreed to assign to him, as collateral security therefor, a bond and mortgage, and thereafter secured the payment of such bond and mortgage, before its matur-

---

* The decision in Sutton v. Newton here referred to was reversed by the general term in the third department, in September, 1885, on appeal from the order entered on said decision. The general term, after discussing other matters, said :

Easton *v.* Cardwell.

ity, by allowing a discount, and applied the money thus realized to
the payment of another note on which his father was an indorser,
is guilty of disposing of his property with intent to defraud such
creditor, and an order for his arrest may be granted in an action
on the note.

(*Decided December* 27, 1886.)

Appeal from order of special **term denying a**
motion to vacate order of arrest.

Sufficient facts are stated in the opinion.

Samuel P. Potter, for defendant-appellant.

James Troy, for plaintiff-respondent.

REYNOLDS, Ch. J.—On October 10, 1884, the defendants were indebted to plaintiff in the sum of $671.25
which was then due. On being pressed for payment
the defendant Cardwell, as an inducement to plaintiff
to take a note at thirty days for the amount, agreed to
assign to plaintiff as collateral security for the note a
bond and mortgage held by defendants for $650, which
Cardwell said would be soon paid and the difference
in the amount paid in cash. The note was accordingly
given, and a written memorandum very inartificially
drawn, by which defendants agreed to deliver to plaintiff the mortgage in question as soon as it was received

---

" But the question whether he [*i. e.*, the plaintiff who succeeded in the reference] is entitled as a matter of right to his
disbursements, has been twice before this general term. Once in
Dodd *v.* Dodd, not reported, again in Miller *v.* Miller (32 *Hun*, 481,
S. C., 67 *How. Pr.* 135). It was again before us indirectly in Webster
v. Nichols (21 *N. Y. Week. Dig.* 566), where costs *and* disbursements
were stricken out of a judgment on such a reference, thus showing
that disbursements were not considered a matter of right.

" As we have twice or three times decided that these disbursements are not a matter of right, we must consider the matter settled,
unless a higher court should reverse our views."

from the register's office, as collateral security for the note. The writing speaks of the mortgage only, but the evidence on the part of the plaintiff shows that the delivery of the bond and mortgage were both contemplated, and of this there can be no doubt. While the plaintiff, relying upon defendant's promise, was waiting for the delivery of the bond and mortgage, the defendants procured the mortgagor to pay the same before its maturity by allowing a discount of $75, and applied the money thus realized to the payment of another note, on which the father of defendant Cardwell was an indorser.

The court at special term held, that in doing this the appellant defendant Cardwell, who appears to have been the active party in this transaction, disposed of his property with intent to defraud the plaintiff, one of his creditors, and accordingly sustained the order of arrest. We think this conclusion is well sustained by the evidence. Defendants obtained from plaintiff an extension of time, upon the promise to turn over the bond and mortgage to him, an although they applied the proceeds of it to the payment of another debt, it was a gross fraud upon the plaintiff, who had acquired a right to hold it as security, or, if paid, to have the money applied to his claim. It was not like the simple case of a creditor applying his property to pay one creditor in preference to another—it was the violation of a legal and honest obligation.

The order should be affirmed with $10 costs and the disbursements.

VAN WYCK, J., concurred.

SCHILLER *v.* MALTBIE, as Trustee, etc.

County Court of Erie County, January, 1887.

§§ 520.

Pleading.— To be subscribed at end.—Indorsement not sufficient.

The Code of Civil Procedure (§ 520) requires that a pleading be
subscribed by the attorney for the party serving it at the end
thereof; and an indorsement of the name and address of such
attorney on the back of the pleading is not a sufficient compliance
with the Code; both the subscriptions and the indorsement are
required, and neither alone is sufficient.

Affidavits showing, or tending to show, that an answer is false, will
not defeat a motion to compel the acceptance of an answer served
in time, but which was returned on account of a slight technical
error resulting from a clerical mistake; the objection should be
taken by motion to strike out the pleading as sham.

While ordinarily, where a party goes into court asking as a favor
to be relieved from his own mistake, he should be required to pay
the costs of opposing his motion; where the mistake is purely
inadvertent, and the objection a technical one, and before motion,
costs have been offered and declined, no costs of the motion should
be allowed.

(*Decided January*, 1887.)

Motion by defendant for an order requiring the
plaintiff's attorney to receive the answer heretofore
served upon him, a copy of which was served with
the moving papers.

The facts appear in the opinion.

Fayette Kelly, for defendant and motion.

Abram Thorn, for plaintiff, opposed.

Schiller *v.* Maltbie.

HAMMOND, Co. J.—It appears from the papers served upon this motion that the original answer, which was verified by defendant, was properly subscribed by his attorney, in accordance with section 520 of the Code of Civil Procedure, which provides, " A pleading must be subscribed by the attorney for the party," &c.,—but in copying the answer the name of the attorney was inadvertently left off from the copy that was served on plaintiff's attorney. But on the outside this copy was properly indorsed with the name and address of defendant's attorney, as required by rule 2 of the supreme court. This copy was thus served on the last day for service, and was returned by plaintiff's attorney the following day, indorsed by him as follows :

" Sir: This copy of answer is returned to you for irregularity. First, it is not subscribed by an attorney. Second, it is not properly verified. Dated," &c.

Defendant's attorney thereupon supplied the omission, by subscribing it, and then tendered the copy thus corrected to plaintiff's attorney, who declined to accept, upon the ground that it was " too late," and thereupon this motion is made.

Defendant's attorney contends that the indorsement on the outside of the answer after it is folded, " Fayette Kelly, attorney for defendant," &c., is a sufficient compliance with the section of the Code above quoted, and cites authorities to sustain that proposition ; but I think this contention cannot be successfully maintained, and that no authority can be found sustaining this precise point. The language of the Code cited is too plain, and it seems to me the lan-of Rule 2 is equally plain.

The Code requires the pleading to be *subscribed,*—

that is, signed at the end, or underneath, or at the
bottom thereof,—while the rule requires that it shall
be *indorsed* with the name, address, &c. Both the
subscription and the indorsement are required, and
neither alone is sufficient.

But as the original answer did fully comply with
both requirements it was in no way irregular or defective; and I think there can be no serious doubt, but
that the irregularity complained of might have been
waived by plaintiff's attorney, either before or after
the correction was made, and it may be obviated by
order of the court, by allowing the defendant to serve
it, or, which is the same thing in substance, by requiring the plaintiff's attorney to accept it.

Plaintiff's attorney submits affidavits in opposition
to the motion which tend strongly to show that the
answer is false, and therefore sham, and insists that
he should not be required to accept service of it for
that reason ; but it appears to me the defendant
should have notice of such a proposition, and an opportunity to meet it with counter affidavits, and be
allowed to show, if he can, that his answer is not false ;
therefore, I do not consider this proposition, or pass
upon it, leaving plaintiff to make such a motion, if he
shall desire so to do.

It appears that when defendant's attorney served
his corrected copy of answer, he offered to pay plaintiff's attorney costs of a motion, but he replied : " We
will consider that you have offered costs of a motion
and it has been refused ;" to which defendant's attorney replied : "I do not wish to spend a day upon a
motion over so foolish a mistake."

Having arrived at the conclusion that this motion
should be granted, this offer to pay costs, to obviate
the necessity of a motion, is proper to be considered
upon the question cf costs. Ordinarily, when a party
goes into court asking, as a favor, to be relieved from

CIVIL PROCEDURE REPORTS.

307

Farmers' Loan, &c. Co. *v.* Bankers', &c. Telegraph Co.

his own mistake, he should be required to pay the
costs of opposing his motion. But where, as in this
case, the objection is a purely inadvertent and technical one, and *before motion costs have been offered and*
declined, no costs of the motion should be allowed.

Motion granted, with costs.

THE FARMERS' LOAN & TRUST COMPANY, *v.*
THE BANKERS' & MERCHANTS' TELE-
GRAPH CO.

SUPREME COURT, FIRST DEPARTMENT, NEW YORK
COUNTY, SPECIAL TERM, JANUARY, 1887.

§ 1675.

Foreclosure—Delivering property to purchaser at sale—When report
should first be confirmed.

Where, upon the motion to compel the delivery of the property of a
corporation to one who had purchased it at a foreclosure sale, it
appeared that the report of sale had not been confirmed; that the
purchaser claimed to have complied with the terms of the sale, but
that the fact of such payment was called in question by one having an interest in the property sold,—*Held*, that the motion should
be denied; that it was the safest as well as the ordinary practice to
have such questions settled by the referee's report of sale, and a
motion to confirm the same.

(*Decided January* 5, 1887.)

Motion by Edward S. Stokes and another, that The
Farmers' Loan & Trust Company be required to deliver
to him certain property of the defendant, claimed to
have been purchased by him at a foreclosure sale.

This action was brought by The Farmers' Loan &
Trust Company, as the trustees of certain bondhold-

ers of The Bankers & Merchants' Telegraph Company, to foreclose a mortgage, covering the property of said telegraph company.

All the property covered by the mortgage, both real and personal and mixed, was sold under a decree of foreclosure and sale, and bid in by Edward S. Stokes for $500,000. Previously receiver's certificates to the amount of more than $600,000 had been issued upon the security of this property. Stokes assigned his bid to the United Lines Telegraph Company, to which the referee and the receiver delivered the possession of the bulk of the property in their hands. The judgment of foreclosure allowed payment to be made partly in receiver's certificates, which were to be received at their proportional share of the purchase money. The referee filed no report of the sale. Stokes and the United Lines Telegraph Company then moved for an order directing the trustee of the mortgage, the Farmer's Loan & Trust Company, to deliver the certificates of the stock of other Telegraph Companies and other securities held by the trustee. Stokes's affidavit stated that he had complied with the terms of the sale and was entitled to all the Bankers' & Merchants' property. The trustee opposed the motion on the sole ground that their securities were subject to a prior mortgage covering a part of the Bankers' & Merchants' property of which it alone was trustee. No notice of the motion was given to any other party to the action. After argument of the motion, Benedict S. Woil, the holder of a receiver's certificate, intervened to oppose it. His affidavit stated that the sale had never been confirmed, and that the referee's report had never been filed, that the intervenor had no knowledge or information as to the amount of certificates deposited by Stokes with the referee. He, however, claimed that Stokes had not paid the full amount of his bid; that the validity of some of the certificates deposited by him were doubtful; and stated that preparations were made to oppose the confirmation of the sale upon the ground of fraud, whenever a motion for that purpose should be made. He further alleged that the Farmers' Loan & Trust Company had refused to object to this application upon the ground that the sale had not been confirmed. The Farmers' Loan & Trust Company objected to the intervention as improper, and denied that it had refused to object to the motion on said ground.

Robert S. Ingersoll, for Stokes and The United Lines Telegraph Co., and motion.

Roger Foster, for the intervenor, opposed.

Contended that Stokes had no right to the possession of the property until an order of the court confirming the sale; citing Clason *v.* Corley, 5 *Sandf. Ch.* 447, 452; Peck *v.* Knickerbocker Ice Co., 18 *Hun*, 183, 186; Mayhew *v.* West Virginia Oil and Oil Land Co., 24 *Fed. R.* 205, 215; *Jones on Mortgages*, 1637; *Rorer on Judicial Sales*, §§ 1, 4, 5, 7, 16, 17, 75, 76

David McClure, for the Farmers' Loan & Trust Co.

POTTER, J.—I do not think this motion should, under the circumstances of this case, be granted. The referee's report has not been filed or confirmed. There is a dispute between the mortgagee and the purchaser at the sale, whether the property of which possession is sought by the motion is embraced in the mortgage or in the property bid off. But the main objection to a delivery of the property in question to the purchaser, is the doubt which is cast upon the payment of the purchase price by some of the defendants and others interested in the proceeds of the sale. It is the safest, as well as the ordinary practice, to have such questions settled by the referee's report of sale, and the motion to confirm the same (Peck *v.* Knicker-bocker Ice Co., 18 *Hun*, 183, and cases cited).

The motion, therefore, should be denied in the present state of the matter, but without prejudice and without costs.

GILMAN *v.* PRENTICE, ET AL.

SUPERIOR COURT OF THE CITY OF NEW YORK, SPEOIAL TERM, NOVEMBER, 1886.

§§ 613, 620, 2265.

*Summary proceedings — Form of undertaking given to stay — When prosecution of, should be enjoined-- When judgment debtor may show that the appearance of attorney for her in action was unauthorized.**

The undertaking to be given by one seeking an injunction restraining the prosecution of summary proceedings before final order therein, should be an undertaking under section 620 of the Code of Civil Procedure, to pay to the party enjoined such damages, not exceeding a sum specified in the undertaking, as he may sustain by the injunction, if the court finally decides that the plaintiff is not entitled thereto, and should not be in the form of an undertaking under section 613 of the Code of Civil Procedure to pay the amount of the judgment with interest.

Summary proceedings may be restrained by an injunction before final order, where an injunction would be granted to stay the proceedings in an action of ejectment.

Where one is without adequate remedy at law,—*e. g.*, where in summary proceedings the defendant has equities which the justice's court cannot protect, or where, from the peculiar circumstances of the case, he is precluded from setting up his defense before the justice,—it is the duty of a court of equity to exercise its equitable jurisdiction by injunction.

---

* See Runberg *v.* Johnson, *ante*, at p. 294, and authorities cited by respondent's counsel in that case, *ante*, 286.

Where a judgment was recovered by one P. against one G. and another, without personal service of the summons and complaint upon G., upon her appearance by an attorney, who, she claimed, she never authorized to appear for her, and certain property belonging to her was sold under an execution issued thereon and afterwards redeemed by a subsequent judgment creditor, T., who received the usual deed from the sheriff, and thereafter instituted summary proceedings against G. to recover possession of said property,—*Held*, that an injunction restraining the prosecution of such proceedings should be granted in an action brought by G. against P. to set aside said judgment and restrain said proceedings; that the case was peculiarly one which needed the protection of a court of equity, inasmuch as the validity of the judgment could not be tried in the summary proceedings, as the justice must render judgment therein in favor of the plaintiff, if it appeared that the judgment and execution were regular upon their face and the applicant showed title thereunder.

Where judgment was rendered against a defendant upon his appearance by an attorney without personal service of the summons and complaint, such defendant can show, in an action brought to set aside the judgment entered therein, that the appearance by the attorney was unauthorized and void.

Burton v. Sherwood (20 *N. Y. Weekly Dig.* 419), followed.

(*Decided November* 8, 1886.)

Motion to continue temporary injunction restraining prosecution of summary proceedings.

The opinion fully states the facts.

Charles R. Crosby and *Henry E. Knox* (*Charles R. Crosby*, attorney), for plaintiff and motion.

Walter R. Leggatt, for defendant, opposed.

TRUAX, J.—The plaintiff was the owner of certain premises in the city of New York.

On August 7, 1884, a judgment was entered in the office of the clerk of the city and county of New York, in an action in the supreme court of the State of New York, wherein the defendant, Augustus Prentice, was plaintiff, and the above named Cornelia Gilman and one Andrew E. Smyth were defendants, for the sum of $1,800.78.

Neither the summons nor complaint in said action was ever served on the plaintiff. She never authorized any attorney to appear for her in said action, and never authorized any person or persons to employ or authorize any attorney to appear on her behalf; and she never had any knowledge of any proceedings in said action, or that any attorney had claimed to appear for her until on or about June 28, 1886; but an attorney, without her knowledge and consent, as aforesaid, did appear in said action, and judgment was entered thereon as on default to answer. Execution was issued on the judgment in favor of said Prentice, and on March 10, 1885, the premises hereinbefore mentioned were sold under said execution, and at such sale Prentice became the purchaser.

On March 1, 1886, one Mary A. P. Tucker obtained a judgment against the plaintiff for the sum of upward of $10,000.

The above named Preble Tucker took an assignment of said judgment and redeemed the premises hereinbefore mentioned from said Prentice. and paid said Prentice the amount of the first mentioned judgment and received a deed of said premises from the sheriff. Thereafter, said Preble Tucker instituted summary proceedings in the district court for the sixth judicial district in this city, and thereupon the plaintiff brought this action to restrain the enforcement of such summary proceedings.

The defendant Tucker contends, that the injunction should be vacated because the undertaking given on obtaining the injunction was given under section 620 of the Code of Civil Procedure, and not section 613, which is the section specifying the security to be given on obtaining an injunction order staying proceedings upon a judgment for a sum of money. It is provided in this last mentioned section that no such order shall be granted until the full amount of the judgment, including interest and costs, shall have been paid into court or an undertaking given to pay the amount of the judgment with interest, and until an undertaking shall have been given to pay to the party injured all damages and costs which may be awarded to him by the court in the action in which the injunction order is granted. Such payment has not been made into court, nor has such an undertaking been given by the plaintiff in this action, and if the proceedings sought to be stayed or enjoined are proceedings upon a judgment for a sum of money, the order must be vacated.

The proceedings which the plaintiff is seeking to restrain are not proceedings upon a judgment for a sum of money. Section 2265 of the Code of Civil Procedure prescribes that an injunction shall not be granted staying or suspending the summary proceedings before the final order in such summary proceedings, except in a case where an injunction would be granted to stay the proceedings in an action of ejectment brought by the petitioner and upon like terms. I cannot find that there is any provision in the Code which specifies the amount of the undertaking to be given upon obtaining an injunction staying the proceedings in an action of ejectment before judgment therein, and I am, therefore, of the opinion, that the undertaking to be given in such a case is the undertaking required by section 620.

Where special provision is not otherwise made by law for the security to be given upon an injunction order, the security to be given is an undertaking to the effect that the plaintiff will pay to the party enjoined, such damages, not exceeding a sum specified in the undertaking, as he may sustain by reason of the injunction, if the court finally decides that the plaintiff was not entitled thereto. Such an undertaking has been given in this case.

The defendant contends that a court of equity has no power to interfere by injunction to restrain the prosecution of summary proceedings, but it seems to me that section 2265, above referred to, implies that an injunction may be granted before the final order in summary proceedings, at least where one would be granted to stay the proceedings in an action of ejectment. See Jessurun v. Mackie (24 *Hun*, 626), where DAVIS, Ch. J., says that section 2265 prescribes the mode by which proceedings for the removal of tenants under that title may be stayed or suspended, both before and after final order (see also Chadwick v. Spargur, 1 *N. Y. Civ. Pro.* 422).

I think that it is settled that where one is without an adequate remedy at law—where he has equities which the justice's court could not protect, or where he is, from the peculiar circumstances of the case, precluded from setting up his defense before the justice —it is the duty of a court of equity to exercise its equitable jurisdiction by injunction (Valloton v. Seignett, 2 *Abb. Pr.* 121; Griffiths v. Brown, 3 *Robt.* 627; Bokee v. Hamersley, 16 *How. Pr.* 461; Chadwick v. Spargur, 1 *N. Y. Civ. Pro.* 422; McIntyre v. Hernandez, 7 *Abb. N. S.* 214).

The case is peculiarly one which needs the protection of a court of equity, for the regularity and validity of the judgment under which the sale of the plaintiff's property was made cannot be tried before the justice. Judgment must be given by him, if it appears that the judgment and execution are regular on their face, and the appellant shows title under them (Brown v. Betts, 13 *Wend.* 29).

The more important question in the case, is the one on which no stress was laid by counsel on the argument, and that is: can the plaintiff show in this action, that the appearance by the attorney was unauthorized and void? That question has lately been answered in the affirmative by the supreme court, in the second department, in the case of Burton v. Sherman, reported in 20 *N. Y. Weekly Dig.* 419.

I shall follow that decision and continue the injunction, with costs.

COOGAN v. OCKERSHAUSEN.

SUPERIOR COURT OF THE CITY OF NEW YORK, SPECIAL TERM, NOVEMBER, 1886.

§§ 2749, *et seq.*, 2759.

Power of sale—When executor can give good title.

Where a testator directed in his will that all his just debts and funeral expenses be paid as soon as practicable, after his decease, and gave all the rest, residue and remainder of his estate to his executors, in trust,—*Held*, that the will by the legal effect of these provisions made the payment of debts a charge upon his real estate; that this charge was an implied and not an express one, and the executor of the will who was the devisee in trust had an implied power of sale for the purpose of paying the debts; that the property could not, therefore, be sold in a proceeding under sections 2749 *et seq.*, of the Code of Civil Procedure, for the payment of debts, etc., and the purchaser at a sale by the executor acquired a good title; that the purchaser was under no obligation to see to the proper disposition of the purchase money.

Hyde v. Tanner (1 *Barb.* 75), distinguished.

The real estate of a testator, which is subject to a valid power of sale for the payment of debts, cannot be sold for the payment of debts and funeral expenses in a proceeding brought for that purpose under section 2749 *et seq.* of the Code of Civil Procedure, unless it appears that it is not practicable to execute the power, and that the creditor has effectually relinquished the same. (*Decided November* 29, 1886.)

Action tried before the court without a jury.

The defendant is the executor of the last will and testament of George G. Taylor, deceased, and as such, on June 7, 1880, entered into an agreement to sell to the plaintiff certain premises, located at No. 246 Lexington avenue, New York City, for the sum of $16,500, and agreed to deliver a deed conveying title thereto, on July 7, 1880, or sooner, if the plaintiff desired. The plaintiff, to bind the contract, paid to the defendant at the time of making it, the sum of $250. The defendant's title as executor was derived under a will in which the testator, after directing that all his just debts and funeral expenses be paid as soon as practicable after his decease, devised the rest, residue and remainder of his estate to the defendant in trust, etc. The plaintiff claimed that this will was such, that the debts of the decedent were a charge upon the property in question, and refused to accept the title, although the defendant was ready to convey. Thereafter, the plaintiff brought this action to recover back the $250 deposited as aforesaid, together with $50, the expense of examining the title. The case came on for trial at trial term, and the parties to the action waived a jury trial and submitted the case upon agreed facts.

Richard S. Newcombe, for the plaintiff.

Thompson & Koss, for the defendant.

SEDGWICK, Ch. J.—The testator directed in his will: "I direct all my just debts and funeral expenses to be paid as soon as practicable after my decease."

All "the rest, residue and remainder of his estate" he devised to his executor, in trust, etc.

The will, by the legal effect of these provisions, made the payment of the debts a charge upon the land (White v. Kane, 7 *N. Y. Civ. Pro.* 267, and the numerous earlier cases). It is to be kept in mind, however, that the charge was not express but implied.

The executor of the will, who was the devisee in trust, had an implied power of sale for the purpose of paying the debts (*Story's Eq. Jurisprudence*, § 1064b and note 3).

The specific objection to the power of the executor to convey a title, is that the land will remain subject to the right of the creditors within three years, and to apply to the surrogate for a decree, that the land be sold for the purpose of paying debts which the personal estate was not sufficient to discharge.

This right of the creditor is claimed to be established by section 2749, *et seq.* of the Code of Civil Procedure. I assume that if, in the present case, the creditors might have a right to proceed under the statute, the objection made to the title would be good. The exception contained in section 2749 would not prevent an application being competently made by the surrogate. The exception is of real estate expressly charged with the payment of debts, etc. The present case concerns an implied charge. But before the surrogate can make a decree of sale he must find (§ 2759) that the property "is not subject to a valid power of sale for the payment of" the debts, with a limitation that will be noticed. The statute does not refer to an express power. If there be an actual and valid, although implied, power, the surrogate cannot make the decree.

I am therefore of the opinion that the creditors have no claims upon the land and will have none excepting through the implied charge and power of sale that have been specified. The plaintiff is under no obligation to see to the proper disposition of the purchase money.

Hyde *v.* Tanner (1 *Barb.* 75), differs from the present case because it had regard to the right of executors, etc., or of creditors through them, to apply to the surrogate for leave to sell under the Revised Statutes. Those statutes permitted the sale of land without regard to the fact that the executor had power of sale, although if there were an express charge the land could not be sold.

It has been shown that under the Code, if there be a valid power of sale, the land cannot be sold with the limitation that will now be examined. Section 2759 declares that if there be a valid power of sale, the surrogate may make the decree, " if it is not impracticable . . . . to execute the power " and " the creditor has effectually relinquished the same." These words do not include the present case, for there is no objection made that the power, if it exist, cannot be practically executed.

I think further, that the powers of sale contained in the devises in trust were valid.

I have said nothing as to the personal property being the primary fund for the payment of debts, because the plaintiff places his objection to the title on the ground substantially that there appears to be a deficiency of personal property to pay debts.

The defendant should have judgment dismissing the complaint on the merits.

VANDEVEER v. WARREN

SUPERIOR COURT OF THE CITY OF NEW YORK, SPECIAL TERM, JANUARY, 1887.

§ 3251, subd. 3.

Term fees—When party entitled to, although he has not noticed cause for trial.

The party to an action who has prevailed therein, is entitled to term fees for the terms the cause is necessarily on the calendar, although he has never noticed it for trial.

(*Decided January* 22, 1887.)

Motion by plaintiff, for new taxation of costs.

This action was begun on January 7, 1885. Issue was joined by the service of an answer on February 4, 1885. The plaintiff noticed the cause for trial, for the November, 1885, and the June, 1886, trial term, but failed to file any note of issue. The defendant duly noticed the cause for trial, at the October, 1886, trial term, and filed a note of issue for that term. The cause thereafter, in January, 1887, appeared on the calendar, was duly tried, and a verdict rendered in favor of the plaintiff and against the defendant. On January 14, plaintiff caused a bill of costs to be served on the defendant's attorney, and among other items charged therein, was $50, term fees; the defendant objected to the allowance of such term fees, and the plaintiff insisted that he was entitled to at least three of them, inasmuch as the cause was regularly upon the calendar for that number of terms. The clerk disallowed the term fees, and the plaintiff thereupon made this motion.

William George Oppenheim, for plaintiff, and motion.

Cited Andrews *v.* Schnitzler, 2 *N. Y. Civ. Pro.* 18 ; Flint *v.* Green (N. Y. City Ct. Sp. T.), *N. Y. Daily Register*, April 19, 1884 ; Sipperly *v.* Warner, 9 *How. Pr.* 332.

H. W. Fowler, for defendant, opposed.

Dugro, J.—The plaintiff prevailed on the trial of the action, but the clerk of the court has refused to allow him any term fees, on the ground that he has never noticed it for trial.

The defendant had regularly noticed it for trial for October term, 1886, and it was on the calendar for that term.

The plaintiff appeals from the clerk's decision. I think the plaintiff is entitled to term fees, even though he never noticed the cause for trial. The general term of this court in March, 1882, in the case of Andrews *v.* Schnitzler* (opinion by Mr. Justice Freedman), say that the true construction of the Code is, that as long as a cause has been noticed for trial, the party finally prevailing at the trial is entitled to costs for all proceedings after notice of trial, and to the costs for each term, though the notice of trial was not given by him but by his opponent. The preparation to be made is the same whether only one or both parties give notice of trial.

From the above it follows that the decison of the clerk should be reversed (without costs), and re-taxation is ordered, with instructions to the clerk to allow the term fees which he disallowed.

* 2 *N. Y. Civ. Pro.* 18.

O'ROURKE *v.* THE HENRY PROUSE COOPER
COMPANY, ET AL.

SUPERIOR COURT OF THE CITY OF NEW YORK,
SPECIAL TERM, DECEMBER, 1886.

§§ 1251, 1429, 1430.

*Summary proceedings.— When injunction to stay, granted.—Form of
undertaking.*

The superior court of the city of New York has jurisdiction to
restrain the execution of a warrant to dispossess, issued in summary proceedings taken by a landlord against his tenant, where it
appears that since the making of the lease, the title of the lessee
to the leasehold premises has been divested, and where that question cannot be properly disposed of by the justice before whom
the proceedings are pending.

Gilman *v.* Prentice (11 *N. Y. Civ. Pro.* 310), followed.

A lease of real property for the term of ten years, is a chattel real ;
and as such, is subject to the lien of a judgment recovered against
the lessee thereof, for ten years after the filing of the judgment-
roll, if the judgment is docketed in the county in which the leasehold premises are situate.

A leasehold interest in real property of a judgment debtor, which has
less than three years to run, although the lease was originally for
ten years, is not real property within the provisions of the Code
relating to the sale of real property under execution, and may
therefore be sold under execution as personal property; and upon
a sale the property sold vests immediately in the purchaser.

(*Decided December* 2, 1886.)

Motion to continue temporary injunction, restraining the prosecution of summary proceedings.

Samuel M. Meeker, as executor, &c., let the premises No. 292 Fifth avenue, to Henry Prouse Cooper
for the term of ten years from May 1, 1879. Cooper

at this time sublet portions of the premises to the
Nippon Mercantile Company of 310 Broadway, for the
same period.   Both these leases were recorded.   In
October, 1883, Cooper assigned the lease from Meeker
to The Henry Prouse Cooper & Co.   After the assignment the Nippon Mercantile Company paid rent to
the Henry Prouse Cooper   Co.

William L. Flagg obtained a judgment by default
against Cooper in July, 1883.   This default was vacated
that there might be a trial on the merits, the judgment
then obtained being allowed to stand as security.   In
May, 1886, the referee to whom the case was referred,
reported in favor of Flagg, and a judgment was entered
on the confirmation of that report May 20, 1886.   Flagg
issued an execution on this judgment, which was returned unsatisfied.   He then issued another execution
on the judgment recovered July 3, 1883, and under that
execution, the sheriff sold, as a chattel real, the interest of Henry Prouse Cooper which he had in the above
lease on July 3, 1883.   Motions were made to set these
executions aside, on the ground of various irregularities, which were denied.   Jeremiah O'Rourke became
the purchaser of Cooper's interest at the sheriff's sale,
and notified the tenants of the building, 292 Fifth
avenue, of his purchase, and demanded from them
the rent due.   At the time of the sale. O'Rourke
received a sheriff's certificate of sale, but no deed was
given.

The Nippon Mercantile Company refused to pay
the rent due, and summary proceedings were commenced against it in the sixth district court by the
Henry Prouse Cooper   Company. These proceedings
were stayed by injunction, and the case removed to
the superior court.

William L. Flagg, for plaintiff.

F. F. Vandeveer, for the Henry Prouse Cooper Co.

Charles H. Murray, for Nippon Mercantile Co.

INGRAHAM, J.—The general term of this court, in the case of Flagg v. Cooper, et al.,[*]held that the execution issued in that action, under which the sale by the sheriff was made, was valid, and that decision is binding upon me on this application.

I think this court has jurisdiction to restrain the execution of a warrant to dispossess where it appears that since the making of the lease the title of the lessor to the leasehold premises has been divested, and where that question cannot be properly disposed of by the justice. It was so held in Gilman v. Prentice, (*ante* p. 310).

The only question remaining, is whether the plaintiff has obtained by the sale under the execution, a valid title to the lease held by the defendants, The Henry Prouse Cooper Co.

By section 5 of article 1 of title 2 of the Revised Statutes, 7th ed., page 2175, it is provided : " Estates for years shall be chattels real." The interest, therefore, of Henry Prouse Cooper, at the time of the entry of the judgment in favor of Flagg against Cooper, was therefore, a chattel real.

By section 1251 of the Code, it is provided : " Except as otherwise specifically prescribed by law, a judgment hereafter rendered, and which is docketed in the county clerk's office, as prescribed in this article, binds, and is a charge upon—ten years after filing the judgment-roll and no longer—the real property and chattels real in that county which the judgment debtor has at the time of so docketing it, or which he acquires at any time afterwards and within the ten years."

By the docketing of that judgment against Henry P. Cooper, the plaintiff acquired a lien upon the lease of the premises in question. Under the execution issued on that judgment, the sheriff advertised the leasehold property for sale, and on July 24, 1886, sold to the plaintiff all the right, title and interest of Henry Prouse Cooper, that he had on July 3, 1883, in and to the leases therein described, and duly delivered to the plaintiff in this action a bill of sale therefor. The sale appears to be regular, and, so far as appears, the sale was made in accordance with the provisions of the Code for the sale of personal property. Article 3, sections 1430 to 1478, do not apply to a sale under this execution, because .at the time of the sale they had less than three years to run.

By section 1430 it is provided that the expression " real property," as used in this and the succeeding article, include leasehold property, where the lessee or his assignee is possessed, at the time of the sale, of at least five years' unexpired term of the lease. The leasehold interest not being real property, it must be sold as personal property, and upon the sale under the execution the property sold vested immediately in the purchaser.

I think, therefore, on the facts as they appear on this application, that the plaintiff has obtained a valid title to the lease by the sale under the execution. The defendant, the Nippon Mercantile Co., having appeared and asked leave to pay the amount of rent due into the court, if such payment is made to the credit of the action within ten days after the service of the order on this motion, the injunction will be con-tinued against the defendant, The Henry Prouse Cooper Co., restraining them from executing any warrant to dispossess the Nippon Mercantile Co. until the further order of this court.

Plaintiff to have $10 costs of this motion, to abide the event.

AARON, Appellant, *v.* FOSTER, Respondent.

CITY COURT OF NEW YORK, GENERAL TERM, DECEMBER, 1886.

§ 3228, sub'd. 1.

Costs.—When question of title to land comes in question.

Where an assignee of a landlord sued a tenant, to recover damages for breach of the covenants contained in the lease, and the complaint alleged title to the premises in the landlord, and the defendant took issue on this allegation,—*Held*, that the question of title to land did not arise, and the plaintiff recovering less than $50, was not entitled to costs.

In an action for breach of covenant contained in a lease, brought by a landlord, the plaintiff is entitled to recover, independent of the question of ownership or title.

The question of title to land does not come in question, unless plaintiff, in order to recover, is bound to allege, and, if denied, prove title on the trial; and unless the title does so come in question, the plaintiff, if he recovers less than $50, is not entitled to costs.

(*Decided December,* 1886.)

Appeal from order of special term, affirming the clerk's taxation of costs.

The opinion states the facts.

Leo C. Dessar, for plaintiff-appellant.

William Foster, for defendant-respondent.

McADAM, Ch. J.—The plaintiff, as assignee of the landlord, sued the defendant for breach of the covenants of an indenture of lease, wherein the defendant agreed "to keep and maintain the plate glass in the windows in proper order and repair." The breach charged is that the defendant caused or permitted "three panes of the plate glass to become broken and out of order," to the plaintiff's damage $60. The jury awarded the plaintiff a verdict for $39, on which the plaintiff undertook to tax a bill of costs. The clerk declined to tax the bill because the verdict was under $50, and from an order of the special term sustaining the ruling of the clerk, the present appeal is taken.

The plaintiff unnecessarily alleged in his complaint title to the premises, and because the defendant took issue on this immaterial allegation, the plaintiff claims that the title to land came in question, and that he was, therefore, entitled to costs, without regard to the amount of his recovery. This claim is unfounded. The trial judge did not certify that the title came in question, nor did the question arise upon the pleadings within the contemplation of the Code (§ 3228, subd. 1). The plaintiff, having sued for breach of covenant, was entitled to recover independently of the question of ownership or title. The question of title does not come in question unless the plaintiff, in order to recover, is bound to allege, and (if denied) prove title on the trial (Muller, v. Bayard, 15 *Abb. Pr.* 449; Rathbone v. McConnell, 20 *Barb.* 311; aff'd, 21 *N. Y.* 466; Learn v. Currier, 15 *Hun,* 184; aff'd, 76 *N. Y.* 625).

It follows, therefore, that the order appealed from must be affirmed, with costs.

NEHBRAS, J., concurred.

DE WITT, Respondent, *v.* GREENER, Appellant.

CHEMUNG COUNTY COURT, DECEMBER, 1886.

§§ 55, 2944.

Attorney— When employment of ends—Power of, to release claim of client—Justices' court— When amendment of pleadings should be allowed.

Where an attorney was employed to prosecute an action to recover possession of a piano, and the case was settled before trial by the making of a verbal agreement, which was to be reduced to writing, providing that the defendant should retain possession of the piano for two years and a half, and keep it in as good repair as it then was, for the purpose of renting the same, and out of the rentals received, reimbursing himself for the money expended in repairing it, and at the expiration of said period should return the said piano to the plaintiff, and this agreement was afterwards reduced to writing, and the provision added that if the piano was not delivered, the defendant should forfeit $75 agreed upon in the writing as liquidated damages in   case of such failing to deliver, and the attorney never delivered such agreement to the plaintiff, but without her knowledge or consent, before the expiration of said two years and a half received $10 and gave a receipt upon the back of the agreement, reciting that that amount was paid in full satisfaction of all claims and demands under said written agreement, and that the agreement was surrendered up to the defendant and the piano therein referred to was regarded as delivered to him to be his property from date,—*Held,* that the attorney did not have authority to receive said money or give said receipt; that his employment ended with the termination of the action, and that he had no further authority, either actual or implied, and the defendant was not entitled to assume that he was authorized, and his authority could be disputed by the plaintiff.

Anderson *v.* Coonley (21 *Wend.* 279); Standard Oil Company *v.* Triumph Insurance Company (3 *Hun*, 591), distinguished.

In such a case, *it seems,* if there had been money due under the agreement its possession by the attorney would have justified the defendant in assuming that he had authority to collect it.

De Witt *v.* Greener.

While an agent to take a bond is not to be deemed as of course
entitled to receive the money under that bond, such agency may
be presumed if he retains custody of it; but it is not to be presumed that he is entitled to such payment before it becomes due;
and his right to release the bond before its maturity or in part payment, is not to be presumed from mere-possession.

Where a complaint in an action in a justice's court set forth a
cause of action for conversion, and the plaintiff on the trial
expressly waived the tort set out in such cause of action, and
asked leave to amend the complaint by setting forth a second cause
of action for liquidated damages under a contract, relating to the
same subject-matter as the first cause of action,—*Held*, that the
change of the first cause of action from tort to contract did not
work injustice to the defendant, as it did not change the nature of
the proof required.

A justice of the peace has the power, and may amend a complaint at
any time before or during the trial, by substituting one form of
action for another; and may change the nature of the action from
one in tort to one on contract.

No uniform independent rule can be laid down under the provision
of the Code of Civil Procedure as to when amendments of pleadings should be allowed in justices' courts regardless of the facts;
every case must be controlled by the facts surrounding it; the test
being whether substantial justice will be promoted by allowing an
amendment.

(*Decided December*, 1886.)

Appeal from an order of a justice of the peace.

The opinion states the facts.

W. Lloyd Smith and *J. Gibson*, attorneys for
defendant-appellant.

· *John T. Davidson*, for respondent.

DEXTER, Co. J.—Some years prior to June, 1883,
the plaintiff was the owner of a piano. She rented it
to a Mrs. Starks, with whom it remained for a long
time. Mrs. Starks finally sold or traded it to the
defendant herein, who is a manufacturer and dealer in

pianos, without the knowledge of the plaintiff. The plaintiff claimed the piano from the defendant. Wm. P. De Witt, her father, acted as her agent. He employed A. V. Murdoch, an attorney at law, to secure a settlement of the claim with Greener. No settlement was secured until he authorized him to bring a suit in justice's court against Greener, to recover the piano or its value. A suit was brought before Justice A. B. GALATIAN. That suit was settled before trial, Mr. Greener, Mr. Wm. P. DeWitt, Mr. Murdoch and the plaintiff being present. Mr. Greener claiming that he had received this piano in good faith from Mrs. Starks, and had expended $50 in repairs upon it, a verbal settlement was arrived at, whereby Mr. Greener was to keep the piano for two years and a half, and keep it in as good repair as it was then, and retain the rents to reimburse him for the repairs made upon the piano, and at the expiration of said two and one half years, he was to deliver the same to the plaintiff. It was suggested that the agreement be reduced to writing, and Mr. Murdoch was authorized by the plaintiff to reduce the same to writing, and secure Mr. Greener's signature to the same, which he did. In the agreement thus made in writing, Greener agreed to deliver the piano to the plaintiff or her agent, at the expiration of the said two and one-half years, in as good condition as it then was, on demand, and if not so delivered. Greener agreed to forfeit $75, agreed upon in the writing as liquidated damages in case of failure to deliver the same, unless such failure to deliver was occasioned by the piano being destroyed by fire.

At the expiration of said time, the plaintiff demanded the piano, and Mr. Greener refused to deliver the same, and this action was brought to recover its value, and the original complaint was one in tort to recover damages for a conversion of the piano.

From the evidence it appears that Mr. Murdoch had never delivered the written agreement to the plaintiff. It was dated June 28, 1883. On March 4, 1884, without the knowledge or consent of the plaintiff or her father, Murdoch received from Greener " ten dollars in full satisfaction of all claims and demands under said written agreement," and he signed a receipt upon the back of the agreement to that effect, in which it was stated further that the written agreement "is hereby surrendered up to him (Greener) and the piano referred to herein, is hereby regarded as delivered to him (Greener) to be his property from date.   " ESTELLE DE WITT

       "by her attorney A. V Murdoch.

"Elmira, March 4, 1884."

The defense offered this receipt as evidence of an accord and satisfaction.

The plaintiff denies the authority of Murdoch to thus dispose of her rights under the written agreement. So far as it is a question of fact, whether Murdoch had express authority or not, that has been settled by the court below in favor of the plaintiff, and is not before us for review. The weight of evidence was certainly with the plaintiff on that issue. The defendant claims, however, that Murdoch had an implied authority, and under the facts appearing, the defendant had a right to assume that he was so authorized, and the plaintiff should not now be allowed to dispute it. In support of this claim, the defendant cites two cases : Anderson v. Coonley, 21, *Wend.* 279 ; and Standard Oil Co. v. Triumph Ins. Co., 3 *Hun*, 591.

In the first, one W. was the agent of A. in buying grain. He made a contract with C. for his barley. C. did not deliver it and A. brought suit for damages for the non-delivery. C. offered to prove that soon after the contract was made, W. sent him word that he did not want his barley, as it was injured, and the trial court refused such proof. The court of review held that this was error ; that a general agent, entrusted by his principal with power to make and enter into contracts for the purchase of grain, has power to modify or waive a contract made by him in respect to such grain.

In the other case, one J. L. Lord, an insurance broker, procured a policy of insurance from the defendants for the plaintiff. The policy gave the right to the defendants to raise the rate of premium or cancel the policy at any time. Subsequently, the defendants demanded of Lord an increase of one per cent. It was not paid by Lord, and nearly sixty days after this, a messenger from Lord's office brought the policy to the defendants' agent who issued the same and directed its cancellation. It also had an indorsement on it indicating that it was to be canceled, which indorsement was made by Lord, or a brother of his who had the general management of his business. The defendants canceled the policy, and a few days after, the property covered by this policy, burned. The plaintiffs brought suit against the defendants on the ground that the policy had been returned unintentionally and through mistake. No question is raised in this case as to the power of Joseph L. Lord, as agent of the plaintiffs in procuring the policy of insurance, to have returned the same to the defendants and canceled, and thereby bind the plaintiffs. He was the only person with whom the defendants dealt. To secure insurance was his business ; but the plaintiffs insisted their agent did not intend to return it. They did not intend to have him return it, but through the mistake of some one in Mr. Lord's office it had been returned. The question litigated was whether the plaintiff's were bound by the mistake of their agent, and the court held that they were, and also affirmed the rule laid down in Anderson v. Coonley, that an agent having authority to make, has implied authority to cancel or modify. The question is, does this rule of law relating to agency have application to the facts of this case. In Anderson v. Coonley the defendant C. had all his dealings with W. the agent of A. In the last case, the defendants had all their dealings with Lord the insurance broker. In neither case had the defendants met the principals, and did not know the principals except through the agent. In both cases the agency was general as to the matter which the agent had in charge for his principal. In neither case did the agent assume to act as an attorney. In the present case Murdoch was known to the defendant to be acting as an attorney. He signed the receipt as "attorney for the plaintiff." Under the evidence of W. P. De Witt and Ryan, he was employed as an attorney to prosecute the claim. His compensation was limited to ten dollars by express agreement in the first suit brought. This court must assume that fact as established by the judgment in the court below. Murdoch says, when the claim was put into his hands, "it was all left to my discretion as to whether I should bring a suit or compromise." The suit was brought. In the settlement of the suit, the plaintiff, her father, Murdoch and defendant were present. The terms of the settlement being agreed upon, it was left to Mr. Murdoch to reduce it to writing and have Mr. Greener sign it. Murdoch says, "I instituted the suit. It resulted in a compromise between the plaintiff and defendant." It is therefore clear that there is a broad distinction between this case and the one cited by the defendant. In this case, the written agreement was but reducing the parol agreement, made between Greener and Mr. Murdoch's principal, to writing. Mr. Murdoch's position in the transaction was that of an attorney prosecuting a claim. The whole matter was disposed of between the parties whereby Mr. Greener was to deliver the piano, not to the agent, but to the plaintiff, at the end of two and one half years. There was nothing pending or undetermined between them until that time had expired. There is no fact from which Mr. Greener had a right to assume that pending that two years and a half Mr. Murdoch had any agency in the premises whatever, unless it is the fact that he brought with him the written agreement. Had there been any money due on this agreement at the time he presented it, his possession of it under the circumstances under which it was made, would have justified Greener in assuming that Murdoch had authority to collect such money. "An agent to take a bond is not to be deemed as of course entitled to receive payment of the money under that bond" (*Story on Agency*, 112). But such agency may be presumed if he retain custody of the bond. *Ib.* (See also Williams *v.* Walker, 2 *Sandf. Ch.* 225).

But it is not to be presumed that he is entitled to receive such payment before it becomes due (*Story on Agency*, 113). His right to release the bond before maturity by a part payment is not to be presumed from mere possession. It seems to us clear that when pending that time Mr. Murdoch appears for the purpose of releasing Mr. Greener from his obligations to the plaintiff, he deals with him at his peril. It is a well settled rule of law that an attorney of record in an action cannot release his client's interest or compromise it, unless he have express authority so to do. Mandeville *v.* Reynolds (68 *N. Y.* 528). Mr. Murdoch did not even occupy the position of an attorney of record. The action in which he was acting as attorney, had, many months before, been settled between the parties themselves before judgment. The plaintiff had in no act, word or writing which had come to the attention of Greener, done anything from which Greener had the right to assume that he was clothed with the power of sale of the plaintiff's rights under the contract. The plaintiff and her father resided in the same place with the defendant. It was an easy matter for him to have demanded the receipt of the plaintiff, or the written authority of the plaintiff to Murdoch to empower him to make this sale or release—and especially where he was paying $10 for that for which he had agreed to pay $75, in the event he did not return the piano at the expiration of the time ; and Mr. Murdoch, as the plaintiff's attorney, had simply reduced such agreement to writing. So far as Greener had any legal right to assume, Murdoch's connection with the matter then ceased ; hence it seems to us manifest that no implied agency remained in Murdoch whereby he could bind the plaintiff against her knowledge and consent in the matter of surrendering her rights against Greener before the expiration of said term of two and one half years.

The plaintiff insists there is another ground of error calling for a reversal of this judgment. As before stated, the original complaint was for a conversion : it set forth an action in tort. After the defendant introduced the receipt and release signed by Murdoch on the back of the agreement of settlement of the first suit, the plaintiff introduced in evidence the agreement itself, to which it referred. The plaintiff clearly had the right to do so. Thereafter the plaintiff asked to amend her complaint, alleging, as a second cause of action, the contract on the part of Greener, contained in the agreement wherein he had agreed to forfeit seventy-five dollars as liquidated damages in the event he should not return the piano at the expiration of the time agreed upon. It was allowed, against the defendant's objection. This left the first cause of action set out in the complaint one in tort, and the second cause of action one in, contract. Thereupon the. plaintiff gave notice that she expressly waived the tort set out in the first cause of action, and an amendment to that effect was allowed. By the amendments thus allowed against the defendant's objection the action was charged from an action in tort to one on contract. Had the justice power to allow such amendments? is the question presented. Section 2944 of the Code, which has direct reference to the amendment of pleadings in justice court, provides that "The court *must*, upon application, allow a pleading to be amended, at any time before the trial, or during the trial, or upon appeal, if substantial justice will be promoted thereby."

Was substantial justice promoted by these amendments? If so, then it was the imperative command of the statute that they be allowed "upon application."

The application was made by the plaintiff.

There is no method provided in justices' courts for making application by motion upon notice as in courts of record. Amendments can only be applied for when the parties are present before the justice; hence no objection can be made to the manner of the application. It may be made before or during the trial. It was made during the trial, hence the application as to time conforms to the statute; hence the only question is, were the amendments of a nature whereby substantial justice was to be promoted by their allowance? The first effect was to change the action from tort to contract: did this work injustice to the defendant? We do not see how it could. Before the amendments an execution against the body might have been issued upon the judgment recovered : after the amendments, a body execution could not be issued. That certainly worked no injustice to the defendant. It relieved him from an odious. incident attaching to any judgment that might be recovered.

To maintain the action the proofs must be the same.

under the amended as under the original complaint: under either, the agreement must be proved, except as to the "liquidated damages:" the expiration of the two years and a half, a demand by the plaintiff upon the defendant, and a refusal to deliver. Beyond relieving the defendant from a body execution issuing upon any judgment recovered, the only question which the amendment effected was that relating to the amount of damages that might be recovered against him in the action.

Under the original complaint, the question of damages turned wholly upon the question of value of the piano at the time of the demand and refusal. Under the amended complaint, the question of its value became immaterial, for the reason that by the terms of the agreement the question of damages had been agreed upon at the time the agreement was made, in case the contingency arose that had arisen, and upon which the cause of action was based. Was any injustice done the defendant by changing the contest upon the question of value, to the fact whether he had made the agreement as to the amount of damages in case he failed to deliver the property? Was it not "substantial justice," that he should be called upon to fulfill his agreement? That he made the agreement was unquestioned. Was not substantial justice promoted by conforming the issues to the truth of the transaction? If we have any just appreciation of what "promoting substantial justice" means, the allowance of this amendment was within the letter and spirit of the provisions of the Code cited above.

The appellant insists this language does not permit an amendment that changes the action from tort to contract. It must be admitted that the language of the statute contains no such limitation. In Bigelow *v.* Dunn (36 *How. Pr.* 120), it was held that a justice of the peace has the power and may amend a complaint

De Witt *v.* Greener.

at any time before trial by substituting one form of action for another. The correctness of this rule then laid down stands unquestioned. The Code gives just as broad a power to the justice to amend *during the trial* as before the trial. In either case, the amendment must be allowed if " substantial justice" will be promoted thereby. In the supreme court an action may be changed from tort to contract, upon motion, where substantial justice will be promoted thereby. It was done in Eighmie *v.* Taylor, 39 *Hun,* 366. It is a mistake to assume that an action cannot be changed from tort to contract by amendment of the pleadings. No uniform unbending rule can be laid down under the provisions of the Code that shall apply to every case regardless of the facts. Each case must be controlled by the facts surrounding it. The test is, will substantial justice be promoted by allowing the amendment? It seems to me unnecessary and idle to enter into a discussion of the various cases relating to amendments that have been cited. It seems to us clear that the amendments allowed in this case promoted substantial justice. Amendments after the trial has begun should not be allowed unless it is clear that substantial justice will be promoted. In determining that question, the facts surrounding that case, and the application, are to guide the justice.

For the reasons above stated, we think the justice did not abuse his discretionary power, but did in fact exercise it in the furtherance of substantial justice. We therefore conclude the judgment should be affirmed. An order will be made accordingly.

Estate of BURGESS CLUFF, Deceased.

Surrogate's Court, New York County, February,
1887.

§§ 2578–2580.

*Appeal from surrogate's court—When undertaking necessary to perfect
appeal.*

The filing of an undertaking is absolutely essential to perfect an
appeal from a surrogate's decree revoking letters testamentary, and
removing a testamentary trustee from office.

A notice of appeal from a decree of a surrogate requiring an executor or trustee to deliver property, or pay or deposit money, is
ineffectual for any purpose, unless an undertaking is given in the
sum of at least $200.

An order extending the time to make and serve a case on appeal,
granted after the time to appeal has expired, in a case in which
an appeal has not been perfected, should be vacated.

(*Decided February*, 1887.)

Motion to vacate order granting time to make case
on appeal.

The opinion states the facts.

Rollins, S.—The decree herein on September 30,
1886, revoked the letters testamentary of Edward E.
Tower, executor of this estate, and removed him from
his office as trustee under his testator's will. It also
settled and adjudicated his account, and directed him
to make immediate deposit in this court of the sum of
$10,037.98, being the principal or *corpus* of the estate
in his hands, and to pay to Mary Cluff the sum of
$2,050.76 due her as income. It still further directed

him to deliver to said Mary Cluff a certain promissory note, and to pay as costs taxed against him the sum of $868.04. This decree was duly served upon the executor's attorneys on October 19.

The executor had the right to appeal, therefore, at any time during the thirty days then next ensuing. Notice of appeal was served by his attorney *before* the thirty days had expired. *After* the expiration, he applied *ex parte* to the surrogate for an order giving him time in which to make a case. By an order entered on November 26 he was allowed twenty days for that purpose.

Counsel for Mary Cluff now moves that that order be vacated, on the ground that at the time it was granted the would-be appellant had neglected to file any undertaking, and that his notice of appeal had therefore become utterly ineffectual.

This contention is unquestionably sound, so far as it relates to the provisions in the decree of September 30, which revoke the respondent's letters testamentary and remove him from his office as trustee. To perfect an appeal from a decree of that character, the filing of an undertaking is absolutely essential (Fernbacher *v.* Fernbacher, 4 *Dem.* 246.)

Whether or not the moving party is correct in claiming that failure to file an undertaking has made inoperative the respondent's effort to appeal from those portions of the decree which direct the delivery of property and payment or deposit of moneys, is a question more difficult of solution.

Counsel for the respondent claims that, although an appeal from a decree containing such directions cannot, in view of the provisions of sections 2578 and 2580 of the Code of Civil Procedure, operate as a *stay of execution*, except upon the filing of an undertaking in a sum not less than twice the sum directed to be paid or deposited, &c., &c., it may, nevertheless, be

·operative for all other purposes without the interposi-
ition of any undertaking at all.

When the second part of the Code of Civil Procedure first came upon the statute-book, an appeal from
a surrogate's decree containing such directions as are
here the subject of consideration, was declared by
section 2578 to be "*not effectual for any purpose*," in
the absence of the special undertaking for which that
section provided—an undertaking sufficient in amount
to secure not only such costs and damages as might be
recovered against the appellant, but the payment or
deposit of money, or the delivery of property directed
by the decree appealed from.

It was at the same time declared by the next preceding section (§ 2577), that "to render a notice of
appeal" (that is, *any* notice of appeal) "effectual for
any purpose *except* in a case specified in section 2578
(*ante*), . . the appellant must give a written undertaking with at least two sureties, to the effect that he
would pay all costs and damages (to an amount not
exceeding $250.00) which might be awarded against
him upon the appeal."

(In the place indicated above by asterisks, there is
set forth another restriction upon the operation of section 2577. This restriction will be ignored as foreign
to the purposes of the present inquiry.)

On July 1, 1882,* the legislature amended section
2578, by substituting in place of the words "*is not
effectual for any purpose*" the words "*does not stay
the execution of the decree appealed from.*"

The respondent claims that so far as regards the
direction of the decree of September 30 for payment,
deposit and delivery, this case is not within the pur-
view of section 2577, because it is "a case specified in
the next section," and that by that section, as it now

stands, no undertaking is required, save for the purpose of effecting a stay of execution.

An interpretation of the act of 1882, so out of harmony with the general scheme of appeals from surrogates' decrees, which is established by article 4 of chapter 18 of the Code, should not be countenanced unless it is absolutely demanded by the phraseology of the amending statute.

Before subjecting that phraseology to critical examination, it may be said in general that its apparent purpose was to relieve executors, administrators, testamentary trustees, guardians, &c., from a hardship to which they had been theretofore subjected—the hardship of giving a bond in double the amount involved in a proceeding culminating in a decree containing some such direction as is specified in section 2578, as a condition, precedent not merely to a stay of execution, but to the exercise of the privilege of appeal.

It would seem, in other words, that the legislature intended to say to a would-be appellant from a decree directing the payment or deposit of money, or the delivery of property—" You must give an undertaking proportioned to the amount of money which you are directed to pay or deposit, or to the value of the property which you are directed to deliver, if you wish, pending your appeal, to avoid compliance with the decree appealed from ; otherwise you must give such an undertaking as is ordinarily required as security for the payment of costs and damages that may ultimately be awarded against you."

I think that this construction may be put upon sections 2577 and 2578 as they now stand without violence to their language. It seems to me, that as regards a case like the present, the following is a fair paraphrase of section 2577 as it was originally enacted and as it stands unaltered to-day : "To render a notice of appeal effectual for any purpose, the appellant must give a written undertaking in the sum of $250 except in cases which are, by the next section, excepted from the operation of this,—*i. e.*, except in cases where the giving of an undertaking regulated by the amount of money directed to be paid or deposited or the value of the property directed to be delivered, is, in the next section, declared to be essential *for rendering a notice of appeal effectual for any purpose.*"

If this is the true interpretation of section 2577, what was the effect of the amendment of 1882 ? Simply this : that since its adoption section 2578 has ceased to specify any cases that fall within the category of exceptions to section 2577. In other words, the amendment to section 2578 has made altogether ineffective—has indeed actually extinguished—such exceptions to the operation of section 2577 as had been worked by section 2578 before it was subjected to amendment. As a case like the present would no longer fall within any exception to the rule of section 2577, it would now fall within the rule itself, and no notice of appeal would be effectual for any purpose unless an undertaking were given in the sum of at least $250.

I hold that this is the law, and that on the day of the entry of the order giving this respondent time to make and serve a case or exception, his right to perfect his appeal had expired by limitation, thirty days having elapsed from the service of the decree without his filing an undertaking.

The order of November 26 must therefore be vacated.

SMITH, APPELLANT, *v.* TOZER, IMPLEADED, ETC., RESPONDENT.

SUPREME COURT, FIFTH DEPARTMENT, GENERAL TERM, OCTOBER, 1886.

§§ 2447, 2457, 2468, 2471.

Supplementary proceedings—Property situate outside of State cannot be reached in—Power of county judge to order delivery of property to receiver.

The title to real property of a judgment debtor vests in a receiver appointed in supplementary proceedings only from the time of filing the order, or a certified copy thereof, in the office of the clerk of the county where the property is situate;[*] and he does not and cannot acquire title to any property, the *situs* of which is not within this State.[*,*]

The power of a county judge in supplementary proceedings is wholly dependent upon the statute.[1]

There is no provision of the statute authorizing the judge before whom supplementary proceedings are pending, to order the application towards the payment or delivery or transfer to a receiver for such purposes, of any other than personal property of the judgment debtor;[*] and an order requiring a judgment debtor to assign or convey real property situate without the State to a receiver, is not within his power, and the judgment debtor is not in contempt if he disobeys it.[2]

It seems, that the equity power inherent in the supreme court having jurisdiction over the person of a judgment debtor, gives it the power to require the judgment debtor to transfer to a receiver appointed in supplementary proceedings, any property vested in the receiver, although such property is beyond the jurisdiction of the court, when such transfer or conveyance is necessary to its proper appropriation in the execution of the trust;[*] and that this equity power will be exercised at the special term upon motion.[4]

Although proceedings supplementary to execution are special proceedings, they are such in the action and ancillary to the purpose

of enforcing the collection of th judgm t, which was one of the
purposes for which the action was brough , and the legitimate
remedies attendant upon the proceedings to render it effectual, so
far as the orders of the court may be regarded as taken in the
action.[5]

It seems, that the property of a judgment debtor, situate without the
State, may be reached by the statutory creditor's bill;[8] and that
in such an action the court may by judgment appoint a receiver,
and direct the judgment debtor to convey to him.[9]

(*Decided October*, 1886.)

Appeal from order of Monroe special term, denying plaintiff's motion to direct and require the defendant to execute and deliver to a receiver in supplementary proceedings conveyance of his interest in lands
situate in the State of Illinois, and to punish him for
contempt for disobedience of the order of the county
judge of Ontario county directing him to make such
conveyance.

The facts appear in the opinion.

H. M. Field, for plaintiff-appellant.

Spencer Gooding, for defendant-respondent.

BRADLEY, J.—The plaintiff recovered in an action
in this court judgment against Seth A. Tozer and
another defendant, upon which execution against the
property of the defendant was returned unsatisfied.
Thereupon proceedings supplementary to execution
were instituted before the county judge against the
defendant Seth A. Tozer, and after his examination a
receiver of his property was appointed by the order of
such county judge ; and by the order such defendant
was directed to execute and deliver to the receiver "a
proper assignment and conveyance of all his lands and
real estate wherever the same are situated, and particularly the lands and real estate in the counties of.
Williamson and Platt in the State of Illinois." This

order was duly filed and recorded in the office of the clerk of Ontario county, January 19, 1886, and the receiver, having duly qualified, served the defendant with such order, and thereafter presented to him for execution quit-claim deeds of the Illinois lands in question, and requested him to execute them, to do which the defendant refused. This motion was then, upon due notice to the latter, made and denied. On the part of the plaintiff, it is contended that the order of the county judge was an effectual requirement for the execution of a conveyance to the receiver of such lands, and that his refusal to do so charged him with contempt and subjected him to punishment as the consequence. No question is made as to the manner of bringing him before the court for that purpose, and it is unnecessary to inquire whether it could be done otherwise than by an order to show cause.*

The question is one of power of the county judge to direct by order the execution of the conveyance to the receiver. It was within the power of the judge in such proceedings given by the old Code, to order any property of the judgment debtor not exempt from execution to be applied towards the satisfaction of the judgment (§ 297), and to appoint a receiver with ample powers to consummate the purposes of such order (§ 298), and it was held that those provisions made an order of the judge before whom the proceedings were had effective and operative upon the judgment debtor in regard to his lands situated outside of the State (Fenner v. Sanborn, 37 *Barb.* 610). In that view, the inquiry here is whether there has been any modification of the statute to deny such effect to the order in question. Those sections were repealed by Laws of 1877, chap. 417, and the Code of Civil Procedure sup-

---

* See Sandford v. Sandford, 9 *N. Y. Civ. Pro.* 289.

plies all the provisions now relating to proceedings supplementary to execution as such. The power ['] of the judge in them is wholly dependent upon the statute. There is no provision of the statute authorizing the judge to order the application toward the payment or the delivery or transfer to the ['] receiver, for such purpose, of any other than personal property of the judgment debtor (*Code Civ. Pro.* § 2447).

The direction in the order to assign or convey the real property situate in the State of Illinois was not within the power of the judge, and therefore the judgment debtor was not in contempt. The judge may appoint a receiver, in whom the property of such debtor becomes vested by force of the statute, subject to certain exceptions (*Id.* § 2468). The powers of the receiver are able to reach and make available the property of the judgment within the jurisdiction of the court. And there is no apparent reason why effect can not be given by the direction of the court, requiring him to transfer to the receiver any of his property outside the State which became vested in the ['] receiver by virtue of the appointment. The equity power is inherent in this court, having jurisdiction of the person of a judgment debtor, to require him to transfer to the receiver, any property so vested in the latter, when such transfer is necessary to the appropriation by him for the purpose of the trust, although such property is beyond the jurisdiction of the court. Mitchell *v.* Bunch, 2 *Paige,* 606, 615 ; Bailey *v.* Ryder, 10 *N. Y.* 663 ; Fenner *v.* Sanborn, 37 *Barb.* 610. And for other purposes the court having like jurisdiction of the party has frequently exercised its power of requiring him to perform acts relating to property beyond the State, when his duty to do so has been judicially declared (Newton *v.* Bronson, 13 *N. Y.* 587 ;

Gardner *v.* Ogden, 22 *Id.* 329 ; Williams *v.* Fitzhugh, 37 *Id.* 444 ; Shattuck *v.* Cassidy, 3 *Edw. Ch.* 152).

[*] This court, in an action by the receiver, might require the defendant to assign or convey to him any property vested in him, which may be in another State, when such transfer or conveyance is necessary to its proper appropriation in the execution of the trust. And this court may and will exercise equity powers at special term, upon motions, in actions where the facts and circumstances are such as not to require a trial of issues in an action for the proper determination of the questions upon which the right depends (Wetmore *v.* Law, 34 *Barb.* 515, 517 ; Hale *v.* Clauson, 60 *N. Y.* 341.)

[*] Although this is a special proceeding, it is such in the action, and ancilliary to the purpose of enforcing the collection of the judgment, which is one of the purposes for which the action was brought. And the legitimate remedies attendant upon the proceedings, and to render it effectual so far as the orders of the court may be regarded, are taken as in the action. When the receiver was appointed he became subject to the direction and control of the court (§ 2471).

No dispute of the facts appears by the papers upon which this motion was heard. And the question presented is whether the direction asked for came within the power of the court. This, in the view taken, depends upon the right the receiver took by his appointment by force of the statute, to the prop-
[*] erty in question. The statute provides that the property of the judgment debtor is vested in the receiver, from the time of filing the order appointing him, subject to the exception, that real property is vested in the receiver only from the time when the order or a certified copy is filed with the clerk of the county where it is situated, &c. (*Code Civ. Pro.* § 2468.)

The real property in Illinois cannot come within the exception, nor is any real property vested in the receiver which does not come within it; because, by the terms of the section, all the real property vested in the receiver is that embraced within the exception, and its *situs* must be in this State.

If the exception, by qualification in term, had limited the real property mentioned in it to that situ-
['] ated in this State, the vesting provision of the
section might have a broader construction, but as
it is, the only real estate the receiver is permitted to
take by force of this section, is that which is situated
in a county where the order may be filed; and our
attention is called to no other provision of the statute
enlarging the power of a receiver appointed in such
proceeding in the respect in question. The plaintiff,
however, is not without remedy. The provisions taking the place of the statutory creditor's bill for discharge authorized by the revised statutes (part 3,
['] ch. 15, title 2, art. 2), and somewhat enlarging
them, furnish a requisite remedy (*Code Civ. Pro.* ch.
15, title 4, art. 1), as in such an action the court may
by judgment appoint a receiver and direct the judgment debtor to convey to him, &c. (*Id.* § 1887). The
difficulty in the way of relief by motion here is found
in the qualified power of the receiver: he is not
vested with the real property of the debtor situa-
['] ted without the State, and therefore could not by
action or any proceeding *in invitam* acquire a
conveyance from him.

The views taken lead to the conclusion that the
order should be affirmed.*

SMITH, P. J., and BARKER, J., concurred.

---

* The following is a report of the opinion of the special term filed
on determining the motion resulting in the order appealed from:

SMITH v. TOZER, Impleaded.

SUPREME COURT, FIFTH DEPARTMENT, MONROE COUNTY, SPECIAL
TERM, MAY, 1886.

§§ 2447-2450, 2464-2471.

Supplementary proceedings.—Power of judge to direct transfer of property without the State to receiver in—Jurisdiction of supreme court— Contempt.

Under the Code of Procedure, a judge could in supplementary proceedings order any property of the judgment debtor not exempt from execution to be applied in satisfaction of the judgment, and could appoint a receiver with like authority as if the appointment was made by the court; and also, had power to order all property of the judgment debtor, without qualification as to where it might be situated, to be applied in payment of the judgment; and that the debtor execute to the receiver a conveyance of such property in such form as might be effectual to transfer title according to the laws of the State where the property was; and to punish the debtor for contempt if he refused so to do.[1,4,5]

Under the Code of Civil Procedure, the property of a judgment debtor cannot be reached in proceedings supplementary to execution, unless the judgment is a lien thereon; and as a judgment of this State cannot become a lien on land situate without the State, the court has not power to direct a conveyance to a receiver appointed in supplementary proceedings of lands belonging to the debtor the *situs* of which is not in this State.[2,6]

Mason v. Hackett, 35 *Hun*, 238, followed:[8] Fenner v. Sanborn, 37 *Barb.* 610;[2,6] Ross v. Wigg, 36 *Hun*, 107,[7] distinguished.

Under the Code of Procedure, supplementary proceedings are proceedings in an action in which judgment was recovered on which they were founded; but under the Code of Civil Procedure they are special proceedings.[8]

Where supplementary proceedings are instituted before a county judge, the supreme court at special term has no jurisdiction over or in them, except such as is provided by the statute, and such as it has by virtue of its general supervisory power over inferior jurisdictions.[4]

The power of the supreme court in proceedings supplementary to execution, pending before a county judge, stated.[4]

The supreme court has not power to direct a debtor in supplementary proceedings, pending before a county judge, to make an assignment of his lands situate in another State,[4] but it would have concurrent jurisdiction with the county judge to punish as a contempt, a refusal to comply with such an order if that judge had power to make it. [⁵]

Where the power of a judge to make order is doubtful, its disregard should not be punished as a contempt. [¹⁰]

(*Decided May*, 1886.)

Motion by plaintiff for an order requiring defendant to execute deeds conveying lands in Illinois to receiver appointed in supplementary proceedings by the county judge of Ontario county, and also that he be punished for contempt in neglecting and refusing to obey an order made by said county judge requiring such conveyance. The facts appear in the opinion of the general term report, *supra*.

H. M. Field, for judgment creditor and motion.

Spencer Gooding, for judgment debtor, opposed.

ANGLE, J.—Under the Code of Procedure (§ 297) a judge could, in supplementary proceedings, order any property of the judgment debtor, not exempt from execution, to be applied in satisfaction [¹] of the judgment, and by section 298 he could appoint a receiver with like authority as if the appointment were made by the court according to section 244 of the same Code. Under these provisions it was held in Fenner *v.* Sanborn, (37 *Barb.* 610, 612, 613), that the title of a debtor to real estate situate out of the State would not, by virtue of the appointment of a receiver, vest in him so as to be effectual in the State where the land was situated, and that as the judge had power to order all property of the debtor, without qualification as to where it might be situated—except property exempt from execution—to be applied in payment of the judgment, and as such power could only be effectually executed by an order that the debtor execute to the receiver a conveyance of such property in such form as to be effectual to transfer the title according to the laws of the State where the property was, the judge had power to make such an order and to punish him for contempt if he refused to do so. Fenner *v.* Sanborn was approved in Clan Ranald *v.* Wykoff (41 *N. Y. Sup.* [9 *J. & S.*] 529), a case under the Code of Civil Procedure, in which the court, upon the motion of the receiver, ordered the debtor to make an assignment of his property situated in another State.

The Code of Civil Procedure (§ 2464) gives to the judge power of "appointing a receiver of the property of the judgment debtor," but omits anything about the power of such receiver. A more [²] important difference between the former Code and the present is, that by the former the judge had power to direct application of any property of the debtor (not exempt from execution), to the satisfaction of the judgment, and it was upon this provision that Fenner v. Sanborn was decided. I am not cited to any clause in the Code of Civil Procedure, giving this power to the judge, nor have I been able to find any such provision, except as the appointment of a receiver itself works out such application under sections 2447, 2449, 2450, 2464, 2465, 2466, 2467, 2469, 2470, 2471. The case of Fenner v. Sanborn is not now an authority for the power claimed, but on the contrary, the implication is that the present Code, by omitting the clause, which in the former Code had been held to confer that power, has designedly withheld the power.

[³] There is a still more important difference between supplementary proceedings under the Code of Procedure, and supplementary proceedings under the Code of Civil Procedure. Under the former, they were proceedings in the action in which the judgment was recovered on which they were founded, and they were said to be in the nature of new remedies or equitable rights arising by force of the statute in the actions in which the judgments were recovered. Wright v. Nostrand (94 *N. Y.* 45-6). They were expressly held not to be special proceedings (Dresser v. Van Pelt, 15 *How. Pr.* 19 ; S. C., 6 *Duer*, 687), but as much proceedings in the action as the issuing of the execution upon the judgment. Wegman v. Childs (41 *N. Y.* 163). Under the Code of Civil Procedure, they are " special proceedings." *Code Civ. Pro.* §§ 2433, 3334, 3343, subd. 10 ; Champlin v. Stodart (64 *How. Pr.* 378); Fiske v. Twigg (5 *N. Y. Civ. Pro.* 41).

[⁴] The proceedings in this matter were " special proceedings " before the county judge under certain statutory provisions, and this court has no jurisdiction over or in them except as provided by statute, and such as it has by virtue of its general supervisory power over inferior jurisdictions. When such proceedings are before a county judge, all the power which the Code gives this court, so far as I am cited, or am able to discover, is to review orders made in the course of such proceedings in certain cases (§ 2433), to vacate or modify an injunction order as provided in section 2451; and it has concurrent jurisdiction with the judge or referee to punish as for contempt a person who refuses, or without sufficient excuse neglects to obey an order of a judge or referee, or to attend before a judge according to the command of a subpœna, section 2457; it also has power in certain cases to control, direct or remove a receiver, or to subordinate the proceedings in or by which the receiver was appointed, section 2466; and under section 2471, a receiver is subject to the discretion and control of the court out of which the exeution issued. I have not found any provision of the present Code or any authority under it, which gives this court the power to inter- fere in proceedings before a county judge and direct the debtor to make an assignment to a receiver of his lands situate in another State, and that part of the motion asking for such order is denied.

[⁵]   The county judge has already made such an order, and under section 2457 this court has concurrent jurisdiction with that judge to punish as a contempt a refusal to comply with it if the judge had power to make the order.*

[⁶]   I need not consider whether the exercise of this concurrent power would be judicious without any reason being given why the jurisdiction in which the proceeding is pending, and which is equal to that of this court in this regard, is not so invoked. As already seen, the statutory provision under which Fenner v. Sanborn held that the county judge had power to order such an assignment, no longer exists. Since that decision, and as part of the same pro- cess by which the change from "supplementary proceedings in an action" to "special proceedings" was made, that provision has been eliminated. As above suggested, the process provided for vesting in the receiver the real estate of the debtor is under section 2468, which declares that "real property is vested in the receiver only from the time when the order, or a certified copy thereof, as the case may be, is filed with the clerk of the county in which it is situated." The order, with the filing of it, appears to be the statu- tory transfer of the real estate of the debtor to the receiver, and to be the only transfer the statute provides for.

[⁷]   In Ross v. Wigg (39 Hun, 654), the general term in the fourth department say, with reference to the declaration in the Code of Civil Procedure that the remedies provided by section 2432 were "special proceedings:" " We do not regard this declaration of the legislature as indicative of any intent to change the character of the proceedings, or as in any way diminishing the force of section 4, chapter 96, Laws 1857." In that case, the question was whether the changes in the Code had ousted the recorder of the city of Oswego from jurisdiction under said section 4, and which under that section he had previously exercised in supplementary proceedings. I do not regard the above quoted sentence as an adjudication that the change from " proceedings in an action " to a " special proceeding " is not a change in the nature and character of the proceedings in the case, and for the purposes I am considering. That it was not such a

---

* Freeman ♦. Richardson, 68 N. Y. 617.

Smith v. Tozer.

change as defeated the jurisdiction of the recorder was all that the court decided, or, I suppose, meant to decide. One of the controlling points in Wright v. Nostrand (*supra*), was in the distinction between regarding such proceedings as proceedings in an action, and regarding them as special proceedings.

[8] There is in our own department a case of some bearing upon the question. In Mason v. Hackett (35 *Hun*, 238), a county judge had made an order in supplementary proceedings on a docketed justice's judgment for $20 damages and $7.85 costs—$27.85; upon which an execution had been issued and returned unsatisfied. A motion was made before the judge to vacate his order for examination, which he denied, and held that, when section 2458,—which provided that, in order to entitle a judgment creditor to take such proceedings, "the judgment must have been rendered . . . for a sum not less than twenty-five dollars, exclusive of costs,"—was modified in 1881 by striking out the words "exclusive of costs;" it was no longer necessary that the judgment should be for twenty-five dollars, exclusive of costs; but the general term reversed this, on the ground that the judgment being for less than twenty-five dollars, exclusive of costs, it was not a lien on real estate; and the court say: "Whenever the proceedings result in the appointment of a receiver, the title of all his (the debtor's) real estate passes in trust to that officer without any assignment or other conveyance by the debtor. Sections 2464, 2468. We think it clear that it was not the intention of the legislature to devote the debtor's property to the payment of judgments against him, unless they, by the same statute, become [9] liens thereon." If this be sound (and the court held it sufficient to repel the argument arising from the change made ·in the statute by striking out the words "exclusive of costs"), then, as the judgment in the present case was not a lien on Illinois lands, the legislature did not intend they should be reached by supplementary proceedings.

[10] In any view of the case, I regard the order of the county judge as of doubtful validity, and therefore the court should not punish its disregard as a contempt. *Rapalje on Contempts*, § 16.

Motion denied, without costs.

SMITH, Respondent, *v.* GRANT, Appellant.

CITY COURT OF NEW YORK, GENERAL TERM,
JANUARY, 1887.

§ 1294.

*Order—When recitals in, conclusive—When provisions inserted in
order by consent not appealable.*

Where a motion to resettle order was denied on the ground that the
same was in conformity to the decision made, and there was no proof
that it was not,—*Held*, that there was nothing in the order denying
the motion to be resettled that could be reviewed on appeal.

Provisions inserted in an order by consent cannot be reviewed on
an appeal taken by the consenting party.

Where the defendant in an action asked an adjournment of the trial
thereof, and the same was granted on stringent terms and conditions
to which he assented,—*Held*, that the order could not be reviewed
on an appeal taken by such defendant.

Recitals in an order or judgment, though not conclusive, are presumptive evidence of their truth, and when uncontradicted are conclusive.

The fact that a case is irregular on the calendar of the court is waived
by an application to adjourn the trial.

Admissions or stipulations and consents given on the hearing of
motions, if not reduced to writing, should as matter of practice, be
incorporated in the order to be entered thereupon, and thus made
part of the record for future guidance, in case the propriety of the
order is afterwards called in question. The judge who decides a
motion like one trying a case, must in the nature of things either on
the settlement of the order or the case on appeal, determine what
occurred before him that the record may record the facts as they
appeared.

(*Decided January*, 1887).

Appeal from an order granting motion that the
trial of action be postponed, upon conditions, and
from an order denying a motion to resettle such
order.

This action was brought on May 14, 1886, against the defendant, to recover $1,600, for the alleged conversion of certain property which the defendant seized under and by virtue of a warrant of attachment, issued to him as sheriff of the city and county of New York, for execution. Issue was joined on May 1, 1886, and on June 1, a notice of trial for June 7, was served, together with a notice that on June 5, a motion would be made at a special term of the court to advance the cause on the ground that the plaintiff was entitled to a preference. This motion was argued and granted on June 5, and the trial of the cause set down for June 9. On the argument of the motion, the defendant presented to the judge at chambers, an affidavit, showing that a material witness for the defendant could not be found, and asked that the cause be set down for some day during the following month. The justice who heard the motion held that he could not consider an application to postpone; that the action being a preferred one, he had no discretion but to advance it, leaving it to the trial term justice to grant such an adjournment as was proper. The cause first appeared on the day calendar on June 15, and on that day the attorneys for the defendant appeared and moved that the cause be adjourned until the next term, on the ground that a material witness was absent from the city temporarily, sojourning in Boston, and that without his evidence the plaintiff could not safely proceed to trial.

The motion to postpone until the next term was denied, and the cause was adjourned for one week by the trial justice; the adjournment being upon condition that the cause be tried on June 21, the adjourned day; and that examination of the absent witness be taken by an open or closed commission at defendant's option, to the issuing of which commission the plaintiff was required to consent, and that an inquest if taken, should be final. To all these terms and conditions the parties assented, and the order was entered to that effect. The defendant claiming that the order should recite that a motion was made to strike the case from the calendar on the ground that no notice of trial had been served with the order advancing it, applied for a re-settlement ; and this motion to re-settle was denied, on the ground that the order was an accurate and complete record of the decision. The defendant thereupon appealed from the order directing the postponement, and also from the order denying his motion to re-settle it.

Cockran & Clark, for defendant-appellant.

David Leventritt, for plaintiff-respondent.

Having stipulated to accept the terms imposed by the court, as a condition of the adjournment obtained, the defendant will not now be heard on appeal. It is universally recognized that a party is bound by any agreement into which his attorney enters relative to the trial of a cause. Corning *v.* Southland, 3 *Hill*, 552 ; Gaillard *v.* Smart, 6 *Cow.* 383 ; Gorham *v.* Gale, 7 *Id.* 739. And in Mark *v.* City of Buffalo, 87 *N. Y.* 184, the court of appeals (p. 188), pointedly asserts that doctrine in the following language : "In all that properly relates to the conduct of a trial, the attorney represents the party and is his authorized agent. The attorney's agreement and stipulation within the boundaries of the authority is the agreement and stipulation of his client, and binds the latter as if he himself had personally made it." Having accepted the benefit of an adjournment of the trial embraced in the order, he cannot now appeal therefrom. The acceptance of any benefit under a judgment or order constitutes a waiver of the right to appeal. McElwain *v.* Willis, 9 *Wend.* 548 ; Lewis *v.* Irving Fire Ins.

Co., 15 *Abb. Pr.* 140, *note;* Lupton *v.* Jewett, 19 *Id.* 320 ; Radway *v.* Graham, 4 *Id.* 468. And in Matter of N. Y. C. & H. R. R. R. Co., 60 *N. Y.* 112, the following language appears : " It is only when a party accepts some benefit under an order, that he waives his right to appeal therefrom." To the same effect, Egbert *v.* O'Connor, 46 *N. Y. Super.* (14 *J. & S.*) 194 ; Taussig *v.* Hart, 33 *Id.* (1 *J. & S.*) 157. Even by compliance with the conditions of an order under protest, the right to appeal is defeated. Dambmann *v.* Schulting, 6 *Hun,* 29 ; People *v.* Rochester & S. L. R. R. Co., 15 *Id.* 188. Having by means of the stipulation acquired an advantage which would not otherwise have been accorded to him, the appellant cannot now avoid the conditions imposed. ... McGuire *v.* N. Y. C. & H. R. R. R. Co., 6 *Daly,* 70 ; Cox *v.* N. Y. C. & H. R. R. R. Co., 63 *N. Y.* 414. To reverse the order would be equivalent to awarding to the plaintiff the benefit of the order, which he has enjoyed, and to relieve him of the conditions of the stipulations into which he entered in order to secure those benefits, and without which stipulation they would not have been accorded to him. This should not be countenanced. Rust *v.* Hauselt, 43 *N. Y. Super.* (11 *J. & S.*) 571. And, moreover, the court has nothing whatsoever to do with the terms of the order, since they were assented to and accepted by the appellant as a condition of the adjournment which he succeeded in obtaining. Jex *v.* Jacobs, 7 *Abb. N. C.* 452. A justice present at hearing and disposing of an application is alone able to say what transpired thereat. Tweed *v.* Davis, 1 *Hun,* 252 ; Bohnet *v.* Lithauer, 7 *Id.* 238.

McAdam, C. J.—The second order refused to resettle the order made June 15, on the ground that "the same was in conformity to the decision made," and there is no proof that it was not, so that there is nothing in the second order which can be reviewed. Nor can we review the first order, for the reasons : (1.) The part granting an adjournment of the trial until June 21 was made on the defendant's application. It was, as far as it went, a decision in the defendant's favor, and as a consequence he cannot complain of it. (2.) The part imposing stringent terms and conditions on the defendant was assented to by the defendant, and we cannot review provisions inserted in an order by consent of the appealing party.

The order recites the consent of the parties, and the recital being uncontradicted is conclusive. The rule is that recitals in an order or judgment, though not conclusive, are presumptive evidence of their truth (Struthers v. Pearce, 51 N. Y. 365 ; Maples v. Mackey, 89 Id. 146 ; Ferguson v. Crawford, 70 Id. 253 ; Porter v. Bronson, 29 How. Pr. 292 ; Wright v. Nostrand, 94 N. Y., at pp. 44, 45 ; Barber v. Winslow, 12 Wend. 102 : Belden v. Meeker, 2 Lans. 473, aff'd, 47 N. Y. 307 ; Dayton v. Johnson, 69 Id. 425). The terms imposed were indeed stringent, and we might have relieved against them were it not that the consent to them forbids us from interfering. (3.) The case on appeal does not show that the defendant made any application to strike the case from the calendar, or that the trial judge decided any such motion. Indeed, the order made by him negatives the idea that any such motion was made. If any such irregularity existed it was therefore waived (Macy v. Nelson, 62 N. Y. 638).

(4.) The printed case does not show what occurred on June 21, and we are therefore uninformed whether the application to adjourn was renewed, granted or denied, or whether the action was tried or dismissed, or whether an inquest was taken or not, so that we cannot review on this appeal the action of the trial judge on that day. In regard to recitals in orders, it may be proper to observe that admissions or stipulations made and consents given on the hearing of motions, if not reduced to writing, should as matter of practice be incorporated in the order to be entered thereupon, and thus made part of the record for future guidance, in case the propriety of the order is afterwards called in question. The judge who decides a motion, like one trying a cause, must in the nature of things, either on the settlement of the order or the case on appeal, determine what occurred before him, that the record may truthfully represent the facts as they appeared. For the reasons aforesaid, the order appealed from must be affirmed, with costs.

NEHRBAS and HYATT, JJ., concurred.

PRICE, APPELLANT, v. PRICE, ET AL, RESPONDENTS.

SUPREME COURT, FIRST DEPARTMENT, GENERAL TERM, OCTOBER, 1886.

§§ 1599, 1600, 1615.

Dower.— What property may be set-off to widow.

Under the Code of Civil Procedure, one of several distinct parcels of land in which a widow is entitled to dower, constituting one-third of the real property of which dower is to be admeasured, may be set-off in satisfaction of her entire claim for dower in the several parcels of property.[6,7]

Instance of a case in which one parcel of real property was held to have been properly set-off to a widow in satisfaction of her claim for dower in sundry distinct pieces of property.[8]

At common law the widow was entitled to dower in each separate and distinct parcels of land whereof her husband was seized of an estate of inheritance at any time during the marriage:[1] but this general right was subordinate to the equitable rights and interest of other parties in the property, and where it would be inequitable and unjust to have assigned dower to any lands conveyed by her husband during his lifetime with warranty, the widow's dower was admeasured to her in other property affected by no such right or interest.[2] This view of the law, however, has been questioned in Illinois.[3,4] Wood v. Keyes (6 *Paige*, 478), followed.[2,5] Schuebley v. Schuebley (26 *Ill.* 116);[3,5] Atkins v. Merrill (39 *Id.* 62), distinguished and not followed.

(*Decided October* 15, 1886.)

Appeal from an order denying a motion to confirm the report of a referee for admeasurements of dower.

The opinion states sufficient facts.

George H. Starr (*Starr & Hooker*, attorneys), for plaintiff-appellant.

William Peet and *David Wilcox* (*Bristow, Peet & Opdyke*, attorneys), for Frank N. Price, and others, defendants-respondents.

Frank L. Hall (*De Forest & Weeks*, attorneys), for The Rector, etc., of St. John the Evangelist's Church, defendants-respondents.

James R. Marvin, for Josephine Little, defendant-respondent.

Hughes & Northrup, for Walter J. Price, defendant-respondent.

Stephen Brown, guardian *ad litem* of Lillie M. Price, and for the Glen Falls Fire Ins. Co., defendant-respondent.

De Witt, Lockman & De Witt, for Mary A. Lockman, defendant-respondent.

DANIELS, J.—The plaintiff has been held entitled in this action to recover dower in the real estate owned by Walter W. Price during the time of her intermarriage with him, and until the entry of a decree annulling that marriage. The controversy as it was then disposed of is reported in 33 *Hun*, 76. Under that decision an interlocutory judgment was recovered directing the plaintiff's dower to be admeasured in the real estate so owned by her husband, who departed this life on June 6, 1876, and a referee was appointed to make such admeasurement of her dower. The property in which under this decision she is entitled to dower consisted of four separate and distinct parcels of land. Two parcels are still owned in severalty by two of the children of Walter W. Price. One, consisting of about fifteen acres, was conveyed by the deceased to his son, the defendant, Walter J. Price, in July, 1875, and that has since been mortgaged to the Glen Falls Fire Insurance Company to secure the sum of $10,000. This property consists of about fifteen acres of land having no substantial rental value. The deceased left a will by which he devised certain premises, consisting of a lot of land on Hammond street, in the city of New York, to his son, Charles G. Price. He sold and conveyed this property to the rector, church wardens, &c., of St. John the Evangelist's Church. The church acquired the title for a valuable consideration without notice of the plaintiff's right to dower therein. The testator also devised to two of his sons as tenants in common, a house and lot known as number 4 Vanness place, in the city of New York, which they conveyed to their sister, Mrs. Ashmead, and she afterwards sold and conveyed the same property to Josephine Little for the consideration of $11,000. And she afterwards conveyed it to Mr. Wedeland. The rental value of this property was found by the referee upon evidence sustaining the conclusion to be the sum of $776, after deducting taxes and water rents, and of the Hammond street lot to be about the sum of $790, after making the same deduc-tions. The remaining property in which the plaintiff was entitled to be endowed consisted of two adjacent pieces of land on the westerly side of Lake George, containing together about seventy-three acres, and a small island situated near these premises in the lake. This land was divided only by a road running in a northerly and southerly direction, and upon that por-tion of it, situated westerly of the road, valuable buildings had been erected prior to the decease of the testator. This piece consisted of 33 and 75–100 acres, and the two pieces together, including the island, pro-duced an annual rental varying from eight to thirteen hundred dollars. The dwelling upon it was designed for a summer residence, and the property had been improved to make it convenient, attractive and desir-able for such a residence.

But the referee considered it to be impractical to assign the plaintiff her dower in this property, and was of the opinion that it should be sold and her dower estimated and paid to her out of the proceeds. It is true that no such express direction was given by him, but that was evidently the opinion upon which his final conclusions were founded. The court, upon the motion to confirm his report, dissented from his conclusion as to the inability to assign the plaintiff's dower in his property, and ordered the case to be referred back to the referee to set off to the plaintiff her dower in that property, and the plaintiff has appealed from that order, considering it to have been unauthorized and not within the power of the court to make it. And her counsel has endeavored to sustain this view in support of the appeal under the general statutory authority, declaring that a widow shall be endowed in the third part of all the lands whereof her husband was seized, of an estate of inheritance at any time during the marriage (2 R. S. [6th ed.] 1121,

['] § 1), and the common law rule maintaining her right to dower in each separate and distinct parcel of such lands.

But it was considered by the chancellor in Wood v. Keyes (6 *Paige*, 478), that this general direction should be subordinated to the equitable rights and ['] interests of other parties in the property. And where it would be inequitable and unjust to assign dower in the lands conveyed by her husband during his lifetime with warranty, that her dower should be admeasured to her in other property affected by no such rights or interests. The authority of the court to make this decision has been drawn in question ['] in support of the appeal, and the case of Scheubley v. Scheubley (26 *Ill.* 116), decided under a like statutory provision, has been relied upon as supporting this objection. And it is true that the court there announced and acted upon the common law principle, which was held to be consistent with the statute, that the widow was entitled to be endowed in each separate parcel of land which had been owned by her husband during the period of the marriage. And ['] the case of Atkins v. Merrill (39 *Ill.* 62), followed this authority. But these cases require no de- ['] parture to be made from the doctrine of that of Wood v. Keyes, for the reason that the provisions of the Code of Civil Procedure concerning the admeasurement of dower, have not only followed but have enlarged the effect of this authority. For by sub- division 1 of section 1609, it has been in the most ['] general manner directed that the referee, or com- missioners, must, if it is practicable, and in their opinion for the best interests of all the parties con- cerned, admeasure and lay off as the dower of the plaintiff a "distinct parcel," constituting one-third of the real property of which dower is to be admeasured. And if that is not practicable, or for the best interests of all parties concerned, then that fact is to be reported to the court.

This phraseology, empowering the referee or the commissioners to set apart a distinct parcel of land for the dower of the plaintiff, was not contained in the provisions of the Revised Statutes concerning this subject. There the direction was that the commissioners should "admeasure and lay off as speedily as possible the one-third part of the lands or premises embraced in the order" (3 *R. S.* [6th ed.] 777, § 13; 578, § 5). And this additional direction empowering the referee or commissioners to admeasure and lay off "a distinct parcel" of the lands must have been designed to enlarge the authority of the court over this subject, and it has been employed by way of contrast to other parcels or portions of the real estate of the deceased husband.

This significance of the phraseology is not only indicated by the language itself, but by the manner in which it has been employed in section 1599 of the Code of Civil Procedure, where a distinct parcel is distinguished from other real estate of which the husband may have died siezed or alienated by one conveyance to one or more other persons.

That the employment of these terms was designed and intended to have their appropriate office and effect in the proceedings further appears from sections 1610 and 1613 of the Code. For care has been taken where that can be done, and the rights and interests of other parties shall be promoted thereby, to restrict the property to be set off as the dower of the widow, to a distant parcel of that in which she may be entitled to be endowed.

It has been urged that this construction should be limited to the class of cases in which the widow indicated her willingness to receive a gross sum in satisfaction and discharge of her right of dower. And where she may consent to receive that sum in the manner provided for by the statute, it has been further directed by section 1319 that a reference shall be ordered to ascertain whether a distinct parcel of the property can be so admeasured and laid off without material injury to the interests of the parties, and if it cannot, that then a sale shall be made, out of the proceeds of which such a sum of money shall be paid to her. The next section has further provided, where the widow may consent to receive the same, for the appropriation to her of a distinct parcel of vacant or unimproved lots, to be owned by her in severalty and fee simple for and as her dower. These sections are substitutes for the enactments contained in chapter 717 of the Laws of 1870, and in no manner affect or abridge the authority provided by the preceding sections for setting off to the widow a distinct parcel of real estate   But they specially provide for a class of cases not enumerated in those sections, and they in no manner enlarge or extend, in the use which they have made of it, this phraseology which has been inserted and repeated in these sections of the Code ; but whenever this language has been employed, the same significance is required to be given to it.   What is a distinct parcel of the property in one case is no more nor less than a distinct parcel in the other, and the phraseology must have been designed and intended to have the same significance and effect wherever it has ['] been employed in this part of the Code. And that was to confer upon the court in all cases the power to set off as the dower of the widow, a separate and distinct parcel of the real estate.   That has been positively required to be done where it can be, and at the same time will be for the best interests of all the parties concerned.

['']   And the referee has concluded from the evidence produced before him, that it was for the

best interests of all the parties concerned that the
dower should be secured to the plaintiff out of the
property situated upon the westerly side of Lake
George. And in this conclusion he is sustained by
the manifest injustice of directing dower to be apportioned to the plaintiff out of the houses and lots on
Hammond street and Vanness place, in the city of
New York. That property has passed into the hands
of purchasers, for value, without notice of the plaintiff's rights, and to assign her dower in those lots,
would necessarily entitle their owners to reimburse-
ment for the amounts paid from the estate of the testator or under the covenants of warranty contained in
the deeds conveying this property, and that should
not unnecessarily be done. The lands conveyed to
Walter J. Price, and situated between what is known
as the Bolton road and the westerly bounds of Lake
George, are in no manner adapted to the plaintiff's use
or enjoyment as her dower, for no income can be
derived from that which would afford her any remun-
eration whatever, for her claim. And in this state of
the property, the seventy-three acres upon which the
buildings were erected by the testator in his life-time,
and still owned by his devisee, seem to be all that can
justly be appropriated to the satisfaction of the plaintiff's right of dower.

The referee concluded that this property could not
be so divided as to set any portion of it off to the
widow in satisfaction of her entire claim for dower in
these four parcels of property. But the evidence
taken by him, very decidedly preponderates in support of the view adopted at the special term, when the
order was made, from which the appeal has been
taken, and that is that this property can well be
divided upon an easterly and westerly line, setting off
to the plaintiff that portion containing the buildings
standing upon it and so much of the land as would

yield to her at least one-third of the rental value of all this property. Three witnesses, whose knowledge of the property sustain their opinion, have expressed their views to the effect that the land can be so divided, and its locality, extent, condition, value and rental seem to sustain that view. The evidence opposed to it was very slight and inconclusive, and failed against the other testimony upon the hearing to sustain the conclusion adopted by the referee. As the interests of the parties were proved and found by the referee, and to which no exception has been taken by either of them, and the evidence was presented concerning the ability to make this division of the land, the order made at the hearing was a proper one and it should be affirmed, with costs and disbursements to abide the event of the action.

BRADY, J., concurred.

RISLEY *v.* RICE AND ANOTHER.

SUPREME COURT, FOURTH DEPARTMENT, ONTARIO COUNTY, SPECIAL TERM, AUGUST, 1886.

§§ 1496, 1497, 1525, 1531.

Ejectment— What to be paid by defeated party on application for new trial.

Upon an application for a new trial in an action of ejectment, after final judgment upon the trial of an issue of fact, the party seeking a new trial is required to pay all costs and damages other than for rent and profits, or for use and occupation awarded to his adversary, where the damages awarded include what was technically known at common law as *mesne profits,* such party is not required to pay them as a condition of obtaining new trial.

(*Decided August* 3, 1886.)

Risley *v.* Rice.

Motion by defendants for new trial in action of ejectment after judgment in favor of plaintiff upon the trial of an issue of fact, under section 1525 of the Code of Civil Procedure.*

The opinion states the facts.

---

* There are three cases in which a new trial will be ordered in an action of ejectment:

First—Where a final judgment was rendered upon the trial of an issue of fact. In this case, the court " at any time within three years after such a judgment is rendered, and the judgment-roll is filed upon application of the party against whom it was rendered, his heir, devisee or assignee, and upon payment of all costs and all damages other than for rents and profits, or for use and occupation awarded thereby to the adverse party, must make an order vacating the judgment and granting a new trial in the action" (*Code Civ. Pro.* §§ 1524, 1525). This order may be made before judgment is perfected, and may be to the effect that when the judgment is perfected, it be thereupon vacated and a new trial granted without further order of the court (Post *v.* Moran, 1 *N. Y. Civ. Pro.* 222; Cook *v.* Passage, 4 *How. Pr.* 360). Under the provisions of the Revised Statutes which were superseded by the Code of Civil Procedure, a new trial could be granted within three years after judgment was rendered (2 *R. S.* 309, § 37). The Code of Civil Procedure was not intended to change the practice as to when such orders might be made. but to fix with greater certainty the exact date from which the absolute right to a new trial runs; and not to exclude the defeated party from the advantages of anticipating the entry of judgment, retaining possession of disputed premises and preventing the issue of an execution to enforce the judgment (Post *v.* Moran, *supra*).

One new trial may be granted in such a case on payment of costs, etc., without showing any cause whatever (Harris *v.* White, 54 *How. Pr.* 113). The right of the plaintiff thereto is absolute (*Ib. ;* Evans *v.* Millard, 16 *N. Y. Super. Ct.* 619). And an order granting a new trial is not appealable to the court of appeals (Evans *v.* Millard, *supra*).

The defendant in an action of ejectment is not deprived of his right to a new trial under the statute, by the fact that all his interest in the land in question was sold to the plaintiff under the execution for costs, issued upon the judgment recovered in such action, and that the plaintiff had received a sheriff's deed therefor (Phyfe *v.* Masterson, 45 *N. Y. Super. Ct.* [13 *J. & S.*] 388).

Second—Where a new trial has been ordered in a case in which judgment was rendered after a trial of an issue of fact, "the court

H. M. Field, for defendant and motion.

A. W. Gardner, for plaintiff, opposed.

ANGLE, J.—The only question on this motion is, whether, in addition to costs, the defendants must pay the judgment for $72 recovered against the defendant, Rice.

Under section 1525, Code Civ. Pro., the defendant is required to pay, in addition to costs, "all damages

---

upon like application, made within two years after the second final judgment was rendered, and, the, judgment-roll is filed, may make an order vacating the second judgment and granting a new trial upon like terms, if it is satisfied that justice will be promoted, and the rights of the parties more satisfactorily ascertained and established " (*Code Civ. Pro. § 1525.*)

This second new trial is discretionary with the court, and it must find that substantial justice requires a new trial (Phyfe *v.* Masterson, 45 *N. Y. Super. Ct.* [13 *J. & S.*] 338).

After a second new trial has been granted, no other new trial can be granted under the statute (*Code Civ. Pro.* § 1525, and see Bellinger *v.* Martindale, 8 *How. Pr.* 113; Bright *v.* Milbrank, 9 *Bosw.* 672).

It seems, however, that the granting of two new trials under the statute, will not prevent the reversal of the judgment for errors occurring on the trial, and that new trials granted for such errors do not count as a part of those authorized to be granted under the statute (*Vide Sedgwick & Wait on the Trial of Title to Land*, §§ 577, 596).

Where final judgment is rendered for the plaintiff in an action to recover real property otherwise than upon the trial of an issue of fact, the court within five years after the judgment-roll is filed upon application of the defendant, his heir, devisee or assignee; and upon the payment of all costs and damages awarded to the plaintiff, must make an order vacating any judgment and granting a new trial if it is satisfied that justice will be thereby promoted, and the rights of the parties more satisfactorily ascertained and established, but not otherwise (*Code Civ. Pro.* § 1526).

EXCEPTION.—The provisions of the Code authorizing the granting of a new trial in an action of ejectment, are not applicable where the action is founded upon the allegation of rent in arrears, or where the summons in an action is served pursuant to an order directing substituted service thereof (*Code Civ. Pro.* § 1528).

other than for rents and profits or for use and occupation awarded" by the jury. An action of ejectment is an action to recover the immediate possession of real property (*Code*, § 3343, sub. 20), and in such action plaintiff may demand in his complaint, and in a proper case recover damages for withholding the property (§ 1496) ; these damages include rents and profits, or the value of the use and occupation when either can be legally recovered by the plaintiff (§ 1497) ; and the plaintiff is entitled to recover as damages, the rents and profits, or the value of the use and occupation of the property for a term not exceeding six years (§ 1531). Under the above provisions damages for detention now include the rents and profits or value of the use and occupation, and the former rule as held in Larned v. Hudson (57 *N. Y.* 151), has been changed. De Lisle v. Hunt (36 *Hun*, 620) ; see, also, Wallace v. Berdell (8 *N. Y. Civ. Pro.* 363).

The complaint here alleges among other things, that defendants are in the wrongful possession of the premises, and wrongfully claim possession thereof, and, although plaintiff has demanded possession, the defendants have refused, and still do refuse, to deliver the premises and the possession to plaintiff, and wrongfully withhold the same from her to her damage $200, wherefore she demands judgment for the possession of said premises and for $200, the plaintiff's damages, by the withholding the said premises by the defendant and use of the same ; and plaintiff has judgment that she "recover of the defendant, Eli Rice, the sum of $72 for the wrongful detention and withholding of said real estate from her." Under the above authorities the damages asked for, and adjudged, included the rents and profits, or the value of the use and occupation (if any was proven), being what at common law was known by the technical

name of *mesne profits*,* and that the damages awarded
in this case were, in fact, for rents and profits, or use
and occupation is quite clear from the affidavits and
printed case ; defendants, therefore, need not pay
them as a condition for a new trial.

Motion granted without costs.

ANSONIA BRASS & COPPER CO., APPELLANT,
v. CONNER, ET AL., AS EXECUTORS, ETC.,
RESPONDENTS.

COURT OF APPEALS, NOVEMBER, 1886.

§ 1366.

Execution—Effect of stay on time to return.

An order made by a court of competent jurisdiction staying the sheriff
from any interference under an execution with the property of a judgment debtor, suspends during its continuance the running of the
statutory term of sixty days given to the sheriff for executing the
process.[5,7,8]

The limitation upon the right of a sheriff to hold an execution issued
to him is for the benefit both of the sheriff and of the judgment
creditor, and intended to fix the time beyond which in the usual and
regular process of payment, the creditor's right to payment shall not
be postponed;[2] but this does not affect the right of any party interested to stay the enforcement of an execution for sufficient cause;[3]
the sufficiency of the cause must be determined by the tribunal to
which an application for a stay has been made, and where it has been
adjudged that sufficient cause exists, its order providing that it has
jurisdiction of the matter and the parties, is obligatory upon them
and must be obeyed.[3]

---

* The common law and statutory rules as to the recovery of *mesne
profits* in action of ejectment are stated in Wallace *v.* Berdell, 8 *N. Y.
Civ. Pro.* 363.

It seems, that the fact that a plaintiff has directed that an execution issued by him should not be returned, or that the sheriff has procured it to be stayed by order of the court, are lawful defenses in an action against the sheriff for not returning execution.[4]

Wehle *v.* Conner (69 *N. Y.* 546), followed.[4] Paige *v.* Willett (38 *N. Y.* 28);[5] People *v.* Carnley (3 *Abb. Pr.* 216),[6] cited and approved.

A judgment debtor whose property has been taken by a sheriff under execution remains its general owner, subject only to the special property acquired by the sheriff, by reason of his levy and his right to dispose of so much thereof by sale, as may be required to satisfy the execution ; the residue of the property remaining unsold, after satisfaction of the judgment, reverts to the debtor by virtue of his ownership, but while still in the hands of the sheriff, it is liable to attachment and levy on behalf of other creditors, and the resulting interest in the surplus constitutes property in the debtor subject to be reached by the creditors generally, under the bankrupt law.[9]

The power of an United States District Court in bankruptcy to restrain interference with the property of a person adjudged by it to be a bankrupt, is not only a necessary incident of the power conferred upon such courts to collect and marshal the bankrupt's assets, and ascertain and liquidate the liens and other specific claims thereon,[10] but is also an express power conferred upon them by section 5106 of the Revised Statutes of the United States.[11]

The Ansonia Brass & Copper Company *v.* Conner (6 *N. Y. Civ. Pro.* 173), affirmed.[12]

(*Decided November,* 1886.)

Appeal from judgment of the New York court of common pleas affirming judgment of the general term of the city court of New York, affirming judgment of its trial term in favor of the defendant.

Reported below (6 *N. Y. Civ. Pro.* 173).

November 22, 1875, the appellant recovered a judgment for $9,594.34, in the supreme court, against one Charles G. Wilson, and on the same day issued execution thereon to the sheriff of the city and county of New York, who, on the same day, levied upon and took into his custody property of said Charles G. Wilson.

On November 27, 1875, Wilson filed a petition in voluntary bankruptcy, in the United States district court, for the southern district of New York, and upon an affidavit alleging that plaintiff's judgment was fraudulent and showing the issuing of plaintiff's execution, and the levy, and that the threatened sheriff's sale would work great prejudice to the other creditors, and that the plaintiff was trying to obtain an undue preference, procured an injunction order which was served by him on the plaintiff herein, and on the sheriff, restraining them and each of them and their agents, employees, etc., "from interfering in any way with the said property of said Charles D. Wilson, a bankrupt, and from any interference therewith until further order of the court." This order was vacated upon motion of plaintiff herein after argument, December 14, 1875, and a copy of the order vacating it served upon the sheriff, who on December 17, sold all the property upon which he had levied, and realized the sum of $480.81. A dispute arose between the deputy-sheriff who made the sale and the plaintiff, respecting the amount of the officer's compensation ; and the sheriff having failed to make a return of the writ, the plaintiff on January 27, 1886, brought this action for failure to return the execution, alleging that more than sixty days had elapsed since the issuing of the same, and demanding judgment for $2,000. On April 4, 1886, after issue joined herein, the sheriff paid the plaintiff the sum of $387.15, and made a return of the execution to the effect that he had made thereon $387.15. This action has been four times tried. On the first trial the plaintiff recovered six cents damages, the defendant entered judgment for costs ; and the judgment was reversed on appeal by the general term of the marine court, without opinion. On the second trial plaintiff had judgment for $80.83, with costs ; and the general term of the court of common pleas reversed it on the ground that the plaintiff had proven no judgment on which to found an action. *Vide* Ansonia Brass & Copper Co. *v.* Conner, 62 *How.' Pr.* 272. On the third trial plaintiff had judgment for $80.79, with costs ; and the general term of the court of common pleas reversed the judgment and granted a new trial. See opinions reported, 3 *N. Y. Civ. Pro.* 88. On the last trial the plaintiff's complaint was dismissed, and the judgment entered in favor of the defendants, which was affirmed by the general term of the New York court of common pleas (Opinion reported, 6 *N. Y. Civ. Pro.* 174), and this appeal was taken from the judgment of affirmance thereupon entered, leave to do so having been granted by the court of common pleas.

The above are all the facts material to the questions considered in the opinion here reported. Other facts and grounds on which the appeal was based, not material to these questions, are not here stated.

Marshall P. Stafford, for plaintiff-appellant.

It was an imperative statutory requirement, that the execution should be returned within sixty days after its receipt by the sheriff. The execution was issued in 1875. By section 290 of the Code of Procedure, then in force, it is provided that " the execution shall be returnable within sixty days after its receipt by the officer." Following this statutory provision, the execution itself commanded the sheriff to return it "within sixty days after its receipt." . . . The time for returning an execution having been fixed by statute, no court had any power to enlarge that time. Jackson *v.* Wiseburn, 5 *Wend.* 139 ; Caldwell *v.* Mayor, 9 *Paige*, 574 ; Bank of Monroe *v.* Widner, 11 *Id.* 529 ; Wait *v.* Van Allen, 22 *N. Y.* 321 ; Salles *v.* Butler, 27 *Id.* 639 ; Humphreys *v.* Chamberlain, 11 *Id.*

275. The statutory provision fixing the time at which an execution must be returned, is solely for the benefit of the party who issues the execution, and the absolute right thus given him cannot be taken from him without his consent. The execution itself, and everything done under it, is for the exclusive benefit of the party in whose behalf it is issued. It is the weapon devised solely to aid the successful party to a litigation in enforcing the judgment he obtains. Root v. Wagner, 30 N. Y. 17; Hathaway v. Howell, 54 Id. 109; Nelson v. Kerr, 59 Id. 225; Hotchkiss v. McVickar, 12 Johns. 407. For this reason, the party who issued the execution has general control over it, and the right to direct the sheriff as to proceedings under it. Root v. Wagner, 30 N. Y. 17; Walters v. Sykes, 22 Wend. 566; Smith v. Erwin, 77 N. Y. 466. After the time fixed by law for its return, an execution is *functus officio*, and the sheriff can thereafter do nothing by virtue of its continued possession. Van Rensselaer v. Kidd, 6 N. Y. 333; Vail v. Lewis, 4 Johns. 450; Sherman v. Boyce, 15 Id. 443; Devoe v. Elliot, 2 Caines, 244. No new levy can be made after the return day, and possession of the execution by the sheriff is not necessary for any other purpose. He can sell property previously levied upon and discharge all his duties and obligations springing therefrom, as well without as with possession of the execution, and after he has made a return. Devoe v. Elliot, 2 Caines, 244; Hathaway v. Howell, 54 N. Y. 114; Hotchkiss v. McVickar, 12 Johns. 407; *Freeman on Executions*, § 106. . . . The party against whom an execution is issued cannot extend the time for its return. Even if he requests the sheriff to retain it beyond the return day, agrees that it may thereafter be enforced and receives a benefit under such agreement, he cannot be held under such agreement, the process is still *functus officio* after the return day; and

the sheriff cannot thereafter do anything by virtue of its possession. Sherman v. Boyce, 15 *Johns.* 426 ; Bigelow v. Provost, 5 *Hill*, 566. The party who issues the execution may extend the time for its return, and such extension will be a legal warrant to sheriff for retaining it and acting upon it after the return day. Humphrey v. Hathorn, 24 *Barb.* 278. . . . Federal courts have no power to extend the time fixed by a State statute for an officer of the State court to return a process issued to him by a State court in an action tried therein. . . . The jurisdiction of the federal courts is strictly defined and limited by the Constitution of the United States, art. 3, § 2. Neither this provision nor any law passed by Congress, in pursuance thereof, gives to any federal court power to interfere in any way with the enforcement of a judgment of a State court, or with the obligations of an officer of that court in the discharge of his duties on its process, much less to disregard an imperative provision of a State statute prescribing the duties of such officer under such process. The claim of such power would be at war with the fundamental-principles that distinguish the functions and jurisdictions of the federal courts, from those of the State courts, as well as with those that govern courts of the same State in their relations to each other. Mead v. Merritt, 2 *Paige,* 404 ; Peck v. Jenness, 7 *How.* (*U. S.*) 624, 625 ; Randall v. Howard, 2 *Black.* 589 ; The Robert Fulton, 1 *Paine*, 625 ; Youley v. Lavender, 21 *Wall.* (*U. S.*), 276 ; Williams v. Benedict, 8 *How.* (*U. S.*) 107. . . . A court cannot accomplish by indirect means that which it has no power to do directly. Caldwell v. Mayor, 9 *Paige*, 575 ; Bank of Monroe v. Widner, 11 *Id.* 532 ; Wait v. Van Allen, 22 *N. Y.* 321 ; Salles v. Butler, 27 *Id.* 639 ; Humphreys v. Chamberlin, 11 *Id.* 275 ; Bryant v. Bryant, 4 *Abb. N. S.* 138 ; Lavelle v. Skelly, 24 *Hun*, 642. An execution and proceedings under it are proceedings in the action which results in the judgment on which the execution issues. United States v. Collins, 4 *Blatchf.* 142 ; Ruggles v. Simonton, 3 *Biss.* 331. The sheriff's possession of property under levy of an execution is the court's possession, his proceedings thereunder are the court's proceedings, and any interference with him in such proceedings is an interference with the court and its proceedings. Johnson v. Bishop, 1 *Woolw.* 326 ; Kuhn v. McMillan, 3 *Dill.* 372 ; Ruggles v. Simonton, 3 *Biss.* 328, 330.

Even courts of the same sovereignty, having co-ordinate jurisdiction, have no power to enjoin each others' proceedings. Grant v. Quick, 5 *Sandf.* 612 ; Bennett v. Le Roy, 5 *Abb. Pr.* 55, 156 ; Minor v. Webb, 10 *Id.* 286 ; Phelan v. Smith, 8 *Cal.* 521. And where two different actions are pending in the same court, the court has no power to make an order in one suit enjoining proceedings in the other (Schell v. Erie R. Co., 4 *Abb. Pr. N. S.* 287 ; Ely v. Lowenstein, 9 *Id.* 39 ; Minor v. Webb, 10 *Abb. Pr.* 286 ; Arndt v. Williams, 16 *How. Pr.* 245; Hunt v. Farmers' L. & T. Co., 8 *Id.* 416; Dederick v. Hoysradt, 4 *Id.* 350 ; Savage v. Allen, 54 *N. Y.* 458 ; Woodhull v. Rosenthal, 61 *Id.* 382), unless the action in which the injunction order is granted is a suit in equity. Erie R. Co. v. Ramsey, 45 *N. Y.* 637. Federal courts belong to one sovereignty ; State courts to another. Pomeroy v. Neff, 95 *U. S.* 932–3 ; Peck v. Jenness, 7 *How. U. S.* 624. Courts belonging to different sovereignties cannot restrain each others proceedings. City Bank v. Skelton, 2 *Blatchf.* 14, 28 ; Ruggles v. Simonton, 3 *Biss.* 330 ; McKinn v. Voorhies, 7 *Cranch,* 279 ; Duncan v. Dant; 1 *How. U. S.* 306 ; United States v. Council of K., 6 *Wall.* 517 ; Riggs v. Johnson Co., 6 *Id.* 194–5.... A Federal court has no power to interfere with the administration or natural operation of a statute of any State (Williams v. Benedict, 8 *How. U. S.* 107 ; Yonley v. Lavender, 21 *Wall.* 276 ; Mead v.

Merritt, 2 *Paige*, 404), or restrain proceedings in any
State court, even where a plenary suit has been instituted expressly for that purpose (Diggs v. Wolcott, 4
Cranch, 179 ; Peck v. Jenness, 7 *How. U. S.* 624–5 ;
Taylor v. Carryb, 20 *How. U. S.* 583 ; Johnson v. Bishop,
1 *Wall.* 324), still less by a mere order, when there is no
suit pending before it to which those sought to be
enjoined are parties (Smith v. Mason, 14 *Wall.* 419 ;
Marshall v. Knox, 16 *Id.* 551 ; *In re* Master, 12 *Nat.
Bank. Reg.* 188 ; Wilson v. Childs, 8 *Id.* 527) ; and,
coming to the precise point involved in this case, where
a sheriff has levied upon property under an execution
issued from a State court, there is no power in a Federal
court to take that property from him, or interfere in
any way whatever with his performance of the duties
imposed upon him by his receipt of the execution.
Tenth Nat. Bank v. Sawyer, 42 *How. Pr.* 179 ; Clark
v. Binninger, 3 *Nat. Bank. Reg.* 518 ; *In re* Campbell, 1
Id. 165 ; *In re* Burns, 1 *Id.* 174 ; *In re* Dudley, 1 *Pa.
L. J.* 302 ; The Oliver Jordan, 2 *Curtis*, 414 ; Blake v.
A. & C. R. R., 6 *Nat. Bank. Reg.* 322 ; Hagan v. Lucas,
10 *Peters*, 400 ; Puliam v. Osborne, 17 *How. U. S.* 471.
Should the respondents claim that the order under discussion operated upon the sheriff *in personam*,
instead of being a direct stay of proceedings in the
State court, the answer is that the United State district court had no power to make him a party to the
bankrupt proceedings by any such *ex parte* order, and
could acquire no jurisdiction over him *in personam*
except by a plenary suit instituted for the express purpose of annulling the judgment on which the execution
was issued to him. Smith v. Mason, 14 *Wall.* 419 ; Marshall v. Knox, 16 *Id.* 551 ; *In re* Master, 12 *Nat. Bank.
Reg.* 188. . . . The United States district court
was prohibited by statute from issuing an injunction
such as is invoked as a defense to the action. " The
writ of injunction shall not be granted by any court

of the United States to stay proceedings in any court of a State, except in cases where such injunction may be authorized by any law relating to proceedings in bankruptcy." *U. S. Rev. Stat.* § 720. The execution here in question, and the sheriff's proceedings under it, were proceedings in the State court. United States *v.* Collins, 4 *Blatchf.* 142 ; Ruggles *v.* Simonton, 3 *Biss.* 331 ; Johnson *v.* Bishop, 1 *Woolw.* 326 ; Keehn *v.* Mc Millam, 3 *Dillon,* 372. The bankrupt law in force when the order in question was made, authorized an injunction against proceedings in a State court, for one purpose only, as follows : "No creditor whose debt is provable in bankruptcy shall be allowed to prosecute to final judgment any suit at law or in equity therefor, against the bankrupt, until the question of the debtor's discharge shall have been determined ; and any such suit or proceedings shall, upon the application of the bankrupt, be stayed to await the determination of the court in bankruptcy on the question of discharge," etc. *U. S. Rev. Stat.* § 5106. As there was already a final judgment against Wilson at the time the order in question was issued section 5106 manifestly had no application to the state of facts existing between him and this appellant, and did not relieve the court from the inhibition of section 720. The bankruptcy act further provided that "the court may also, by injunction, restrain the debtor and any other person, in the mean time, from making any transfer or disposition of any part of the debtor's property, not excepted by this title from the operation thereof, and from any interference therewith." *U. S. Rev. Stat.* § 5024. . . . This provision refers exclusively to cases of involuntary bankruptcy ; whereas Wilson was a voluntary bankrupt. It authorizes an injunction only where there is an order for the debtor to show cause why he should not be declared a bankrupt, and for the purpose of restraining any disposition of his property "in the mean time."

It is manifest from the very terms of this provision that it has no reference whatever to legal proceedings, or to the transfer of property under judicial process, but relates solely to voluntary transfers by the debtor himself, or by parties acting in his interest, by sale and purchase. The power of the court to issue an injunction under this section is strictly limited to cases of involuntary bankruptcy, in which an order for the debtor to show cause why he should not be declared a bankrupt is pending. It confers no power to issue an injunction in a case where the debtor has already been adjudicated a bankrupt, and any injunction issued under it ceases to be of any force or vitality the moment the debtor has been adjudged a bankrupt. *In re* Mary Irving, 14 *Natl. Bank. Reg.* 293–4; *In re* Moses, 6 *Id.* 182. . . Sections 5024 and 5106 are the only ones that remove the prohibition of section 720, and, as neither of these had any application to the facts in Wilson's case, the United States district court was under the prohibition of section 720 at the time the order invoked in this case was issued. . . . When any court assumes to do what it has no power to do under any circumstances, its action is *coram non judice*, and void. Quimbo Appo *v.* People, 20 *N. Y.* 531; People *ex rel.* Tweed *v.* Liscomb, 60 *Id.* at pp. 571, 591; Bigelow *v.* Forrest, 9 *Wall. U. S.* 351; *Ex parte* Lange, 18 *Id.* 163, 177; *Ex parte* Page, 49 *Mo.* 291. . . The sheriff would not have been in contempt had he proceeded to sell the property under the execution before the United States court order was vacated. *In re* Marter, 15 *Natl. Bank. Reg.* 185; *In re* Mary Irving, 14 *Id.* 293–4; *In re* Moses, 6 *Id.* 182; Ansonia *v.* Babbitt, 8 *Hun*, 161–2. Even if the United States district court had had power to extend the statutory time for returning the

execution, the order invoked in this case would not
have worked such an extension. . . . Even where
courts are authorized to extend the time fixed by the
statute for taking any steps in legal proceedings, such
an extension is not worked by a mere stay of proceedings in the action. Thompson v. Erie R., 9 *Abb. Pr.
N. S.* 233 ; Platt v. Townsend, 3 *Abb. Pr.* 9 ; White v.
Smith, 16 *Id.* 109 (note). A stay of proceedings, and
every other kind of injunction is always strictly construed. It covers nothing except what it expressly
assumes to cover in clear and unequivocal terms.
Weeks v. Smith, 3 *Abb. Pr.* 214 ; Glover v. Witten-
hall, 6 *Hill*, 600 ; Lowber v. The Mayor, 5 *Abb. Pr.*
268. The time for the sheriff to return an execution
is not extended by an appeal from the judgment on
which the execution issued (Bowman v. Cornell, 39
Barb. 70) ; nor by the institution of a suit to replevin
the property he has levied upon (Sweezy v. Lott, 21
N. Y. 481) ; nor by service upon him of attachments
against the property of the execution creditor (Wehle
v. Conner, 63 *N. Y.* 260 ; Parker v. Bradley, 46 *N. Y.
Super.* [14 *J. & S.*] 244). . . Property under levy of a
final process is not the debtor's property. It has
already been appropriated to the payment of a final
judgment. It is in the custody of the court under
whose process it was taken, and its officer, the sheriff,
holds the legal title for the benefit of the judgment
creditor. 3 *Black. Comm.* 146 ; Hall v. Tuttle, 2
Wend. 478 ; Hartwell v. Bissell, 17 *Johns.* 128 ;
Ansonia Brass and Copper Co. v. Babbitt, 8 *Hun*,
161 ; The Robert Fulton, 1 *Paine*, 625. The property
held by the sheriff, therefore, was not Wilson's, and
was not in any way affected by an order relating to
the property of Wilson. The fact that the order
points specifically to the property held under the
execution, and calls it "said property of Charles G.
Wilson," does not make it his property, and is of no

consequence whatever, for the United States supreme
court has expressly held that the district court has
no power thus to determine the ownership of property,
and that an *ex parte* order assuming to do so is an
absolute nullity. Smith *v.* Mason, 14 *Wall.* 419;
Marshall *v.* Knox, 16 *Id.* 555.

Henry Thompson (*Vanderpoel, Green & Cuming,*
attorneys), for defendants-respondents.

The statute which gives a sheriff sixty days in
which to execute and return process, means sixty free
days, and the time during which he is enjoined and
restrained by law from selling, or in any way interfering with the property seized under the execution, is
not to be included in the time within which a return
must be made. The sixty days allowed by the statute
to the sheriff to execute and return process is for the
benefit of the sheriff, to prevent an action, etc.,
against him, until he has had a reasonable time to
execute such process. Renaud *v.* O'Brien, 35 *N. Y.*
99. The statutes requiring a return of process, and
giving a right of action for a failure to make "due
return" (*Code of Proc.* § 290, and 3 *R. S.* 6th ed. 100,
p. 725), do not contemplate a return in all cases within
sixty days, under the penalty of fining the officer the
amount of the execution. They are to be construed
together, and with regard to the meaning and intent
of the legislature in enacting them. Prior to the
statute of 1840 (*Laws of* 1840, p. 334, § 24), writs of
execution were returnable only in term time, and were
required to be made returnable on a particular day.
Livingston *v.* Cleveland, 5 *How. Pr.* 397. By the
statute of 1840, executions were allowed to be issued
or tested at any time, in term or vacation. *Laws of*
1840, p. 335, § 24. The law remained thus until the
enactment of the Code of Procedure of 1848. Section
244 of the Code of that year prescribed the form of the

execution, and section 245 enacted that "in all cases" it must be returned within sixty days. . . . The amended Code of 1849 repealed section 245 of the Code of 1848, and substituted, in lieu thereof, section 290 of the Code of 1849. . . It was under this provision of the statute, which remained in force until the adoption of the new Code (*Laws of* 1877, chap. 416), that the execution here sued on was issued. Under section 245 of the Code of 1848, it might be plausibly urged that the sheriff was bound "in all cases," whether under injunction or not, to return the execution within sixty days; but, it is submitted, that the legislature of 1849, by repealing that section, and merely making the execution "returnable within sixty days," and that for the officer's benefit (Renaud *v.* O'Brien, *supra*), meant to and did allow the sheriff, where his proceedings were stayed by injunction, to retain the execution beyond sixty days, without being liable to an action. Bernheim *v.* Daggett, 12 *Abb. N. C.* 317; aff'd, without opinion, 84 *N. Y.* 670; Van Gelder *v.* Van Gelder, 26 *Hun,* 357; aff'd, on opinion below, *sub nomine;* Van Gelder *v.* Hallenback, 89 *N. Y.* 633; Dorrance *v.* Henderson, 92 *Id.* 406; aff'g S. C., 27 *Hun,* 206; People *v.* Carnley, 3 *Abb. Pr.* 215; Paige *v.* Willett, 38 *N. Y.* 28; Renaud *v.* O'Brien, 35 *Id.* 99; Mills *v.* Thursby, 11 *How. Pr.* 121; Wehle *v.* O'Conner, 63 *N. Y.* 258; 69 *N. Y.* 546, 550, and 83 *N. Y.* 231; *Freeman on Executions*, 105 (ed. 1882), and cases cited. Ansonia Brass & Copper Co. *v.* Conner, 3 *N. Y. Civ. Pro.* 88; Same *v.* Same (3d. appeal), 67 *How. Pr.* 157. . . . The mandate of the execution is not alone to "return" it, but is "to satisfy the said judgment out of the property of the judgment debtor . . . and return." An injunction which restrained the sheriff from all interference with the judgment debtor's property, would manifestly prevent satisfying the judgment. The plaintiff not having required the return, without satisfaction of the judgment, the court will not hold the officer liable for a penalty for a mere failure to "return," when the preceding requirement of "satisfying the judgment" was made impossible by order of the court. See authorities cited, *supra*.

The order of injunction, issued out of the United States district court in bankruptcy, and served upon plaintiff and defendants' testator, was of binding force upon them, and the seventeen days of its continuance is not to be computed as part of the sixty days granted by law to the defendants' testator, in which to satisfy and return the process against Wilson. It was granted by the court, upon the special, verified application of the bankrupt and judgment debtor, upon facts which clearly warranted its interference. In this respect the order differs from that considered by this court in Dorrance *v.* Henderson (92 *N. Y.* 406), which was granted by the clerk, *ex parte*, upon filing the creditors' petition. It was the act of a court having a general jurisdiction of the subject-matter, and which had acquired jurisdiction of the insolvent in this particular case. *U. S. Rev. Stat.*, §§ 4972, 4991, 5132. The issuing of the injunction restraining the sheriff and The Ansonia Brass & Copper Company from all interference with Wilson's property, until the further order of the court, was within the power of the court, notwithstanding the previous levy under a State writ, and the most the sheriff could do was to hold his levy and keep possession of the property, as he did. It had this power, the court says (*In re* Ulrich, 6 *Ben.* 483), under three separate sections of the bankruptcy act. (1) In the exercise of the plenary jurisdiction conferred by the first section of the act. *U. S. Rev. Stat.* § 4972. (2) Under section 21 of the act. *U. S. Rev. Stat.* § 5106. (3) Under section 40 of the act, involuntary bankruptcy. *U. S. Rev. Stat.* § 5024.

Authority to make such an order has never been seriously questioned. It was exercised by the bankruptcy court, and acquiesced in by the State court, when levy had been made under an execution in the following cases, among many others: *In re* Schnepf, 2 *Ben.* 72; *In re* Bernstein, 2 *Id.* 44; *In re* Wilber, 1 *Id.* 527; *In re* Price Fuller, 4 *Natl. Bank. Reg.* 115; *In re* Lady Bryan Mining Co., 6 *Id.* 252; *In re* Donaldson, 1 *Id.* 181; *In re* Atkinson, 7 *Id.* 143; *In re* Mallory, 6 *Id.* 22; *In re* Dillard, 9 *Id.* 8; Sutherland *v.* Lake Superior Co., 9 *Id.* 298; Traders' Bank *v.* Campbell, 14 *Wall.* (*U. S.*) 87. . . .

It is a well-established rule that a party who has had notice of and been heard on a motion is bound by the decision, and this is true *a fortiori* if he himself invokes the interposition of the court. Acker *v.* Ledyard, 8 *N. Y.* 62; Dorrance *v.* Henderson, 92 *Id.* 406; O'Brien *v.* Weld, 2 *Otto* (*U. S.*) 81; approving People *ex rel.* Jennys *v.* Brennan, 3 *Hun,* 666.

RUGER, Ch. J.—The main question in this case is whether an order made by a court of competent jurisdiction staying the sheriff from any interference under an execution with the property of a judgment debtor suspends, during its continuance, the running of the statutory term of sixty days given to the sheriff for executing the process.

The execution in question was issued under section 290 of the Code of Procedure, which provided that an "execution shall be returnable within sixty days after its receipt by the officer to the clerk with whom the record of judgment is filed." This was substantially a re-enactment of section 24, chapter 386, Laws of 1840, which was suspended temporarily by section 245 of the Code of Procedure, adopted in 1848, and amended by section 290 in 1849. Previous to the act of 1840, executions were made returnable in term time, and no fixed period of time intervened between their receipt and return by the sheriff.

It will thus be seen that the period of sixty days for the service of such process was originally provided by the act of 1840, and has ever since remained the same, with the exception of a few months in ['] 1848 and 1849. The reason why this period was adopted has been stated to be for the "benefit of the sheriffs" (Renaud v. O'Brien, 35 N. Y. 99), but we think this hardly comprises all the reasons for the provision, which are obvious from its nature. It undoubtedly contemplates a reasonable opportunity for the sheriff to execute the process free from unreasonable demand of an impatient creditor for more peremptory service, and authority to the sheriff to extend indulgence for a limited time to a delinquent and embarrassed debtor (*Crocker on Sheriffs*, § 488 ; McDonald v. Neilson, 2 *Cow.* 139). The opportunity for indulgence afforded by the section is certainly not for the creditor's interest, as he is justly entitled to his money upon the recovery of his judgment.

['] The limitation upon the right of the sheriff to hold the execution was undoubtedly for the benefit of the judgment creditor, and intended to fix a time beyond which, in the usual and regular process of collection, his right to payment should not be postponed. This, however, does not affect the right of any party interested to stay the enforcement of an execution for sufficient cause. The sufficiency of the cause must of course be determined by the tribu-['] nal to which the application for a stay is made, and when it has adjudged that sufficient cause exists, its order, provided that it has jurisdiction of the matter and the parties, is obligatory upon them and must be obeyed. It was said by Judge MILLER, in Wehle v. Conner (69 N. Y. 546), in an action ['] against the sheriff for not returning an execution, that "proof that plaintiff had directed the execution not to be returned, or that the sheriff had procured it to be stayed by order of the court, are lawful defenses."

[*]   In the case Paige *v.* Willett (38 *N. Y.* 28), it was held that the sheriff was not chargeable with interest accruing upon moneys collected by him on execution, but retained beyond the return day in obedience to an order restraining him from paying them over to the judgment creditor. The principle of this case seems clearly to recognize the exemption of the sheriff from liability when acting under the order of the court. In People *v.* Carnley (3 *Abb. Pr.* 216), [*] it was decided that an order by a court of competent jurisdiction staying the sheriff's proceedings excused him from returning the writ according to its requirements, and that he could not, while thus restrained, be adjudged guilty of contempt in disobeying the mandate of the writ or the notice of the judgment creditor to make return. This decision was made at special term, but was rendered by the late Judge DAVIES, and accords with the analogies of the law.

[']   The statute of limitations suspends its bar against parties who are incapacitated from commencing an action by reason of disability, and the law frequently deducts from the time within which an act is to be performed those *dies non* upon which the party is unable to act. So, too, the time limited for the issue of an execution, or making an application for leave to do so, does not run while the plaintiff is stayed by an injunction or other order from proceeding in the matter (§ 1382, *Code Civ. Pro.*). The policy of the statute could not be accomplished if the sheriff should be deprived of the advantageous use of the time extended to him by injunction orders or stays of proceedings covering the whole, or even a material portion of that time allowed to him to serve the writ. Suppose the sheriff is stayed during the first fifty days of the life of the process, and the remaining time does not afford him sufficient opportunity to discover property and make the money therefrom by a sale, is it reasonable that he should be visited with a penalty for not returning the process according to its requirement ? Or suppose, after a levy and before a sale, his proceedings are stayed until after the return day, can he be adjudged liable for the judgment debt because he did not make return ? We cannot think so. Would the sheriff be justified in the case last supposed in abandoning his levy and returning the execution at the end of sixty days from its receipt, and yet if not, under the plaintiff's contention, he would become liable to pay the judgment. Can a sheriff be made liable for the amount of a judgment which he is debarred from collecting, but which on the sixtieth day he has secured by a levy upon property sufficient to satisfy it, but which he is unable to advertise and sell by reason of the necessity of returning his writ ? We think not.

It is claimed if he does not return his writ he becomes liable, and certainly if he does return it he not only abandons the levy but makes himself liable for the debt as for a false return. He could not, under these circumstances, protect himself from suit by advancing the money to the plaintiff and retaining the execution to reimburse himself; for this, it has been held, he could not lawfully do (Carpenter *v.* Stillwell, 11 *N. Y.* 61; Mills *v.* Young, 23 *Wend.* 314; Sherman *v.* Boyce, 15 *Johns.* 443). And thus, under the plaintiff's contention, the officer would be made liable for the debt in any event, although he is entirely without fault, and has by his *vis major* been disabled during the whole period of the life of the writ from executing its command.

If the stay is granted for some alleged vice in the process or the judgment upon which it is founded, as it usually is, is there any reason why the sheriff should bear the loss occasioned by such delay, and the offending party be exempted therefrom? The law does not sanction such manifest injustice, and will give the statute a reasonable construction to avoid such a result.

We think the true policy of the statute can be satisfied only when the sheriff has sixty full days in which to perform the duties enjoined upon him. The onerous liabilities which the law imposes upon him for not returning process, for a false return, and for non-performance of his official duties, require that his time for their performance should not be curtailed or limited by periods of disability to act.

Although the sheriff cannot levy upon property except during the life of the execution (Devoe v. Elliott, 2 *Caines*, 244 ; Hathaway v. Howell, 54 *N. Y.* 114), he yet can complete the act already initiated by the levy by selling after the return day (Devoe v. Elliott, *supra*) ; and it is often indispensable to the security of the rights of the plaintiff that he should retain his writ for that purpose.

[*] . It is not questioned but that a stay procured by an appeal and security given thereon, operates as a suspension of the time within which the sheriff is required to return the writ, and in such a case the sheriff retains the execution and a levy made thereon until the final determination of the appeal, even though years lapse, and then in case of affirmance of the original judgment, makes the amount by virtue of his original levy. The stay effected by an appeal simply restrains the officer from collecting the execution. His power to return the writ is not in terms extended or restricted and is not effectual, unless the right to enforce the writ suspends its requirement to

make return within sixty days. Yet I think it has never been doubted that it was the duty of a sheriff to hold his execution and levy after appeal, and until the final determination of the case. The analogy between such a stay and the one under discussion seems perfect, and requires us to hold that any stay which restrains the sheriff from enforcing the execution, suspends the running of the time in which he is required to return the writ.

It is also claimed by the appellant that the bankrupt court had no authority to make the order in question restraining the sheriff from selling the property. We think this point is not sustainable.

[*]   It cannot be questioned but that the judgment debtor, whose property has been taken by a sheriff, under execution, remains its general owner, subject only to the special property acquired by the sheriff by reason of his levy and his right to dispose of so much thereof by sale as may be required to satisfy the execution (Scott *v.* Morgan, 94 *N. Y.* 508). The residue of property remaining unsold after satisfaction of the judgment, reverts to the debtor by virtue of his ownership. While, however, still in the hands of the sheriff it is liable to attachment and levy on behalf of other creditors, and the resulting interest in the surplus constitutes property in the debtor subject to be reached by creditors generally under the bankrupt law (Ansonia Brass & Copper Co. *v.* Babbitt, 74 *N. Y.* 401.)

The order in question was made by the district court of the United States for the southern district of New York in a proceeding in bankruptcy instituted by the judgment debtor, and upon an application by him showing, among other things, the seizure by the sheriff of his property under an execution issued upon a judgment recovered in the supreme court by the plaintiff herein, and which was alleged to have been

Ansonia Brass & Copper Co. v. Conner.

obtained fraudulently, and in violation of the provisions of the bankrupt act. The order was made on November 27, 1875, and purported to restrain the plaintiff herein and the defendant "from interfering in any way with the said property (held by the sheriff under levy) of said" bankrupt until the further order of the conrt. The plaintiff herein assumed the validity of this order, and appeared in the bankrupt court upon an application to vacate it and for leave to the sheriff to sell under his execution. Upon this application an order was made by the bankrupt court on December 17 thereafter, vacating the stay and granting leave to the sheriff to sell; and plaintiff availed itself of such leave (Dorrance v. Henderson, 92 *N. Y.* 406).

["] Without entering a general discussion of the jurisdiction of the bankrupt court, we may say that we entertain no doubt of their power to examine into the validity of alleged claims upon the bankrupt's property, and restrain by temporary injunction the sale and disposition thereof, during the pending of proceedings in bankruptcy in such court. This must result from, and is the necessary incident of, the power conferred upon them to collect and marshal the bankrupt's assets, and ascertain and liquidate the liens and other specific claims thereon (*U. S. R. S.* § 4972). Any other view would render such courts powerless to enforce the provisions referred to.

["] Express power to stay proceedings instituted in any court by the creditors of a bankrupt, for the collection of debts provable in bankruptcy against him, and for stay of execution thereon, is also ["] given by section 5106 of the Revised Statutes of the United States.

The judgment should be affirmed.

All concurred.

DOHERTY, et al., as Grantors of Charles Jones,
v. MATSELL and Another.

Superior Court of the City of New York, General Term, November, 1886.

§§ 365, 368, 369, 370.

Ejectment — Title necessary to maintain — When possession will be presumed — What amounts to adverse possession.

Deeds made in 1786 and 1793 to one " H." of certain lands, and proof that said " H." resided on said lands in 1828, together with a series of conveyances from " H." down to one " D.," show a paper title in said " D." which coupled with the actual or constructive possession of " H.," constitutes seizin and a *prima facie* title in him, which inures to the benefit of his successor in interest.[']

In an action of ejectment the plaintiff must depend for success on the strength of his own title ; not on the weakness of that of his adversary ; and must prove his right to immediate possession, and that he has been seized or possessed of the premises in question within twenty years before the commencement of the action.[²] The mere production of isolated conveyances as proof of the title without possession is not enough ;[³] there must also be possession of the grantor or accompanying the deeds, and without this the plaintiff proves no title ;[³] but if it is found or conceded that a party has title that is sufficient, his possession will be presumed, and the occupation by any other person is presumed to be subordinate to the legal title, unless it appears that the premises have been held adversely twenty years before action was brought.[⁴]

Where in an action of ejectment there was proof of a paper title and actual possession in the plaintiff's grantors in 1829, — *Held*, that a legal seizin and constructive possession which inured for the benefit of such grantor's successors in interest was presumed ; and that the burden of proving adverse possession for twenty-years before the commencement of the action rested on the defendant.[⁵]

The occupation of one who enters into possession of real property, under a tax lease having no other paper title, does not constitute adverse possession against the owner of the fee, and he cannot during the continuance of the lease sustain a claim to any higher title than that of lessee for a term of years.[⁶]

An entry under a deed, even though it be invalid, coupled with actual

Doherty *v.* Matsell.

possession in the grantee, is entry under a colorable title, and the possession is adverse.[1]

In order to the establishment of possession as against the owner in fee of real property defeating his title, the possession must be adverse to the legal title and founded upon a written instrument and under a claim of title exclusive of any other right;[8] and during the time of possession claimed to be adverse, the owner in fee must not be under a disability preventing him from asserting his title by action of ejectment against him who holds adversely:[9] no possession can be deemed adverse to a party who has not at the time the right of entry and possession.[10]

Possession of real property and claim of title under a municipal tax lease is not adverse to the title of the owner in fee.[11] Possession of land to establish the title in fee must be accompanied by a claim of title in fee.[12]

The owner of the fee of real property in order to maintain ejectment must be legally entitled to immediate possession.[13]

Where one has been in possession of real property for a term of years, the law will not from the mere fact of his possession adjudge him to be in possession under a higher right or larger estate [14]

Where real property was sold for taxes in 1848, and a lease for twenty-five years given to one G. W. M., who entered into occupation of the premises thereunder, and in 1857 executed a quit-claim deed thereof to one M., and assigned to him the tax lease, and about a year thereafter said G. W. M. dissiezed M. and resumed occupation of the premises, and continued to occupy them until 1864, when he conveyed them to one G. M. by an absolute deed; and G. M. thereupon entered into possession of the premises and continued in possession of them until 1853, when an action of ejectment was brought against him by the owner of the fee; and in 1861 the said premises were again sold for unpaid taxes, and the lease thereof for fifteen years executed to one F. O., who assigned it to G. W. M.,—*Held,* that the possession of G. M. was not adverse to the plaintiff;[7,13,14] that even if the possession was adverse it was adverse only during the period there were no outstanding tax leases which prevented the plaintiff from bringing an action of ejectment to recover immediate possession of the property.[15]

(*Decided November* 10, 1886.)

Motion by plaintiff for new trial on exceptions ordered to be heard in the first instance at general term.

The opinion states the facts.

John Townshend and *Alexander Thain* (*Thain & Kearney*, attorneys), for plaintiff and motion.

The possession of Yallis Hopper having been established under conveyances to him, and a complete chain of conveyances from his executors and their grantees down to the plaintiffs and their grantor, entitled the surviving plaintiffs to recover, unless an adverse possession of twenty years has been established in favor of the defendants. *Code Civ. Pro.* § 368. Possession having been shown in Yallis Hopper, possession of his grantees and those claiming under him will be presumed until twenty years adverse possession has been established in some other person. *Code Civ. Pro.* § 368. The possession of George W. Matsell, Sr., having been commenced in 1849, and there being no evidence of title to him other than the tax lease, it will be presumed that his possession was under that lease. . . . The lease to Matsell shows that he took the same because of the neglect of the owner to pay the taxes ; and he took for the term of twenty-five years, and for that term only, against the owner of the fee, for the reason that "the person claiming the title" had not redeemed. This is more than presumptive—it is direct evidence that Matsell entered "under and subordinate to the legal title." *Code Civ. Pro.* § 368. The tax lease continued in operation for twenty-five years from September 25, 1848, and expired on September 25, 1873, so that George W. Matsell and his successors in interest were rightfully in possession during the continuance of that lease, and had the right to remain in possession for one month thereafter, for the purpose of removing buildings, etc. Robinson *v.* Phillips, 65 *Barb.* 418 ; S. C. aff'd, 56 *N. Y.* 634. The plaintiffs had no cause of action by way of ejectment, they not attacking the lease until September or October, 1873, and then it was that the adverse possession began ; or about ten years before the commencement of this action. No adverse possession could be acquired under the tax lease. Gross *v.* Welwood, 90 *N. Y.* 638; Bedell *v.* Shaw, 59 *Id.* 46 ; Hoyt *v.* Dillon, 19 *Barb.* 644. The case of Sands *v.* Hughes (53 *N. Y.* 287) is not in conflict, but rather in confirmation of this doctrine. There the plaintiff attacked the lease, and the court ruled that if there was no lease, then defendant's possession was not subordinate to, but rather averse to the legal title ; while if the lease was conceded, defendants could not be ejected until after the expiration of the term.

John C. Shaw (*Thomas H. Barowsky*, attorney), for defendants, opposed.

In order to maintain this action the plaintiffs must show conclusively that their ancestor, predecessor or grantor, was seized or possessed of the premises in question within twenty years before the commencement of the action. *Code Civ. Pro.* § 365 ; Sherman *v.* Kane, 86 *N. Y.* 64 ; Hansee *v.* Mead, 2 *N. Y. Civ. Pro.* 175. . . . The mere production of copies of deeds of an action of this kind, without any proof of the actual possession of the *locus in quo* by the plaintiffs, or their alleged predecessors or grantors named in the deeds, has been held not to be sufficient evidence to enable the plaintiffs to establish a legal title. Dorning *v.* Miller, 33 *Barb.* 386 ; Thompson *v.* Burhans, 79 *N. Y.* 93–99 ; Roberts *v.* Baumgarten, 51 *N. Y. Super.* (19 *J. & S.*) 482, 484 ; Miller *v.* Downing, 54 *N. Y.* 631 ; Gardner *v.* Heartt, 1 *Id.* 528 ; Stevens *v.* Hauser, 39 *Id.* 302. The strictness of the rule required in cases of ejectment is illustrated by the decision of the court of appeals in the case of Carroll *v.* Carroll (60 *N. Y.* 121, at p. 125), MILLER, J., delivering the opinion of the court, says :

"It will also be noticed that this is a case where the claim of title is made to real property in an action of ejectment to recover the same, where more strict proof is required than in cases where the question arises incidentally and collaterally. See 2 *Greenl. Ev.* § 303; 2 *Phil. Ev.* 93. The plaintiffs, to recover in this action, must, before the defendant is put upon his defense, conclusively show that they have the legal interest and a possessory title to the premises in controversy, not barred by the statute of limitations; and they can in any event only recover on the strength of their own, and not on the weakness of the defendant's title. 2 *Greenleaf Ev.* § 303; *Adams on Ejec.* 32, 285; *Chitty on Pleadings*, 172, 209 (7th ed.); Christy v. Scott, 14 *How.* (*U. S.*); Lamont v. Cheshire, 65 *N. Y.* 30–43. . . . The principle requisites to constitute an adverse possession under color of title, or naked possession under a claim of title founded upon no written instrument, are substantially the same. *Code Civ. Pro.* §§ 371, 372. . . . The possession and occupation of the premises in question by the defendant, his predecessor and grantor during the twenty-five years prior to the commencement of these actions, meets with all the requirements of law to originate and complete a perfect title to the same by adverse possession under the statute of limitation. The possession of the defendant's grantor during the six years from 1858 to 1864, when he conveyed the same to this defendant, was actual, continuous, open, hostile and exclusive. . . . . This defendant has likewise been in the actual, continued and exclusive possession of the same since November 1, 1864, under said two deeds, and received and collected the rents and profits thereon, paid all taxes, assessments and other charges, and claimed the sole and exclusive ownership of the same. Bolton v. Schriever, 49 *N. Y. Super. Ct.* (17 *J. & S.*) 168; 2 *Washburn on Real Prop.* 501; Thompson v. Burhans,

79 *N. Y.* 93, 99 ; Sherman *v.* Kane, 86 *Id.* 57, 69 ; Shriver *v.* Shriver, 86 *Id.* 575 ; Humbert *v.* Trinity Church, 24 *Wend.* 587 ; School District *v.* Lynch, 33 *Conn.* 334 ; Thompson *v.* Pioche, 44 *Cal.* 517 ; Foulke *v.* Bond, 12 *Vroom* (*N, J.*) 541 ; Samuels *v.* Borrowscate, 104 *Mass.* 201 ; 2 *Smith's Lead. Cases,* 565 ; Bell *v.* Denson, 56 *Ala.* 448 ; Poignard *v.* Smith, 6 *Pick.* (*Mass.*) 172, 178 ; Jackson *v.* Warford, 7 *Wend.* 62.

The two periods of time during which this defendant and his grantor and predecessor, George W. Matsell, Sr., had possession of the premises, when joined or attacked together, form one continuous and uninterrupted possession from 1858, when Matsell, Sr., disseized Andrew H. Mickle and entered for the second time into possession, down to the time of the commencement of these actions is 1883, a period of over twenty-five years.   There was a privity of estate between them by purchase, and their consecutive possessions joined together make a continuity of disseizin. Simpson *v.* Downing, 26 *Wend.* 320 ; Haynes *v.* Boardman, 119 *Mass.* 115 ; Wheeler *v.* Moody, 9 *Texas,* 377 ; Benson *v.* Stewart, 30 *Miss.* 57 ; Chandler *v.* Rushing, 38 *Texas,* 595 ; Riggs *v.* Fuller, 54 *Ala.* 146 ; Day *v.* Wilder, 47 *Vt.* 583 ; Howland *v.* Newark Cemetery Ass'n, 66 *Barb.* 366 ; Dowell *v.* De La Lanza, 20 *How. U. S.* 32 ; 2 *Washburn on Real Prop.* 489, 493 ; *Id.* book 3, § 7, ch. 2. . . . . If Matsell, Sr., entered into possesion under the first of these tax leases—and this was the only right he had to the possession of the property, he could still grant the land in fee to Mickle. An entry under that grant, and claiming title from the latter, is a sufficient foundation for an adverse possession under claim of title.   Sands *v.* Hughes, 53 *N. Y.* 287.   Possession of land under a deed given without right is adverse to the rightful owners, and a subsequent deed executed by them during such adverse possession is void.   Jackson *v.* Smith, 13 *Johns.* 406 ;

Thurman *v.* Cameron, 24 *Wend.* 87; Bradstreet *v.* Clark, 12 *Id.* 602; Sands *v.* Hughes, 53 *N. Y.* 287.

O'GORMAN, J.—This is an action in ejectment to recover possession of four lots of land on the north side of Eighty-third street, between First and Second avenues, in this city. A verdict was rendered for the defendants by the direction of the court below, and it was ordered that the exceptions should be heard in the first instance at the general term, judgment meanwhile to be suspended. The plaintiffs excepted, and the defendants also excepted to the denial of their motion to dismiss the complaint. It was conceded by both sides that there was no question of fact to go to the jury.

The plaintiffs put in evidence as the origin of the title, conveyances made in 1786 and 1793, to one Yallis Hopper, of a tract of land in Harlem, and also a map of the same, the correctness of which was supported by the evidence of experts, showing that the lots in suit were part of the tract covered by these conveyances.

Plaintiffs also gave evidence that Yallis Hopper was living in 1828, and then resided on a farm known as the Yallis Hopper farm, which was situate between lines now known as Eighty-third street and Eighty-fourth street and Second avenue; and also that the lines of fences of that farm, which ran east and west and north and south, existed within recent memory; and that the tract of land thus bounded was substantially the same as that covered by the map.

['] This paper title is carried by a series of conveyances down to the plaintiff's, and coupled with actual or constructive possession in Yallis Hopper constitutes seizin, and a *prima facie* title in him which inures to the benefit of his successor in interest. Pope *v.* Hanmer, 74 *N. Y.* 243. Yallis Hopper died in 1830, and there is no evidence that the plaintiffs, or any of their ancestors or grantors, other than he, had any actual possession of this tract of land, or any part thereof.

['] In an action of ejectment the plaintiff must depend for success on the strength of his own title,* not on the weakness of that of his adversary, and must prove his right to immediate possession, and that he was seized or possessed of the premises in question within twenty years before the commencement of the action. *Code Civ. Pro.* § 365. The ['] mere production of isolated conveyances as proof of title, without proof of possession, is not enough. Stephens *v.* Hauser, 39 *N. Y.* 304; Gardner *v.* Heartt, 1 *Id.* 528. In addition to paper title the plaintiff in an action in ejectment must show also possession in the grantor or possession accompanying the deeds— without this he proves no title.

['] But where it is found or conceded that a party named has title, that is sufficient—his possession will be presumed, and the occupation by any other person is presumed to be subordinate to the legal title,† unless it appears that the premises have been held adversely twenty years before action brought. Stephens *v.* Hauser, *supra;* Carleton *v.* Darcy, 46 *N. Y. Supr. Ct.* 493 ; Roberts *v.* Baumgarten, 51 *Id.* 488.

---

* See Bond *v.* Collins, 18 *N. Y. Weekly Dig.* 90; Hunter *v.* Starin, 26 *Hun,* 529 ; Wallace *v.* Swinton, 64 *N. Y.* 188 ; Henry *v.* Reichert, 22 *Hun,* 394; Richardson *v.* Pulver, 63 *Barb.* 67; Roggan *v.* Avery, 63 *Id.* 65; S. C., 65 *N. Y.* 592.

† It is presumption of law that possession of real property is in accordance with the right, and that it is not adverse to the lawful owner. Alexander *v.* Polk, 39 *Miss.* 738; Alexander *v.* Stewart, 50 *Vt.* 87; Parker *v.* Banks, 79 *N. C.* 480; Davis *v.* Bowmar, 55 *Miss.* 671; Bedell *v.* Shaw, 5? *N. Y.* 46; Cook *v.* Travis, 20 *Id.* 400; Hart *v.* Boswick, 14 *Fla.* 162; Brandt *v.* Ogton, 1 *Johns.* 156; Jackson *v.* Vredenburgh, 1 *Id.* 159–163; Jackson *v.* Parker, 3 *John. Cas.* 124; Buchanan *v.* King, 22 *Gratt.* (*Va.*) 414.

[°]   The paper title and actual possession being proved to have been in Yallis Hopper, in 1829, a legal seizin and constructive possession, which inured for the benefit of his successors in interest, is presumed, and the burden of proving adverse possession for twenty years before commencement of the action rests on the defendants. *Code*, § 368.

To maintain this defense the defendants have proved that in 1848, the tract of land within which these lots were situated, was vacant and unfenced; that the lots were sold for unpaid taxes, and that a lease for a term of twenty-five years from date was made on September 5, 1848, to George W. Matsell, who thereupon entered into occupation of the lots and built five houses thereon. The term of this lease expired on September 5, 1873.

[°]   The occupation by Matsell under this tax lease (and no other paper title is proved in him), did not constitute adverse possession against the owners of the fee, and he could not, during the continuance of the lease, sustain a claim to any higher title than that of lessee for a term of years. Bedell *v.* Shaw, 59 *N. Y.* 50.

In February, 1857, Matsell executed a quit claim deed of these lots to one Andrew Mickle, and the deed was duly recorded in March, 1857. Mickle thereupon entered into occupation of the lots, and collected the rents of the houses built thereon.

On February 29, 1857, Matsell assigned to Mickle the tax lease, and that assignment was also duly recorded without delay, and the tax lease continued in possession of Mickle until the end of the term.

After Mickle had been in possession of the premises for about one year, he was disseized by Matsell, who resumed occupation of the premises, and continued to occupy them for his own benefit until November 1, 1864, when he conveyed them to his son George

Matsell, Jr., by an absolute deed. This deed was duly recorded on November 11, 1864, and thereupon Matsell, Jr., entered into actual possession of the premises, and continued in possession until the commencement of this action.

On November 15, 1861, the lots had been again sold for unpaid taxes, and a lease thereof of that date and for the term of fifteen years had been executed by the city to one Francis Owens, who assigned the lease to George Matsell, the elder, on December 2, 1862. The term of this tax lease did not expire until November, 1876. Thus, from September 5, 1848, to September 5, 1873, and from that time to November, 1876, a period of twenty-eight years, the premises were held subject to one or other of these tax leases.

The defendant, Matsell, Jr., claims that he has held adverse possession of these lots for nineteen years, that is to say, from November 1, 1864, when he received the deed from his father, to October 9, 1883, when this action was begun, and that he is entitled to add to that period the period when his father held also adverse possession, which periods, together, would exceed twenty years.

The question is whether this claim can be maintained.

['] As to the title acquired by Matsell, Jr., by the deed from his father to him, it has been held that an entry under a deed, even although an invalid deed, coupled with actual possession in the grantee, is entry under a colorable title and adverse possession. Sand v. Hughes, 53 *N. Y.* 287, 294, 295.*

The same doctrine may apply also to the title acquired by Mickle under deed from Matsell, Sr., under which Mickle held possession for a year.

---

* See also Pope v. Hanmer, 8 *Hun*, 265 ; aff'd 74 *N. Y.* 240 ; Hilton v. Bender, 2 *Hun*, 1 ; rev'd 69 *N. Y.* 75.

[⁸]   But in order to the establishment of a posses-
      sion as against the owner in fee, defeating his title,
the possession must be adverse to the legal title, and
founded on a written instrument and under a claim of
title exclusive of any other right.

[⁹]   During the time of possession claimed to be
      adverse, the owner in fee must not be under any dis-
ability preventing him from asserting his title by action
      of ejectment against him who holds adversely.

[¹⁰] No possession can be deemed adverse to a party
      who has not at the time the right of entry and
possession. Robinson v. Phillips, 65 *Barb.* 418 ; aff'd,
      56 *N. Y.* 634. Possession and claim under a

[¹¹] municipal tax lease is not adverse to the claim of
      the owner in fee. Bensel v. Gray, 62 *N. Y.* 633.

[¹²] Possession of land to establish a title to the fee
      must be accompanied by claim of title in fee.
Bedell v. Shaw, 59 *N. Y.* 50 ; approved in Hilton v.
      Bender, 69 *Id.* 79.*

[¹³]   The only paper title that Matsell, Sr., could
      claim was for a term of years, and the law will
not from the mere fact of his possession adjudge him
to be in, under a higher right or larger estate. Bedell
v. Shaw, *supra.* Any occupation which he may have
had of the premises before receiving the tax lease,
was without any paper title, and was not, from all that
appears in assertion of any claim of special title or
otherwise, openly adverse to the title of the plaintiffs.
Crary v. Goodman, 22 *N. Y.* 175.† During all the
twenty-eight years under which the premises were
subject to possession under the tax lease, the plaintiff could have maintained no action of ejectment.

---

* See *Sedgwick and Wait on Trial of Title to Land,* §§ 754 *et
seq.;* Sturges v. Parkhurst, 50 *N. Y. Super.* (18 *J. & S.*) 306, and cases
cited.

† Not v. Carroll, 18 *N. Y. Week. Dig.* 405.

["]   In order to maintain an action of ejectment, the plaintiff must be legally entitled to immediate possession, and that would be impossible while the right to possession was in the tax lessee. Kurkel v. Haley, 47 *How. Pr.* 75.*

Again, the defendants' title depends on the alleged disseizin of Mickle by Matsell, Sr.   Matsell had before that, conveyed the lots to Mickle, who had entered ; and but for the disseizin, the title would have been in him.

The facts on which this legal result of "disseizin" is predicated do not appear in the evidence ; and if, in fact, there was no disseizin but only a re-entry by Matsell, Sr., by consent and acquiescence of Mickle, no new or stronger title was acquired by Matsell, and he held only by mere occupation, without any paper title or any claim of any specific title as against the plaintiffs, which would establish adverse possession.

["]   But putting the argument solely on the fact that during the thirty-five years, which had elapsed from 1848, when Matsell, Sr., entered in occupation of the lots, to the time of the commencement of the action in 1883, there was for twenty-five years some one holding a tax lease of the premises, and in possession, or having right to take possession of the lots under the tax lease, and that during that period

---

* See also Trull *v.* Granger, 8 *N. Y.* 115 ; People *v.* Mayor, 10 *Abb. Pr.* 111; Bryan *v.* Butts, 27 *Barb.* 503; aff'd, 28 *How. Pr.* 582, *n.*; McLean *v.* McDonald, 2 *Barb.* 534 ; Hunter *v.* Trustees of Sandy Hill, 6 *Hill,* 407 ; City of Cincinnati *v.* White, 6 *Peters* (*U. S.*) 431 ; Jackson *ex dem.* Livingston *v.* Selover, 10 *Johns.* 368; Jackson *ex dem.* Starr *v.* Richmond, 4 *Id.* 483 ; Reformed Church *v.* Schoolcraft, 65 *N. Y.* 134 ; Betz *v.* Mullin, 62 *Ala.* 365 ; Taylor *v.* Horde, 1 *Burr* (*Eng. K. B.*) 60 ; Price *v.* Osborne, 12 *Ired.* (*N. C.*) 26 ; Kile *v.* Tubb, 82 *Cal.* 332 ; Meeks *v.* Kirby, 47 *Id.* 168; Clay *v.* Ransome, 1 *Munf.* (*Va.*) 455 ; Colston *v.* MacVay, 1 *A. K. Mar.* (*Ky.*) 251.

the plaintiffs could not have successfully maintained an action of ejectment, or recovered immediate possession of the lots, I am of opinion, that, during that period, they were not occupied adversely under claim of title hostile to the plaintiffs, and their cause of action was not barred.*

The plaintiff's exceptions are sustained, and a new trial is ordered, with costs to abide the event.

DE SILVA v. HOLDEN.

SUPERIOR COURT OF THE CITY OF NEW YORK, SPECIAL TERM, OCTOBER, 1886.

§ 572.

Discharge from imprisonment—When not granted, because of failure to issue execution.

Prior to the amendment of section 572 of the Code of Civil Procedure by chapter 672 of the Laws of 1886, an execution against the person could be set aside for the reason that it was not issued within three months after the entry of the judgment upon which it was based, only where the defendant was in actual custody ; but the amendment abolishes the requirement of actual custody, and, except in a case where an order of arrest can be granted only by the Court, enables the defendant, in any event, to make the motion upon proof that the plaintiff neglected to issue the execution within three months after the entry of the judgment.

A motion to set aside an execution against the person, on the ground

---

* When there is existing any relation or agreement between the owner of lands and the occupant thereof, in pursuance of which the latter is in possession, his possession cannot be adverse (Rosewell v. Davis, 38 *Conn.* 562), and where possession is begun in subserviency to the owner's title, proof of disseizin must be very clear. Foulke v Bond, 12 *Vroom* (*N. J.*) 538; Sherman v. Kane, 86 *N. Y.* 57; Zeller v. Eckert, 4 *How. U. S.* 296. See also Whiting v. Edmunds; 94 *N. Y.* 309; Jackson v. Stiles, 1 *Cow.* 575; Thayer v. Society of United Brethren, 20 *Pa. St.* 62; Towne v. Butterfield, 97 *Mass.* 105.

De Silva *v.* Holden.

that it was not issued within three months after the entry of judgment, should be denied whenever reasonable cause is shown why
the application should not be granted. An absence of neglect on
the part of the judgment creditor is such reasonable cause.

Where a judgment in an action was entered on January 18, 1884, and
an appeal taken therefrom, a judgment of affirmance entered
thereon in April 18, 1884, an execution upon these judgments was
issued against the defendant's person on May 21, 1886 ; another
execution issued thereon July 28, 1886, and returned not found,
September 27, 1886, and an alias execution issued October 2, 1886,
—*Held*, that the plaintiff in the executions was not chargeable with
neglect ; that his execution, issued on October 2, 1886, should not
be set aside on the ground that it was not issued within three
months after the recovery of the judgment.

(*Decided October* 29, 1886.)

Motion to set aside execution against the defendant's
person.

The opinion states the facts.

Edward P. Wilder, for defendent and motion.

C. Bainbridge Smith, for plaintiff, opposed.

FREEDMAN, J.—This is a motion to set aside two executions against defendant's person. Of the grounds assigned
only one requires serious consideration. The others are,
under the circumstances shown, clearly untenable. The
ground which does present a grave question is, that the
said executions were not issued within three months after
the entry of the respective judgments upon which they
are based. Prior to the amendment of section 572 of the
Code of Civil Procedure, passed June 15, 1886,* the ground
stated was available only to a defendant in actual custody,
which is not the case of the present defendant.

The amendment of 1886 abolishes the requirement of
actual custody, and, except in a case where an order of
arrest can be granted only by the court, enables a defendant in any event to make the motion upon proof that the

* Laws of 1886, chap. 572.

plaintiff neglected to issue the execution within three months after the entry of the judgment.

In the case at bar the first judgment was entered upon a demurrer to the complaint on or about January 18, 1884, for the sum of $2,643.98. The defendant appealed from said judgment to the general term, which affirmed the same. Judgment of affirmance was entered in April, 1884, with $66.10 costs. Upon these judgments executions against defendant's person were issued May 21, 1886, and returned unsatisfied July 20, 1883. Thereupon executions against defendant's property were issued July 28, 1886, and the same having been returned September 27, 1886, with the indorsement: "Not found," alias executions against the person were issued October 2, 1886. Defendant's motion is to set aside the alias executions.

Upon these facts it is clear that the plaintiff did not issue the executions against defendant's person within three months after the entry of the judgments. But is he chargeable with any neglect? A neglect in such a case consists of the omission to perform the duty of entering the judgment within the proper time. But prior to the amendment of 1886 the plaintiff was under no duty to enter judgment unless the defendant was in actual custody, which was not the case. Moreover, as matter of fact, the plaintiff did issue executions against defendant's person in less than two months after the amendment took effect.

No neglect within the meaning of the law has, therefore, been established, and the defendant, upon whom the burden of proof in this respect rests, has not brought himself within the statute. Moreover, this failure to establish neglect constitutes also a sufficient reason, in another respect, why the defendant's application should be denied. Section 572, as amended in 1886, is not peremptory. It authorizes, in express terms, a denial of the application, whenever reasonable cause is shown why the application should not be granted. The facts disclosed and the absence of neglect do constitute such reasonable cause.

The disposition of the motion renders it unnecessary to determine whether cases, pending at the time the amendment of 1886 went into effect, do or do not remain wholly unaffected by said amendment.

The motion must be denied, with $10 costs.

WRIGHT *v.* GRANT.

SUPREME COURT, THIRD DEPARTMENT, CLINTON COUNTY, SPECIAL TERM, JANUARY, 1887.

§§ 111, 572–575.

Discharge from imprisonment—When defendant who has given bail cannot be, under section 111 of the Code of Civil Procedure —When defendant should not be discharged from imprisonment under order of arrest on ground that more than three months have elapsed since recovery of judgment without the issuing of an execution against the person.

A defendant arrested on an order of arrest who has given bail under Code of Civil Procedure, § 575, subd. 3, to the effect that he will at all times render himself amenable to any mandate which may be issued to enforce a final judgment recovered against him in the action, and has been thereupon discharged from arrest, is not, either in fact nor in contemplation of law, a prisoner ; and cannot be discharged from imprisonment under section 111 of the Code of Civil Procedure as enacted by chap. 672 of the Laws of 1886.

Section 111 of the Code of Civil Procedure, as enacted in 1886, has reference only to that class of defendants who are actually confined in jail or within the jail liberties by virtue of an undertaking given pursuant to Code of Civil Procedure, § 150 ; conditioned that the person so in custody shall remain a prisoner and shall not at any time or in any manner escape or go without the liberties of jail until discharged by due course of law ; and makes provision for their discharge under certain circumstances.

Where a defendant in an action was arrested on an order of arrest and gave bail under the Code of Civil Procedure, § 575, subd. 3, and a judgment was recovered in the action, from which he took an appeal, and the defendant moved for an order releasing him from the liability to arrest on the judgment, on the ground that an execution against his person had not been issued within three months after the entry of judgment, and it appeared that the defendant was not and had not been imprisoned in the action, and that he was not imprisoned in any action nor liable to be,—*Held,* that the granting of the application rested in the discretion of the court, and that under the circumstances the motion should be denied.

It seems, that in such a case it is not now necessary that the defendant, to be entitled to make such a motion, should be in custody.

(*Decided February,* 1887.)

Motion by the defendant that he be discharged from imprisonment under order of arrest issued in this action, and from any liability to be arrested upon an execution issued upon the judgment herein.

The facts appear in the opinion.

Gilbert & Kellogg, for defendant and motion.

Cantwell, Badger & Cantwell, for plaintiff, opposed.

POTTER, J.—This is a motion made at the Clinton county special term in January, 1887, for the discharge of the defendant from arrest under an order of arrest heretofore issued in this action, and from any liability to be arrested upon any execution that may be issued upon the judgment in this action, &c.

The order under which the defendant was arrested was granted by a judge, and the defendant was arrested thereunder by the sheriff of the county of Franklin, on February 13, 1885, and upon such arrest the defendant on the day following gave the sheriff an undertaking pursuant to sections 573, 574 and 575 of the Code of Civil Procedure, and was thereby discharged from such arrest.

The undertaking was under the 3d subdivision of section 575, to the effect that the defendant would at all times render himself amenable to any mandate which may be issued to enforce final judgment in the action.

The affidavits upon the motion also show that the action has been tried and a judgment recovered therein upon the 17th of March, 1886, for $660.22 damages and costs, and that in due time the defendant brought an appeal from said judgment, which is still pending, but gave no undertaking upon such appeal, and that the plaintiff has neglected to issue execution for more than three months after the entry of judgment. The motion is based upon two grounds,—one, that more than six months having elapsed since the arrest of defendant under said order, the defendant is entitled to be discharged under Code Civ. Pro. § 111, as amended ; the other, that the plaintiff having neglected to issue execution against the body of defendant within three months after the entry of judgment, the defendant is entitled to be relieved from liability to arrest under any execution that may be issued in said action pursuant to section 572 of the Code of Civil Procedure as amended in 1886.*

My impression upon the argument was that the defendant was not entitled to be discharged under the decisions made by me in Lust v. Grant and Solomon v. Same,† and reported in the 10 N. Y. Civ. Pro. 158, and cited upon the argument in support of the motion, even if that

---

* Laws of 1886, chap. 572.

† An appeal was not taken from the decision in People ex rel. Lust v. Grant, but in People ex rel. Solomon v. Grant (4 cases) appeals were taken to the general term of the supreme court, in the first department (Van Brunt, P. J., Brady and Daniels, JJ.), and the orders appealed from affirmed by that court on January 23, 1887. The court did not write any opinion, but filed a memorandum of its decision reading as follows : " Orders affirmed with $10 costs and disbursements in one case, on opinion of Potter, J."

decision in all respects should be affirmed ; but as that decision was undergoing review by the general term, in the first department, and might be reversed as to the principle which the defendant's counsel contended was applicable to this case, I thought it best to withhold any decision upon this motion until the decision of the general term in the above mentioned cases.

Recently I have seen that the decision in those cases was affirmed, and the question now presented is whether the motion should be granted upon either of the grounds of defendant's contention.

The first ground arises upon the amendment of the several sections of the Code, made by chaps. 672 and 648, Laws of 1886.

It will be observed, upon reference to those amendments, that they all relate to the duties of officers and in relation to imprisonment of persons confined in the jail or within the jail liberties by virtue of an undertaking pursuant to section 150, conditioned that the person so in custody,—that is, under an order of arrest, surrender by bail or execution against the person,—shall remain a prisoner, and shall not at any time or in any manner escape or go without the liberties of the jail until discharged by due course of law.

Section 111 has only reference to that class of defendants, and makes provision for their discharge under certain circumstances, viz. : Those " imprisoned within the prison walls of a jail" and those " imprisoned within jail liberties of any jail."

Prisoners of the first class may become prisoners of the second class by giving the undertaking specified in section 156, above referred to, and in no other way. Prisoners of the second class may again become prisoners of the first by their surrender to the sheriff through their bail or sureties.   These two classes only are mentioned in the various sections of the Code, notably in sections 111, 149, 150, 152, 153, 154, 155, 158, 160, 162, 572, as prisoners.

Each of these classes is mentioned as prisoners, whether confined within the walls of a jail, or within the jail liberties and in custody of the officers, in these sections of the Code, and were regarded as in the custody of the law before these provisions of the Code were enacted (Peters *v.* Henry, 6 *Johns.* 272; Brown *v.* People, 75 *N. Y.* 438, 440).

The defendant does not fall within either of these classes. He is neither a prisoner within the walls, nor within the liberties, of the jail. The undertaking he has given to the sheriff does not obligate him "not to escape in any manner or at any time or to go without the liberties of the jail." He may go when or where he pleases, without or within the county, with this one limitation, that he will, when required, be somewhere in the county amenable to a mandate issued upon final judgment in this action. He is not, in fact nor in contemplation of law, a prisoner, and these provisions of the law in relation to imprisonment of persons in civil actions and their discharge therefrom have no application to his case.

There is no hardship in this case of which the defendant can justly complain. He had his choice of what condition he should be in when arrested under the judge's order in this action. He could have given an undertaking for the liberties of the jail, and suffered in those restricted liberties for six months, and then had unrestrained liberty to go where he pleased for all time ; or give the undertaking—which he gave—for the other kind of liberty, which is only restricted by his agreement to be in the county in case he shall be required upon final judgment against him in the action.

As a further illustration of the humane character of this law, I see no reason why, if the defendant made a bad choice when he decided what kind of liberty he would have and is dissatisfied with it, he cannot now obtain the other kind by a surrender to the sheriff and then giving the undertaking for the jail liberties, and after submitting to such restriction for six months,—in dull times or unpleasant weather, perhaps,—obtain that larger liberty more desirable with a larger business and wider range of travel with the change of times and the seasons.

My conclusion is that the first ground on which the motion rests is untenable.

The defendant invokes section 572 as amended by the same chapter, 672, above referred to, as entitling him to an order releasing him from liability to arrest upon the final judgment in this action. That section as amended is rendered somewhat obscure, no doubt, in the effort to adapt it to the amendments of the other sections, and to avoid dividing its substance into additional sections.

Assuming that the Legislature intended to change the law upon this subject, as it existed in the Revised Statutes and the provisions of the Code and their amendments from time to time, and the decisions of the courts, requiring that the defendant, when making this motion, should be in custody (see 3 R. S. 5 ed. 870 ; Code Procedure, § 288 ; Bostwick v. Goetzel, 57 N. Y. 582, and cases there referred to), and permitting a defendant not in custody to make the motion, it results that the granting of the motion in this case is a matter resting in the discretion of the court.*

I will not here undertake to decide that question. If it were necessary, I should be inclined to the opinion that. the law was changed by the amendment ; but as a matter discretion, I am not inclined to grant that part of the motion.

As we have seen, the defendant has not been, and is not, imprisoned in this action, though a judgment was rendered against him, and from which he has appealed. The defendant is not now imprisoned in any other action, nor liable to be, so far as shown by the papers upon this motion. It is to be presumed that the defendant expects

---

* See De Silva v. Holden, ante, p. 404.

to reverse the judgment against him in this action as illegal or unjust. If he is not disappointed in his expectations, the judgment will be reversed, and he will never be imprisoned or arrested upon its mandate.

Should the defendant be heard to complain that the plaintiff has forborne to imprison him upon an unjust and erroneous judgment, and, if the judgment is reversed finally, will never have the right to imprison him? That would be a novel and extraordinary use to apply the provisions of that humane legislation to a defendant complaining that the plaintiff has been so considerate and humane as not to imprison him on an unjust judgment; and because he had not imprisoned the defendant, when the defendant claims that plaintiff ought not to, that the plaintiff should not imprison him when the court holds he ought to, if judgment should be affirmed.

Motion denied, with $10 costs.

STICHTER, ET AL., RESPONDENTS, v TILLINGHAST, APPELLANT.

SUPREME COURT, FOURTH DEPARTMENT, GENERAL TERM, JANUARY, 1887.

§§ 803 et seq.

Inspection of books and papers— When ordered. *

An application for an order for the inspection of books, etc., after issue joined, must show that the discovery is sought to aid the applicant to prove his cause of action or his defense.

A discovery of the books, etc., of a party to an action may be had at the instance of his adversary after issue joined, under Code of Civil Procedure, sections 803 *et seq.* and on grounds other than those specified in rule 14 of the supreme court.

Where the papers upon which an order for the inspection of the

---

* See Note on Discovery of Books and Papers, 1 *N. Y. Civ. Pro.* 176.

books, etc., of the party to an action was granted did not show or even allege that the books would furnish evidence which would aid the plaintiffs to establish their cause of action, and no excuse appeared for the omission of definite allegations, such papers are insufficient to support the order.

(*Decided January*, 1887.)

Appeal from order permitting the plaintiffs to inspect books and accounts of defendant's assignor.

The facts sufficiently appear in the opinion.

B. T. Wright, for the defendant-appellant.

Frank H. Hiscock, for plaintiffs-respondents.

FOLLETT, J.—Appeal from an order permitting plaintiffs to inspect the books and accounts of defendant's assignor. This order was applied for and granted after issue was joined; but it has been twice held that a discovery may be had after issue joined, under article fourth, title sixth, chapter eighth of the Code of Civil Procedure,* and for grounds other than those specified in the fourteenth rule of the supreme court (Amsinck *v.* North, 2 *N. Y. Month. L. Bul.* 67;† aff'd, 62 *How. Pr.* 114; S. C., 12 *N. Y. W. Dig.* 573; Babbitt *v.* Crampton, 1 *N. Y. Civ. Pro.* 109).

An application after issue joined must show that the discovery is sought to aid the applicant to prove his cause of action, or his defense (Douglas *v.* Delano, 20 *N.Y. Week. Dig.* 85; Andrews *v.* Townshend, 2 *N.Y. Civ. Proc.* 76; Shoe & Leather Reporter Assn. *v.* Bailey, 49 *N. Y. Super.* (17 *J. & S.*) 385; Mott *v* Consumers' Ice Co., 52 *How. Pr.* 148; 2 *Wait's Pr.* 531; *Baylies Trial Pr.* 120; *Hare on Discovery*, 3 Am. ed. 197). The general terms of the

---

* Section 803 *et seq.*　　　†S. C., 1 *N. Y. Civ. Pro.* 180, *note.*

supreme court, of the superior court, and of the court of common pleas are in accord on this question.

This court held in Adams *v.* Cavanaugh (37 *Hun,* 232), that a party cannot be examined under article one, title three, chapter nine of the Code of Civil Procedure,* except for the purpose of proving the applicant's cause of action, or defense.

The papers upon which this order was granted do not show, or even allege that the books will furnish evidence which will aid the plaintiffs to establish their cause of action. There seems to be no excuse in this case for the omission of definite allegations, as the plaintiff's counsel has been permitted to examine the books for two days, and the defendant offered a further examination, and to permit them to be examined by an expert, to be agreed upon by the parties. An examination under an order seems to be sought because defendant refused to permit an examination by an expert unknown to him and not named by plaintiffs.

We think the allegations in the moving papers insufficient to support the order.

The view taken of the merits of this appeal renders it unnecessary to consider whether the supreme court rule 37 was a bar to granting this order upon an order to show cause returnable out of the judicial district in which the venue of the action was laid.

The order is reversed, with $10 costs and printing disbursements, and the motion denied, with $10 costs, but without prejudice to the right of the plaintiffs to make a new application for discovery, upon the payment of the costs.

HARDIN, P. J., and BOARDMAN, J., concurred.

* Section 870 *et seq.,* relating to examination of party before trial.

JONES, Respondent, v. SHERMAN, Appellant.

City Court of New York, General Term, February, 1887.

§§ 2433, 2455, 2456, 3240.

Supplementary proceedings—Costs.

The only costs that can be allowed on appeal from an order made in proceedings supplementary to execution committing defendant for contempt, are motion costs,—*i.e.*, $10 and disbursements.

Although proceedings supplementary to execution are no longer regarded as proceedings in an action, but as distinct special proceedings, yet the mode of reviewing orders therein and the practice relating thereto are the same as if the orders had been made in an ordinary action.

Appeals from orders are, for the purpose of determining the amount of costs, merely regarded as motions.

(*Decided February* 25, 1887.)

Appeal by defendant from order of special term made on retaxation of costs.

The defendant, a judgment debter, was adjudged guilty of contempt in proceedings supplementary to execution, and an order made for his committal. He appealed from that order to the general term of this court, which reversed it, with costs; he presented a bill of costs to the clerk, claiming $60 costs besides disbursements, and the clerk allowed the same; the plaintiff thereupon moved at special term for a new taxation, and the court reduced the amount of costs to $10 and disbursements; and the defendant took this appeal from the order thereupon entered.

L. F. Post, for defendant-appellant.

N. Quackenbos, for plaintiff-respondent.

Jones *v.* Sherman.

McADAM, Ch. J.—Proceedings supplementary to execution are no longer regarded as proceedings in an action, but distinct "special proceedings " (*Throop's Code*, § 2433 and notes), yet the mode of reviewing orders made therein, and the practice relating thereto, are the same as if the order had been made in an ordinary action (§ 2433, subd. 2). The amount of costs recoverable in such proceedings is regulated by sections 2455 and 2456. The motion to punish for contempt went to the general term. It was therefore nothing more than a continuation of the motion on appeal in the same court. There it was in the category of motions, and no more than $10 could be allowed as costs, besides disbursements (Phipps *v.* Carman, 26 *Hun*, 520). The rule is that appeals from orders are merely regarded as motions for the purpose of costs (*Parsons on Costs*, 9.). * As the costs in these proceedings are specially prescribed, section 3240, which relates only to costs in special proceedings " not otherwise regulated," has no application to the present contention. The court below was right in limiting the costs on appeal to $10 costs and disbursements (People *v.* Cooper, 10 *N. Y. Week. Dig.* 77), and the order must be affirmed, with costs.

HYATT, J., concurred.

---

* The cases cited in *Parsons on Costs* to sustain the proposition are : Savage *v.* Darrow, 4 *How. Pr.* 74 ; S. C., 2 *Code R.* 57 ; Pennell *v.* Wilson, 5 *Robt.* 674 ; S. C., 2 *Abb. Pr. N. S.* 466.

CANARIE, Respondent, v. KNOWLES and Another,
Appellants.

Supreme Court, First Department, General Term,.
March, 1887.

§ 1294.

Appeal—When right to waived by conditional acceptance of benefit..

Where an injunction order was continued unless the defendants
stipulate that the plaintiff should recover a certain sum as damages if he succeeds in the action and the defendants gave such
stipulation, but in their stipulation stated that the same was
made and served under protest and was not to be considered as a
waiver of the defendants' right to appeal therefrom, —*Held*, that
the defendants thereby waived their right to appeal; that the protest did not prevent the defendants' action operating as a waiver
of such right; that the defendants did not act under duress in
serving the stipulation, for had the proviso been omitted
their only remedy would have been an appeal from the order, and
that remedy was equally open to them, the proviso being added.
A party who avails himself of provisions in his favor contained in
an order thereby waives the right to appeal from other provisions
therein which are adverse to him.

{Decided March 18, 1887.)

Appeal by defendants from an order continuing injunction during the pendency of the action.

The facts are fully stated in the opinion.

George W. Wingate (*Hirsch & Rasquin*, attorneys), for
defendants-appellants.

W. Bourke Cockran (*Cockran & Clarke*, attorneys), for
plaintiff-respondent.

CHURCHILL, J.—December 10, 1885, plaintiff procured an order of injunction forbidding defendants to allow any person other than the plaintiff to occupy for dramatic purposes the building known as the "Grand Opera House," in the city of Brooklyn, during the week commencing December 21, 1885, or until the further order of the court; and also ordering the defendants to refrain from interfering in any manner with the right of the plaintiff to occupy the same during that week.

The order further required the defendants to show cause at a special term to be held at chambers in New York, December 19, 1885, why the injunction should not be continued during the pendency of the action. On the 19th, cause was shown, and an order made by the court continuing and making permanent the injunction, but with the following proviso added:

" Provided, however, that in case the defendants shall serve a written stipulation that the damages to be recovered by the plaintiff in this action (in case he shall be decreed to be entitled to recover damages from the defendants therein) will be $2,000, less the expenses of the salaries of the company for the week in question, which the plaintiff will not be bound to pay; that upon the service of such stipulation, signed by the defendant's attorneys, upon the plaintiff's attorney, the injunction hereby granted shall thereupon stand dissolved."

December 21 the defendants executed and served the stipulation called for by the proviso, and the injunction was thereupon dissolved. Indorsed upon the stipulation as served was the following notice:

" Please take notice that the within stipulation is made and served in pursuance of the injunction order of the 19th instant, and that the same is made and served under protest, and is not to be considered as constituting our assent to such order or any waiver of the defendant's right to appeal therefrom. Dated December 21, 1885.

HIRSH & RASQUIN,
Attorneys for defendants.

"To W. BOURKE COCKRAN, Esq.,
Attorney for plaintiff."

December 22 the defendants appealed from the order of December 19 and every part of it to the general term.

The proviso of the order was a favor to the defendants. It put within their power to obtain, what in showing cause they were seeking to obtain, i. e., a dissolution of the injunction. They availed themselves of the provision and thereby obtained such dissolution.

[¹]   This action on their part was inconsistent with and a waiver of their right to appeal from the order (Smith v. Rathbun, 75 N. Y. 122; Baylies on New Trials, 19 et seq. and cases cited; 4 Wait Pr. 216).

[²]   It cannot be said that the defendants acted under duress in serving the stipulation. Had the proviso been omitted, their only remedy would have been an appeal from the order. This remedy was equally open to them, the proviso being added (Chapin v. Foster, N. Y. Ct. of Appeals, 33 Alb. L. J. 33).

[³]   The case just cited recognizes the rule "that a party who has availed himself of provisions in his favor contained in an order has thereby waived the right to appeal from other provisions therein which are adverse to him."

[⁴]   The defendants, in acting upon the proviso and serving the stipulation, made the plaintiff's situation less favorable than it was when the order appealed from was made, since by their action the injunction was dissolved, and they could not after that insist upon their right to appeal (Grunberg v. Blumenlähl, 66 How. Pr. 62).*

* See Claflin v. Frankel, 3 N. Y. Civ. Pro. 109; Jayne v. Jayne, 8 Id. 94.

[*]   The protest served did not prevent the defendants'
action operating as a waiver of their right to appeal
(Dambman *v.* Schulting, 6 *Hun*, 29).

The order appealed from should be affirmed, with $10
costs and usual disbursements.

DANIELS and BRADY, JJ., concurred.

FLAGG, RESPONDENT, *v.* COOPER, APPELLANT.

SUPERIOR COURT OF THE CITY OF NEW YORK, GENERAL TERM,
NOVEMBER, 1886.

§§ 724, 1240.

*Judgment—When leave to defend after entry of, does not affect its
validity.*

Where judgment was entered by default and an order thereafter made
permitting the defendant to defend, but directing that the judgment stand as security, and that no execution issue thereon until
the determination of the action, the judgment is not vacated by
the entry of a subsequent judgment in the action, but it can then
—the action having been determined—be enforced in the way provided by law.

A defendant against whom judgment has been entered by default
who accepts leave to defend, is bound by the order granting such
leave, and cannot thereafter insist that the terms are irregular.

On a motion to set aside an execution under which real property has
been advertised for sale, it is not necessary to determine whether
the judgment is a lien on such real property, as, if it is not, no interest will pass on the sale.

(Decided November 10, 1886.)

Appeal by defendant from order denying his motion
to set aside an execution issued against his property.

July 3, 1883, plaintiff obtained judgment by default. This default was opened for purpose of permitting a trial on the merits, but on condition that " the judgment stand as security but no execution to issue thereon until after the determination of the action." In May, 1886, after trial on the merits, judgment was again entered in favor of plaintiff, upon which he issued an execution, which being returned unsatisfied, he issued execution on the judgment recovered July 3, 1883. Defendant moved to set aside such execution. From the order denying that motion this appeal was taken.

Other facts appear in the report of the decision in O'Rourke v. Henry Prouse Cooper Co., *ante*, p. 321.

D. H. Robinson, for defendant-appellant.

William L. Flagg, for plaintiff-respondent.

PER CURIAM.—[SEDGWICK, Ch. J., and INGRAHAM, J.]—The judgment entered by default July 3, 1883, was a final judgment within the provisions of section 1240 of the Code, and an execution on such judgment was regular.

The defendant applied to the court for leave to defend the action, and that application was granted, but the judgment as entered was not vacated, and as a condition for the favor granted it was provided "that the judgment stand as security, but no execution to issue thereon until after the determination of the action."

The defendant, having accepted the favor granted, was bound by the conditions imposed, and on the determination against him of the defense interposed, under the provisions of the order the conditions upon which the leave leave was granted became binding upon him.

The subsequent judgment entered did not have the effect of vacating the original judgment. That stood under the terms of the order, and, the period during which no execution was to issue having expired, we can see no reason why the judgment originally entered should not be enforced in the way provided by law.

It is not necessary to determine whether the judgment

is a lien upon the property advertised for sale. If the judgment is not a lien upon such property no interest therein will pass under the sale, and, the judgment and execution being regular, the plaintiffs had the right to enforce the judgment against all the property upon which it is a lien.

The defendant having accepted the leave to defend granted by the order, it is too late for him to insist that the terms upon which such leave was granted were irregular. We think the order appealed from should be affirmed, with $10 costs and disbursements.

LERCHE, APPELLANT, v. BRASHER, AS ADMINISTRATOR, ETC., RESPONDENT.

COURT OF APPEALS, JANUARY, 1887.

§§ 829, 933.

Evidence—When testimony as to conversations and transactions with decedent, not admitted—When admission of, material—When transcript of record of power of attorney, properly received in evidence.

Evidence by the plaintiff, in an action against an administrator, to the effect that he had not been paid for services rendered by him for the decedent, negatives a personal transaction with the decedent, and is equivalent to a declaration that neither the deceased, nor his administrator had paid for the services rendered, and is improperly admitted. [1]   But where there is no evidence of payment,—the defense of payment being an affirmative defense, and the burden of proving it upon the defendant,—such testimony in no possible respect affects the result and is not a ground for reversing the judgment. [2]

The plaintiff in an action to recover for services rendered the decedent of the defendant cannot testify to an employment or request by such decedent ; but, where such employment or request was proved by other evidence, he may describe simply the things which he did, provided such acts could have been done in the absence of the deceased, and without his immediate personal participation. [3]

Lerche v. Brasher.

In an action to recover for services rendered the decedent, brought against his administrator, a question addressed to the plaintiff inquiring, "What was done by you—excepting, of course, personal transactions or communications with the deceased....—from the time you first commenced your labor down to his death?" is not incompetent as calling for a personal transaction with the deceased; the question was proper in form; it called for no objectionable proof; and, if any was proffered under it, the defendant's duty was to object specifically and move to strike out so much of the answer as exceeded the legitimate scope of the inquiry. [4]

Objection to testimony after it is given may possibly be treated as a motion to strike out such testimony. [5]

In an action brought against an administrator to recover for services rendered his decedent, in matters pertaining to two actions, evidence that the plaintiff went to the office of the decedent's attorneys and got the papers in one of the cases, and went to Albany to prepare his case with the decedent's counsel, for the court of appeals, is evidence of independent facts in which the deceased was not a personal participator; and which if living he could not for that reason have contradicted, and does not necessarily involve a personal transaction with him. [6]

If, in such a case, the employment or request in any manner or to any extent rested upon inference drawn from the character of the acts done, the evidence would be incompetent; but where no such error was committed, and the jury were expressly charged that before they could find the fact of employment they must be satisfied of it, by testimony other than plaintiff's, the evidence is properly admitted. [7]

Where in an action brought against the personal representative of a decedent to recover for services rendered under a power of attorney, the plaintiff testified without objection that he had had the original in his possession, but lost it; and a certified transcript, from the register's office in New York county, of the power of attorney, was offered in evidence, and the power of attorney related to real estate of the defendant which it was shown was situate in New York county,—Held, that said power of attorney was properly read in evidence. [3]

Lerche v. Brasher (8 N. Y. Civ. Pro. 115), reversed. [7]

(Decided January, 1887.)

Appeal by plaintiff from an order of the general term of the supreme court in the second department, affirming an order made at circuit, setting aside a verdict for

$750, in his favor, and granting a new trial on defendant's
motion, made at the close of the trial upon exceptions.
Reported below, 8 *N. Y. Civ. Pro.* 115.

The action was brought by the plaintiff to recover
$2,675 for services alleged to have been rendered Pierre M.
Van Wyck, the defendant's decedent, in his life-time; and
the answer put in issue the rendering of the services and
the value thereof; and also set up a counter-claim that
the decedent was the owner of certain bonds and mortgages worth $9,675; and that plaintiff became possessed
of the same, and, for the purpose of defrauding his estate,
transferred said bonds and mortgages to Francis Xavier
Huber; that an action was commenced against said Huber,
in the supreme court, to recover said bonds and mortgages, in which judgment was recovered by the defendant
herein; and that, in prosecuting such action, and recovering such judgment, the defendant necessarily expended
the sum of $2,000.   On the trial, the jury found a verdict
for $750 in favor of the plaintiff, and the justice presiding
at the circuit, upon defendant's motion, directed a new
trial on the exceptions, and an order entered upon his
decision was affirmed by the general term on appeal.
Other facts are stated in the opinion.

G. A. Clement (*King & Clement*, attorneys), for plaintiff-
appellant.

There was no error in regard to the admission of
evidence concerning a lost power of attorney.   The instrument in question,—a certified transcript of a record,—was
offered in evidence by plaintiff's counsel and was objected
to on the ground that it was secondary evidence.   The
court admitted it as proof only that a paper of that kind
was on record.   It being a certified transcript of a record,
there was more reason for the plaintiff to except than the
defendant, as the statute expressly makes such a transcript competent evidence as the original. *Code Civ. Pro.*

§ 933.	The cases cited by the court below in its opinion obviously have no application to the facts of this case. In both the cases cited (Hadsale v. Scott, 26.*Hun*, 617, and Pease v. Barnett, 30 *Hun*, 525), the witness was questioned and testified to the contents of the lost instrument. In this case, there was no such question or evidence whatever, other than what plaintiff testified to on cross-examination ; his only testimony in relation to the lost power of attorney was that he had had the original, that he had made search for it, and that it was lost, and to this evidence there was on objection or exception. The case of Holcomb v. Holcomb, 95 *N. Y.* 325, cited by the court below, does not apply to this case.	By reading the whole opinion of the court of appeals in that case, it is clear there was a violation of the statute in receiving certain specified evidence. There is no such evidence whatever in this case.	The statute is limited in its legal operative force to personal transactions and communications ; a case must be within the letter as well as the spirit of the statute ; the exclusion of evidence must be made out by the party alleging its incompetency as to the particular matter. Pinney v. Orth, 2 *N. Y. Civ. Pro.* 1 ; Cary v. White, 59 *Id.* 339 ; Severn v. National State Bank, 18 *Hun*, 223, 229 ; Ham v. Van Orden, 84 *N. Y.* 257; Pratt v. Elkins, 80 *Id.* 201 ; Wadsworth v. Hermann, 85 *Id.* 639.	There was no error, requiring a new trial, in the allowance of the question: "Has any part of this been paid? Ans. No." Neither the question nor the answer called for or disclosed any personal transaction or communication with deceased. *Non constat* it was paid by defendant himself, the administrator, or by an agent of Mr. Van Wyck.	Pratt v. Elkins, 80 *N. Y.* 201.	If, as the court states in its opinion, the question should have been limited to the administrator, that was really the only ground of objection.	But there was no such objection made or taken.	If it had, it might have been obviated.	It cannot therefore, under well settled rules be considered on appeal.	Ward v. Kilpatrick, 85

N. Y. 417. It is obvious that neither the question nor answer prejudiced the defendant, and this is conceded by the court below. And see Rowland *v.* Hegeman, 1 *Hun,* 491; affd., 59 *N. Y.* 643. There was no error in the charge of the trial court to the jury : "That the statute does not prohibit a man, after his employment has been shown by other evidence, from testifying as to the services which he has performed." If there was anything in response objectionable, defendant's proper remedy was by motion to strike out or request to charge jury to disregard. But there was no such motion or request. See Platner *v.* Platner, 78 *N. Y.* 91; Pontius *v.* People, 82 *Id.* 347.

Morris & Pearsall, for defendants-respondents.

The court erred in allowing plaintiff to testify, against defendant's objection to the question : "Has any part of this been paid? Answer. No." It is well settled that a negative fact cannot be proved by a witness who is a party and brought within section 829. Dyer *v.* Dyer, 48 *Barb.* 190 ; Howell *v.* Van Siclen, 6 *Hun,* 115 ; Haughey *v.* Wright, 12 *Id.* 179 ; Boughton *v.* Bogardus, 7 *N. Y. Civ. Pro.* 252.

The question: " Has any part of the claim been paid ? " should have been excluded. Wilson *v.* Reynolds, 31 *Hun,* 47 ; Howell *v.* Van Sicklen, 6 *Id.* 115 ; Somerville *v.* Crook, 9 *Id.* 664; Baldwin *v.* Smith, 5 *Id.* 454; Williams *v.* Davis, 7 *N. Y. Civ. Pro.* 282; Hill *v.* Heemans, 17 *Hun,* 470 ; Haughey *v.* Wright, 12 *Id.* 179 ; Fooley *v.* Bacon, 70 *N. Y.* 34; Chadwick *v.* Fonner, 69 *Id.* 406 ; Brague *v.* Lord, 2 *Abb. N. C.* 1 ; Pease *v.* Barnett, 30 *Hun,* 525 ; Hadsell *v.* Scott, 26 *Id.* 617. The court erred in permitting plaintiff to testify to the various services rendered by him for deceased. Williams *v.* Davis, 7 *N. Y. Civ. Pro.* 282; Holcomb *v.* Holcomb, 95 *N. Y.* 316 ; Fisher *v.* Verplank, 7 *Hun,* 150 ; Boughton *v.* Bogardus, 7 *N. Y. Civ. Pro.* 252.

FINCH, J.—The plaintiff brought this action claiming to recover about $2,600 as compensation for services rendered to the defendant's testator in the character of his agent and attorney. The contract of employment was proved beyond all question, by evidence wholly uncontradicted, and of a kind open to no criticism. The services rendered began a few days before January 14, 1880, on which day the plaintiff collected a judgment of about $500 in favor of Van Wyck. On that day, the latter, by a written instrument, the signature to which was proven, and not questioned, appointed plaintiff his "attorney in fact" for all matters pertaining to two actions which were specified. That the employment was earlier than that, is evident, from a letter of Van Wyck, dated December 30, 1879, in which he speaks plainly of the existing relation. Other letters are quite as decisive, and on February 10, 1880, Van Wyck gave to plaintiff a general power of attorney, covering substantially the transaction of all his business. The employment was further proved, by at least one witness, who swore to the statements of the testator to that effect.

The general character of the services contracted for and rendered, was also shown by evidence outside of anything which fell from the plaintiff. The property of the testator had been taken from him on account of his intemperate habits, and placed in the hands of a committee. Van Wyck had become restored to health and capacity, and entitled to receive back and manage his property. The committee had placed the estate in the hands of Morris & Pearsall, his attorneys, and in a letter, dated February 27, Van Wyck notifies plaintiff, that they had agreed to deliver the papers, if he (Van Wyck) would care for them, and adds: "I shall not go, and so shall answer. They shall settle with you alone." That they did so settle, the defendant himself proved. The amount of property thus delivered over, was about $28,000. The defendant also proved the payment of the Walsh mortgage of $5,500, and the interest upon it, to plaintiff. There was thus clear evidence of the employment, and the general nature of the services rendered, outside of any testimony given by the plaintiff in his own behalf. A verdict was rendered in his favor for $750, or about one quarter of his claim. A motion was made upon the minutes, and the exceptions taken, to set aside the verdict, and for a new trial, which was granted upon two grounds, relating to the admission of evidence. On appeal, the general term affirmed the order, but for other and different reasons.

The trial judge specified two such errors as the ground of his action. On the hearing, after the plaintiff had described the work he had done, he was asked if he had been paid for it. To this inquiry, the defendant objected, as involving a personal transaction with the deceased. The objection was overruled, an exception taken. and the witness answered "No." The answer negatived a personal transaction with the testator, and was equivalent to a declaration, that neither the deceased nor his administrator with the will annexed had paid for the services rendered. But while the objection was a good one, the evidence was wholly immaterial. The plaintiff was not required to prove the negative, and payment was an affirmative defense, the burden of establishing which was upon the defendant. No evidence in that direction was offered or given, and striking out the inadmissible answer would, in no possible respect, affect the result reached. We ought not to reverse a judgment on so narrow a ground.

The trial judge further held, that it was error to admit the transcript from the register's office of New York of Van Wyck's power of attorney. When first offered, it was objected to, as secondary evidence, and as no proof of the original. The court said, "It is no proof that Van Wyck executed it; it is simply proof that a paper of this kind is on record;" and thereupon overruled the objection, and defendant excepted. The plaintiff then testified, without objection, that he had had the original in his possession, but had lost it, and on a careful search had been unable

to find it.   At a later period of the case, the power of
attorney was read in evidence, against an objection that
there was no proof that Van Wyck ever executed it and
the paper was incompetent.

By the revised statutes (vol. 3, 6 ed. p. 1151, § 73) a
power of attorney, authorizing, as did the one in question,
the conveyance of real estate, may be recorded in the
clerk's office of any county in which the land affected is
situated, and the record be received in evidence with like
effect as a conveyance. My first impression was that there
was not sufficient proof that Van Wyck owned land situated in New York county, but a careful reading of the evidence shows that, while the proof was not direct and
pointed, there is an abundance of it from which the
natural and necessary inference of such locality follows.
The Code provides (§ 933) that a transcript from a record
kept "pursuant to law" in a public office of the State
whose incumbent has an official seal, when properly certified by the officer, is evidence, as if the original was
produced. Under these provisions the transcript was
properly received in evidence.*

The general term, in affirming the order for a new trial,
placed no reliance upon the objections thus considered,
but rested its action upon the much more serious ground,
that the plaintiff was permitted to state, in detail, the services he rendered, in the face of an objection, that such
proof involved a personal transaction with the deceased.
The trial judge stated distinctly and carefully what he
intended to rule. He said that the plaintiff could not
testify to an employment or request, but where that was
proved by other evidence the party might describe simply
the things which he did, provided such acts could have
been done in the absence of deceased, and without his
immediate or personal participation.   Acting upon this
basis, the court excluded all evidence of visits to Van
Wyck's residence or of facts which Van Wyck, if living,

* See George *v.* Toll, 39 *How. Pr.* 497.

could have directly contradicted by his own oath, and limited the proof to independent facts. These were that plaintiff collected the Erie judgment, the Walsh mortgage, and the assets in the hands of the committee, and to effect those results, made certain calls upon the committee, and his attorneys, and examinations of records in other counties.

The only objection taken was a general one to the question with which the inquiry began, and that question was: " What was done by you—excepting, of course, personal transactions, or communications with the deceased, Mr. Van Wyck—from the time you first commenced your labor down to his death? * The objections were thus phrased: " as incompetent and calling for transactions with deceased." The question was proper in form. It called for no objectionable proof, and, if any was proffered under it, the defendant's duty was to object specifically, and move to strike out so much of the answer as exceeded the legitimate scope of the inquiry. Nothing of this kind actually and in terms occurred. The only further objection taken to the evidence under the provision of the Code, was to the inquiry, "how much time" his detailed services occupied?

At the close of the case there was an exception to the charge to the jury, in which the judge explained the reasons why he permitted the plaintiff to testify to what he did. Whether those reasons were sufficient, or in all respects correct, was immaterial. The sole question was whether any of the evidence objected to, and admitted, was competent under the Code. Some of it we think was. Possibly one objection might be treated as a motion to strike out an answer. To the inquiry, proper in form, because excluding personal transactions, or communications, the witness said : " I went to Morris & Pearsall's

---

* See Bristol v. Sears, 3 N. Y. Civ. Pro. 328.

office, and got the papers in the case of Van Wyck, by committee, against Ostermeyer and Brasher, and went to Albany, to prepare the case with Judge, HAND, for the court of appeals." The record adds: "Objection to this evidence renewed, as calling for a transaction with the deceased."

If we indulge in the latitude of treating this, which is the sole specific objection taken, as fairly equivalent to a motion to strike out, we are still of opinion that the two facts related were independent facts, in which the deceased was not personally participator, and which, if living, he could not, for that reason, have contradicted. They might have been done without his authority, or knowledge, as were some other acts of the plaintiff, and did not necessarily involve a personal transaction with him. When that inquiry arose by reason of his employment, or request, the mouth of the witness was closed. If that employment or request in any manner, or to any extent, rested upon an inference drawn from the character of the acts done, the evidence would be incompetent.* But no such error was committed. The jury were expressly warned against it, and told, " Before you can find the fact of the employment, you must be satisfied of it by testimony other than his own."

On this state of the record, we think the ruling of the trial was not erroneous, and especially for the reason that the facts specifically challenged were substantially proved by the deceased's own written communications.

The general term intimated a doubt whether defendant's counter-claim was not erroneously excluded. The court admitted the facts as a defense and excluded them as a counter-claim, and with this ruling the defendant seems to have been contented, for he took no exception.

---

* *Vide* Jacques *v.* Elmore, 7 *Hun*, 675 ; Burnett *v.* Noble, 5 *Redf.* 69 ; Fisher *v.* Verplanck, 17 *Hun*, 150 ; Freeman *v.* Lawrence, 43 *N. Y. Super.* (11 *J. & S.*) 288; Somerville *v.* Crook, 9 *Hun*, 664; Clarke *v.* Smith, 46 *Barb.* 30 ; Ross *v.* Ross, 6 *Hun*, 182.

The orders appealed from should be reversed, and judgment for plaintiff ordered on the verdict, with costs.

All concur, except RAPALLO, J., not voting.

BAUER, RESPONDENT, *v.* SCHEVITCH, ET AL., APPELLANTS.

SUPREME COURT, FIRST DEPARTMENT, GENERAL TERM, FEBRUARY, 1887.

§§ 559, 575.

Undertaking on order of arrest—Amount of—Defects in not jurisdictional.

Where an order of arrest requires that more that one person be arrested and held to bail, the undertaking given to procure it, should be for not less than one-tenth of the aggregate of bail required of such defendants. Accordingly,—Held, where an order was granted for the arrest of three defendants and directed that they be held to bail in the sum of $2,000, that an undertaking in the sum of $500 was insufficient.

Where an undertaking on which an order was granted for the arrest of three persons was conditioned for the payment of the sum therein mentioned to the defendants or either of them,—Held, that it was insufficient ; that under the obligation created by it, the defendants could only secure protection in case judgment was rendered in favor of the three ; for if a judgment was rendered against one, and in favor of the others, the undertaking would protect but one of the two ; that it should have provided for the payment of the damages which each of the defendants might sustain by reason of the arrest.

An undertaking on an order of arrest which is defective in form, or insufficient in amount, or both, may be amended by the substitution of such an undertaking as the nature of the case and

the provisions of the Code of Civil Procedure require should
be given.

Where, on appeal from an order denying motion to vacate an order
of arrest, on account of defects of the undertaking on which it
was granted, it appeared that the order to show cause on which
the motion was made did not specify such defects ; but it did
not appear that any objection was taken to it on this account on
the hearing of the motion, it will be presumed that it was heard
and disposed of without reference to the omissions in the order to
show cause.

(*Decided February* 18, 1887.)

Appeal from order denying motion to vacate order of
arrest.

This action was brought to recover damages for the
publication by the defendant of an alleged libel in a newspaper, known as the *New Yorker Volks Zeitung,* consisting
of a notice calling upon workingmen to boycott a
hotel, etc., kept by the defendant, on account of his
alleged breach of faith toward waiters employed by him.
The plaintiff procured an order for the arrest of the
defendants (three in number) requiring the sheriff to
arrest the defendants, and hold them and each of them to
bail in the sum of $2,000. To procure this order of
arrest, he gave an undertaking in the usual form, conditioned that "the plaintiff in said action will pay all costs
which may be awarded to the defendants or either of
them, and all damages which they or either of them may
sustain by reason of the arrest in said action not exceeding the sum of $500." The defendants were arrested
under this order of arrest, and, after having giving bail,
moved to vacate the order of arrest on the ground that
the plaintiff's undertaking was insufficient. The application was denied, and this appeal taken from the order
thereupon entered.

Simon Sultan and Theodore Sutro, for defendants-appellants.

The undertaking is clearly insufficient in amount and

does not meet the requirements of the statute. . . . The Code prescribes that the sum specified in the undertaking "must be at least equal to one-tenth of the amount of the bail required by the order, and not less than two hundred and fifty dollars." The object of the undertaking is, that "if the defendant recovers judgment, or if it is finally decided that the plaintiff was not entitled to the order of arrest, the plaintiff will pay all the costs which may be awarded to the defendant and all damages which he may sustain by reason of the arrest." *Code Civ. Pro.* § 559. In this case, there are three defendants; the order of arrest requires the sheriff to hold each of them to bail in the sum of two thousand dollars. According to section 559 of the Code, the sum specified in the undertaking should have been " not less than two hundred and fifty dollars " as to each defendant, or $750, instead of $500. Each defendant is entitled to the indemnity against damages and costs prescribed by said section of the Code. . . . The aforesaid defect in the undertaking is jurisdictional. It is not a mere irregularity, but rendered the order of arrest void *ab initio.* The language of the Code is that the judge, " before " he grants the order, " must " require a written undertaking, &c. Godfrey *v.* Pell, 4 *N. Y. Civ. Pro.* 448 ; Kroszinski *v.* Volkowicz, 1 *N. Y. Month. Law Bull.* 89.

Benjamin Patterson, for plaintiff-respondent.

If there should be any defect in the undertaking, it does not avoid the order for want of jurisdiction, but is subject to the amendment, and is an irregularity merely, which defendant could waive, and for which the court, in the exercise of its discretion, could refuse to vacate the order of arrest. Irving *v.* Judd, 20 *Hun,* 562 ; Kissam *v.* Marshall, 10 *Abb. Pr.* 424 ; Pember *v.* Schaller, 58 *How. Pr.* 511 ; Bellinger *v.* Gardner, 12 *Id.* 381 ; Wilson *v.* Allen, 3 *Id.* 369; Schermerhorn *v.* Anderson, 1 *N. Y.* 430 ; Beach *v.* Southworth, 6 *Barb.* 173 ; O'Shea *v.* Kohn, 33

Hun, 114. The defect, if any, not being jurisdictional, the court was not bound to vacate the order of arrest, and the defendants having moved upon the papers upon which the order of arrest was granted only, and not having specified the irregularity (if any) in the undertaking. G*o*dfrey *v.* Pell, 4 *N. Y. Civ. Pro.* 443 ; *General Rule of Practice,* 37.

DANIELS, J.—The application to set aside and vacate the order proceeded upon the insufficiency of the undertaking given on the part of the plaintiff.

There are three defendants in the action, and the order directed the sheriff to arrest them and to hold them, and each of them, to bail in the sum of $2,000. The undertaking was given for the payment of such costs and damages as the defendants, or either of them, might sustain by reason of the arrest, not exceeding the sum of $500.

To obtain this order of arrest, section 559 of the Code of Civil Proceedure required the undertaking to be at least equal to one-tenth of the amount of bail required by the order ; and as this order directed each of the defendants to be held to bail in the sum of $2,000, it is very clear that this undertaking was not one-tenth of that amount.

By section 575 of the same Code, it has also been provided that the defendant when arrested shall be discharged on bail consisting of an undertaking that the defendant to be discharged will at all times render himself amenable to any mandate which may be issued to enforce a final judgment against him in the action. And this undertaking to comply with the order of arrest would uecessarily be given in the sum of $2,000. The undertaking given by and on behalf of the plaintiff obligated the persons executing it to pay the damages mentioned in it to the defendants, or either of them. And under the obligation created by it, they all could only secure protection in case judgment was rendered in favor of the three ; for if judgment was recovered against one and in favor of the others, the undertaking would protect but one of the two. What it should have provided for was for the payment of the damages which each of the defendants might recover by reason of the arrest, which would be a protection if judgment proceeded in favor of two and against the other. Neither in form nor amount was it such an undertaking as the law required to be given to entitle the plaintiff to the order which was made.

But, defective as it is, it may still be amended by the substitution of such an undertaking as the nature of the case and these provisions of the Code required should be given (Irwin v. Judd, 20 *Hun*, 562).

The order to show cause upon which the motion was made did not specify the defects in the undertaking as it should have done, but it does not appear that any objection was taken to it on this account on the hearing of the motion, and, from the order afterwards entered, it has to be presumed that it was heard and disposed of without reference to this omission in the order to show cause.

The order appealed should be reversed and an order made setting aside the order of arrest, unless, within ten days after notice of the decision, the plaintiff shall obtain and as practice requires that to be done, a further undertaking in the sum of one thousand dollars conditioned to pay to the defendants and to each of them the damages sustained by reason of the arrest, if judgment shall be recovered by them, or either of them, in the action, or it should be decided that the plantiff was not entitled to the order; and upon such an undertaking being given and the payment of the costs of opposing the motion and the appeal within the time already mentioned, the order should be affirmed. But in a case of a failure to comply with these conditions, the order should be reversed and the order of arrest vacated with like costs.

All concurred.

MORRISSEY, et al., as Administrators, etc., v.
LEDDY et al.

Supreme Court, Fourth Department, Onondaga County,
Special Term, December, 1886.

§§ 484, 1627.

*Foreclosure—When two causes of action properly joined in same com-
plaint.*

Two causes of action to foreclose two mortgages upon the same real
estate, both of which are held by one party and past due, but
which were not given at the same time, nor by the same parties,
and which are accompanied by bonds executed by different persons, may properly be joined in one complaint, where it is alleged
that all the defendants have, or claim to have, some interest in or
lien upon the mortgaged premises subsequent to the lien of the
mortgages therein described, and that notwithstanding that the
persons, against whom a deficiency judgment was sought on
different causes of action, were not the same.

Two or more causes of action to foreclose mortgages on the same property, the parties to which are the same, may properly be united
in the same complaint, where no relief for deficiency is sought.

(*Decided December* 28, 1886.)

Demurrer to complaint by defendant John Leddy, on
the ground that two causes of action are improperly
joined therein.

The action was brought to foreclose two mortgages
upon real estate. Both were held by plantiffs, were past
due, and covered the same property. They were not
given at the same time, nor by the same parties. They
were accompanied by bonds made by the mortgagors.
Subsequent grantees of the mortgaged premises, by assuming and agreeing to pay the first mortgage, had become

personally liable for that mortgage debt with the mortgagor, and the defendant, John Leddy, although not a mortgagor, joined in the execution of the bond accompanying the second mortgage.

The complaint contains two causes of action—one upon each bond and mortgage.

In each cause of action, it was alleged that all the defendants have or claim to have some interest in or lien upon the mortgaged premises, subsequent to the lien of the mortgage therein described. In the first cause of action, it was also alleged that a portion of the mortgaged premises were conveyed to John Leddy, the defendant who demurs, after the first mortgage was given.

The defendant, John Leddy, by his demurrer, claims that plaintiffs cannot in this action foreclose these two mortgages and have judgment against the defendants separately for deficiency as to the two mortgages according to the respective personal liability of the several defendants.

W. M. Morrissey, for plaintiffs.

M. E. Driscoll, for defendant.

WILLIAMS, J.—If the action was one to foreclose the two mortgages, and no relief was sought for deficiency against the defendants personally liable therefor, then the action would be properly brought, and the two causes of action could be properly united in the same complaint (*Code Pro.* § 167; *Thomas on Mort.* 267, etc.; *Code Civ. Pro.* §§ 484, 1627).

Both causes of action were connected with the same subject of action—the real property covered by the mortgages—and both affect all the parties to the action. These facts are alleged in the complaint and are therefore admitted by the demurrer.

If the action was one to enforce the bonds and personal liability of the defendants, and no relief was sought foreclosing the mortgages, then there would be an improper joinder of causes of action, because both causes of action would not affect all the parties to the action. Each one would affect only part of the parties to the action.

The action as brought does seek both kinds of relief— the foreclosure of the mortgage and the recovery of judgments against the defendants (liable personally therefor) for deficiencies resulting from the foreclosure of the two mortgages

By section 1627 of the Code of Civil Proceedure, it is provided that in an action brought to foreclose a mortgage, any person who is liable to the plaintiff for the payment of the debt secured by the mortgage may be made a defendant in the action, and the final judgment may award payment by him of the residue of the debt remaining unsatisfied after a sale of the mortgaged property and the application of the proceeds pursuant to the directions contained therein. An exception is thus created to the rule prescribed in section 484, that the causes of action must each affect all the parties to the action in order to permit them to be united in the same complaint. It is claimed this section cannot be applied and made use of in an action where two mortgages are being foreclosed together, and where the personal liability is several, a liability of some of the defendants for one mortgage debt ˙and of other defendants for the other mortgage debt.

It is said by counsel there are no authorities, the one way or the other, on this question ; that the question is a new one. I have not been able to find any authority myself upon the question, and must, therefore, determine it without precedent and according to my own judgment.

The object of the provision of section 484 was to enable several causes of action to be joined in the same complaint and to be litigated in the same action, and thus avoid several actions and unnecessary cost and expense. It was provided, however, that the causes of action should each affect all the parties to the action.

There was an exception to this last provision, which referred to mortgage foreclosure actions, and section 1627 provided the bond and mortgage might be enforced in the same action, although the general rule prescribed by section 484 was thus deviated from—that each cause of action should affect all the parties to the action. The object of this provision, like the other, was to save multiplicity of actions and avoid unnecessary expense and cost.

The action under this last provision is one to foreclose a mortgage. The enforcement of the personal liability is merely an incident to the real cause of action under this branch of the Code of Civil Procedure, and I can perceive no reason why the section should not be held to authorize the enforcing of the personal liability of the defendants in a case where two mortgages are being foreclosed as well as where one alone is involved.

It may also be said there are especial reasons in this case why all the matters involved in the action, as commenced, should be settled and determined in this one action. First, in 1856, a bond and mortgage for $8,600 was given. To these John Leddy was in no way a party. In 1857, however, he became owner of some of the mortgaged property. From time to time other parties became liable for this mortgage debt, and finally, in 1879, another bond and mortgage were given, the mortgage covering the same property and John Leddy joining in the bond. John Leddy, it will be seen, is therefore a necessary party to an action brought to foreclose the first mortgage. He is interested in protecting the part of the property that was deeded to him by compelling a sale of the other part first, and he has an equitable interest in having the first bond paid by persons who have become liable therefor, it may be, to the exclusion of saving the mortgaged property or some part of it, to the end that so much of it as possible may be left to be sold upon the second mortgage, and so save him from liability upon the bond, wholly or in part. Especially is this so, if, as it may be claimed, he joined in the bond merely as a surety for the mortgagors, .the owners of the mortgaged property.

These suggestions may have no real bearing upon the legal question involved, but they lead one to inquire what possible interest John Leddy can have in separating these causes of action and increasing the cost and expense which are so liable to result to his injury in the end.

My conclusion is that the demurrer should be overruled, and an order entered accordingly, directing judgment for plaintiff, with leave to defendant John Leddy to answer on payment of costs.

Let formal order be prepared by plaintiffs' counsel, and submitted to defendant's counsel for approval as to form, and to me for signature.

WATSON v. PHYFE ET AL.

SUPREME COURT, FIRST DEPARTMENT, NEW YORK COUNTY, CHAMBERS, MARCH, 1887.

§ 977.

New trial—Notice of trial not necessary—Right to have case restored to calendar.

Where a new trial is ordered on appeal from a judgment, either party has an absolute right to have the case placed on the day calendar for trial, without filing a new note of issue, and a new notice of trial is not necessary.

(*Decided March* 7, 1887.)

Motion to restore this cause to the calendar of the court, and placed upon the day calendar thereof.

The opinion states the facts.

C. N. Bovee, Jr. (*Arnoux, Ritch & Woodford,* attorneys), for defendant and motion.

George H. Curtis, for plaintiff, opposed.

ANDREWS, J.—Plantiff's counsel is mistaken in supposing that the court has any discretion in regard to granting or denying this motion. The action has been once tried, and upon such trial the complaint was dismissed. On appeal, the decision of the court below was reversed and a new trial ordered. The defendant desires that a new trial should be speedily had, but the plaintiff wishes the new trial postponed.

It is perfectly well settled that in a case like this either party has a right to have the case placed on the day calendar for trial. It is not a question of whether the action shall have a preference, which is addressed to the discretion of the court, but a matter of absolute right.

There has been some difference of opinion in regard to the status of an action which has been once tried, and where, on appeal, a new trial has been ordered. Section 977 of the Code provides that in this district an action once noticed for trial shall remain on the calendar until it has been disposed of. Whether an action which has been tried has been disposed of, depends upon whether an appeal is taken, and upon the disposition of such appeal which is made by the general term. If a new trial is ordered, the case cannot be said to have been disposed of.

In cases of this character, it is considered by some of the judges that the action is to be regarded as holding the same position as though it had been marked generally reserved, and that either party has the right to have it put on the day calendar on two days' notice. It is thought by others that in cases of this character the action must, in this district as well as in others, be re-noticed for trial and a new note of issue filed with the clerk.

So far as I am aware, however, it has always been held that in cases of this description either party has a right to have the case placed on the day calendar. An order must therefore be entered directing the clerk to place this action on the day calendar. The order will be settled on notice.

HOWE, JUDGMENT CREDITOR, v. WELCH, JUDGMENT DEBTOR.

CITY COURT OF NEW YORK, SPECIAL TERM, MARCH, 1887.

§§ 854, 2442, 2443, 2444, 2457.

Supplementary proceedings —Reference in—Refusal af witness to submit to examination—Contempt.

The right of a judge granting an order for examination in proceedings supplementary to execution, to appoint a referee to take the testimony of the debtor and the right of a party to such proceedings to examine witness, is undoubted.

One upon whom a subpoena issued by a referee duly appointed in proceedings supplementary to execution, requiring her to appear and testify as a witness, was duly served, who appears in obedience thereto, but refuses to be sworn as a witness, and leaves the room where the reference is being held, in direct disobedience of the order of the referee, under advice of her counsel, is clearly guilty of a contempt of court.

(*Decided March 14, 1887.*)

Motion to punish Hattie B. Welch, for refusal to testify as a witness in proceedings supplementary to execution.

The facts are stated in the opinion.

Nelson S. Spencer (Stickney & Shepard, attorneys), for judgment creditor and motion.

Cited, as to power of the referee to issue subpœna: *Code Civ. Pro.* §§ 854, 2436, 2442, 2444; Knowles v. De Lazere, 8 *N. Y. Civ. Pro.* 386. As to witness's conduct being a contempt : Reynolds v. Parkes, 2 *Dem.* 399.

Albert A. Abbott, for judgment debtor and witness, opposed.

HALL, J.—The proceeding supplementary to execution herein was duly instituted, and the same was directed to proceed before a referee named in the order. The referee duly issued a subpœna requiring the witness to appear and testify, as he was authorized to do by section 854 of the Code. The subpœna was duly served upon the witness, and she appeared in obedience to it, but refused to be sworn as a witness, and left the room where the reference was being held, in direct disobedience to the order of the referee, under the advice of defendant's counsel.

It was clearly a contempt of court for the witness to refuse to be sworn, and it was also a contempt for her to leave the room, contrary to the oral direction given directly to her by the referee (§ 2457, Code Civ. Pro.).

There can be no question of the right of the judge granting the order for examination to appoint a referee to take the testimony of the debtor (Code, § 2442), nor of the right of the party to examine witnesses (Code, § 2444).

Section 2443 does not apply to an order of reference to examine the debtor or witnesses in the proceeding, but applies only to incidental questions of fact arising at any stage of the proceeding before a judge to whom the order is returnable ; this is the plain reading of the section.

There can, therefore, be no question but that the witness is guilty of a contempt, and it remains only to determine what punishment should be inflicted.

She claims to have acted under the advice of counsel. She was not entitled to counsel as a witness, but she took the advice of defendant's counsel. This she had no right to do, but she might, and probably did, believe that she had such right. The counsel misinterpreted the law in giving such advice ; but I am inclined to think that he acted in good faith in the matter. By reason of such advice, and the witness leaving the referee's room, the plaintiff's counsel has lost his time before the referee, and has been compelled to make this motion.

The witness is adjudged guilty of contempt, and is fined the sum of $20, to be paid to the plaintiff's attorney, and is directed to appear for examination before the justice at special term, on Monday, March 14, at 1 :30, and in default thereof a commitment will issue.

LYNCH, RESPONDENT, *v.* WALSH, APPELLANT.

CITY COURT OF NEW YORK, GENERAL TERM MARCH, 1887.

§§ 545, 546.

*Pleading—Striking out irrelevant and redundant matter—Making com-
plaint more definite and certain—Penalty for not obeying order
so to do.*

A denial, in an answer to a complaint in an action for rent, that the
defendant is indebted to the plaintiff in the sum claimed, is
irrelevant, and, where it forms a part of an entire defense, cannot
be reached by demurrer, and should be stricken out by motion.

Where the answer in an action for rent of real property admitted
that the defendant hired the premises described in the complaint
and occupied the same for some time, but denied having hired
and occupied the same for the time therein mentioned, the defendant is properly required to make the answer more definite and
certain as to the time he occupied the premises.

Lynch *v.* Walsh.

Where in such a case the defendant fails to make his answer more definite and certain, pursuant to an order requiring him to do so, the court has jurisdiction to make an order precluding him from giving evidence upon the trial "of, concerning, contradicting or tending to contradict" the allegation of the complaint as to the time he occupied the premises therein described.

(Decided March 25, 1887.*)*

Appeal by defendant from an order of the special term striking matter out of his answer as irrelevant and requiring of the defendant to make such answer more definite and certain, and from order precluding the defendant from giving evidence of the defense he was required to make more definite and certain on account of his failure so to do.

The complaint set forth three causes of action, the first of which was as follows : " For a first cause of action, that heretofore and prior to September 1, 1882, the defendant rented from the plaintiff a portion of certain premises at No. 80 West Broadway, in the City of New York, and entered into the occupancy thereof, and continued to occupy, hold, use and enjoy the same up to and including the month of March, 1885 ; that the sum of $8 per month, being $240 for the term from September 1, 1882, to March 31, 1885, was a reasonable rent for said premises for said term, but the defendant has not paid said sum or any part thereof."

The first paragraph of the defendant's answer was as follows : " First, he denies being indebted to the plaintiff in the sum of $2_0 claimed in the first paragraph or cause of action of the complaint. He admits having hired the premises for $6 per month, and having occupied the same for some time ; but denies having hired and occupied the said premises for the time in the complaint mentioned ; and, except as admitted or denied, denies the other allegations of said first cause of action." In the sixth paragraph of the answer, the defendant denied each and every other allegation in the complaint, except those before admitted or denied in the answer. On November 23, an order was made, upon motion after argument, by the special term of the city court of New York, striking out the words, "he denies being indebted to plaintiff in the sum of $240, claimed in the first paragraph or cause of action in the complaint," as irrelevant and redundant, and requiring the defendant to make his answer more definite and certain, by stating the time he occupied the premises described in the· first cause of action contained in the complaint. The defendant failed to make his answer more definite and certain, and on December 29, 1886, an order was entered precluding the defendant from giving evidence upon the trial "of, concerning, contradicting or tending to contradict" the allegation of the complaint that the defendant occupied the premises therein described from prior to September 1, 1882, to March 31, 1885.

Thomas Brennan, for defendant-appellant.

The defendant denied being indebted to plaintiff in the sum of $240, claimed in the first cause of action. It was a denial of plaintiff's claim, and put in issue plaintiff's right to recover the $240 alleged to be due. It was a material allegation of defense, and was not "irrelevant, redundant and immaterial." See Walter v. Fowler, 85 *N. Y.* 621. Where there is a semblance of defense or cause of action, set up in a pleading, it cannot be stricken out as being "irrelevant or redundant." Bangs v. Allan National Bank, 53 *How. Pr.* 1. "Matter which is merely evidence, and not defense, will be stricken out as irrelevant or redundant." The order made December 29, 1886, should not have been granted. It prevents the defendant from giving evidence upon the trial, concerning, contradicting or tending to contradict the allegation of the complaint as to occupancy. This order deprives the defendant of the right to offer evidence on the trial. It is believed that this could not be lawfully done, and it should be reversed. The complaint makes the time of occupancy both definite and certain, namely, from September 1, 1882, to March 31, 1885. This is positive and certain enough, and defendant could not make it more so, and if the plaintiff proves the facts, he can recover.

Hy. Huffman Browne, for plaintiff-respondent.

The motion to strike out the first phrase in the first paragraph of the answer, which reads as follows : " He denies being indebted to the plaintiff in the sum of $240, claimed in the first paragraph or cause of action of the complaint," was properly granted. This is not a denial of any fact alleged in the complaint, but merely a denial of a conclusion of law, which, although it is deducible from the facts therein alleged, is not contained in the complaint. The denial of a conclusion of law raises no issue. Kay *v.* Churchill, 10 *Abb. N. C.* 83. The Code authorizes a denial of "a material allegation of the complaint " or a statement of "new matters constituting a defense or counter-claim." *Code Civ. Pro.* § 500. A denial of indebtedness is not a denial of a material allegation (Drake *v.* Cockroft, 4 *E. D. Smith*, 34 ; S. C., 1 *Abb. Pr.* 203 ; 10 *How. Pr.* 377), and is not a sufficient denial. Piersou *v.* Cooley, 1 *Code R.* 91. Matter out of which no cause of action or defense could arise between the parties is irrelevant. Lee Bank *v.* Kitching, 11 *Abb. Pr.* 435 ; S. C., 1 *Bosw.* 664.

The order requiring that the first paragraph of the defendant's answer be made more definite and certain by stating the time the defendant occupied the premises described in first cause of action was properly granted. *Code Civ. Pro.* § 516 ; Heywood *v.* City of Buffalo, 14 *N. Y.* 534. . . .

The order precluding the defendant from proving the defense which he was required to and failed to make more definite and certain should be affirmed. It is well settled

that where a defendant fails to serve a bill of particulars
as required by an order therefor, the court will exclude
proof of the facts as to which particulars were required.
Dwight v. Germania Life Ins. Co., 84 *N. Y.* 507; Whitehall &
Plattsburg R. R. Co. v. Myers, 16 *Abb. Pr. N. S.* 34. The
rule where the answer is required to be made more definite and certain, and the reasons for the granting the relief are the same.   See, as to nature and office of bill of particulars, Note on Bill of Particulars, 2 *N.Y. Civ. Pro.* 240.
See also McKinney v. McKinney, 12 *How. Pr.* 22.   If the
court had merely stricken out the words " some time," as
the defendant's attorney claims it should have done, or
even it had stricken out the clause containing that word,
the failure of the defendant to obey the order requiring him
to make his answer more definite and certain would have
resulted in a positive advantage to him, for the drag-net
denial of "each and every other allegation" contained in
paragraphs 1 and 6 of the answer would then have put in
issue every allegation of the first paragraph of the complaint.   The only adequate relief was that granted by the
court; to hold that it had not power to grant it will be to
hold that the court is without power to enforce its own
order in a case like the present.

EHRLICH, J.—The order dated December 29, 1886, is
conditional only.   The court below had the jurisdiction
to make such an order upon the refusal or failure of
defendant to comply with its former order; and I am
inclined to the opinion, therefore, that in the present case,
unless the first order should be found erroneous, both
orders should be sustained.

The matter objected to as irrelevant, was properly
stricken out as such, for the reason that it stated no
issuable fact in an issuable form; the same being alleged
as an entire defense, could not be reached by demurrer;*

---

* A demurrer lies only "to a counter-claim or a defense consisting

Lynch v. Walsh.

and the denial contained in the sixth clause of the answer afforded ample protection to the defendant. It is quite clear that the discretion of the court below was properly exercised in requiring the defendant to make more definite the expression "some time," referring to his admission of occupancy of the premises, for the rent of which plaintiff seeks to recover. The order should be affirmed, with costs.

HALL, J., concurred.

---

of new matter." *Code Civ. Proc.* § 494. Where no new matter is set up in an answer a demurrer does not lie to it. Smith v. Greening, 2 *Sandf.* 702 ; Ketcham v. Zerega, 1 *E. D. Smith*, 553 ; Thomas v. Harrop, 7 *How. Pr.* 57 ; People v. Barker, 8 *Id.* 258 ; Reilay v. Thomas, 8 *Id.* 266 ; Lund v. Seaman's S. Bank, 37 *Barb.* 124 ; Rice v. O'Connor, 10 *Abb. Pr.* 362 ; Maretzek v. Cauldwell, 19 *Id.* 35. New matter is that which admits and avoids the cause of action set up in the complaint and constitutes or is intended to constitute a defense. Gilbert v. Cram, 12 *How. Pr.* 455 ; Radde v. Ruckgaber, 3 *Duer.* 684 ; Brazil v. Isham, 12 *N. Y.* 9 ; Bellinger v. Craigue, 31 *Barb.* 537 ; Carter v. Koezley, 14 *Abb. Pr.* 147 ; Walrod v. Bennett, 6 *Barb.* 144. It is matter extraneous to the matter set up in the complaint as the basis of the cause of action. Manning v. Winter, 7 *Hun*, 482. Matter which merely denies essential allegations of the complaint is not new matter. Radde v. Ruckgaber, 3 *Duer*, 684. An answer which denies a fact or conclusion of law, which, although not expressly alleged in the complaint, is to be implied from averments contained in it, does not set up new matter. Stoddard v| Onondaga An. Con., 12 *Barb.* 573. A demurrer will not lie, in any case, to matter in the answer which goes merely in denial of the complaint. Ketcham v. Zerega, 1 *E. D. Smith*, 553 ; and see cases cited *supra.* A demurrer will not lie to any but a separate defense. Cobb v. Trazee, 4 *How. Pr.* 413 ; Welsh v. Hazelton, 14 *Id.* 97.

THE GERMAN AMERICAN BANK *v.* CHAMPLIN
AND ANOTHER.

COUNTY COURT OF ERIE COUNTY, MARCH, 1887.

§§ 417, 421, 520.

Folioing papers—When not necessary—Pleadings—What address should be thereon.

Where an answer and the verification taken together were more than two folios in length, but neither taken alone contained two folios, —*Held*, that they were not required to be folioed; that the answer and verification were not one paper and should not be taken together in determining how many folios they contained.

A pleading must be subscribed by the attorney for the party making it, and, where it is the only notice of appearance in the case, the attorney must add his office address to his signature; otherwise he need not.

Where an answer was subscribed by the defendant's attorney, and there was indorsed on the back of it, after it was folded, the title of the action; the name and address of the defendant's attorney, and immediately thereunder a notice of appearance, which was also subscribed by the defendant's attorney, but to which his address was not added,—*Held*, that the answer and notice of appearance fully complied with the requirements of the Code of Civil Procedure in respect to the signature and address thereon, and gave the plaintiff all the information he desired or was entitled to.

(Decided March 4, 1887.)

Motion by defendant to vacate and set aside a judgment entered herein by plaintiff as for want of an answer.

The facts appear in the opinion.

A. C. De Witt, for defendant and motion.

Fred. Griner, for plaintiff, opposed.

HAMMOND, Co. J.—Defendant served her answer upon the last day for service, which was returned by plaintiff within twenty-four hours, but after the expiration of the twenty days for service, with the following indorsement:

"This answer is respectfully returned to you within the time limited so to do, upon the following grounds. First, it does not comply with rule 19 of the general rules of practice, in that the same is not folioed. Second, it does not comply with section 421 of the Code of Civil Procedure in that you have failed to add your office and post-office address to your signature. Third, your notice on the answer is defective on the same point." Dated, signed, etc.

The answer was not folioed, but it was less than two folios in length; but the answer and the affidavit of verification, taken together, are over two folios.

Rule 19 only requires pleadings, affidavits, etc., *exceeding* two folios in length to be folioed. Neither the answer, nor the affidavit of verification were required to be folioed by this rule, as neither contained two folios. The contention of the plaintiff that both must be taken together, and are only one paper, I think cannot be maintained.

Section 417 of the Code of Civil Procedure, in prescribing the requisites of a summons, among other things, says: "And it must be subscribed by the plaintiff's attorney, who must add to his signature his office and post-office address, and, if in a city, street and number," etc.

Section 421, among other things, provides: "*A notice or pleading so served* must be subscribed by the defendant's attorney, who must add to his signature his office address, with the particulars prescribed in section 417," etc.

It will be observed by a careful reading that section 421 provides for the *appearance* of the defendant; and this may be either by a notice *or* service of a copy of demurrer or answer, and in either case the defendant's attorney must add his office address, etc. : because, it being the appearance of the defendant, the plaintiff must be informed of the office address, etc., of the defendant's attorney; while section 520 provides for a pleading, which is not an appearance, and only requires that it shall "be subscribed by the attorney for the party;" and does not require any other or further addition than the signature of the attorney.

Taking these provisions of these sections together, we are plainly led to the conclusion, that a pleading must be subscribed by the attorney for the party; and, when such pleading is the *only* notice of appearance, then the attorney must add his office address, etc., to his signature, otherwise he need not.

In this case the answer was properly subscribed, and upon the back of the paper, after it was folded, was indorsed the title of the action, and the name and address of the defendant's attorney, and immediately beneath this was a notice of appearance, which was also subscribed by the defendant's attorney, but the office address was not added beneath this. I think this was not necessary, as it was written in full immediately preceding it, and gave the plaintiff's attorney all the information he desired, or was entitled to, and must be held to be a full compliance with the requirements of the sections of the Code above referred to (Falkner *v.* N. Y. etc. R. R., 100 *N. Y.* 86; Schiller *v.* Maltbie, 11 *Civ. Pro.* 304).

Motion granted, with $10 costs to the defendant.

INDEX.

***

466 INDEX.

H

Lightning Source UK Ltd.
Milton Keynes UK
UKHW011553040119

334726UK00009B/519/P

9 780266 175025